Future of Business and Finance

The Future of Business and Finance book series features professional works aimed at defining, analyzing, and charting the future trends in these fields. The focus is mainly on strategic directions, technological advances, challenges and solutions which may affect the way we do business tomorrow, including the future of sustainability and governance practices. Mainly written by practitioners, consultants and academic thinkers, the books are intended to spark and inform further discussions and developments.

Andreas Krämer • Thomas Burgartz
Christina Muzzu

Customer Value-centered Management

Understanding and Leveraging Value-to-Value, Pricing, Big Data, and Controlling

 Springer

Andreas Krämer
exeo Strategic Consulting AG
Bonn, Germany

Thomas Burgartz
University of Europe for Applied Sciences
Iserlohn, Germany

Christina Muzzu
University of Europe for Applied Sciences
Iserlohn, Germany

ISSN 2662-2467   ISSN 2662-2475   (electronic)
Future of Business and Finance
ISBN 978-3-031-90496-7   ISBN 978-3-031-90497-4   (eBook)
https://doi.org/10.1007/978-3-031-90497-4

This Springer imprint is published by the registered company Springer Nature Switzerland AG
The registered company address is: Gewerbestrasse 11, 6330 Cham, Switzerland

If disposing of this product, please recycle the paper.

Preface

For management, the challenge of having to make decisions under extreme time pressure and increased uncertainty is growing. On the one hand, businesses have adopted the military acronym VUCA to describe their increasingly complicated working environment, but on the other hand, innovations in fields such as big data and artificial intelligence promise solutions in decision-making that may provide significant relief to management. In this context, customer *centricity* is often described as a major driver of success for companies, not least after the success of US e-commerce giant Amazon over the last decade. However, in practice, customer *value* is the parameter companies look to most as a key factor in the success chain of relationship marketing: customer centricity, satisfaction, and loyalty. The concept of customer value in turn encompasses two different perspectives, namely the customer's view (value-*to*-the-customer) and the company's view (value-*of*-the-customer). Both facets can be combined in an integrated approach we call value-to-value segmentation. Doing so is particularly important because companies often find it difficult to implement customer value concepts in practice, even as they are propagated by academics as the "measure of all things" and constantly being expanded to include new aspects.

In the value-to-value approach discussed in this book, price management is a key anchor point, which, however, must not be viewed in isolation nor one-sidedly in terms of sacrifices to be made by the customer vs. monetization of the service. Like "customer value", the term "value-based pricing" is sometimes misleading if it is equated with the exploitation of customers' willingness to pay. It is recommended to avoid analyzing and evaluating in isolation, but rather to gain a deeper understanding of the interaction between the cornerstones or core functions of customer benefit, price, and costs, with a particular focus on their respective interactions.

Customer value-centered management requires an approach to corporate management that is both data-driven and overarching.

Although many articles and books on individual facets of value-based corporate management have been published to date, there is no integrative consideration of the two customer value perspectives. This is addressed by the title of this book, "Customer value-centered management", in contrast to "value-oriented management" or "customer-centered management".

It is a personal concern of ours to place and present the lines of thought developed in numerous joint essays in a combined context. While, on the one hand, we

v

bring different topics, which are not new, into a different structure, at the same time we counter current mainstream and narratives and come to conclusions such as:

- The stronger functional orientation and specialization has had the negative effect of creating a tunnel vision, while the changed framework conditions require a networked view.
- Although big data and AI are revolutionizing how business is conducted, it requires an understanding of business to make data usable as a basis for value creation.
- Unfortunately, the term "customer value" is very amorphous, and a precise interpretation is required. This also applies to derived terms such as "value-based pricing".
- The profitability of the customer relationship is a central point of reference for management, even if it cannot be calculated with 100% accuracy.
- Although customer centricity appears interesting as a buzzword or as a "new maxim" for marketing, it is one-sided because it lacks the value perspective of the company.
- The central dimensions of value management, serving the basic needs of customers ("value-to-the-customer") and generating contribution margins via the customer relationship ("value-of-the-customer") can be integrated using the segmentation approach discussed in this book. This value-to-value approach provides the basis for customer value-centered management.
- The compromise between a radical value orientation from the company's perspective (shareholder value) and a radical value orientation from the customer's perspective (customer centricity) is customer value-centered management.

Double customer value centricity is a philosophy that can only be successfully applied in practice if interdependencies are considered holistically and comprehensively. Simplicity is not a maxim, true to the motto "As simple as possible, as complicated as necessary." Or to quote Albert Einstein: "Everything should be made as simple as possible, but no simpler." However, this also requires a radical rethink in management that goes far beyond the implementation of modern technologies or the proclamation of new guidelines ("we must act in a customer-centric manner").

We would like to thank the team of reviewers (Dr. Gerd Wilger and Dr. Robert Bongaerts) for their careful examination of the texts and many suggestions regarding content. Our special thanks go to the interview partners who gave us brief insights into their industry:

- Fabian Beger, MEDICE Arzneimittel Pütter GmbH & Co. KG
- Dr. Sandra Böhrs and Susanne Ilemann, simpleshow GmbH
- Prof. Dr. Stefan Diefenbach, Telekom Deutschland Business Solutions GmbH
- Carsten Dürselen, Hamburger Verkehrsverbund (hvv)
- Cosimo Franco, CERTIQUALITY Srl
- Tobias Hartmann, Scout24
- Sebastian Hense, KiK Textilien und Non-Food GmbH

- Prof. Dr. Regine Kalka, Hochschule Düsseldorf
- Markus Kalt, Swiss Federal Railways SBB AG
- Prof. Dr. Wolfgang Merkle, University of Europe for Applied Sciences
- DI Thomas Posch, WESTbahn Management GmbH
- Dr. Michael Scheidler, Skymetrix
- Tom Shelton, TNS Consulting/MINDSwork
- Luke van Skyhawk, Hypatos.

We hope that the contributions of this book will stimulate an appreciation for as well as further discussion and deepening understanding of this extremely interesting topic. We expressly encourage further exchange and look forward to suggestions, critical feedback, and constructive ideas.

Bonn, Germany	Andreas Krämer
Menden, Germany	Thomas Burgartz
Wetter, Germany	Christina Muzzu

Competing Interests The authors have no competing interests to declare that are relevant to the content of this manuscript.

Contents

About the Authors

Andreas Krämer is CEO of exeo Strategic Consulting AG in Bonn and Director of the Value Research Institute (VARI e.V.), Iserlohn. Among other things, he teaches price management, CRM, market research, and statistics. After studying agricultural economics and completing his doctorate, Andreas Krämer worked for two leading international consulting companies from 1996 to 2000 before founding his own consulting company in 2000. Since its foundation, exeo has focused on data-driven decision support in marketing, generally based on empirical studies. Andreas Krämer is co-initiator of the "Pricing Lab," "MobilitätsTRENDS," and "OpinionTRAIN" studies and author of numerous specialist articles and books.

andreas.kraemer@exeo-consulting.com

Thomas Burgartz is Dean of the Faculty of Business at the University of Europe for Applied Sciences and Director of the Value Research Institute (VARI e.V.), Iserlohn. He is Professor of Performance Measurement and his teaching and research focuses on key figure-based customer relationship management and controlling and in marketing and sales controlling. After studying economics, he was a research assistant and doctoral candidate at the Chair of Management Accounting and Controlling at the Technical University of Dortmund. Subsequently, he has worked for many years in a medium-sized consulting company and is the author of numerous specialist articles and co-editor of various books.

thomas.burgartz@ue-germany.com

Christina Muzzu received her Master in Business Administration and Master of Spanish degrees from the University of Houston. She has published articles on the evolving influence of digitalization on education and taught Marketing, Corporate Social Responsibility, English and Ethics at the University of Europe for Applied Sciences in Iserlohn, Germany since 2004. Before joining UE, she worked as a Portfolio Analyst for General Investment & Development in Boston, Massachusetts and served as a Language Specialist for the Federal Bureau of Investigation.

christina.muzzu@ue-germany.com

Part I

Introduction and General Conditions

1.1 Why This Book?

1.1.1 The Desire for Simplicity

"Everything should be as simple as it can be, but not simpler!"—Einstein (1950)

The desire for simplicity and a clear, well-organized structure is great, both in private life and in management, as the opening quote from Albert Einstein expresses. Simplicity creates transparency and conveys the feeling of being able to make good decisions and prepare targeted decisions. As Rego (2010) states, undesirable complexity is usually countered by processes designed to increase simplicity.

For example, along with the shareholder value approach, the simplification approach was one of the core values of General Electric championed by Jack Welch (Elderkin and Bartlett 1993): "We found in the 1980s that becoming faster is tied to becoming simpler .... If we're not simple we can't be fast ... and if we weren't fast we can't win." Acceleration through simplification is therefore not a new objective. Nevertheless, complexity is increasing overall in the new millennium, which is also creating a lack of orientation. It is not only the increasing number of interrelationships that is problematic, but also the impact of four key developments on them: volatility, uncertainty, complexity, and ambiguity. It is not so much the perceived complexity that is challenging, but the interplay with other facets. This is described by the acronym VUCA (Volatility, Uncertainty, Complexity, and Ambiguity) (Mack et al. 2016). These factors determine expectations regarding aspects such as predictive accuracy and the amount of information available in decision-making situations, which implies a new behavior in leadership and at all levels of value-based management. Simplicity is not only aimed at the convenience of receiving and processing information, but also at the effectiveness of communication. The so-called KISS principle (keep it simple, stupid) is seen as an effective sales principle, with Macintosh and Gentry (1999) coming to the conclusion: "Higher performers seem to be able to focus on key characteristics of sales prospects regardless of the complexity of the decision task, suggesting that higher performers, at least implicitly, know when to keep it simple." However, the attempt at simplification can also be dangerously exaggerated, as implied by Einstein's "but not simpler" indicating that there are things that cannot be simplified (Wandke 2018).

1.1.2 Changing Framework Conditions for Management Decisions

As VUCA factors have increased, the framework conditions for companies have changed. The following aspects can be named as particular drivers:

- (Modern) societies are subject to a constant change in values. The debate on climate change and the "Fridays for Future" movement, for example, not only led to intense public discussion but also reflected a change in values over the generations (Gutmann 2019). Extreme weather and unusual flooding reinforce the impression that a significant and rapid rethink is required. The changes brought about by the coronavirus crisis affected almost all social and economic interaction (Krämer and Hercher 2020), and the geopolitical upheavals on the European continent and the Middle East have the potential to destabilize societies worldwide for years to come across several areas, from agriculture and energy to security. Currently, the world is grappling with interconnected crises including climate change, war, economic instability, public health threats, and rising political polarization, all of which demand coordinated global responses and interdisciplinary action (IMF 2025).
- The effects of digitalization have been observed for some time but are less obvious in terms of their extent and impact. Bughin et al. (2018) note that managers' understanding of what digital means is already very vague and imprecise. They themselves provide the following definition: "We view digital as the nearly instant, free, and flawless ability to connect people, devices, and physical objects anywhere." In English-speaking countries, the terms digitization and digitalization are used to describe these effects more holistically. According to Bloomberg (2018), digitization tends to refer to the formal step of converting analogue processes into digital ones ("taking analog information and encoding it into zeroes and ones so that computers can store, process, and transmit such information"), whereas the term digitalization is less clearly defined and relates more to the associated changes in behavior ("the way in which many domains of social life are restructured around digital communication and media infrastructures").
- Globalization and specialization are the drivers of global economic growth. The theory of comparative cost advantages formulated by economist David Ricardo (1821) is probably the most important and most frequently cited contribution describing the relationships between specialization and international trade and in which the actor (in a two-country model) who has absolute price disadvantages

due to higher costs in the production of goods can achieve a higher level of prosperity. The prerequisite for profitable trade affecting all participants is therefore not the absolute production costs, but the ability of the two trading partners to specialize in those goods that can be produced relatively more cheaply compared to other goods. In contrast to specialization, the concept of globalization is less clearly defined. Academics have not succeeded in reaching a consensus on the meaning of the term (Kessler and Steiner 2009, p. 25). Since the outbreak of the coronavirus crisis, the trend toward globalization, in terms of a closely coordinated and networked global economy, has been called increasingly into question (Saxer 2020). This affects various forms of isolation of entire economies, but also the rethinking of supply chains and sources. The tariff conflicts of 2025 have led to economic and political tensions across the world.

- Acceleration and disruption are in turn partly consequences of the drivers already mentioned (this is expressed, e.g., by the term "digital disruption"; see Skog et al. 2018). However, they also have an independent character. Advances in data technology (more data, better availability of data in companies, powerful analysis options and automation of processes, use of AI-Tools) inevitably lead to an acceleration in management.

Because of these special drivers and the VUCA framework conditions, optimization efforts are also intensifying around the conflict between simplification and complexity (see Fig. 1.1). On the one hand, companies—if they want to grow—must rely on a functional organization and disaggregated competencies.

Increasingly, people are thinking in terms of areas that take on specific functions. The basic idea behind this is to gain efficiency through specialization and focus. In this logic, the establishment of hierarchy makes sense because it leads to coordinated decisions and rapid implementation, both of which are prerequisites for dynamic growth of the company. However, this perspective also has its shortcomings, namely, when the separately operating divisions develop a life of their own,

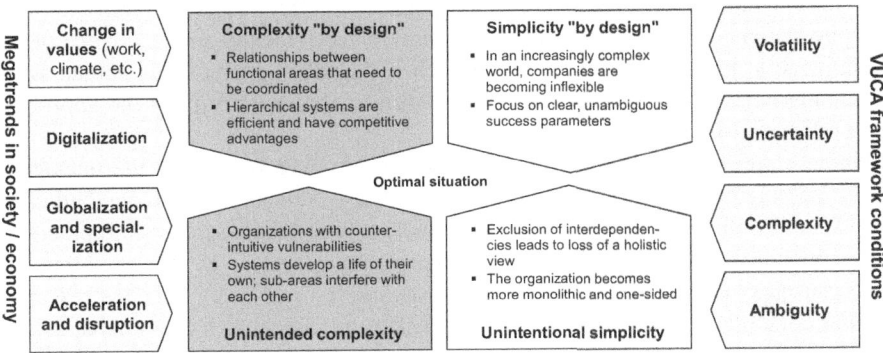

Fig. 1.1 Simplicity and complexity in companies

which not only makes decision-making more difficult, but also makes companies appear sluggish and paralyzed. This is where the counter-perspective comes into play, which attempts to eliminate the inefficiencies caused by complexity. This calls for simplified correlations and explanatory approaches that create transparency, are comprehensible to those involved, and lead to rapid coordination and decision-making. But even this perspective—agility as the "last resort", however logical and intuitively correct it may be—has its limits. If the maxim of simplification is exaggerated, there is a risk of disregarding essential correlations in operational processes and in operative market cultivation. In the worst-case scenario, there is a risk that companies will become more monolithic and ultimately more one-sided and lose sight of market opportunities because the creation and use of unique selling points (USPs), differentiation, creativity, and entrepreneurial curiosity are lost.

1.1.3　The Search for the One (All-Explanatory) Number

A particularly prominent example of excessive simplification is the Net Promoter Score (NPS) developed by Fred Reichheld of Bain & Company (Reichheld 2003) and published in 2003, which has had a major influence on market research and corporate management ever since. The title alone of the article in the Harvard Business Review "The one number you need to grow," which caused a sensation at the time, underlines the promise of performance and the potential for maximum simplification. If it is possible to use just one key figure to identify growth opportunities and to measure the company's prospects, there is no need for lengthy and complicated customer surveys. Instead, customers are simply asked whether they would recommend a particular company to their friends or acquaintances (scale from 0 to 10 with 0 = "not at all likely and 10 = "extremely likely"). The Net Promoter Score is calculated by subtracting the corresponding percentage of detractors (total % of scale points 0-6) from the cumulative percentage of promoters (total % of scale points 9 or 10). The idea of being able to identify a company's growth prospects based on a single central indicator led to a huge media response. Since its much-noticed publication, the NPS has achieved enormous popularity among management, while the scientific community has been less euphoric (Artz 2017). Despite criticism from the research community, which lacked clear evidence of its effectiveness, the use of the NPS approach in business practice has spread very dynamically, as the results of the study confirmed the superiority of the approach over other instruments.

In an empirical study, Bendle and Bagga (2016) even found that the managers surveyed perceive the NPS approach as a particularly scientifically proven and validated set of tools, a set of tools that has been transferred from science into practice, so to speak. In this context, however, the impression should not be conveyed that the NPS is useless as a tool. Our own application examples in projects and other research studies conclude that the NPS can be used well as an indicator of customer satisfaction and loyalty in many cases (although other instruments can also be used) but is not very suitable as a forecasting tool for company growth (Kristensen and Eskildsen

2014). According to our own study results, for example, the very different growth rates of companies in the German food retail sector can be explained well using NPS (dm, e.g., achieves top NPS values and is growing faster than its competitors), but hardly in the airline sector (Ryanair recorded significantly higher sales growth than Lufthansa but only achieves very moderate NPS values).

It gradually became clear in practice that the informative value of the NPS as an isolated figure is relatively limited without the availability of further information. Reichheld himself takes up this deficit later and speaks less of "The one number" rather than an NPS system, i.e., a research approach that collects further information from the customer's perspective in addition to determining the NPS (Reichheld and Markey 2011). The supposedly extremely simple approach has evolved into a more complex approach. As a result, the original promise of being able to control an entire company or customer relationship using just one indicator (NPS) has evolved into a classic example of over-simplification.

1.1.4 New and More Intensive View of the Customer Relationship

Simplification is not an end in itself, but a survival strategy. When behavioral researchers talk about judgment heuristics, they are simply talking about simplification approaches that ensure survival in a complex world. After all, decision-makers generally do not have unlimited resources in terms of time, knowledge, and processing capacity. This also applies to "survival" in modern companies. As Hoffrage et al. (2005) explain, "simple heuristics that require little information can nevertheless lead to astonishingly accurate judgments." For management, the challenges of making decisions under greater time pressure and at the same time with greater uncertainty are currently increasing. On the one hand, the VUCA framework conditions lead to increased uncertainty and complexity, while on the other hand, topics such as big data and artificial intelligence promise solutions in the decision-making process, which in the best-case scenario can even relieve management of decisions.

In this context, the aspect of customer centricity plays an important role. Extremely dynamic competitive pressure, increasingly comparable products and services from the customer's perspective, and a bundle of customer expectations that can hardly be met by many companies in pretty much every industry mean that customer centricity is seen as a success-driving factor for companies in terms of organization, management style, new functions, a customer experience (CX) culture, etc. (not least following the success of the US e-commerce giant Amazon over the past 10 to 15 years and its claim to be the most customer-centric company in the world). Jeff Bezos, as CEO, focused on the optimization of customer processes and interfaces, thus underlining the importance of customer experience (Morgan 2019):

"We see our customers as invited guests to party, and we are the hosts. It's our job every day to make every important aspect of the customer experience a little bit better."—Jeff Bezos

More than almost any other company, Amazon proves that a total focus on customer needs can be a real competitive advantage. This is also expressed in the following definition of "customer centric" (www.businessdictionary.com): "Creating a positive consumer experience at the point of sale and post-sale. A customer-centric approach can add value to a company by enabling it to differentiate itself from competitors who do not offer the same experience." The emphasis should be on "can add." However, when it comes to the example of Amazon, which is currently being discussed almost effusively, it is often forgotten that the world's leading e-commerce provider has long been viewed very critically by financial analysts and others. Many experts feared that Amazon would not be able to generate stable earnings and achieve recognizable, sustainable profitability.

It is astonishing that the interpretations of the term "customer centricity" cited above differ widely in some areas. In some cases, there is even an impression of contradiction. Fader (2020), for example, begins his introduction to customer-centric management with the following statement:

"The customer is not always right. Rather, the right customer is always right. And yes, there is a difference."—Fader

In this interpretation, customer value in the sense of customer lifetime value is actually the central parameter (as the final link in the success chain of relationship marketing consisting of customer proximity, satisfaction, and loyalty). Unfortunately, it becomes apparent at this point that the concept of customer value is multifaceted and at the same time a source of misunderstandings. After all, the concept of customer value encompasses at least two different perspectives, namely, the customer's view ("value-to-the-customer") and the company's view ("value-of-the-customer").

Both facets can be combined in an integrated approach ("value-to-value approach", Chap. 9). This is particularly important because companies often struggle with the practical implementation of customer value concepts, while the customer value concept is propagated by academics as the "measure of all things" and, as mentioned earlier, is constantly being expanded to include new aspects (Bohari et al. 2011). These different strands are also recognizable in the scientific orientation. For example, customer preference measurement, in contrast to customer value analysis, is geared toward measuring the benefits of products and services from the customer's perspective (Krämer and Wilger 1999 or Krämer et al. 2001). If customer needs are recognized and addressed, this is not only a prerequisite for customer satisfaction but can also be a source of competitive advantage, as Woodruff (1997) put it. The term customer insights is increasingly favored over market research because it emphasizes a deeper, behavior-driven understanding of individual consumer needs rather than broad market trends (Bloomfire 2023).

In the conception of the value-to-value approach (see Krämer et al. 2005 for early work), price management is an important anchor point, which, however, must not be viewed in isolation and one-sidedly (sacrifices to be made by the customer vs. monetization of the service): The term value-based pricing is therefore partly misleading if it is often equated with exploiting customers' willingness to pay (Krämer and Schmutz 2020). In the dual interpretation of customer value described above, deliberately not exploiting customers' willingness to pay can also generate value, both for the customer in the short term (high consumer surplus) and for the company in the medium term (e.g., through positive customer loyalty or word-of-mouth marketing). It is also advisable to not only analyze and evaluate in isolation, but also to generate an understanding of the interaction between the cornerstones (core functions) of customer benefit, price, and costs, with a particular focus on the interfaces. In this context, customer value-centered management requires a different approach to corporate management: on the one hand, more data-driven and on the other hand, more comprehensive and networked.

1.2 Increasing Functional Specialization

1.2.1 Ever Deeper Detailed Knowledge

Specialization is a supposedly unavoidable response to the challenge of complexity. At first glance, this results in advantages for both suppliers and buyers. This can be observed not only in research, but also in many other areas, such as the service sector. The effects can be briefly illustrated using the example of professional services such as management consultancies—a consideration of medical services or legal advice would also lead to similar results. The framework condition here is that the use of consultants in accordance with the information economic triangle is characterized by a low degree of search and experience characteristics and a high degree of trust characteristics (Deelmann and Krämer 2020).

Building trust is therefore one of the central challenges in the marketing of consulting professions. However, the question arises as to how trust can be built if there is no personal relationship between the consultant and client (e.g., if no joint projects have been carried out to date). In this case in particular, substitute indicators play a role. Within this spectrum, the aspect of specialization again has a special position:

- Firstly, the simultaneous specialization of the consultant in an industry and function offers the opportunity of particularly high added value for the client. Highlighting a specialization suggests that the consultant not only has above-average methodological skills for projects but also knows the industry and client company inside out. From the client's perspective, the aspect of specialization therefore becomes a surrogate for high quality as well as efficient and targeted support.
- Secondly, further discussion of the chain of effects reveals that specialization can lead to advantages in the argumentation of fees. If the efficiency advantages of the consulting offer are emphasized, the risk of a "price discussion" is also reduced. In a phase in which not only large companies but also medium-sized and smaller companies are professionalizing the procurement of management

consultants and relying on transparent procurement processes and organizations, this is a crucial point. Ultimately, this reduces the pressure on prices.

- Thirdly, consulting firms with a high degree of specialization often have greater flexibility in terms of pricing (Krämer 2011). They are more likely to be able to offer alternative fee models such as fixed or contingency fees instead of daily rates.

The interrelationships shown lead to a win-win situation. By highlighting a high degree of specialization from the perspective of a potential client, the access barriers to consulting are reduced. As a result, the specialized consultant improves his competitive position. Not least the strong growth rates of specialized medium-sized management consultancies seem to confirm these correlations.

However, this should not give the impression that the specialization trend is a one-way street. As Friedrich (2007, p. 9) explains:

"No other strategy is as controversial as the unconditional focus on a few products, services or problem solutions. Supporters of specialization strategies consider it a magic bullet that can solve all common problems of corporate management - regardless of whether they relate to marketing, organization, innovation or knowledge management."—Friedrich

Prominent examples of specialized consultancies include Simon-Kucher & Partners for pricing, Barkawi for digitalization and supply chain management, Horváth for controlling, and Kerkhoff for procurement optimization. Nevertheless, not all consultancies are jumping on the supposedly inevitable bandwagon. Again, there are understandable reasons for this.

1.2.2 The Limits of Specialization

To briefly and concisely illustrate the disadvantages of specialization, the example of management consultants will be used. Specialization can be advantageous if the need for action and the specific task for the consultant are clearly defined. However, this is not always the case: It is not uncommon for the use of consultants to deliberately provide an unbiased view of the company or business processes. It is sometimes argued that specialization leads away from holistic solutions (Hofmann 2013, p. 206). It is also feared that a concentrated focus on a specific problem area could obstruct the view of the "big picture."

In principle, a further conflict of objectives becomes clear: The consulting professions are desperately looking for ways to standardize their own services internally, while at the same time "selling" consulting services tailored to the client company to the outside world. This standardization makes it possible to complete certain tasks more quickly within the consulting team because familiar structures and dependencies are assumed. At the same time, however, this approach inevitably entails a certain degree of operational blindness. Ultimately, there is the following risk: The solution approaches turn out to be wrong, research into symptoms rather than causes is carried out, and too little consideration is given to "networking with other problems" (Hofmann 1987, p. 242).

1.2.3   Tunnel Vision in Many Areas and Functions

Specialization undeniably brings clear advantages, but also disadvantages. The aspect of specialization, which in negative cases can lead to tunnel vision, was discussed using the example of management consulting. Similar basic features can be seen in many other areas. As Fig. 1.2 illustrates, corresponding focal points or specialization deepening can be observed in different fields of research over time. The areas of the strands described below are only examples that can easily be expanded:

- Initially, customer preference research primarily used empirical surveys in which direct methods were used to measure customer needs (e.g., querying the importance of features or feature characteristics on a standardized scale). Next, methods that enable indirect measurement of customer benefit came to the fore. This heralded the widespread adoption of conjoint analysis in market research (for more on its particular significance for market research, see Kuß et al. 2014, p. 276). The increased availability of data in the context of increasing networking and digitalization then led to a strong focus on purchase data in the estimation of customer preferences. The reasoning is initially plausible: Purchase data has a higher degree of hardness than survey data. In this logic, it seems only logical to include other data in the analysis in addition to transaction data, such as search activities or customer history.

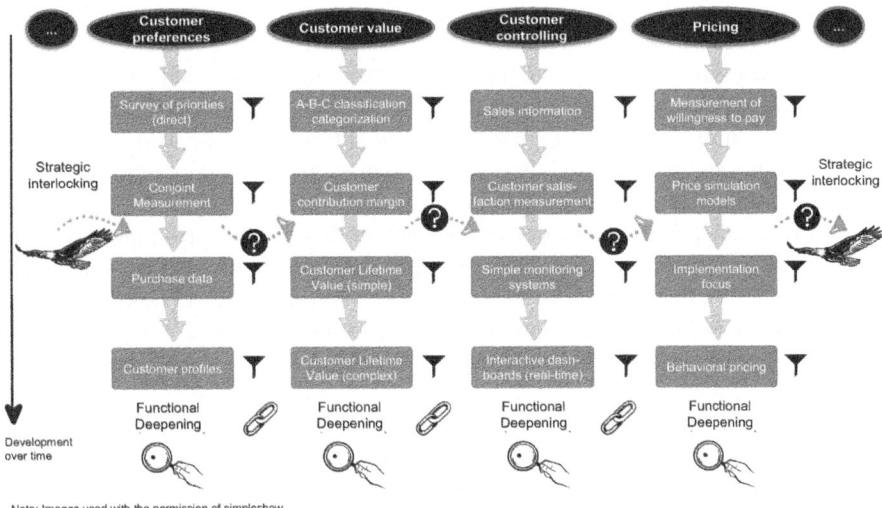

Note: Images used with the permission of simpleshow

Fig. 1.2 Increased specialization in various marketing areas

- In the case of the customer value perspective, customer-specific contribution margin, ABC analyses, which are easy to use, were quickly replaced by the customer profit calculations (reasoning: turnover is a poor predictor of customer profitability). In addition, customer profit calculations were dynamized and converted into a simple Customer Lifetime Value (CLV). The contribution margins are to be aggregated over the individual years of the customer relationship and related to a point in time (usually the current year). With the measure of customer equity ("the total of the discounted lifetime values of all the firm's customers"), a revolution was seemingly achieved in the 1990s. Theoretically at least, different activities can be measured and compared in terms of efficiency and effectiveness based on the question of how much a marketing measure is able to increase customer equity. The research of Lemon, Rust, and Zeithaml is exemplary here (Lemon et al. 2001; Rust et al. 2004). Driven by the realization that complex effects emanate from a customer relationship, many attempts have since been made to further refine corresponding CLV models (Helm et al. 2017). As a result, the specific customer-individual data requirements are increasing (Ghiadi et al. 2020).
- For a long time, companies concentrated on data to control and measure customer relationships that could be provided by the sales department without much additional effort. In a further wave, customer satisfaction was discovered as a central indicator (a strong boost from the discussion about the value of customer orientation in the 1980s, based on the publication of the bestseller "In Search of Excellence" by Peters and Waterman; Dahlgaard-Park and Dahlgaard 2006). The discussion about customer orientation not only triggered an increased analysis of customer needs, but also focused on taking stock and monitoring customer satisfaction (Edvardsson et al. 2014). Other factors, such as a stronger focus on understanding the competitive situation and the harmonization of product quality led to an era of customer satisfaction measurement (Fornell et al. 1996), which in many cases fueled the expectation that it was sufficient to measure customer satisfaction scores and their changes and to react accordingly to be optimally positioned in the market. The consequence of a rather one-sided focus on customer satisfaction has given way to instruments combined with key performance indicators. In the context of digitalization and automation, customer dashboards are currently being discussed that provide management with key information in real time or at least very quickly.
- For a long time, the focus of price management was on measuring individual or segment-specific willingness to pay to enable the estimation of a price-sales relationship on this basis. In a further step—also with the focus on strategic pricing—more complex market simulation models were developed, for example, to be able to depict interdependencies in a multiproduct scenario. A further refocusing occurred with an increased focus on the actual enforcement of prices and the implementation of optimized prices in the market. The subsequent increased discussion of behavioral sciences has also led to a relatively strong rethink in the context of price management. For example, it has become generally accepted that even with identical prices, the presentation of prices alone (color, contrast,

etc.) can have an influence on the price assessment (Spreer 2018; Husemann-Kopetzky 2020; Krämer 2025).

These different lines of development, rather exemplary and abbreviated, are evident in research and in practice. The advantages of the in-depth perspective, which attempts to better explain and understand the individual subject areas, are offset by disadvantages, for example, when it comes to networking perspectives. However, this is elementary for decision-oriented management. In an environment that is perceived as complex, this necessity is even greater.

1.3   Potential Through a Networked Perspective

While it has been shown that there are good reasons for a constant deepening of research in individual functional areas and ultimately a progressive specialization, these developments reach their limits when it comes to the networking of perspectives. The current VUCA framework conditions reinforce this necessity and accelerate the expectation of a management that recognizes cause-and-effect relationships and incorporates them into decision-making. This will first be explained using an example.

1.3.1   Networked Thinking Using the Example of the Decision to Implement Dynamic Pricing

If there is one firm, unquestioned statement in the field of price management, it is certainly the statement that significantly higher sales can be achieved with price differentiation than with undifferentiated pricing (Fassnacht 2009; Frohmann 2018). While some sectors have been implementing flexible pricing for decades—revenue management was already established in the airline industry in the 1980s—dynamic pricing is now also being discussed in bricks-and-mortar retail (Krämer et al. 2015). As Fig. 1.3 shows, several facets need to be examined to support a decision. These can be divided into two strands (internal and external perspective) (Merkle and Krämer 2021). In the internal perspective, the following aspects must be examined:

- Does dynamic pricing fit in with the corporate strategy and does the company have the right skills to implement this pricing philosophy?
- Does the existing and available data allow for fine-tuned, time-controlled price determination or which technology should be used for price management?
- What cost effects result from dynamic pricing? For example, can warehousing costs be significantly reduced?

In addition to these already challenging questions, which can only be clarified within the company, there are further open questions that concern competitors,

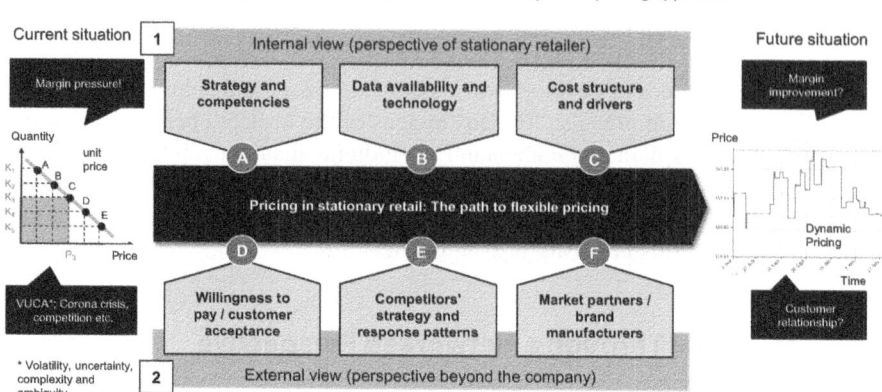

Fig. 1.3 Factors influencing the implementation of a dynamic pricing approach (bricks-and-mortar retail)

customers, and partners in the market. The following questions need to be answered from this external perspective:

- To what extent does customers' willingness to pay for identical products vary depending on the shopping situation, e.g., the start or end of a typical working day vs. Saturday morning? This is a basic prerequisite for dynamic pricing. In other words: If customers' willingness to pay only varies within a narrow band and is stable over time overall, the potential for dynamic pricing is low. Another question also needs to be answered: How would customers rate a flexibilization of prices? Is the approach accepted (e.g., because customers are in favor of the measures and consider them sensible)?
- How will the most important competitors react to the change in price management?
- How do important business partners, e.g., suppliers of branded goods, view the potentially greater price fluctuations in the retail sector?

While in the past the possibilities of dynamic price differentiation tended to fail because insufficient data and corresponding algorithms could not be used or the technical conditions (fixed price tags instead of digital displays) were simply not available, this does not mean that what is now technically feasible is necessarily advantageous for retail companies. Some dependencies are obvious: For example, there are opportunities for retailers to stimulate demand through a targeted price reduction for perishable goods and, for example, to avoid destroying food with an expired shelf life and ultimately achieve a positive cost effect. Other influencing factors are less clear in their scope at first glance. For example, the study by Krämer et al. (2015), which included interviews with retail pricing managers, revealed that there were two main reasons for not implementing dynamic price changes: Firstly, companies fear that their customer relationships would be damaged by making prices more flexible and dynamic (including loss of customer trust, negative image effects, etc.). They also lack personnel and technical know-how, combined with the fear of high resource costs. Expert interviews with marketing decision-makers in 2021 confirmed the sometimes considerable reservations (Krämer and Hercher 2021; Krämer and Merkle 2021). On closer inspection, it becomes clear which organizational changes, in addition to the "customer relationship construction site," companies that take the step toward implementing dynamic pricing will face.

The change in pricing will undoubtedly also attract the attention of key competitors. However, it is unclear how the parties involved will interpret this. In a worst-case scenario, individual competitors will relate the price changes to themselves and fear a loss of market share. This could trigger the initial impetus for price competition or even a price war (Krämer et al. 2016; Krämer 2025).

There may also be a conflict of objectives between the manufacturers of branded products that supply retailers and the retail company that sells the branded product to the end customer (and has pricing authority). In the study conducted by exeo Strategic Consulting AG and Rogator AG, "Pricing Lab" test subjects were presented with various statements for evaluation. Of eight randomly presented statements, the statement that brand products should not be changed in price very frequently (i.e., daily or several times a day) received the highest level of agreement (65%). The rejection rate here is only 9%. Nevertheless, there is an understanding that retail prices should be adjusted at certain intervals depending on the situation (38% agreement). Overall, it is also clear that consumers have high expectations in terms of price stability and reliability—especially for branded products. More than half of consumers (55%) are in favor of branded products having the same price at a retailer, regardless of whether they are sold online or in stores (Krämer 2016).

While brand manufacturers tend to take care not to allow large price variations to become noticeable in the market, dynamic pricing uses price variation to control demand in a targeted manner. This entails risks if consumers adjust their internal reference prices (e.g., the expected usual price or the favorable price for a product) downward, which consequently means a reduction in willingness to pay.

In conclusion, there is a need for networked thinking that combines different effects and does justice to the complexity of the topic. What is needed is less tunnel vision and more eagle eye.

1.3.2 Case Study: Dynamic Pricing (DP) as a "One-Way Street"

As described, flexible pricing has found its way into many areas of life. This is not always viewed positively. A worldwide media response followed the announcement by hamburger chain Wendy's that it would be introducing flexible pricing from 2025. The predominantly negative reviews were largely based on the assumption that the prices for a Frosty and fries would be categorically increased. Helhoski (2024) explains that it seems as if the fast food chain's supposedly insidious plans had already failed on arrival and reports that Wendy's quickly made it clear that it was not a price increase, but on the contrary about creating a technological basis for targeted price promotions ("To clarify, Wendy's will not implement surge pricing, which is the practice of raising prices when demand is highest"). This example alone illustrates how emotionally charged and communicatively explosive the term "dynamic pricing" is. Paraschiv et al. (2024) also refer to corresponding problems and emphasize that dynamic pricing is tantamount to a loss of control for many consumers. In case of doubt, consumers recognize how prices change over time but are unable to understand the patterns and the reasons behind them.

Today, DP is used in many industries, including entertainment, sports, and the ski industry. DP does not only promise a smoothing and increase in demand in the ski industry on the one hand and 0.5% to 7.5% higher sales on the other (Malasevska et al. 2020). However, there appear to be limits to the system of dynamic pricing. As Vomberg et al. (2024) point out, due to the use of pricing algorithms in online markets, for example, prices are increasingly fluctuating, which at the same time contradicts consumers' desire for price stability. The authors argue that algorithmic dynamic pricing (ADP) would reduce trust in the ADP retailer, but this negative effect diminishes after consumers become accustomed to ADP. The fact that Amazon has been using dynamic pricing for a long period of time seems to confirm their arguments. Other examples seem to confirm that the use of DP is not a one-way street: Following the implementation of dynamic pricing in many ski resorts in recent years, the results a few years later are less than euphoric. Some Swiss ski resorts (e.g., Andermatt-Sedrun-Disentis) have decided to abolish dynamic pricing for day tickets. In the meantime, it has become clear that what sounds good has a catch. It is true that day tickets purchased in advance are cheaper. "In this case, however, guests are also buying a pig in a poke because they don't know what kind of weather awaits them on the day of skiing," writes Andermatt Sedrun Disentis Marketing AG (NN 2024). Instead, the management relies on transparency to ensure customer satisfaction. These examples make clear that DP is also associated with risks, such as customers not understanding the pricing or perceiving it as unfair (Bambauer-Sachse and Young 2024). The new price system will have three fixed price levels from the 2024/2025 ski season: One price for customers who buy their ticket by 11:59 pm before the ski day, one price for customers with spontaneous purchases (on the ski day itself), and a third price for purchases on premium ski days from December 26 to January 7 and on weekends from January 25 to March 30, i.e., a peak price.

1.3.3   Interview Tom Shelton

Dynamic pricing (DP) has long been known and established in many industries (e.g. in the airline industry). The term Revenue Management (RM) is also used here. Do both terms describe the same thing?

Tom Shelton: Revenue Management is a relatively broad term that encompasses many different mechanisms and controls to optimize revenues.

In the 1980s and 1990s, RM or Yield Management as it was called in its infancy attempted to maximize yields within a fixed capacity environment by adjusting the availability of seats in specific booking classes that were associated with fixed price ranges. This type of RM/YM utilized the following:

- Inventory control systems to manage booking classes availability
- Forecasting demand for booking classes
- Estimating price elasticity by customer segment and booking class
- Optimization algorithms to establish optimal allocation levels based on EMSR (Expected Marginal Seat Revenue).

Many still use this approach but RM is now seen by many not only as a mechanism to improve yield but also optimize overall network revenue and profitability through using forecasts, optimization, and real-time controls to not only change booking class availability but also:

- Tactically adjust prices based on real time availability and demand data
- Tactically adjust capacities to increase overall profit by either eliminating excess capacity or adding capacity if those actions are profitability positive.

DP is one variation of this approach. In many ways, DP is analogous to bid pricing. That is, with real-time data about how many remaining units of inventory are available and the actual up to the minute demand data for the units, companies can establish the price for the unit without having to set booking class authorization controls that generally are changed once a day and are therefore slow in responding to demand anomalies. By responding to demand changes overnight and not in real time, booking class controls often take effect too late to really address demand deviations. In DP, the price would change in real time (dynamically) with each unit that is sold/booked/canceled or if capacity is added or deleted. Theoretically and within an airline, hotel, or car rental environment the fare, room price or daily rate could change every time there is a new booking or cancelation.

How does RM affect companies and consumers? Is there a win-win in every case? What are your personal experiences as a consultant and as a consumer?

Tom Shelton: While it is not a win-win in every case, RM can contribute significantly to the bottom line for companies if their RM approach is able to incorporate demand/supply anomalies that cannot always be modeled based on historic customer behavior data. My experiences as consultant with RM are only partially satisfying. The projects I have worked one can clearly show that RM has significantly improved overall revenues as well as capacity planning. RM gives a company a better understanding of long-term historic and granular demand patterns as well as providing an alert mechanism to show where current demand deviates from the norm, thereby giving companies more time to react to demand anomalies through either pricing or capacity adjustments.

As a consumer, my personal experiences are that RM is not the great equalizer. RM theory basically discriminates against consumers who have very little flexibility in terms of when they require the product/service with the assumption that the consumer that is less flexible is more willing to pay a higher price and of course on better economic footing than the consumer that is more flexible (retired, student, etc.). Furthermore, RM theory assumes that the price conscious consumer has competitive alternatives. I am not certain that real life bears out those assumptions. An argument has always been made that RM enables the cost conscious and also potentially the lower income customers to find bargains during off time periods. This does seem to be the case when applied to the leisure travel industry. However, I would challenge that this approach benefits customers in the food, basic necessity, and medical industries.

Recently, the implementation in system gastronomy or in stationary retail has been discussed, e.g., also for food. What is different here than in other sectors (airlines, hotels, rental cars, etc.)?

Tom Shelton: The food industry customer segmentation differs drastically from the airline and hotel customer segmentation where you have business/leisure segments with very different requirements and price sensitivities. Where would implementation of airline style RM end in the food industries or even medical services? Customers coming home from work at 6 pm (peak time) would pay 20% more for the same basic stable as a customer who shops at 2 pm? A patient who is willing to put off surgery to a non-peak hospital day would get a 20% discount? I believe this poses an ethical dilemma. On the positive side, the idea that the application of DP or RM in the retail food sector will reduce spoilage is something to consider as long as it does not result in higher overall costs to the already beaten down low and middle income consumer.

The announcement by the CEO of Wendy's to use DP in combination with artificial intelligence processes from 2025 has received a lot of media attention. Many interpreted this to mean Wendy's would be introducing surge pricing—a term often associated with the dynamic pricing models used by companies like Uber, where prices increase during periods of high demand.

Tom Shelton: Customer and media reaction have been unanimously negative. Hence the DP in the fast-food company has been put on hold. Instead, Wendy's and McDonald's are now back to offering $5 value meals. I have no doubt though that DP in the grocery/food industry will reemerge at some point.

The big promise for the customer is of course that somehow lower income customers will benefit by DP and/or surge pricing and for the company that DP will add significantly to their bottom line. The latter I agree with as long as customers don't abandon the company as we are seeing with their first attempt.

The interview partner: Tom Shelton is a consultant specializing in Pricing and Revenue Management. He spearheaded and managed the early development of airline-based YM for the passenger railway industry in the USA and Europe in both operational and consulting roles. As senior consultant, Tom has advised on and managed RM projects in the passenger rail, hotel, logistic, and public transport sectors for more than 25 years.

1.3.4   The Need for Networked Thinking

The challenge of finding the most holistic approach possible when making management decisions is essentially driven by the realization that optimal decisions can no longer be based on common patterns or casuistics (e.g., "we have always done it this way in comparable situations") because the interactions and dependencies are almost impossible for individuals to grasp. In this context, relying on "gut feeling" is only of limited help. The world is more dynamic, more networked, and ultimately more unpredictable, making common decision-making rules drop in value. According to Probst (2013), the following mistakes are made in this scenario:

* Insufficient problematization: This includes the uncritical adoption of values and goals and the uncritical perception of the situation. These are often distortions of perception, which also became known when failed major projects were investigated regarding the reasons for their failure (Jenner 2015).
* Unrealistic modeling and interpretation of the problem situation: This is possible if the company's situation is defined too narrowly or if interactions and control loops are excluded. For example, side effects could be ignored for reasons of simplification.
* Lack of openness to new solutions: There is no actual search for creative solutions that question everything. Instead, the focus is on the "tried and tested." Known cause-and-effect chains that have been observed in the past are applied to the current situation, even though the framework conditions no longer allow this.
* Inappropriate initiation and realization: Virtually overwhelmed by complexity, the watchword is to start with implementation first so that we can then react accordingly. At the same time, however, there are no indicators of an early warning system or there is only a delayed reaction to "disruptions".

Organizations often seek more information than they need, in the spirit of "more is better," but more information does not necessarily lead to better decisions, e.g., when it can lead to information overload and overconfidence (Russo and Schoemaker 1990). Experts generally rely on relatively few factors when making decisions. Exceptions are cases where feedback is prompt and precise, e.g., weather forecasts. However, these few factors can be used efficiently as a basis for decisions, which Gigerenzer (2007) calls "fast and frugal decision-making." Unfortunately, however, decision-makers often do not apply these factors consistently. When presented with irrelevant information, they tend to become more confident in their decisions. The list of perceptual biases presented to us by modern behavioral science is long. It ranges from confirmation bias (people see their own convictions confirmed rather than rejected by others) to availability bias (people rely on their own experiences or reports in the mass media when estimating probabilities).

The trick is to concentrate on just a few parameters. These must be highly relevant (core drivers of a given result), have a sensitive effect and capture, and map significant dependencies.

1.4   From Tunnel Vision to Eagle-Eye View: Book Structure

Several steps are required to identify these core parameters (Fig. 1.4). Chapter 2 first discusses the VUCA environment, in particular the effects catalyzed by the corona crisis and continued by multiple areas of disruption such as ongoing geopolitical instability, inflationary trends, sustainability issues, electromobility, and growing use of artificial intelligence. Current research results from our own studies are also included. The focus will deliberately be on a holistic approach, with the customer relationship being described as the core of entrepreneurial activity. This customer relationship is the key to the company's success. As many hopes are associated with the use of networked and large amounts of data, the topic of "A better understanding of big data" is the focus of Chap. 3, which examines the question of what big data can and cannot achieve.

In the following section (section B), the key points for customer value-centered management are highlighted: the triangle of benefit, price, and cost. The first core function, namely, customer benefit, is discussed in Chap. 4. This chapter deals with the question: What are actual customer needs? The first step is to create an understanding of customer benefits and needs, which will then allow customers to be segmented. The challenges of a 1:1 customer relationship are also addressed in this context. Chapter 5 then concentrates on the second core function, pricing, which includes an explanation of what is meant by the construct of the "optimal price".

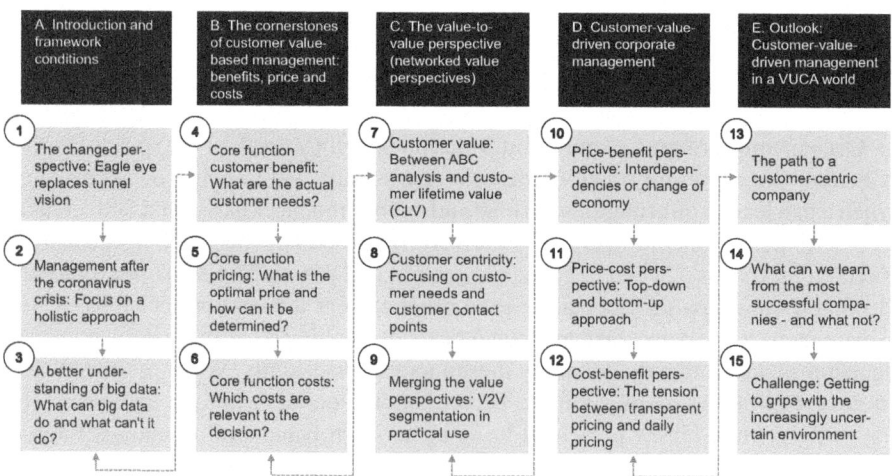

Fig. 1.4 Structure of the book and sequence of chapters

This requires a brief introduction to the importance of price as a marketing instrument and a differentiation between B2B and B2C markets. In addition to the profit potential that is attributed to effective pricing, there are also risks that can arise, for example, from triggering a price war. In this context, we also discuss the opportunities that arise from price differentiation, as well as the limits that restrict these opportunities. Thirdly, the core function of costs is analyzed in Chap. 6, which raises the question of which costs are relevant to decision-making. It also examines how costs are perceived by consumers and companies and how they differ. In this context, cost-related pricing methods (cost-plus pricing) are examined, as is the resilience of the marginal cost = zero assumption.

Section C explains the value-to-value perspective, whereby the different facets of customer value are initially presented as individual strands. Chapter 7, for example, first examines customer value from the company's perspective, i.e., the "value-of-the-customer" and shows the transitions from simple ABC analysis to relatively complex customer lifetime value calculations. It also reveals a balancing act between simple and complex implementations, the advantages and disadvantages of which are described. At the same time, the chapter also deals with a supposed theory-practice gap and explores the question of why the implementation of CLV in companies is more difficult than expected and fails more frequently. The second customer value strand (Chap. 8) deals with customer value from the customer's perspective, i.e., value-to-the-customer. The concept of customer centricity, i.e., the company's focus on customer needs and processes, is also discussed. In this context, the central importance of customer experience in customer management has been repeatedly emphasized in recent years. This gives the impression that it is a function that has not been given (sufficient) consideration in the world of CRM to date. However, it remains to be seen how far the requirement of satisfying customer needs can go. Only after the two value strands have been discussed separately will the value perspectives be brought together in Chap. 9: A networking of both views is proposed in the further course, which also enables self-contained customer segmentation (value-to-value segmentation). Using various project examples from different industries, firstly the broad scope of application will be explained and secondly a concrete use of the segmentation approach to answer strategic and operational questions will be demonstrated.

Section D deals with the design of customer value-centered corporate management: The focus is on the management and controlling of the interfaces between benefit, price, and costs, which are analyzed separately. In the first step, Chap. 10 examines the special features of the price-benefit perspective. This concerns the approach of value-based pricing, a method that has become popular in the last 20 years and which has been identified as the "non-plus-ultra" within the pricing consultant community. Essentially, the aim is to find a way to exploit these willingness-to-pay values as far as possible based on the customer's individual willingness to pay and thus monetize the customer benefit. In this context, the challenges of measuring willingness to pay and implementing value-based pricing are discussed. Chapter 11 examines the price-cost perspective. It deals with the possibilities and limitations of target costing to optimize price and costs and to develop products in such a way that the price is particularly attractive to customers. The orientation toward the competition and customer requirements determines the cost framework, the target costs, for products, and components. Chapter 12 deals with the interface between costs and benefits. In the sense of incremental change, the effects of different performance characteristics (products or services) on the costs and perceived benefits from the customer's perspective must be examined, which is a major challenge in practice. This question leads to application examples for target costing and target pricing (based on Chap. 11). Advancing digitalization in particular enables the provision of individual services with high potential customer benefits, while costs remain low based on automation.

Section E provides an outlook on customer management in a VUCA world after the coronavirus crisis. Section 13 first attempts to take up the previous argumentation and, building on this, to point out concrete steps on the way to a customer value-centered company. Aspects that have already been addressed are also included here (Why do managers need to rethink? What role does the changed data situation play? Why it ultimately comes down to the employees?). Because it always makes sense to look at particularly successful companies and to expect special insights for one's own business, Chap. 14 poses the question "What you can learn from the most successful companies - and what not." Against the background of the previous argument, the examples of Amazon and Apple, both of which are among the most valuable companies in the world, but whose view of customer (value) differs fundamentally, are examined. Finally, Chap. 15 takes up the VUCA scenario discussed at the beginning and illustrates how a company can be aligned using the key performance indicator of customer value.

The structure of the book is shown in Fig. 1.4:

Three main questions will be discussed:

- Why is customer value considered a key performance indicator in customer-centric management?
- Why is centering the customer essential for the success of a company?
- What exactly is new about this way of thinking and what needs to be considered when implementing it?

The thought processes outlined in this chapter show very clearly that modern management needs to reinvent itself. It is also advisable to rethink customer value. In view of the discussion at the beginning of this chapter, there is certainly no question that customer value plays a significant role as a central entity and is becoming increasingly important. However, the extent to which existing patterns of thought and behavior of companies are sufficient or need to be expanded, supplemented, or even structured innovatively from the ground up to do justice to the clearly groundbreaking framework conditions will be answered by the end of the book.

References

Artz M (2017) NPS—the one measure you really need to grow? Control & Manag Rev 61(1):32–38

Bambauer-Sachse S, Young A (2024) Consumers' intentions to spread negative word of mouth about dynamic pricing for services: role of confusion and unfairness perceptions. J Serv Res 27(3):364–380. The following section contains an interview with Tom Shelton, a leading specialist in the field of dynamic pricing

Bendle NT, Bagga CK (2016) The metrics that marketers muddle. MIT Sloan Manag Rev 57(3):73–78

Bloomberg J (2018) Digitization, digitalization, and digital transformation: confuse them at your peril. Forbes. Accessed 25 Aug 2020

Bloomfire (2023) Customer insights vs. market research: How do they differ? Jan 04, 2023, https://bloomfire.com/resources/customer-insights-vs-market-research/. Accessed 9 May 2025

Bohari AM, Rainis R, Marimuthu M (2011) Customer lifetime value model in perspective of firm and customer: practical issues and limitation on prospecting profitable customers of hypermarket business. Intern J Bus Manag 6(8):161–169

Bughin J, Catlin T, Hirt M, Willmott P (2018) Why digital strategies fail. McKinsey Quarterly 1:61–75

Dahlgaard-Park SM, Dahlgaard JJ (2006) In search of excellence–past, present and future. Kreativ und konsequent 2(3):57–84

Deelmann T, Krämer A (2020) Consulting: Ein Lehr-, Lern- und Lesebuch. Erich Schmidt Verlag, Berlin

Edvardsson B, Gustafsson A, Olsen LL, Witell L (2014) Turning customer satisfaction measurements into action. J Serv Manag 25:556–571

Einstein A (1950). https://quoteinvestigator.com/2011/05/13/einstein-simple/. Accessed 25 Aug 2020

Elderkin K, Bartlett C (1993) General Electric: Jack Welch's second wave. Case 9-391-248. Harvard Business School, Boston

Fader P (2020) Customer centricity: focus on the right customers for strategic advantage. Wharton Digital Press, Philadelphia

Fassnacht M (2009) Preismanagement: Eine prozessorientierte Perspektive. Mark Rev St Gallen 5:8–13

Fornell C, Johnson MD, Anderson EW, Cha J, Bryant BE (1996) The American customer satisfaction index: nature, purpose, and findings. J Mark 60(4):7–18

Friedrich K (2007) Erfolgreich durch Spezialisierung: Kompetenzen entwickeln, Kerngeschäfte ausbauen, Konkurrenz überholen. Redline Wirtschaft, Heidelberg

Frohmann F (2018) Digitales Pricing. Springer Gabler, Wiesbaden

Ghiadi S, Chroqui R, Chafik OKAR (2020) Marketing performance measurement criteria: which measure to choose? Strategy Manag Logistics 2(4):1–5

Gigerenzer G (2007) Gut feelings. Penguin Allen Lane, New York

Gutmann J (2019) Der Greta-Effekt, FAZ online vom 22.3.2019. https://www.faz.net/aktuell/politik/inland/was-fridays-for-future-aktivisten-antreibt-zeigt-eine-studie-16103010.html. Accessed 25 Aug 2020

Helhoski A (2024) Wendy's isn't the first: dynamic pricing is everywhere. Nerdwallet.com v. 14.3.2024, https://www.nerdwallet.com/article/finance/dynamic-pricing. Accessed 2 June 2024

Helm S, Günter B, Eggert A (2017) Kundenwert. Springer Fachmedien, Wiesbaden

Hoffrage U, Hertwig R, Gigerenzer G (2005) Die ökologische Rationalität einfacher Entscheidungs- und Urteilsheuristiken. In: Siegenthaler H (Hrsg) Rationalität im Prozess kultureller Evolution: Rationalitätsunterstellungen als eine Bedingung der Möglichkeit substantieller Rationalität des Handelns. Mohr/Siebeck, Tübingen, S 65–89

Hofmann M (1987) Management Consulting: Ausgewählte Probleme und Entwicklungstendenzen der Unternehmensberatung. Kohlhammer

Hofmann M (ed) (2013) Theorie und Praxis der Unternehmensberatung: Bestandsaufnahme und Entwicklungsperspektiven. Springer, Wiesbaden

Husemann-Kopetzky M (2020) Preispsychologie: In vier Schritten zur optimierten Preisgestaltung. Springer

IMF (2025) World economic outlook update: Navigating economic turbulence. International Monetary Fund. May 9, 2025

Jenner S (2015) Why do projects 'fail' and more to the point what can we do about it? The case for disciplined, 'fast and frugal' decision-making. Management 45(2):6–19

Kessler J, Steiner C (2009) Facetten der Globalisierung: Zwischen Ökonomie, Politik und Kultur. In: Facetten der Globalisierung. VS Verlag, S, pp 19–27

Krämer A (2011) Alternative Honorarmodelle im Anwaltsgeschäft. In: Staub L, Hehli-Hidber C (Hrsg) Management von Anwaltskanzleien. Manz, Wien, pp 581–591

Krämer A (2016) Flexibles Pricing: Risiko für starke Marken? Mark Theory 78(12):62–65

Krämer A (2025) Preiskommunikation in Zeiten des "Behavioral Pricing". In: Preiskommunikation: Strategische Herausforderungen und innovative Anwendungsfelder Wiesbaden: Springer Fachmedien Wiesbaden, pp. 29–53

Krämer A, Hercher J (2020) OpinionTRAIN 2020: Rogator/exeo untersuchen die Sicht der Bevölkerung auf das Krisenmanagement der Regierungen sowie die Beeinträchtigung der Arbeitswelt durch die Corona-Pandemie. https://www.rogator.de/unterstuetzung-regierungencorona-krise/. Accessed 25 Aug 2020

Krämer A, Hercher J (2021) Dynamic Pricing im stationären Handel: Die Sicht von Handelsexperten. 18 May 2021. https://www.pressebox.de/pressemitteilung/rogatorag/Dynamic-Pricing-im-stationaeren-Handel-Die-Sicht-vonHandelsexperten/boxid/1059425?utm_source=Belegmail&utm_medium=Email&utm_campaign=Aktiv. Accessed 24 Aug 2021

Krämer A, Merkle W (2021) Dynamic Pricing im stationären Handel – betriebswirtschaftliche Chance oder unternehmerisches Risiko? Forschungsbericht des Value Research Institute (VARI) Nr. 1, 1.8.2021, Bonn

Krämer A, Schmutz I (2020) Mythos Value-Based Pricing: Der Versuch einer (wertfreien) Einordnung. Mark Rev St Gallen 37(2):44–53

Krämer A, Wilger G (1999) Messung von vielschichtigen Kundenpräferenzen mittels Conjoint Measurement. Planung Anal 18(5):50–56

Krämer A, Wilger G, Dethlefsen H (2001) Es muss nicht immer Conjoint sein: Kundensegmentierung als Basis des neuen Preissystems der Deutschen Bahn. Planung Anal 20(6):74–79

Krämer A, Wilger G, Böhrs S (2005) Value-to-Value-Segmentation—Die Integration von Kundennutzen und Kundenwert als Ansatz für das Kundenmanagement. Planung Anal 24(4):55–59

Krämer A, Kalka R, Ziehe N (2015) Personalisiertes und dynamisches Pricing aus Einzelhandelsund Verbrauchersicht. Mark Rev St Gallen 6:28–37

Krämer A, Jung M, Burgartz T (2016) A small step from price competition to price war—understanding causes, effects and possible countermeasures. Int Bus Res 9(3):1–13

Kristensen K, Eskildsen J (2014) Is the NPS a trustworthy performance measure? TQM J 26(2):202–214

Kuß A, Wildner R, Kreis H (2014) Marktforschung: Grundlagen der Datenerhebung und Datenanalyse. Springer, Wiesbaden

Lemon KN, Rust RT, Zeithaml VA (2001) What drives customer equity? Mark Manag 10(1):20–25

Macintosh G, Gentry JW (1999) Decision making in personal selling: testing the "KISS principle". Psychol Mark 16(5):393–408

Mack O, Khare A, Krämer A, Burgartz T (2016) Managing in a VUCA world. Springer, New York

Malasevska I, Haugom E, Hinterhuber A, Lien G, Mydland Ø (2020) Dynamic pricing assuming demand shifting: the alpine skiing industry. J Travel Tour Mark 37(7):785–803

Merkle W, Krämer A (2021) Händler brauchen für Dynamic Pricing eine Gesamtstrategie. Lebensmittelzeitung 12(3):46

Morgan B (2019) 101 of the best customer experience quotes, Forbes online v 342019. https://
    wwwforbescom/sites/blakemorgan/2019/04/03/101-of-the-best-customer   experiencequotes/.
    Accessed 2 Sept 2020
NN (2024) Zu drei verschiedenen Tarifen auf die Skipiste: Andermatt-Sedrun-Disentis setzt auf
    Transparenz. Urner Zeitung v. 10.10.2024, https://www.urnerzeitung.ch/zentralschweiz/uri/
    andermatt-sedrun-disentis-fertig-mit-dynamic-pricing-in-andermatt-gehts-wieder-zu-fixen-
    preisen-auf-die-piste-ld.2683386. Accessed 15 Oct 2024
Paraschiv C, Ayadi N, Rousset X, Turinici M (2024) Consumer vulnerability to dynamic pricing in
    online environments. Appl Econ 56(25):3032–3047
Probst GJ (2013) Vernetztes Denken: Unternehmen ganzheitlich führen. Springer, Wiesbaden
Rego A (2010) Complexity, simplicity, simplexity. Eur Manag J 28(2):85–94
Reichheld F (2003) The one number you need to grow. Harv Bus Rev 12:2–10
Reichheld F, Markey R (2011) The ultimate question 2.0: how net promoter companies thrive in a
    customer-driven world. Rev. and expanded ed. Harvard Business Review Press, Boston
Ricardo D (1821) On the principles of political economy and taxation. John Murray, London
Russo JE, Schoemaker PH (1990) Decision traps decisions—how to make the right decision first
    time. Simon & Schuster
Rust RT, Lemon KN, Zeithaml VA (2004) Return on marketing: using customer equity to focus
    marketing strategy. J Mark 68(1):109–127
Saxer M (2020) Das Ende der Globalisierung, wie wir sie kennen, Der Spiegel Online v.
    11.04.2020.   https://www.spiegel.de/wirtschaft/corona-krise-das-ende-der-globalisierung-
    wiewir-sie-kennen-a-af9f2dd4-f5ce-4402-903f-c6b4949bd562. Accessed 25 Aug 2020
Skog DA, Wimelius H, Sandberg J (2018) Digital disruption. Bus Inf Syst Eng 60(5):431–437
Spreer P (2018) PsyConversion. Springer Fachmedien, Wiesbaden
Vomberg A, Homburg C, Sarantopoulos P (2024) Algorithmic pricing: effects on consumer trust
    and price search. Int J Res Mark. In press
Wandke H (2018) Failure in use of technology. In: Kunert S (ed) Strategies in failure management.
    Springer, Cham, pp 287–306
Woodruff RB (1997) Customer value: the next source for competitive advantage. J Acad Mark Sci
    25(2):139–153

Management in a Multi-crisis Environment

2

2.1 Consequences of the Corona Crisis

"Character proves itself in a crisis"—Helmut Schmidt

Former German Chancellor Schmidt observed that crisis situations require or bring out special character traits. In retrospect, the significance of the long-serving and frequently criticized Federal Chancellor Schmidt is particularly evident in his actions in crisis situations, be it flood disasters or terrorist attacks. In general, business management defines the term crisis as the state of a company that calls its viability into question, whereby the company's potential for success, net assets, and/or liquidity have developed so unfavorably that its existence is acutely threatened (Niering and Hillebrand 2020). The pandemic triggered by COVID-19 can be described as one of the most influential economic crises in modern history (So et al. 2021). Economic cycles and ecosystems were hit hard at both regional and international levels (Sansa 2020). The effects affected financial markets as well as the labor market, which has experienced lasting changes triggered or accelerated by the crisis in individual sectors (Bartik et al. 2020).

The entire world population is therefore currently facing a global challenge. COVID-19 can be seen as a mere episode among a plethora of rapidly developing megatrends and geopolitical upheavals impacting firms. It is clear that the subsequent economic crisis alone could be huge. In addition, climate change will bring serious changes for companies, as will digitalization, which has received an additional boost from the virus crisis (Lawrence et al. 2024). In subsequent years, a landscape of multiple and partially overlapping crises has developed (Lawrence et al. 2024).

Thriving despite these disruptions cannot be achieved alone: The era of the omniscient manager who guides his employees through implementation is definitely over. The task of the leader of tomorrow is to bring together and coordinate different perspectives. This is not just about interdisciplinary thinking and multi-perspective action. Complementary personalities are also needed in management teams. For example, a manager who is more security-oriented would do well to bring in people who think differently, less risk-averse, more open, and more dynamic. In this context, it is important to differentiate between management and leadership: Management is oriented toward results that can be evaluated based on past experience, whereas leadership describes the process that leads to a specific result. Both disciplines will have to continue to develop or redevelop.

2.2   Volatility and Uncertainty as Management Challenges

Uncertainty is one of the defining attributes of the current economic era (Bordo et al. 2001). Although previous periods of economic development have been characterized by a high degree of volatility and uncertainty, the current situation appears to be more strongly influenced by these aspects than ever before, particularly in terms of the extent and the speed of change.

Developments such as globalization and digitalization have significantly accelerated the cycle of change in the business world (Bordo et al. 2001). Key examples in this book include elected economic crises and their cycle times, which have been subject to significant change since the 1970s. Research such as that by Dow (2015) and Carriero et al. (2018) also notes that the increasing level of uncertainty and the associated difficulty of long-term forecasts (and therefore long-term strategies) represent a challenge for business leaders. Strategy development is increasingly being described as a part of risk and crisis management, with intervals between key economic crises such as the oil crisis in 1973, the new economy crisis in 2001, and the financial crisis in 2008 (Dow 2015) seen as occurring with a certain rhythm.

Falling transaction costs due to new information and communication technologies and the general reduction of protectionism between countries with regard to the flow of financial capital, human resources, and manufactured goods are some of the reasons for an increasingly networked and crisis-prone global economy. The accelerated pace at which new economies and trends are gaining traction, as seen in China's rapid growth and the rise of social media in less than a decade, also requires adequate tools to plan for and respond to such challenges. Companies must constantly adapt to new circumstances such as new products, technologies, or management concepts. The competitiveness of organizations is strongly determined by managers' ability to formulate concepts and strategies that correctly identify future trends and anticipate market changes.

Even though managing and doing business in a threatening, globalized, and uncertain environment has become more challenging, it also offers opportunities if planned effectively (Thießen 2014). Agile allocation of financial resources to create the potential for future flexibility is key to responding to volatility and economic downturns. According to Bennett and Lemoine (2014), gathering information both internally and externally and analyzing input from different angles is critical to reducing uncertainty. Restructuring a business operation to encounter external complexity helps to reduce it, and intelligent experimentation enables the determination of beneficial strategies. In other words, their findings suggest that organizations can best address the uncertain environment by thinking about multiple potential scenarios that are controlled and supported by flexible planning of financial resources as part of the strategic decision-making process.

2.3 Resilience Management in Times of Crisis

Resilience describes a mixture of individual characteristics and abilities to successfully adapt to challenges, stressful situations, and even crises, to overcome them without personal harm, but also to grow internally from these experiences (Bleiber 2021). Studies on resilience focus on characteristics, later increasingly on skills. Numerous studies and measurement tools now exist to determine relevant resilience indicators. For development measures for companies, changeable concepts are of particular interest—after all, innate characteristics cannot (or can hardly) be changed (Heller and Gallenmüller 2019). Modern approaches describe organizational resilience as an aspect of organizations that can be influenced by various means.

Organizational resilience is the ability of a system to return to a stable state after a disruption (Burnard and Bhamra 2011). Luthans describes resilience as the ability to recover from or withstand adversity, conflict, failure or even positive events, progress, and increased responsibility (Luthans 2002). In times of uncertainty, crisis, and rapid market change, only flexible and resilient organizations can not only survive but also thrive (Lengnick-Hall et al. 2011). Despite the common perception of a crisis as a threat to organizational well-being, it can be seen as an opportunity for resilient organizations, as those companies that can easily adapt and change can evolve along with a dynamic environment and turn threats into opportunities and their competitive advantage (Fleming 2012).

There are two main perspectives on organizational resilience: Some authors see organizational resilience as the ability of a company to recover its performance after a crisis (Gittell et al. 2006; Tugade and Fredrickson 2004; Walker et al. 2004). Companies are considered resilient as soon as they are fast enough to return to their original state after a damaging experience (Luthans 2002).

The second perspective on organizational resilience goes beyond the ability to recover from a crisis and implies that an organization, after being affected by negative events, can not only return to where it was before the crisis but can also increase its capacities and knowledge and thus even improve its competitive advantage compared to the pre-crisis state (Vogus and Sutcliffe 2007). This view offers a transformational approach to organizational development. It implies that by constantly learning, adapting, applying new strategies, and being ready to respond to upcoming challenges with an adaptive strategy, an organization subsequently increases its chances of growth in times of a new crisis, as knowledge tends to accumulate (Lengnick-Hall et al. 2011).

With regard to crisis management, reference must first and foremost be made to the large number of different crises and their varying degrees of complexity (Damodaran 2007). Crisis management as such is therefore not described as a standardized procedure, but rather as a combination of different approaches and strategies that must fit the respective crisis situation. Janssen et al. (2015), for example, explain this by saying that a fundamental distinction must be made between different types of crises. In this regard, the nature of these crises in particular is described as central. Accordingly, crises can be triggered by internal factors or caused by external conditions, for example. Combinations of these two cause constellations can also occur naturally and are a typical situation, especially in practice (OECD 2025).

2.4   The Management Challenge of Megatrends

Highly dynamic changes in the environment are forcing more and more companies to constantly question and realign their strategies and business models, processes, products and services, organizational forms, communication structures, and much more. In addition to the aftermath of the coronavirus pandemic described above, other megatrends will have a major impact on management activities. Megatrends describe extremely complex dynamics of change and are a model for how the world is changing. They involve the observation of long-term developments with great relevance for all areas of the economy and society. Megatrends are the concentrated result of new developments in the economy and society. Analyzing these always means being able to identify their impact on industries, companies, and markets at an early stage but ultimately also on each individual (customer). As the biggest drivers of change, megatrends generate eminent changes that shape the economy in the medium to long term. They develop their momentum over decades and can form the basis for comparatively rapid breakthroughs on the markets and for disruptions. In the long term, they influence entire societies and often force entire industries to reorganize their structures and business models. Against this backdrop, the examination of megatrends is an indispensable tool for decision-oriented management and strategic planning and determines the future thinking and actions of companies (Rump and Eilers 2020).

One major trend, for example, is climate change and its associated impact on the environment. Organizations are called upon to develop sustainable environmental concepts and implement environmentally friendly business practices in order to meet the challenges of climate change and guarantee the careful use of increasingly scarce natural resources. The growing demand for sustainability is reflected in the European Union's decision to adopt the EU Taxonomy in a move from voluntary to required nonfinancial reporting frameworks for a growing number of companies.

This makes sense both for cost reasons and due to increasing consumer demand and means that managers with strong strategic and conceptual skills are in demand. They should be able to strike a balance between competition, social responsibility, financial success, and environmental protection. For companies, business processes are changing due to the fusion of modern technologies. As a result, cooperation and cross-industry partnerships are becoming increasingly important. The challenge for managers is to realize the potential of these innovations for their functional areas and to establish concepts for implementation and further development.

Another megatrend is digitalization, which combines the digital lifestyle and the digital way of working. Both companies and workplaces are becoming more virtual due to technological developments, blurring the boundaries between private and working life. The young generation (Y/Z) has technical know-how that is often lacking among more experienced specialists, a quality now considered a prerequisite for innovation. From a manager's perspective, it is important to bring these two groups of employees together and pool their knowledge in order to be and remain competitive in the long term (Akin and Rumpf 2013).

New digital technologies mean that many companies must face a changed competitive situation. The barriers to market entry for companies that are repositioning themselves on the market, such as Uber, Airbnb, and Netflix, have fallen. Digitalization has led to a change in customers' expectations of companies. Customers expect companies to have a presence on the Internet and to be accessible. However, a distinction must be made here between different customer expectations: On the one hand, the customer of an online store may wish to be able to use individual offers by collecting and evaluating a lot of data. On the other hand, other customers expect to be able to shop anonymously in the online store. In addition to the challenges described, however, digitalization also offers opportunities. The Internet is making it increasingly easy to expand into other countries, reach your own customers throughout the day, and thus offer them the best possible shopping options (Henriette et al. 2016). It is therefore even more important for companies not to use the latest technologies without hesitation. Instead, a detailed analysis must first be carried out and the opportunities and risks associated with the technology must be considered. The aim should be to develop both the right approach and an appropriate response when dealing with technologies (Harwardt 2020a).

Digital transformation is not specifically aimed at introducing digital technologies into companies. This is the fundamental distinction from digitalization (Biesel and Hame 2018). Digital transformation indicates a focus on transformation and restructuring processes in the world of business and work based on digital and virtual application potential.

This implies a fundamental change in the factors of place, time, and the nature of work, including its reorganization (Schröter 2018). New technologies can be introduced during the digital transformation, but they do not necessarily have to be. This is because digital transformation always pursues certain goals, such as increasing productivity and sales, implementing new communication infrastructures and business models, revising existing business models, or generating new value and competitive advantages through new ways of communicating with customers (Ebert and Duarte 2018). Consequently, digital transformation is a process that uses digital technologies to bring about targeted, holistic changes and is focused on specific goals (Harwardt 2020b).

2.5   Sustainable Drivers for Balanced Post-Corona Management

> "Crisis is a productive state. You just have to take away the taste of catastrophe."— Max Frisch

Crises are always accompanied by a wealth of negative associations. Nevertheless, crises also always offer the opportunity for a new beginning or a necessary change. This is what Max Frisch means when he describes the "productive state." In the search for simple solutions, three facets of long-term, sustainable management appear to be of crucial importance in view of the challenges and megatrends outlined above. Traditional leadership is being replaced by a modern, open leadership concept that integrates the experiences of the crisis.

"Cushioning" and predicting future crises is possible through transparent risk management and controlling. And the rapid developments, particularly in the course of digitalization and the transformation of business processes, raise the question of the "right" business model. This is primarily about business model innovations that go beyond pure product or service innovation that change the fundamental structure of a business and satisfy customer needs better than existing business models. All three cornerstones are significantly shaped by the customer relationship, but at the same time aim to actively influence it. The topic of customer risks is therefore only one facet of risk management. However, this facet will often become the driving force in the future. The same applies to corporate management and the business model (Fig. 2.1).

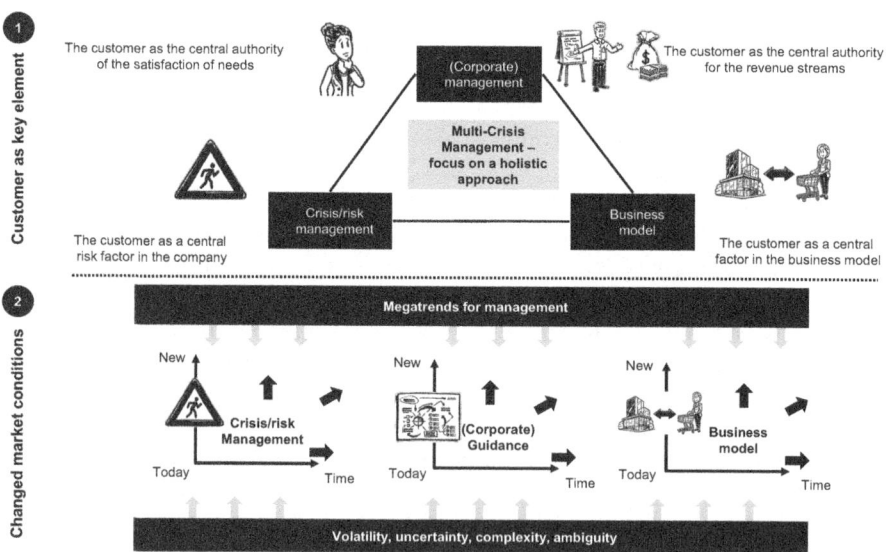

Fig. 2.1 Drivers for sustainable management in a period of multiple crises

2.5.1   Risk Management and Controlling of Customer Relationships in a VUCA Environment

Successful entrepreneurship without the management of opportunities and risks is unthinkable. Risk management comprises the systematic analysis, evaluation, planning, and control of corporate risks. The main task of risk management is to recognize critical situations in the course of the company's activities at an early stage and to avoid or reduce them. In particular, it is about avoiding and reducing risks and improving the ability to control and plan in critical situations, as well as recognizing risks at an early stage and then combating them effectively and as quickly as possible. The early identification of risks serves as an early warning system for company management (Brauweiler 2019).

Efficient and effective risk management is one of the elementary control and management instruments of top management and has established itself as a key success factor for all functional areas. Particularly in times of extreme crisis, the early identification, prompt analysis, and appropriate management of risks are the predominant challenges for value-oriented, sustainable controlling (Reichmann et al. 2017).

A risk management system to be established therefore consists of the entirety of all tasks, regulations, and risk management bodies and aims to ensure that a risk situation is evaluated in its entirety at regular intervals. For example, long-term, profitable customer relationships must be analyzed to determine the extent to which the targeted customer values (customer equity) exhibit a risk pattern from the outset over the duration of the relationship that jeopardizes its continued existence. The strategy can therefore be to focus on the long-term effects of customer loyalty and exploit growth opportunities or, if necessary, to seek to terminate the customer relationship (Shin et al. 2012; Krämer and Burgartz 2019).

Derived from such a primary objective, customer-oriented risk management must ensure that all risks relevant to business activities are identified at an early stage. In order to identify risks, particularly those that could jeopardize the company's success, sufficient information must first be available on the consequences of assuming the respective risks. A market-related analysis of the fundamental risks to be taken into account serves as the first step in order to assess the fundamental market conditions, competitive market attractiveness, and industry-specific market risks in terms of risk awareness (Fig. 2.2).

At the same time, the risks in customer relationship management can be differentiated according to whether the "value-to-the-customer" aspect (is the perceived value of a provider's service stable in the market?) or the "value-of-the-customer" aspect (is the profitability of individual customer relationships at risk?) is affected (Burgartz and Krämer 2016).

This shows that the risk management process must be flexible enough to take account of the company's individual circumstances and requirements in a natural way in a VUCA market environment (Fig. 2.3). In addition, an open process is required for new developments and changing framework conditions. This dynamization requires individually retrievable data and information in order to be

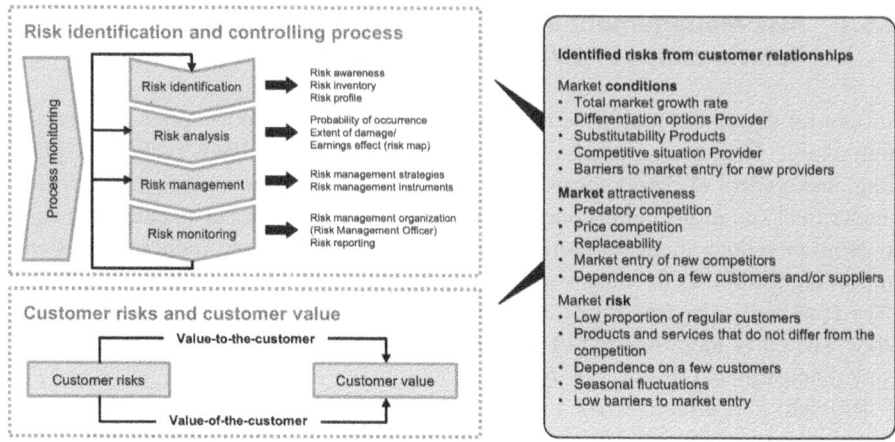

Fig. 2.2 Risk identification in customer relationship management

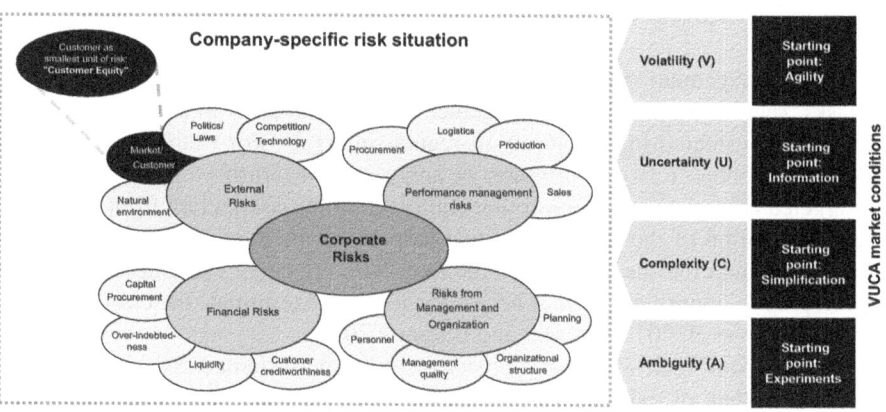

Fig. 2.3 Customer risk identification: General risk profile

able to guarantee the maximum possible return through long-term customer relationships.

The starting point for subsequent considerations is the consideration of the ideal-typical causal chain of relationship marketing. An essential feature of this is thinking in terms of cause-and-effect relationships, whereby the focus is on the effect between individual isolated constructs (Burgartz 2008). From a risk perspective, the company's activities as an input of the company (e.g., relationship marketing measures), the effects of the company's activities on the customer (psychological effects, e.g., in the form of positive quality perception and behavioral effects, e.g., in the form of customer loyalty) and economic success as an output of the company (e.g., sales) are decisive (Bruhn and Homburg 2017). Ideally, this success-relevant information should be translated into meaningful key figures.

A VUCA environment, described as a rapidly changing, highly turbulent and almost unpredictable environment for companies, presents them with additional challenges (Burgartz and Krämer 2016). In the socio-cultural environment, demographic developments and consumer-related social trends should be mentioned. They manifest themselves in heterogeneous customer behaviors that are difficult to assess and are based on differentiated expectations and different levels of knowledge. Furthermore, fast-moving trends have an impact on companies' product range policies. This requires a well-founded risk identification using suitable tools (e.g., market research, especially on customer needs and trend developments) in order to ultimately derive targeted measures with regard to customer approach, product policy, and product range design. If the focus is on the value of a customer relationship, the customer can be regarded as the smallest unit of risk (customer equity) and is to be assigned to a risk identification, as shown in Fig. 2.3.

2.5.2 Leadership Against the Backdrop of the Multi-Crisis-environment and VUCA

The triad of drivers for sustainable management after corona also shows the special responsibility of a company's management. If customer centricity becomes the focus of a holistic management approach, the new challenges must be addressed and secured together with employees and from the customer's perspective.

According to the principles of modern leadership theories, such as transformational leadership, leaders today are seen more as role models, coaches, and mentors. Every good leader is characterized by basic management skills and a confident approach to challenges. The special leadership challenges and areas of tension in the digital age, combined with the COVID-19 crisis and the increasing demands of the VUCA world, place high demands on the roles, skills, and behavior of managers (from Au 2020). On the one hand, managers must acknowledge the digital transformation processes and acquire new skills themselves, while on the other hand they are faced with the task of inspiring employees to use new technologies.

The new requirements of this changed world of work are increased cost and innovation pressure, networked technologies, and big data. New markets are leading to constant change, the loss and reorganization of jobs, and uncertainty about the future. The idea of New Work has experienced an abrupt boost due to the outbreak of the coronavirus crisis and at the latest since the first lockdown (Mar./Apr. 2020) and has gone from being a much-discussed postulate to a practiced working reality in many companies. All of these developments also have an impact on management.

Mobile working is only one facet. According to study results from BITKOM (2020), the proportion of employees working from home has risen from around 18% (before coronavirus) to 45% in Oct./Nov. 2020 (start of the second lockdown) and is expected to be 35% after the crisis. According to most forecasts, this corona-related leap will not be completely reversible but rather will become the norm for many employees. This has far-reaching consequences for the organization of work, for the flow of information, for hierarchies and decision-making channels, and even for communication. Some years later, remote work remains a significant component of the labor landscape in both the United States and Europe. In the U.S., approximately 40% of employees engage in remote work at least one day per week, reflecting a substantial shiftfrom pre-pandemic norms (Barrero et al. 2023). In Europe, the adoption of remote work varies across regions, with urban areas and capital regions adapting more swiftly due to a higher concentration of occupations amenable to telework. These new framework parameters are also accompanied by another aspect, the new leadership. There is no doubt that the question of maximum corporate success always goes hand in hand with the question of maximum customer focus. Creating added value for the customer therefore leads to "customer-oriented management." This means that entrepreneurs and managers must succeed in aligning internal fields of activity in favor of customer management and at the expense of ineffective meetings, emails, and reports. Otherwise, there is a risk that the focus on internal, tightly knit processes due to an outdated management culture will mean that the customer is not at the center of activities geared toward customer benefit.

2.5.3   Business Models Put to the Test: Managing Customer Relationships in VUCA Times

"The greatest danger in times of turbulence is not the turbulence; it is to act with yesterday's logic."—Peter Drucker

2.5.3.1 How Companies Take Off After Crisis: The Focus Is on the Customer

The corona crisis is reforming companies' business models, structures, and processes. Key topics are virtual management in the mobile office, the need to adapt cost management, and targeted investments. Various studies analyze the situation and provide tips for a successful "restart." Studies have concluded that the crisis is driving digitalization forward and that the focus will be on customers more than ever. Decision-makers in companies are under enormous pressure to act when it comes to digitalization. Decision-makers not only need to correctly assess the changed framework conditions, but they also need to question whether familiar patterns of argumentation and decision-making are and will remain effective. This is what Peter Drucker means when he warns against acting "with yesterday's logic." In particular, the areas of data strategy, digital business models, digital products and services, as well as operational processes should be mentioned here. The transformation begins at the digital customer interface and must extend across the company's entire value chain.

2.5.3.2 Business Model Grid in Times of Digitalization

In this situation, a guide to a business model that is resilient to the crisis can help. A clear and generally recognized definition of the term "business model" does not currently exist (Werani et al. 2017). The term is frequently discussed in the relevant literature, especially in the course of transformation processes, but there are many different interpretations that assign a wide variety of functions to business models. In this context, it is probably apt to recognize that literature operates in thematic silos (Jaekel 2015). Business model definitions are often considered and defined in the context of research, which is why there is no universal validity. Depending on the industry, company, or research focus, different aspects of a "business model" are mapped, focused on, and analyzed in more detail.

So the term "illustration" is certainly also well met by "description." A business model attempts to present the complexity of a company in as structured and simplified a way as possible. Sometimes, however, the function of a business model goes beyond the descriptive part, as it can also be regarded as an analytical construct (Becker et al. 2017). In terms of content, the resources or resource transformation and exchange relationships mentioned by Wirtz (2021) are too short-sighted. The customer benefit, which is becoming increasingly important in digitalized business practice, as well as the monetization model, are just as much a part of the holistic business model as a description of the core activities in the course of the value creation process. According to Schallmo (2013), a business model should therefore always explain how the company generates revenue from value creation for the customer. Osterwalder and Pigneur (2010) make a similar point:

> "A business model describes and analyzes the process of how a company creates customer value, distributes it to relevant target groups and uses suitable mechanisms to make it usable for itself."—Osterwalder and Pigneur

2.5.3.3 Elements of a Customer Value-Oriented Business Model

Even though some elements can be found in almost all approaches, Osterwalder and Pigneur's Business Model Canvas is probably the most comprehensive and established overview of business model elements. In addition to the previously dominant characteristics of revenue, customer benefit, and value creation, they add the business idea, channels, costs, customers, customer relationships, the company network, products and product life cycles, as well as company activities (Osterwalder and Pigneur 2010).

However, Osterwalder and Pigneur do not undertake a further clustering into dimensions. Only later research, which mostly refers to the Business Model Canvas, shows attempts to bundle the individual elements. One possibility for this is the three dimensions of value proposition, operational model, and commercial model (Grgurevic 2017).

The commercial model includes all activities that are intended to generate sales growth (Fig. 2.4). The elements of customer relationships, customer segments, channels, and revenue structure relate primarily to the corporate divisions of marketing, sales, and customer management. Internal company structures, on the other hand, are described by the operational model. This includes the elements of corporate activities, resources, and partners, as well as costs. The benefit at the end of value creation forms the center of the model. Although Schallmo also works with the elements of Osterwalder and Pigneur in his grid for business model dimensions

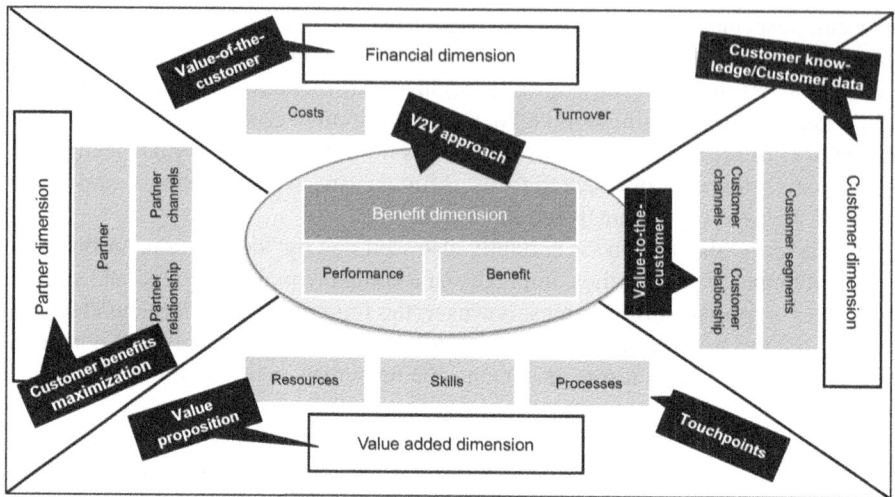

Fig. 2.4 Business model grid (based on Schallmo 2013)

and elements, he supplements these and organizes them into a total of five dimensions: value creation dimension, customer dimension, partner dimension, financial dimension, and benefit dimension (Schallmo 2013).

He also flanks his model with the soft factors of vision and leadership in order to ensure the long-term orientation of a business model on the one hand and to take a closer look at critical success factors on the other. However, a successful business model is only successful when all elements are linked together so efficiently that they reinforce each other. After all, individual elements can be imitated, but the process of their unique combination cannot. As it has a clear and comprehensible classification of elements into structuring dimensions and, like Grgurevic (2017), places the customer benefit at the center of all considerations, this model is recommended as a basis for structuring and detailing. However, due to the strong reference to the value creation process, corporate partnerships should not be understood as independent, but rather as part of the value creation dimension.

Benefit Dimension

The value that a company creates for its customers is at the end of the value creation process and determines success or failure. A company equipped with ample resources and expertise that produces without meeting the needs of the customer and does not focus on the maximum possible benefit for its target groups will be inferior in the long term to organizations that may have fewer skills and resources but achieve customer value in an efficient manner. Customer value is completely dependent on the perception of the customer and therefore cannot be objectively assessed (Botzkowski 2018). It is not only determined by the product in the narrower sense, but rather by a holistic performance system that includes both rational and emotional aspects (Bieger et al. 2011). In principle, customer benefit is achieved by satisfying customer needs.

Customer Dimension

In order to achieve the greatest possible benefit at the end of the value chain, the customer must be at the beginning. Knowing the customer has never been as important as it is today. In a market situation in which there seem to be several providers with a solution for every problem, concentrating on products and services is no longer sufficient. Who is our customer? What exactly does he want? How do they want to communicate? All these questions have become increasingly important in recent years and will play an ever greater role for companies in the future. The customer is gaining power and importance, as Büllingen (2017, p. 4) describes it:

"The digital age gives 'King Customer' more power than ever before and demands considerably more attention from providers. If you want to prevail in the battle for his favor, you should focus your business model entirely on him - and adapt it if necessary."—Franz Büllingen

In order to emerge as a winner from this intense competition, detailed customer knowledge is required in addition to good products. This dimension can be divided into areas such as customer segments, relationships, and channels and largely comprises the classic tasks of marketing (Schallmo 2013).

In general, the principle of long-term profitable customer loyalty to the company applies to customer relationships. Instead of short-term, one-off customer relationships, which are usually limited to a single transaction, the focus should be on customer relationship management (CRM) and therefore long-term success (Burgartz 2008). The CRM value chain provides information about the various phases of a customer relationship and can serve as a business model for customer value-centered management. It is also clear that economic success at the end of the chain is the result of a high level of customer loyalty.

The first step in customer management is therefore acquisition, which results in initial contact or a first transaction. If the subjective customer evaluation of the service provided is positive, the customer is satisfied. However, long-term customer loyalty and recurring transactions require suitable retention measures, which is why a satisfied customer does not automatically become a loyal customer.

There are opportunities to actively involve the sales team in the customer management process in all phases of the customer success chain. Under VUCA conditions, this is even mandatory, and not just in the operational business (when it comes to implementing defined measures). The sales team should also be strategically well positioned in this regard (e.g., how is the price measure justified? What is the price-performance perception of competitors?) In B2B markets in particular, employees in direct contact with customers play a leading role in the creation of the customer success chain (Fig. 2.5). This causality is the basis of a modern understanding of CRM (Bruhn and Homburg 2017). The more uncertain the framework conditions, the greater the focus on the management of customer relationships. In an ideal-typical cycle, customer orientation develops into increased satisfaction, which in turn induces increased customer loyalty and then brings with it the possibility of generating customer value.

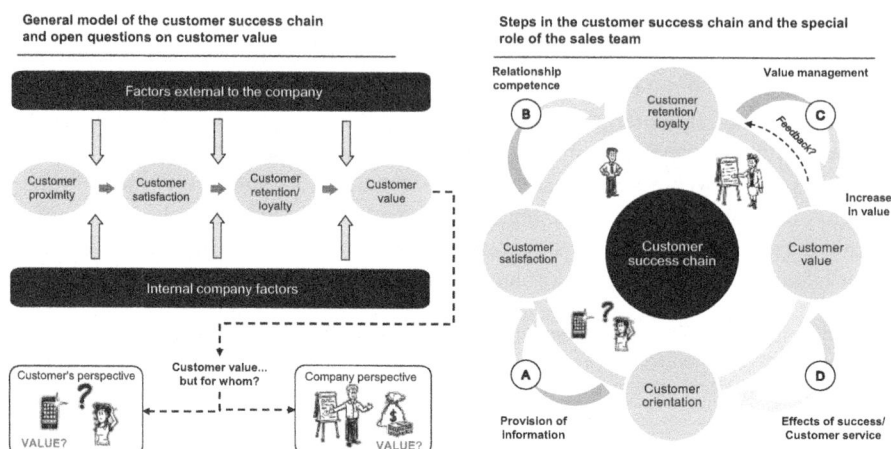

Fig. 2.5 General and specific impact chain (sales team) in customer value-centered management

Different customer segments can adopt and prefer different forms of relationship. After all, they are the ones who determine the type and nature of the relationship with a company. Segments differ in terms of their needs, their willingness to pay, and their value for the company (Schallmo 2013). This already shows the enormous increase in importance of reliable customer data.

Value-Added Dimension

In order to fulfill the communicated value proposition, the value creation process ensures that services can be produced in the required quantity. At the beginning of the value chain are resources that are to be transformed into products or services with the help of skills and processes.

Because they are tradable and not company-specific, only the unique combination of resources provides a competitive advantage that cannot be imitated (Bieger and Reinhold 2011). They can be divided into tangible, intangible, and human resources. Material resources are usually reported on the balance sheet and often include land, machinery, raw materials, or capital. Intangible resources such as the brand name, customer contacts, and customer knowledge are more difficult to value, although they can also be very valuable for companies. Finally, strong human capital is characterized by qualified employees, a high level of motivation or anchored skills (Gilbert 2011). Processes are defined as "a set of tasks to be completed in a sequence" (Schallmo 2013, p. 69).

The process-specific know-how ensures the controllability of the value proposition by making it repeatable. Skills, on the other hand, are necessary to operate processes and can be described as process-specific know-how. Together with resources, they form the competencies of a company and can also be taken over by company partners.

Partner Dimension

Specialists try to generate economies of scale by focusing on a single process step. In contrast, integrators take on all stages of value creation themselves and therefore have full control over all processes. Orchestrators are a combination of the two, as they generally control all stages but hand over individual sub-processes to specialized companies. The so-called market makers do not carry out any processes themselves; they mediate between individual stages of the value chain and the companies involved. Above all, they ensure an adequate supply of information across all stages. The various illustrations clearly show that a suitable value creation network is essential for maximizing customer benefit. Accordingly, the integration of partnerships into the value creation dimension is obvious. Partners can usefully supplement and complete the business model by providing resources and skills that are not available within the company itself. Typical partners are, for example, suppliers, sales, or logistics partners. Long-term partners are more valuable than one-off collaborations (Bieger and Reinhold 2011).

Financial Dimension

Although costs are also a component of the financial dimension alongside sales, it essentially describes the process of how the value created for the customer flows back to the company in the form of income (Bieger and Reinhold 2011). It is therefore about the transformation of customer value into company value (Gilbert 2011). The revenue structure is considered an important strategic decision, as the success of a business model ultimately depends on it. It forms the basis for further growth opportunities by siphoning off the previously created customer value. When choosing the revenue model, there are several decision areas to consider. Different revenue streams arise depending on the orientation of the business model. In addition to the usual sale of products or services, lending models, licensing, transaction fees, or advertising revenue can also be used to finance company activities. The combination of several revenue sources is not only possible, but also well established in practice (zu Knyphausen-Aufseß et al. 2011). This reduces dependence on a single source of revenue and minimizes the risk of environmental influences and changes in customer requirements. The choice of suitable channels also plays a role here. Trends such as mobile payment are currently emerging, which makes payment transactions even easier and possible from anywhere.

Costs are incurred in the course of the value creation process or during the operation of the business model. Typical cost items are, for example, the use of resources, the development of skills, and the execution of processes or partnerships. Depending on the cost type, they are divided into directly and indirectly attributable costs and thus determine the efficiency of the business model. The costs can be used to calculate how much needs to be invested for a certain output, providing a starting point for optimization potential. Processes that create enormous customer value but also require large investments must be streamlined in the long term in order to be profitable. Resources can possibly be procured more cheaply, or processes can be automated in order to reduce personnel requirements.

Ultimately, it is the profit, i.e., the difference between sales and costs, that gives a business model its credentials and thus determines the long-term success of a company. All elements of the business model must be combined as efficiently and uniquely as possible so that they provide an advantage over competitors. Those who create customer value and find ways to monetize it are very likely to have a functioning business model.

2.5.4 Business Model Innovations

Business models that bring success today do not automatically guarantee it in the future. In a dynamic and rapidly changing environment, it is very rare for one and the same model to remain competitive for years. In recent years, "the development and design of innovative business models to improve competitiveness has become increasingly important" (Gilbert 2011, p. 24). As a key driver of sales growth, business model innovations are therefore increasingly becoming the subject of business management research (Becker et al. 2018b). Similar to the definition of the business model, there is no uniformly applied definition of business model innovation. Schallmo describes it as "the strategic decision to restructure or redesign an existing business model" (Schallmo 2013, p. 29) and, in contrast to some other approaches, refers not only to the change but also to the development of completely new business models.

Similarly, Becker et al. (2018a) also describe both the holistic renewal of the company and the change of one or more elements "in favor of a new type of value generation" as a business model innovation. There is general agreement that the volatile environment of companies is the starting point for innovation processes.

Due to the technological advances, focus on ecology, and globalization associated with the global economy, companies are exposed to increasing competitive pressure, which requires an innovative design of corporate structures. However, in addition to external factors, internal company factors can also promote innovation. The literature often speaks of an agile and innovation-friendly corporate culture that sees innovation as an opportunity and can make companies successful in the long term. The skills of employees can also contribute significantly to innovative business structures (Reinhold et al. 2011). The value creation process is particularly important, as companies need to question the way they generate value for their customers. Having previously highlighted the unique combination of resources as a competitive advantage that is difficult to imitate, the constant recombination of these resources is an important component of innovation. Osterwalder and Pigneur, who define four epicenters of business model innovation (Osterwalder and Pigneur 2010), show that they also affect all other dimensions of a business model in addition to value creation. According to them, innovations can be resource-related, supply-related, customer-related, or financial-related. They are resource-related if the aforementioned recombination takes place or the company has new resources at its disposal. Supply-driven and customer-driven innovations are closely related, as a realignment to changing customer needs generally also entails a new value proposition for the customer. Financial innovations result from new sources of revenue as well as leaner cost structures. It is not only possible but also likely that a combination of two or more epicenters will take place, which determines the extent and strength of innovations. As the above definitions already indicate, there are various forms of innovation in the context of the business model. Whereas in the past, product, service, and process innovations were at the center of entrepreneurial activities, the holistic development of business models is now playing an increasingly important role. In this context, Zollenkop (2006) speaks of incremental and radical innovations and compares them in his four-field options cube with the number of business model elements affected in order to make the extent of innovations tangible. Incremental innovations are defined as "comparably minor changes to an existing business model" (Becker et al. 2018b, p. 27), whereas radical innovations result in completely new models. Even if the trend tends toward holistic changes, different forms cannot be assessed across the board. It is not always disruptive innovations that give a company its strong competitive position. A change of perspective on internal structures and the market situation can also be promising. Above all, innovations should have an individual basis for decision-making.

Radical innovations generally require different resources than incremental ones. They are therefore less likely to be adopted in established companies with fixed structures than in young companies and start-ups (Zollenkop 2006). Even if every company, regardless of size and structure, should consider business model innovations as a prerequisite for future success, the type and manner of change must always be assessed individually. Both successful global players and small- and medium-sized enterprises cannot rely on established business models because they are permanently exposed to volatile environmental influences (Piller et al. 2016).

2.6   Interview with Prof. Dr. Stefan Diefenbach, Telekom Deutschland Business Solutions GmbH

Question: How has the coronavirus changed leadership at Deutsche Telekom?

Stefan Diefenbach: Telekom is fundamentally geared and equipped for mobile working. The prerequisites for this are in place for all employees and this work style is also traditionally used intensively within the company. For example, all business trips involve working on the move. This was already the case before the outbreak of the coronavirus crisis. However, Deutsche Telekom's situation is special: Technologically, it is certainly 10–15 years ahead of some other companies in this respect. The company is therefore well-prepared in terms of "management after corona." During the corona pandemic, Deutsche Telekom had over 80% of its employees working from home. In a sense, little has changed as a result of working from home. As Telekom operates throughout Germany, employees are used to working via Unified Communication Solutions (e.g., WebEx), email, or telephone, and this has been established for years.

What has changed completely and that is dramatic: There has been a significant decline in face-to-face interactions. All "side conversations" no longer take place or only to a very limited extent. Only technical discussions take place. All rumors and information that are not directly related to the project are no longer part of the communication between employees. As a result, new projects usually became known very quickly within the company, even among those not involved in the project: Employees were able to put together individual "pieces of the puzzle" from several "side conversations" to form a picture. In times of the pandemic, these kinds of preliminary ideas were not known even after 4 months. As a result, the "salt in the soup" is missing, so to speak. When new employees start, they often encounter difficulties in building up personal relationships. They are increasingly underinformed about what has worked well in the company, and this restricts their scope for action. Another effect is the loss of corporate identity, emotional passion, and identification with the corporate culture.

New team members hardly could fully "feel" this culture, as comprehensive interaction that takes all human emotions into account is only possible to a very limited extent. It is therefore a very difficult situation when half of a team is in the office and the other half has dialed in by phone. If the entire team is working from home, this works almost better as an experience shared by all.

If there are already good personal relationships within the company, informal collaboration is also possible; if not, pragmatism is difficult. Our group has predefined processes. For example, fixed appointments with customers must be kept punctually. In the meantime, face-to-face meetings are being used again to build and strengthen a personal basis. As a manager at Deutsche Telekom, the need for control is not as pronounced as in medium-sized companies. Tasks are completed with a high degree of reliability, so management works quite well even in corona times—at least in terms of the work result.

Question: What significance will working from home have in the future and what consequences will this have?

Stefan Diefenbach: Before coronavirus, the home office rate was around 10%. The problem now is that employees have to come into the office. Employees are currently no longer prepared to go back to the pre-coronavirus presence. At the moment, the rate is 80%. The target is 50%.

Our experience with productivity development has been rather positive: Human error has decreased in corona times; effective working hours have increased. The lack of informal discussions "in the corridor" may have hindered effectiveness, which is probably difficult to measure, but has certainly had a negative impact on the sense of community and the culture of the company. Ultimately, the issue of emotionality falls by the wayside. I have already noticed that employees tend to become "tools that produce." In the medium term, we must try to find a better balance.

Question: How much more dynamic is or will working at Deutsche Telekom become as a result of VUCA?

Stefan Diefenbach: People are trying to counter VUCA with a certain form of agility. In recent years, we started to introduce a fully agile organization but then scaled it back to some extent. One of the problems was that only the line manager made decisions. However, employees bound by collective agreements showed great uncertainty, as they want their line manager to know them, guide them, and make decisions for their career on the basis of this close relationship. A significant proportion of employees ultimately did not cope well with the given framework conditions. This has led to a countermovement. However, parts of the agile organization are being retained. In corona times, thousands of customers wanted more bandwidth, which was not entirely possible due to the enormous volume.

It just could not be realized quickly. We therefore had to recognize that we as an organization were not able to react quickly enough to changing customer needs. The consequence is that process chains are now becoming more modular, which means that individual parts can be renovated more quickly. Implementation for the group as a whole will take 4 to 5 years. In the Business Customers segment, we always have to contend with volatility due to the large order volumes: It makes a big difference to the resource situation whether an order worth around EUR 100 million comes in or not. Mechanisms have therefore been developed to deal with this uncertainty.

Business customers want to get to know each other personally and not just communicate digitally. Agility in terms of uncertain delivery dates is not an option for large-scale projects: Customers are dependent on receiving a clearly defined service at a fixed time and having defined interim milestones. Telecommunications projects have a significant impact on the competitiveness and current situation of business customers. If, for example, a call center for an insurance company were not to function perfectly or even fail, this could quickly put an end to the company. For this reason, business customers also want to run a rather waterfall-like (i.e., classic, non-agile, or only slightly agile) projects.

Question: To what extent will the business model of Telekom or customers change after corona?

Stefan Diefenbach: The business model will change enormously for our customers. In the aviation industry, for example, sales plummeted by 80% at one point and it is possible that these companies will no longer achieve their previous sales volumes with the existing business model. Business travel may well decrease to a considerable extent, so a complete realignment is required. The end customer structure is changing, so the business model for business customers must change. Numerous strategy projects are being relaunched. There are no answers yet, but a lot will happen.

Software providers for the travel industry and logistics companies are further examples. A large German logistics company hopes that online trade will continue on this scale. E-mobility is also picking up speed here. These companies are all thinking very broadly. If other trends are observed, they will be incorporated into the new business model. The automotive industry, for example, has also launched projects that will see sales switch even more strongly to virtual technologies and artificial intelligence.

The interlocutor:

Prof. Dr. Stefan Diefenbach.

Vice President Program Management.

Telekom Deutschland Business Solutions GmbH. Email: s.diefenbach@ telekom.de.

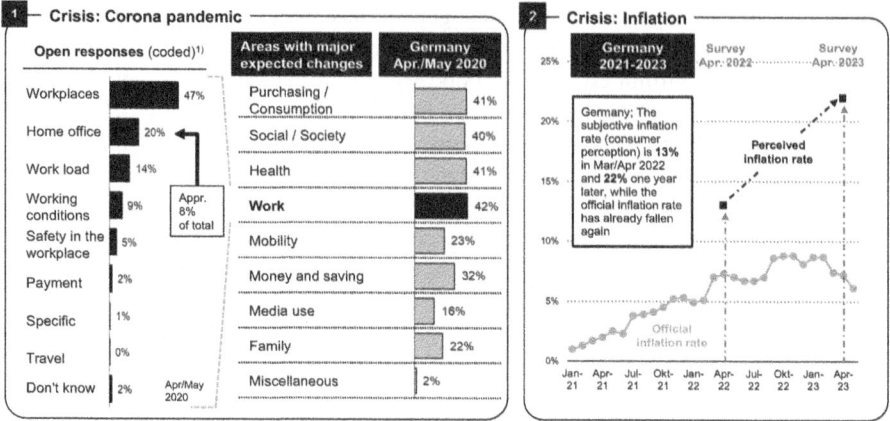

1) Do you believe that the coronavirus crisis will lead to lasting changes in society? In which areas do you expect particularly strong changes? Multiple
    answers possible. And: What changes do you expect in the area of work? Open question.
2) In your opinion, how have consumer prices developed over the last 12 months? Compared to last year, currently … (categories "prices have risen sharply"
    to "Prices have fallen"). And: In your opinion, by what percentage have consumer prices risen / fallen in the last 12 months?

Fig. 2.6 Expected sustainable change in the area of work (2020) and perceived inflation (2022 and 2023)

2.7 Outlook: Focus on the Customer Relationship in a Rapidly Changing Environment

Individual companies and the economy as a whole must succeed in focusing on long-term stability instead of short-term efficiency. In addition to modern, future-oriented management, orderly risk management, and adaptation of the business model, continuous market observation is required. The lack of planning certainty in a professional environment increasingly marked by VUCA characteristics demands great agility from companies. Agile management methods in all business areas that react quickly to changing situations are helpful here—but only as they are tailored to meet staff needs.

The coronavirus crisis—and this is just one factor in the VUCA environment—is having a variety of effects in different areas. The OpinionTRAIN study conducted by exeo and Rogator measured the areas expected to undergo major changes from the population's perspective both after the start of the coronavirus crisis (Apr./May 2020), during the second lockdown (Nov./Dec. 2020) and in the phase with a vaccination rate of greater than 50% of the population (Aug./Sep. 2021). The results are shown in Fig. 2.6. At the beginning of the crisis, work is the area with the strongest expected lasting changes. This is followed by health and consumption. In a more digitalized world, with greatly changed consumer habits or a changed value system, there is an immediate impact on the customer relationship. Some companies recognized this immediately after the outbreak of the crisis and reacted. Just think of perfume manufacturers who switched their production to disinfectants in order to serve society (at least that is how it was communicated), while others used the economically uncertain situation to cut costs (e.g., when a well-known sporting goods manufacturer suspended rent payments while at the same time the state put up rescue packages—also or especially for large companies). Corresponding positive and negative examples can of course also be cited in the subsequent crisis in 2022, the Ukraine conflict. Another problem area is a sharp rise in perceived inflation. This was triggered by the sharp rise in consumer prices in 2022 and 2023 (Fig. 2.6. Nr. 2). Even after the official inflation rate in Germany approaches 2% again from 2024, perceived inflation will remain high. In Apr. 2025, the Ipsos Global Advisor study "What Worries the World" sees the issue of price increases as the most important concern for consumers (IPSOS 2025).

In any case, companies will continue to have the opportunity to gain competitive advantages if they build up a close relationship with their customers, recognize them as individuals, and develop an understanding of what customers actually expect from providers.

References

Akin N, Rumpf J (2013) Führung virtueller Teams. Gr Organ 44(4):373–387

Au von C (2020) New Leadership—Führungspersönlichkeiten im digitalen Zeitalter. In: Harwardt M, Niermann PF-J, Schmutte AM, Steuernagel A (eds) Führen und Managen in der digitalen Transformation—Trends, Best Practices und Herausforderungen. Springer Gabler, Wiesbaden, pp 99–113

Barrero JM, Bloom N, Davis, SJ (2023) The evolution of work from home. Journal of Economic Perspectives, 37(4): 23–49

Bartik AW, Bertrand M, Lin F, Rothstein J, Unrath M (2020) Measuring the labor market at the onset of the COVID-19 crisis (No. w27613), National Bureau of Economic Research, pp 1–29

Becker W, Ulrich P, Botzkowski T, Eurich S (2017) Digitalisierung von Geschäftsmodellen. In: Schallmo D, Rusnjak A, Anzengruber J, Werani T, Jünger M (Hrsg) Digitale Transformation von Geschäftsmodellen. Wiesbaden, pp 283–309

Becker W, Ulrich P, Stradtmann M (2018a) Geschäftsmodellinnovationen als Wettbewerbsvorteil mittelständischer Unternehmen, Wiesbaden

Becker W, Eierle B, Fliaster A, Ivens B, Leischnig A (2018b) Geschäftsmodelle in der digitalen Welt—Strategien. Prozesse und Praxiserfahrungen, Springer, Wiesbaden

Bennett N, Lemoine GJ (2014) What a difference a word makes: understanding threats to performance in a VUCA world. Bus Horiz 57(3):11–317

Bieger T, zu Knyphausen-Aufseß D, Krys C (eds) (2011) Innovative Geschäftsmodelle: Konzeptionelle Grundlagen. Gestaltungsfelder und unternehmerische Praxis, Springer, Wiesbaden

Bieger T, Reinhold S (2011) Das wertbasierte Geschäftsmodell—Ein aktualisierter Strukturierungsansatz. In: Bieger T, zu Knyphausen-Aufseß D, Krys C (Hrsg), Innovative Geschäftsmodelle—Konzeptionelle Grundlagen, Gestaltungsfelder und unternehmerische Praxis. Heidelberg, S 13–70

Biesel HH, Hame H (2018) Vertrieb und Marketing in der digitalen Welt. So schaffen Unternehmen die Business Transformation in der Praxis, Springer Gabler, Wiesbaden

BITKOM (2020) Mehr als 10 Millionen arbeiten ausschließlich im Homeoffice. Presseinformation v. 8. Dezember 2020. https://www.bitkom.org/Presse/Presseinformation/Mehr-als-10-Millionenarbeiten-ausschliesslich-im-Homeoffice. Accessed 23 Aug 2021

Bleiber R (2021) Erfolgreiches Krisenmanagement—Prävention, Unternehmensstrategien. Haufe-Lexware-Verlag, Freiburg, Wege aus der Krise

Bordo M, Eichengreen B, Klingebiel D, Martinez-Peria MS (2001) Is the crisis problem growing more severe? Eco pol 16(32):52–82

Botzkowski T (2018) Digitale Transformation von Geschäftsmodellen im Mittelstand—Theorie. Empirie und Handlungsempfehlungen, Springer Fachmedien, Wiesbaden

Brauweiler H (2019) Risikomanagement in Unternehmen—Ein grundlegender Überblick für die Management-Praxis. 2 Aufl. Springer Gabler, Wiesbaden

Bruhn M, Homburg C (2017) Handbuch Kundenbindungsmanagement: Strategien und Instrumente für ein erfolgreiches CRM. 9 Aufl. Springer, Wiesbaden

Büllingen F (2017) Digitale Geschäftsmodelle Themenheft Mittelstand-Digital, Themenheft Mittelstand-Digital, hrsg. vom Bundesministerium für Wirtschaft und Energie, Berlin

Burgartz T (2008) Kennzahlengestütztes Kundenbeziehungs-Controlling: Ein konzeptioneller Ansatz zur entscheidungsorientierten Planung und Kontrolle von Kundenbeziehungen. Lang, Frankfurt a. M

Burgartz T, Krämer A (2016) Measures to understand and control customer relationship and loyality. Managing in a VUCA World, S:99–11

Burnard K, Bhamra R (2011) Organisational resilience: development of a conceptual framework for organisational responses. Int J Prod Res 49(18):5581–5599

Carriero A, Clark TE, Marcellino M (2018) Measuring uncertainty and its impact on the economy. Rev Econ Stat 100(5):799–815

Damodaran A (2007) Strategic risk taking: a framework for risk management. Pearson Prentice Hall, New Jersey

Dow SC (2015) Addressing uncertainty in economics and the economy. Camb J Econ 39(1):33:47

Ebert C, Duarte CHC (2018) Digital transformation. IEEE Softw 35(4):16–21

Fleming N (2012) VARK: a guide to learning styles. https://vark-learncom/. Accessed 31 Jan 2021

Gilbert DU (2011) Erfolgreich durch innovative Geschäftsmodelle. Controlling & Management:S 24–32

Gittell JH, Cameron K, Lim S, Rivas V (2006) Relationships, layoffs, and organizational resilience: airline industry responses to September 11. J Appl Behav Sci 42(3):300–329

Grgurevic K (2017) Geschäftsmodellstrategien im globalen, digitalen Wettbewerb. In: Werani T, Jünger M (eds) Schallmo D, Rusnjak A Anzengruber J. Digitale Transformation von Geschäftsmodellen. Springer Gabler, Wiesbaden, pp 127–157

Harwardt M (2020a) Digitalisierung in Deutschland—Der aktuelle Stand. In: Harwardt M, Niermann P F J, Schmutte A M Steuernagel A (Hrsg), Führen und Managen in der digitalen Transformation. Trends, Best Practices und Herausforderungen. Springer Gabler, Wiesbaden, 18–34

Harwardt M (2020b) Management der digitalen Transformation—Eine praxisorientierte Einführung. Springer Gabler, Wiesbaden

Heller J, Gallenmüller N (2019) Resilienz-Coaching: Zwischen "Händchenhalten" für Einzelne und Kulturentwicklung für Organisationen. In: Heller J (ed) Resilienz für die VUCAWeltResilienz für die VUCA-Welt. Springer, Wiesbaden, pp 3–18

Henriette E, Feki M, Boughzala I (2016) The shape of digital transformation: a systematic literature review. In: Kokolakis S, Karyda M, Loukis EN, Charalabidis Y (eds) Information systems in a changing economy and society: MCIS2015 proceedings. Universität der Ägäis, Samos, pp 431–443

IPSOS (2025) Stimmungslage in Deutschland - Sorgenbarometer. Press Release from 6.5.2025. https://www.ipsos.com/dede/meinungsumfragen/sorgenbarometer?utm_source=chatgpt.com#top-5-sorgen. Accessed 8 May 2025

Jaekel M (2015) Die Anatomie digitaler Geschäftsmodelle. Springer, Wiesbaden

Janssen C, Sen S, Bhattacharya CB (2015) Corporate crises in the age of corporate social responsibility. Bus Horiz 58(2):183–192

Krämer A, Burgartz T (2019) Kundenwert und Kundenprofitabilität: Nicht zu komplex und nicht zu einfach. Sales Excellence 2(7/8):40–43

Lawrence M, Homer-Dixon T, Janzwood S, Rockström J, Renn O, Donges JF (2024) Global polycrisis: The causal mechanisms of crisis entanglement. Global Sustainability, 7:E6. https://doi.org/10.1017/sus.2024.1

Lengnick-Hall CA, Beck TE, Lengnick-Hall ML (2011) Developing a capacity for organizational resilience through strategic human resource management. Hum Resour Manag Rev 21(3):243–255

Luthans F (2002) The need for and meaning of positive organizational behavior. J Org Beh: Int J Ind Occ Orga Psyc Beh 23(6):695–706

Niering C, Hillebrand C (2020) Krise—der Anfang vom Ende? In: Niering C, Hillebrand C (eds) Wege durch die Unternehmenskrise—Sanieren statt Liquidieren—Ein Praxisleitfaden für Unternehmer und Berater. Springer, Wiesbaden, pp 1–19

Osterwalder A, Pigneur Y (2010) Business model generation: a handbook for visionaries, game changers, and challengers. Wiley

OECD (2025) States of fragility 2025. Organisation for Economic Co-operation and Development. 18 February 2025 https://www.oecd.org/en/publications/states-of-fragility-2025_81982370-en.html. Accessed 9 May 2025

Piller F, Gülpen C, Lüttgens D (2016) Systematische Geschäftsmodellinnovation—Die Geschäftsidee von morgen muss kein Zufallsprodukt sein. In: Granig P, Hartlieb E, Lingenhel D (eds) Geschäftsmodellinnovationen. Springer Gabler, Wiesbaden, pp 145–153

Reichmann T, Kißler M, Baumöl U (Hrsg.) (2017) Controlling mit Kennzahlen. Die systemgestützte Controlling Konzeption. 9 Aufl., Vahlen, München

Reinhold S, Reuter E, Bieger T (2011) Innovative Geschäftsmodelle—Die Sicht des Managements. In: Bieger T, zu Knyphausen-Aufseß D, Krys C (Hrsg) Innovative Geschäftsmodelle—Konzeptionelle Grundlagen, Gestaltungsfelder und unternehmerische Praxis. Springer, Berlin, pp 71–91

Rump J, Eilers S (eds) (2020) Die vierte Dimension der Digitalisierung. Spannungsfelder in der Arbeitswelt von morgen. Springer Gabler, Berlin

Sansa NA (2020) The impact of the COVID-19 on the financial markets: evidence from China and USA. Elec Res J Soc Sci Hum 2:29–39

Schallmo D (2013) Geschäftsmodelle erfolgreich entwickeln und implementieren. Springer, Wiesbaden

Schröter W (2018) Von der "nachholenden Digitalisierung" zu "autonomen Software Systemen". In: Cernavin O, Schröter W, Stowasser S (eds) Prävention 4.0. Analysen und Handlungsempfehlungen für eine produktive und gesunde Arbeit 4.0. Springer, Wiesbaden, pp 290–303

Shin J, Sudhir K, Yoon DH (2012) When to "fire" customers: customer cost-based pricing. Man Sci J 58(5):932–947

So MK, Chu AM, Chan TW (2021) Impacts of the COVID-19 pandemic on financial market connectedness. Financ Res Lett 38

Thießen A (2014) Handbuch Krisenmanagement. 2 Aufl., Springer, Wiesbaden

Tugade MM, Fredrickson BL (2004) Resilient individuals use positive emotions to bounce back from negative emotional experiences. J Pers Soc Psy 86(2):320–333

Vogus TJ, Sutcliffe KM (2007) Organizational resilience: towards a theory and research agenda. 2007 IEEE international conference on systems, man and cybernetics. IEEE, pp 3418–3422

Walker B, Holling CS, Carpenter SR, Kinzig A (2004) Resilience, adaptability and transformability in social–ecological systems. Eco Soc 9(2):5

Werani T, Schauberger A, Martinek-Kuchinka P, Freiseisen B (2017) Wertdisziplinen und digitale Transformation von Geschäftsmodellen. In: Schallmo D, Rusnjak A, Anzengruber J, Werani T, Jünger M (eds) Digitale Transformation von Geschäftsmodellen. Springer, Wiesbaden, pp 237–263

Wirtz BW (2021) Business Model Management Business Model Management, Design—Instrumente—Erfolgsfaktoren von Geschäftsmodellen. Springer Gabler, Wiesbaden

zu Knyphausen-Aufseß D, van Hettinga E, Harren H, Franke T (2011) Das Erlösmodell als Teilkomponente des Geschäftsmodells. In: Bieger T, zu Knyphausen-Aufseß D, Krys C (eds) Innovative Geschäftsmodelle—Konzeptionelle Grundlagen, Gestaltungsfelder und unternehmerische Praxis. Springer, Berlin, pp 163–184

Zollenkop M (2006) Geschäftsmodellinnovation: Initiierung eines systematischen Innovationsmanagements für Geschäftsmodelleauf Basis lebenszyklusorientierter Frühaufklärung. Springer, Wiesbaden

3.1 Digitization

"Computers are useless. They can only give answers."—Pablo Picasso

Digitalization and numerous associated technological innovations are currently a much-discussed topic in literature and research (Groß and Pfennig 2019; Hippman et al. 2017; Blosch and Fenn 2019; Samulat 2017). These developments always entail the risk of an exaggerated technology-oriented approach. In the spirit of Pablo Picasso, computers can at best provide answers, but they are not able to ask the right questions. Nevertheless, the social and economic relevance of the subject area is so considerable that the number of works published on digitization has increased exponentially in recent years, suggesting a saturation of information. The fact that many of those "affected" in this context are nevertheless struggling to remain competitive without a fixed objective and suitable action plans suggests that the need for research will continue to grow.

There is no longer any doubt about the importance of digitalization for securing the long-term existence of a company, but hardly anyone in charge knows the exact consequences for their company. This is not to say that digitalization only became significant with the business models of Netflix, Uber, or Spotify. Amazon's business model was not only customer-centric from the outset but also designed as a digital platform as far as possible. The low-cost carriers established in the early 2000s rely on a distribution system with a maximum degree of digitalization (Ryanair has perfected this approach). To this day, both research and corporate practice are primarily concerned with the digitalization of products, services, or partial aspects of an organization (Keimer et al. 2017). However, as a company can only be successful in the long term if technological innovations can be transferred into the value creation concept of a business model and thus a continuous customer orientation and processing can be generated with the associated success, it is urgently necessary to

© The Author(s), under exclusive license to Springer Nature Switzerland AG 2025
A. Krämer et al., *Customer Value-centered Management*, Future of Business and
Finance, https://doi.org/10.1007/978-3-031-90497-4_3

include the concept of one's own business model in further considerations and, if necessary, to realign it according to the value chain through big data.

The growing market power of the customer (including customer transparency and far-reaching comparison options)—in addition to increasing competition and growing maturity in numerous product markets—is due in particular to the far-reaching possibilities of modern information technology and the globalization of the product range (Burgartz and Krämer 2014, 2016). In terms of customer value management features, digital technologies allow for a new form of customer journey that can be supported by data across various channels. Companies know the customer relationship status and can tailor their communication accordingly (Krämer and Burgartz 2015). The number of communication channels has multiplied enormously, which is why the customer needs communication that is as simple and barrier-free as possible, e.g., for complaints or other services. Some companies create digital networks or platforms where they not only communicate with customers but also allow customers to communicate with each other. From the client perspective, digitalization offers increased transparency and comparability, which intensifies competition. Examples include price search engines such as idealo.de or billiger.de. The same applies to comparison portals such as Verivox or Check24 in Germany, with similar services available in the US—for example, EnergySage for electricity and The Zebra for car insurance. Digital processes can also be incorporated into the management of resources and key activities. For example, collaborative platforms can manage know-how within a company or recruitment processes can run via digital channels. Business intelligence systems (analytics) and new technology infrastructures can manage processes at all stages of the logistics value chain and make them transparent for commercial analysis. Sales processes can be optimized using computer-aided selling and supported by CRM systems (Werani et al. 2017).

3.2   Big Data: Better Understanding and Explanation

"Information is the oil of the 21st century, and analytics is the combustion engine"—Peter Sondergaard

Big data is a much-cited aspect and particular driver of digital growth (Lee 2017). Analogous to the importance of the exploration and provision of the raw material oil at the beginning of the last century for the global spread of combustion engines as the starting point for the industrialization and automation of society, a century later the aspect of big data is seen as the starting point for a further innovation cycle (Industry 4.0). In this respect, Peter Sondergaard places the "raw materials" oil and data on the same level in terms of content. On the one hand, the amount and variety of data available today presents companies with significant challenges, but on the other hand it also offers the opportunity to optimize structures and processes and, above all, to work in a more customer-centric way. Constantly changing customer requirements are the trigger for a paradigm shift from a product-centric to a customer-centric way of thinking. Where product innovation used to be at the beginning of the value chain, the individual customer with his needs and problems is now the focus. Those who are able to solve these problems will survive the competitive pressure and dominate the competition (Tiefenbacher and Olbrich 2018). Digitalization and, in particular, the new possibilities of data management serve as a tool to expand and build customer proximity and to break new ground in value creation.

3.2.1 Big Data: Basic Understanding

Big data is not a clearly defined term, nor is its authorship clear (Klein et al. 2013). Only a small number of scientific definitions have been published (Loos et al. 2011). An early definition comes from Gartner analyst Doug Laney, who simply defined big data in 2001 as "data volumes that are larger than we are used to" (Laney 2001). Big data represents a major trend in the corporate world and creates enormous (added) value for many companies and municipalities. The term big data generally describes particularly large amounts of data from areas such as the Internet and mobile communications, the financial industry, the energy sector, healthcare and transport, and credit and customer cards (Fasel and Meier 2016). The main characteristics of data are its size, complexity, fast-moving nature, and generally weak structure. Experts generally also speak of mass data, although the definition is identical. First perceived as a phenomenon or as hype, the term can be summarized under two aspects. On the one hand, big data allows large volumes of data to be stored, processed, and analyzed (Saggi and Jain 2018). On the other hand, special technologies enable the processing of data volumes that relational databases cannot process. In essence, this is about new and powerful IT solutions and systems that enable companies to process the flood of information in an advantageous way (e.g., with the help of machine learning). Mainly unstructured data, for example, from social networks, makes up a significant proportion of mass data. Grid computing is a special form of distributed computing that enables computationally and data-intensive processing. Big data now stands for a completely new era of digital communication and corresponding processing practices. In social terms, this circumstance is even being held responsible for a fundamental change—or upheaval—in society.

In the economic debate, the use of big data is often touted as the ideal way to achieve greater success in realizing additional business with existing customer relationships. Companies are faced with the challenge of facing up to the digital revolution and dealing with the use of big data in order to create added value for customer relationships using big data and at the same time meet the resulting challenges (Steinberg 2019).

There are basically five digital technologies that are responsible for the global increase in digitalization: cloud computing, big data, mobile applications, social media, and the Internet of Things (IoT). These five topics/technologies are essential for the transition to digital and data-based business models. The topic of big data is therefore becoming increasingly interesting, also for the general public. Big data makes it possible to analyze extremely large volumes of data in order to identify interrelated patterns, trends, and connections, particularly with regard to behavior and interactions between the customer and the company (Hackett 2016).

The use of big data ensures greater information transparency of the collected data, while at the same time increasing the continuity of data processing and analysis (Fasel and Meier 2016; Krämer et al. 2016).

One focus of technological progress lies in its use in connection with dealing with and supporting customers. Consumers leave many traces every day using data, which can be of great importance for companies in terms of customer acquisition or customer retention. Large amounts of data can no longer be processed with conventional hardware and software. Big data solves these problems with special hardware and software that work in a distributed manner, i.e., in a cluster of many computers. This means that the data in big data systems is no longer stored on one server but is distributed across many computers that can communicate with each other. This combination makes it possible to store and process enormous amounts of data. Well-known software (big data) systems for processing enormous amounts of data are, for example, Apache Hadoop and Apache Spark (Freiknecht and Papp 2018).

3.2.2   Big Data: Properties, Uses, and Benefits

The big data concept is usually explained and characterized in detail on the basis of certain dimensions. The majority of these approaches include the main characteristics of volume, velocity, variety, and veracity, which are often referred to as the four V's (König et al. 2018). In terms of a complete understanding of customer value-centric management, it appears to make sense to characterize big data with additional dimensions (De Mauro et al. 2015). In addition to the main characteristics mentioned, these can include other dimensions that relate specifically to the company level (validity, visualization, or value). This is why, for example, we also talk about the 7 Vs of big data (Fig. 3.1).

Big data is characterized above all by a rapidly increasing volume of data, which significantly exceeds traditional and previously existing data from ERP systems and CRM databases (Fasel 2014). It is now in the terabyte and even petabyte range. According to Statista 2017, the volume of data produced worldwide each year will increase tenfold to 163 zettabytes by 2025. The amount of data and its scope depends on the number of data sources and the depth of data or the level of resolution (Barnaghi et al. 2013).

Velocity is aimed at the high speed at which new data is created or used and defines the speed at which data is produced and changed so that it can be analyzed as time-efficiently as possible and decision-making can be supported in the best possible way (Sivarajah et al. 2017).

The speed at which the data itself can change is described as velocity (König et al. 2018).

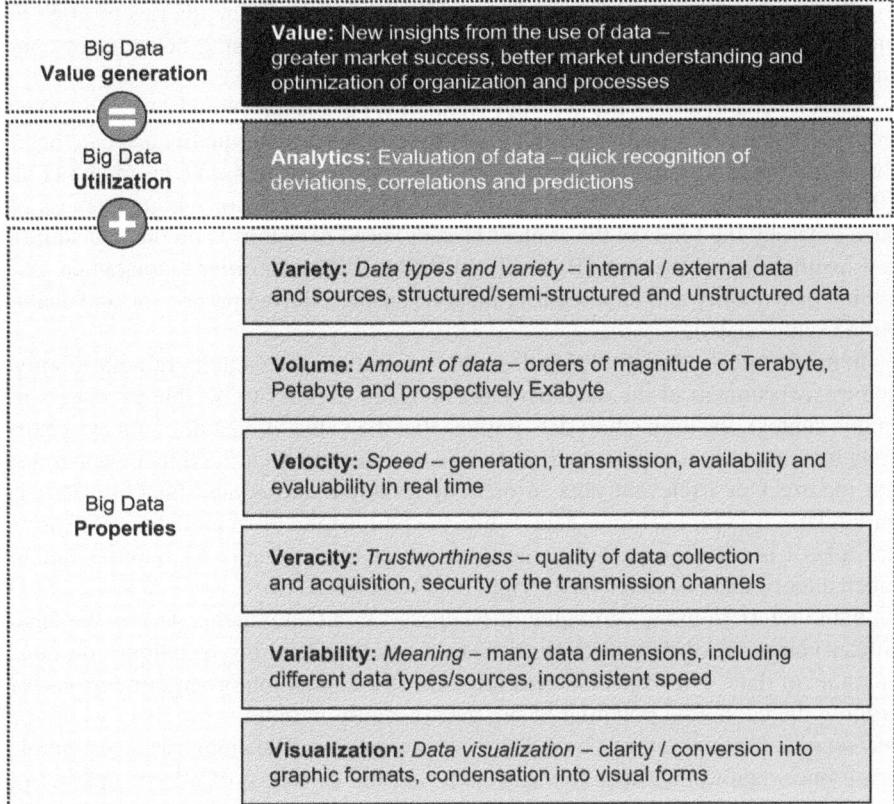

Fig. 3.1   The 7 Vs of Big Data—value generation, use and properties

The variety of data is also increasing enormously, as it now comes from different internal and external sources (data sources and types) and often does not appear in a structured form, but in so-called polystructured forms (Chen et al. 2013). Around 90% of stored data is saved in unstructured formats such as text, images, or videos. Today, real-time processing plays a major role for many companies and can provide a decisive competitive advantage. Machine learning contributes to classification and analysis by applying appropriate algorithms to big data and creating a model from it. Unstructured data is qualified, analyzed, and immediately usable in the shortest possible time, at least according to the widespread narrative. Structured data is, for example, data from a table with a person's name, age, and income (Finlay 2014).

Unstructured data, on the other hand, takes the form of documents, videos, images, or emails. In addition, internal company data pools with important customer data are crucial, which occur in the form of a classic CRM system or databases with product and sales information (Deutscher Dialogmarketing Verband e. V. 2016). Another variety of information is provided by public data pools as well as databases from production processes within a company or Internet information such as emails, communication in social networks, or search engine queries through to movement data, location data, or information on the purchasing behavior of consumers via their credit or discount cards (König et al. 2018).

Veracity characterizes the accuracy (reliability) of the data and data quality. Data from various sources sometimes does not arrive in the desired quality and can therefore not be used as intended or has to be laboriously reprocessed (Vasarhelyi et al. 2015). The quality is influenced by possible inconsistencies or incompleteness of data, whereby the focus in the context of data-based decisions is on the traceability and justifiability of the data (Baumöl and Berlitz 2014). In order to guarantee reliability, data quality and data security must be ensured during processing and evaluation (Schön 2016).

In his definition, Jaekel (2015) describes veracity as the meaningfulness, quality, and trustworthiness of the data that must be given in order to be able to process it. In this context, the term smart data implies that the value of data does not automatically increase with the quantity. Rather, it is necessary to filter the right data and sort out incorrect or irrelevant data in order to generate subsequent benefits. This is particularly true for customer data. While the philosophy of "a lot helps a lot" often prevails, it is actually clear that the focus on customer centricity requires not so much a lot of data, as much as the right data (Gotsch 2022).

Value refers to the added value or business value that is generated by the large (linked) amounts of data through the use of machine learning techniques on huge amounts of data. This aspect is certainly one of the most important dimensions for arguing the economic potential of big data, because without value there would be few reasons for this very resource-intensive proposition. The emphasis on economic sense once again underlines the statement that the existence of a large amount of data does not necessarily bring added value. The core of big data management is therefore not the accumulation, but above all the adequate use of data so that value is created.

Variability refers to data whose meaning is constantly changing. Companies often need to develop sophisticated programs to understand the context in the data and decipher its exact meaning. This is particularly the case when data collection is based on language processing.

Natural language processing (NLP) is used to capture natural language and process it on a computer using rules and algorithms. NLP uses various methods and results from linguistics for this purpose and combines them with modern computer science and artificial intelligence. The aim is to create the widest possible communication between humans and computers using language. Words do not have static definitions and their meaning can vary greatly depending on the context (Sivarajah et al. 2017).

The visualization of big data is about presenting data of almost any kind in a graphical format that makes it easy to understand and interpret. This enables decision-makers to examine data sets in order to identify correlations or unexpected patterns.

The networking of different data sources illustrated in Fig. 3.2 (Gleich et al. 2014; Tröbs and Mengen 2018; Krämer and Tachilzik 2016) is a prerequisite for the

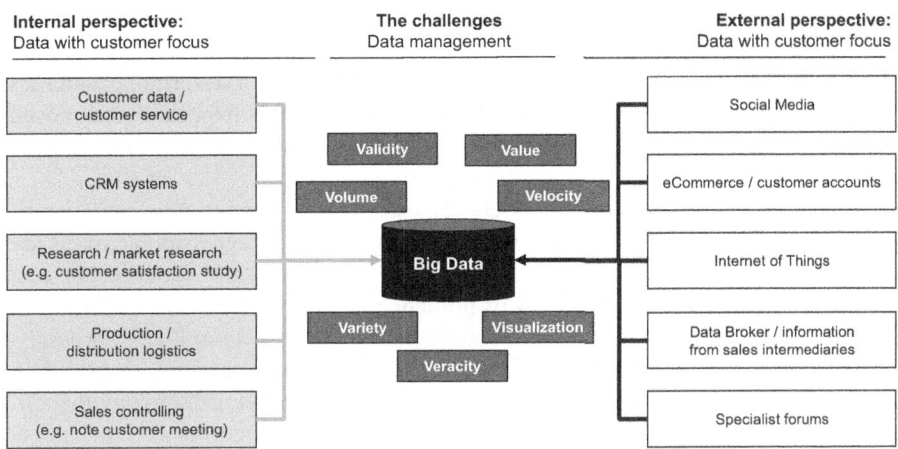

Fig. 3.2 Value chain for big data: focus on customer-related data sources

resulting benefits (value generation). In concrete application, this can be seen in the creation of a basis for decision-making, the optimization of business processes, the calculation of risks, the increase in profitability, dynamic pricing, and a focus on the customer in order to exploit market potential as a result of a better understanding of the market.

An overall view shows that the term big data is relatively vague, as data characteristics, technologies, and other related aspects are combined. It makes sense to expand the term big data. From a business perspective, big data structures exist when companies put themselves in a position to analyze a previously unmanageable amount of polystructured data in real time due to its volume and to validate and use it accordingly.

This requires the use of modern methods, processes, and technologies, which can be summarized under the generic term big data technologies. What needs to be clarified here is how the process of turning data into value should be structured. Big data analyses offer an answer to this.

3.3   Generating Competitive Advantages with Big Data Analytics

Since the beginning of the 2000s, digitalization, especially the increasing networking via the internet, has facilitated the transformation of traditional analytics into the new era of Analytics 2.0. Building on previously dominant descriptive analysis methods, predictive big data analyses can be used to generate concrete statements about future facts. More detailed knowledge of future developments is a decisive competitive advantage for companies (Schneider and Grieser 2016).

Gadatsch (2017) talks about different target areas of big data and shows ways in which data can create value. On the one hand, the most obvious and common form of use is probably past- or present-oriented data analysis. Based on the Gartner Group's "Analytics Value Escalator," data analysis is concerned with the core topics of descriptive analytics and diagnostic analytics. The scope of descriptive analytics has a descriptive function and clarifies the question of what has happened. Diagnostic analytics is also related to the past but attempts to uncover more precise causes for events.

Descriptive analyses are used to determine correlations and trends from historical data, e.g., via frequency distributions. Methods such as regression analyses are then used to derive forecasting models, e.g., to form price-sales functions or cost functions. By measuring indicators or influencing variables, an expected value is then formed with regard to the future variation of the target variables. If necessary, various scenarios are considered and their probability of occurrence is calculated. If, for example, reports of a new competitor entering the market accumulate, this circumstance is recognized by the system, and the effects on the company's own price/sales situation are calculated immediately. This enables strategic controlling to submit proposals for countermeasures to management more quickly than before (Horváth et al. 2020; Gluchowski 2014).

Predictive and prescriptive analytics are designed to generate future-oriented insights. They address the questions of what is most likely to happen and how a company should respond effectively. Increasingly, artificial intelligence (AI) enhances these analytics by enabling more accurate pattern recognition and decision automation in dynamic business environments (QuantumBlack 2025). Although they are more complex, they can sometimes create enormous value by supporting the earliest possible and, above all, correct decisions. The knowledge gained and the conversion of data into relevant insights represents a value in their own right because they generate new information and key figures that would otherwise not be available in this form. Similar to other products, data also undergoes a kind of production process in which investments are made and which can therefore also optimize a company's added value.

However, collected data and new insights are not only interesting for the company's own value creation, but also for other companies and can therefore be traded. According to Gadatsch (2017), this added value of generating sales revenue is another target area of big data. Regardless of who ultimately uses it, whether it serves internal purposes or external companies, data always brings with it a changed decision-making culture. The aforementioned analysis methods create a new, reliable way of making decisions (Dorschel 2015). Responsibilities and activities are shifting from people to information systems because many processes can be automated. The susceptibility to errors is generally much lower, as recommendations are based on algorithms and stored information rather than gut decisions. Other authors even speak of a changed corporate culture through big data as a new basis for decision-making. The main advantages are the speed, quality, and transparency of decision-making, which have increased enormously (Dorschel 2015). Analyses therefore not only add value by providing additional information, but also by saving time (Altmann 2013). They can no longer only be carried out retrospectively, but at best also provide relevant information in real time. Results can be accessed anytime and anywhere, giving a company a high degree of flexibility. Increased transparency is achieved by making analyses and findings quickly accessible to everyone digitally. In terms of the various company activities, data has a wide range of possible applications along the value chain. It can be used for marketing, sales, research and development, customer service, production, or logistics and can optimize existing processes or initiate completely new ones.

In marketing, a much more individualized customer approach can be achieved by first having more information available about customers and then segmenting them more precisely. Services and communication can thus be optimally tailored to individual customers or customer groups in order to maximize benefits and gain a competitive advantage (Krämer and Tachilzik 2016). In terms of predictive analytics, customer expectations and market trends can also be forecast. Subsequent product development can be based on these findings and identified market conditions, which can reduce risks. The probability of successful products increases with increasing proximity to the customer. Greater customer focus can also be achieved in the area of customer service, as customer data can be accessed more quickly and to a greater extent. This enables service employees to react faster and better to requirements and increase customer satisfaction (Krämer and Mauer 2023).

In this context, a standardized database that aggregates all customer data, i.e., master data, transaction, and relationship data, is also important. In order to obtain a holistic view of production processes, big data applications can also link and aggregate individual subsystems. The increasingly complex supply chains of industries can thus be integrated and made more manageable (e.g., by harmonizing operationally used information systems and standardized file formats for information exchange) (Krafft et al. 2021). The entire network of suppliers, logistics companies, buyers/customers, and other partners becomes more transparent as relevant data can be made available to every member of the network in near real time.

3.3.1   Big Data: Effects and Challenges

Big data offers great potential for companies when setting up new companies, developing new products and services, and improving business processes. The use of big data analytics can bring benefits such as cost savings, better decision-making, and higher product and service quality (Davenport 2014). Management realizes that big data has a potential impact on companies, but there are still difficulties in using the data. The following effects of big data can be mentioned:

- Personalized marketing
- Improved pricing
- Reduction of costs
- Improved customer service
- Reporting and consolidation
- Planning and forecasting
- Organization and qualification.

The challenges lie, for example, in the selection of big data software. This problem is not completely new for companies, as the amount of data available has increased continuously in recent years in particular. Rather, the challenge for companies is to implement the often increasing, self-imposed requirements for data processing and evaluation. Over the past few years, business intelligence software has become increasingly strategically important for companies. This in turn has led not only to an increase in the number of users, but also to their expectations regarding the timeliness and short-term availability of data. In addition, the relevance of the query performance of the respective systems also increased. Overall, these high requirements simply illustrate the challenges of the business world. Above all, fast reacting companies can use big data analytics to gain a competitive edge in a highly competitive business environment.

Big data is one of the relevant technologies of the future and helps companies to generate high-quality competitive advantages. The technology is already at a very good stage of development but will certainly experience a further boost, as the rapidly growing flood of data means that managing it is one of the most important aspects when designing digital solutions for corporate success. Only a good big data approach can provide companies with the holistic and detailed overview they urgently need. Big data will therefore have a significant impact on the way companies, organizations, and their IT experts solve tasks in the future (Fig. 3.3).

Big data is also a challenge for data protection. The linking of inherently unproblematic information can lead to problematic findings, and the statistics may make customers appear to be at risk. Information ethics asks about the moral implications of big data in relation to digital paternalism (big data as big brother), informational autonomy, and informational justice. Economic ethics and legal ethics are also required. Data protection laws and institutions can go some way toward preventing excesses and ensuring consumer protection. It is understandable that the way in which personal data is collected and used as a basis for marketing and how this is ultimately communicated to the customer/buyer has an influence on their

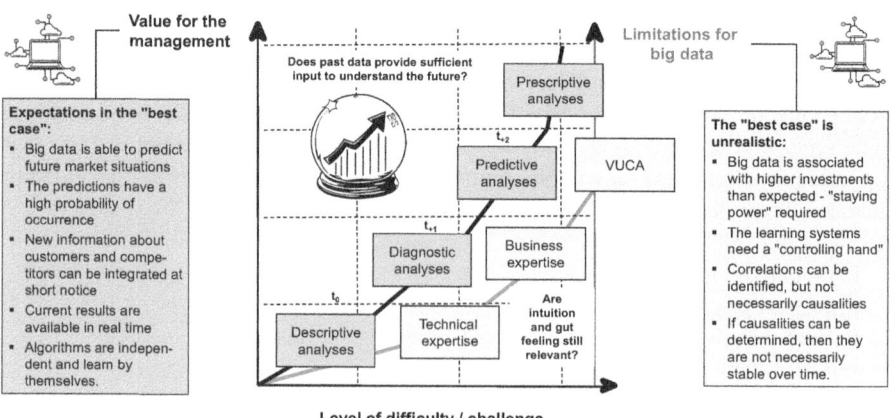

Fig. 3.3 Expectations vs. limitations in big data management

purchasing decision. This connection is particularly strong in the case of personalized pricing. Consumers will include in their evaluation whether offering behavior-based prices serves their self-interest or not (van Boom et al. 2020).

The most important point to consider is the legal situation: as online services tend to personalize prices by using cookies to identify, track, and categorize customers, it can be concluded that the European Data Protection Regulation is relevant for online stores in most cases. Consequently, a company that uses a personalized pricing system must inform its customers about the purpose of the processing of personal data on the basis of a legal basis.

This perspective can also be extended and does not only apply to individually tailored prices. Based on algorithmic pricing, prices can be set both dynamically over time and personally depending on individual consumer information. Although dynamic pricing is legal, the ethical justifiability of such approaches must be examined on a case-by-case basis because they often trigger moral concerns and sometimes outrage among end customers (Seele et al. 2021).

Critical issues to be discussed include different options for the application and use of big data. The analyst behind the software, who derives actual correlations from numerous connections between the data and basically has a final evaluative function in the sense of a plausibility check, possibly without sufficient knowledge of the business model or the market effects, can be problematic. This necessary qualification will be of crucial importance for companies in the future. In addition, big data is considered innovative and is currently being highly acclaimed. Behind some of this hype lies a dangerous misalignment that reduces people to data traces and seems to reduce intuition, management experience and industry knowledge to a minimum of importance (Fig. 3.3). Developments in the IT environment tend to take place over time in an evolutionary rather than "revolutionary" way, as the hype surrounding the buzzwords sometimes suggests. Peter Mertens, one of the founding fathers of business informatics in German-speaking countries, relativizes the term digitalization in some places with the question of what is really new, especially since a kind of digitalization already existed at the beginning of the Internet age in the early 1990s, which has basically continued to accelerate to this day (Mertens et al. 2018). Digitalization itself is not new and is only being used more comprehensively and extensively (e.g., Covid vaccination certificates as apps during 2020–2022).

Comprehensive change requires internal organizational resources—especially employees—who not only apply IT solutions, but also implement them and contribute their interface knowledge. Ultimately, the best tool is of little use if employees do not understand it, interpret it, and are unable to improve its use. Training and further education in IT systems are a key driver for the successful application and implementation of digitalization.

3.4   Interview with Sebastian Hense (KiK Textilien und Non-Food GmbH)

Question: In your opinion, how has corona changed the relationship and decision-making behavior of customers?

Sebastian Hense: It's certainly difficult to make a general assessment. In my experience, retailers who have had to temporarily close their brick-and-mortar stores have found that the proportion of sales generated by regular customers was the most reliable, as it was possible to communicate with them in a better and more targeted manner. Retailers would certainly have performed significantly worse without their regular customer data. Covid-19 is just one extreme example and other fundamental issues await. What companies also need to focus on (now) are supply chains and the impact on the entire value chain. Unpredictable things will continue to occur in the future and are likely to increase. The question is, how dependent is my company on issues such as Covid-19 and will data and analyses help me to be more independent or more capable of acting?

Question: What developments do you see in your work with customer and market data?

Sebastian Hense: I can assess the topic from the perspective of multichannel retailers in particular. Ultimately, this topic is very dependent on the company and business model. I see the issue of purchase data as crucial. Transaction data is the hardest currency for me. Therefore, many retailers started offering special discounts (only) to customers which give their personal and transactional data. Other sources must also be integrated, such as market research or other data sources. The accuracy and reliability of the data is crucial for me. It is becoming increasingly difficult for management (who are often not "at home" with technological details due to their own role) to analyze and interpret data and understand the possibilities. In my view, one of the most important steps for companies is to know what I am measuring, what valid data I can rely on, and, in particular, what I want to do with the results.

You often read, "we are a totally data-driven company!" But hardly anyone in these companies understands the data and can interpret it. More and more frequently, other buzzwords are being used alongside big data and people are talking about a data lake, for example. As long as I don't know what I want to do with the data, a data lake usually makes no sense. I also believe that "old school" entrepreneurial behavior and new ways of using data need to complement each other. Clear, well-founded and binding decisions are still needed. However, these can increasingly be made or supported on the basis of data. However, there needs to be a connection between the two. I always find it exciting to look at key figures every day, such as turnover. What do we do if sales are bad again tomorrow? What do I conclude from this and can data help me with this?

In other words, linking analyses and translating them into instructions for action applies to me for both large and small data sets.

Question: What do you understand by big data? Which applications are feasible for you?

Sebastian Hense: In the basic description of big data, I often find generalized or similar wording in everyday working life or from service providers, but that is also the problem. Big data or similar terms are not just words and not just collecting data, and that's where the whole topic often fails. The VUCA world is actually making everything even more complex, which makes simple and hard, measurable causalities even more difficult. I believe that development has progressed technologically but will continue to do so significantly.

In practice, however, it is more likely that companies will only be able to work in this world if they have very clear boundaries and know what benefits they will derive from it. Breaking it down to company-specific issues and asking what I want to achieve and what I need for this are crucial and will then show what exactly data or "big data" can do for the respective company. You also have to look the reality of the company in the eye. If, for example, I run predictive analyses and in the end someone decides on a completely different solution, then I don't need this analysis and I certainly don't need big data. Ultimately, the question is which analyses are relevant for action. The most important thing is to reduce the complexity of your own company, coupled with staying in power and adherence to clearly defined courses of action. For me, the topic really is a corporate management issue. This requires you to have certain management qualities, which you need to know, you shouldn't have blinkers, a certain openness is important. What value drivers do I have and what data do I need for them? And finally, what do I do with the results of the analysis or does it help me in my business model or can I align processes with it? Very basic examples: If, as a retailer, I have very long order cycles or lead times, I have to ask myself which analyses of sales volumes or trends make sense during the year or in the short term if I can no longer adjust my quantity structures. For example, if a fashion retail brand decides to offer blue suits for the next season and I, as a retailer, find out from analyses and market research that customers actually (will) primarily buy green suits this year—what do I do then? Does this analysis help me or do I have to start at other points in the value chain? I have to decide for my company what the control parameters are. It is then important to look at what data is relevant for your own company, how much effort is required to obtain this data, and how additional data sources can improve the quality of my analyses. For example, if a company has a very low purchasing frequency per customer per year, it can be challenging to develop a model from the amount of data that helps me predict (well enough that I can monetize it) what the customer buys next.

If, as a retailer, I also purchase goods from third parties that I cannot significantly influence for the future except through selection, I have to ask myself about the additional value of such an analysis. In my view, there is often a lack of a well-founded definition of values and clear procedures for determining this value on a company-specific basis.

Question: What positive and negative experiences have you had with big data?

Sebastian Hense: I see a low cost-benefit effect as soon as the efforts of big data or data collection are not oriented toward corporate management and also include the point of data use through decision-making/action derivation. Only then will big data bring the desired success. Working with small data sets, testing, and acting on a small scale, i.e., I consider "back to the roots" to be very helpful here in order to work out which data (use), delivers which added value on a company-specific basis. Real value drivers are then usually easily scalable. I also see a certain contradiction between big data and the associated "promise of salvation" that everything will (automatically) be better or clearer. Simply because of the uncertainty driven by VUCA. If big data is associated with the expectation that everything, including important parameters that determine our business, will be simple and easy to predict thanks to extensive data and analyses, but at the same time we recognize that the world is becoming more complex and volatile, then it must be recognized that this is at least not an automatism or a logical consequence.

Interview partner:

Sebastian Hense. Head of Marketing & Customer Relationship Management, KiK Textilien und Non-Food GmbH, Bönen.

Email: Sebastian.Hense@kik.de.

3.5   The Future of Big Data and AI

The emergence of big data is not limited to a few sectors or technology areas but has broad applications across all industries. In light of this reality, companies must pursue big data capabilities as necessary foundational developments that can in turn enable competitive advantage. Companies face significant challenges in integrating big data, but the potential use cases of big data promise positive impacts on business, marketing, customer experience, and more. Using tools to assess and understand big data, such as the integrated view of big data dimensions presented here, will help organizations realize the individual benefits of big data integration, achieve integration, and position themselves within the context of technological change as big data becomes a part of mainstream business practices. By integrating big data and artificial intelligence, companies can make more accurate predictions and automate decision-making processes, which in turn significantly improves responsiveness and operational efficiency in complex environments (Joshi 2025).

There is a need for more practical research to investigate and address these challenges associated with big data in business, as well as changes in the industry to support talent and infrastructure development. This big data reality that companies find themselves in is large, complex, comprehensive—and it is here to stay. However, cost-benefit considerations will increasingly dominate the discussion in the future.

References

Altmann G (2013) Neue Entscheidungskultur Personalmagazin 3:22–23

Barnaghi P, Sheth A, Henson C (2013) From data to actionable knowledge: big data challenges in the web of things. IEEE Intell Syst 28(6):6–11

Baumöl U, Berlitz P (2014) Big Data als Entscheidungsunterstützung—Herausforderungen und Potentiale. Controlling und Big Data—Anforderungen, Auswirkungen, Lösungen. Haufe Finance Office Premium, München, pp 159–176

Blosch M, Fenn J (2019) Understanding Gartner's hype cycles (Gartner Inc. Research, Hrsg.). https://www.gartner.com/en/documents/3969607-understanding-gartner-s-hype-cycles

Burgartz T, Krämer A (2014) Customer relationship controlling—IT-gestütztes customer value management. Controlling 26(6):264–271

Burgartz T, Krämer A (2016) Measures to understand and control customer relationship and loyalty. In: Mack et al (eds) Managing in a VUCA world. Springer, New York, pp 99–114

Chen J, Chen Y, Du X, Li C, Lu J, Zhao S, Zhou X (2013) Big data challenge: a data management perspective. Front Comp Sci 7(2):157–164

Davenport TH (2014) Big data at work: dispelling the myths, uncovering the opportunities. Harvard Business Review Press, Boston

De Mauro A, Greco M, Grimaldi M (2015) What is big data? A consensual definition and a review of key research topics. AIP conference proceedings, pp 97–104

Deutscher Dialogmarketing Verband e.V (2016) Dialogmarketing Perspektiven 2015/2016: Tagungsband 10. wissenschaftlicher interdisziplinärer Kongress für Dialogmarketing. Springer Gabler, Wiesbaden

Dorschel J (2015) Einführung und Überblick. Praxishandbuch Big Data. Springer, Wiesbaden, pp 5–14

Fasel D (2014) Big Data—Eine Einführung. HMD Prax Wirtschaftsinform 51(4):386–400

Fasel D, Meier A (2016) Big Data: Grundlagen, Systeme und Nutzungspotenziale. Edition HMD. Springer Vieweg, Wiesbaden

Finlay S (2014) Predictive analytics, data mining and big data: myths, misconceptions and methods. Palgrave Macmillan, Basingstoke, Hampshire

Freiknecht J, Papp S (2018) Big Data in der Praxis: Lösungen mit Hadoop, Spark, HBase und Hive. Daten speichern, aufbereiten, visualisieren. 2. Aufl, Carl Hanaser, München

Gadatsch A (2017) Zielsetzung von Big Data Projekten. In: Gadatsch A, Landrock H (eds) Big Data für Entscheider. Springer, Wiesbaden, pp 11–16

Gleich R, Grönke K, Kirchmann M, Leyk J (2014) Controlling und big data. Anforderungen, Auswirkungen, Lösungen, Haufe, München

Gluchowski P (2014) Aktuelle trend in der business intelligence. Controlling—Zeitschrift für erfolgsorientierte Unternehmensführung 26(4/5):235–243

Gotsch ML (2022) Customer Centricity & Datenschutz—Die Geschichte eines Missverständnisses. Mark Rev St Gallen 2022(2):888–894

Groß C, Pfennig R (2019) Digitalisierung in Industrie, Handel und Logistik. Leitfaden von der Prozessanalyse bis zur Einsatzoptimierung, 2. Aufl. Springer Fachmedien, Wiesbaden

Hackett D (2016) Big data in life insurance: December 2016. MLC life insurance. https://www.mlc.com.au/content/dam/mlc/documents/pdf/media-centre/big-data-report.pdf. (Siehe Seiten ii, 2)

Hippman S, Klinger R, Leis M (2017) Digitalisierung—Anwendungsfelder und Forschungsziele. In: Neugebauer R (ed) Digitalisierung. Schlüsseltechnologien für Wirtschaft & Gesellschaft. Springer Vieweg, Berlin, pp 9–18

Horváth P, Gleich R, Seiter M (2020) Controlling, 14. Aufl., München

Jaekel M (2015) Die Anatomie digitaler Geschäftsmodelle. Springer Gabler, Wiesbaden

Joshi S (2025) The synergy of generative AI and big data for financial risk: Review of recent developments. IJFMR-International Journal For Multidisciplinary Research 7(1):1–17

Keimer I, Zorn M, Gisler M, Fallegger M (2017) Dimensionen der Digitalisierung im Controlling—Grundlagen und Denkanstöße zur Selbstanalyse und Weiterentwicklung. Expert Focus 11:827–831

Klein D, Tran-Gia P, Hartmann M (2013) Big data. Informatik-Spektrum 36(3):319–323

König C, Schröder J, Wiegand E (2018) Big Data: Chancen, Risiken, Entwicklungstendenzen. Schriftenreihe der ASI—Arbeitsgemeinschaft Sozialwissenschaftlicher Institute. Springer Fachmedien, Wiesbaden, pp 8–11

Krafft M, Kumar V, Harmeling C, Singh S, Zhu T, Chen J, Rosa E (2021) Insight is power: understanding the terms of the consumer-firm data exchange. J Reta 97(1):133–149

Krämer A, Burgartz T (2015) Customer value controlling—combining different value perspectives. Bus Manag Stud 1(2):11–19

Krämer A, Tachilzik T (2016) Die Zukunft von Big Data im Vertrieb. Sales Manag Rev 2:64–71

Krämer A, Mauer R (2023) Datenschutz für Entscheider in Marketing und Vertrieb. Springer Books, Wiesbaden

Krämer A, Tachilzik T, Bongaerts R (2016) Automatisierung im Kundenbeziehungsmanagement: Chance oder Risiko für Unternehmen? Marketing Review St Gallen 4:10–17

Laney D (2001) 3D data management—controlling data volume, velocity, variety, metagroup Inc. (Hrsg). http://blogs.gartner.com/doug-laney/files/2012/01/ad949-3D-Data-Ma-nagement-Controlling-Data-Volume-Velocity-and-Variety.pdf

Lee I (2017) Big data: dimensions, evolution, impacts, and challenges. Bus Horiz 60(3):293–303

Loos P, Lechtenbörger J, Vossen G, Zeier A, Krüger J (2011) In-Memory-Datenmanagement in betrieblichen Anwendungssystemen. Wirtschaftsinformatik 53(6):383–390

Mertens P, Barbian D, Baier S (2018) Digitalisierung und Industrie 4.0—eine Relativierung. Springer Vieweg, Wiesbaden

QuantumBlack (2025) The state of AI. How organizations are rewiring to capture value. March 2025. https://www.mckinsey.com/~/media/mckinsey/business%20functions/quantumblack/our%20insights/the%20state%20of%20ai/2025/thestate-of-ai-how-organizations-are-rewiring-to-capture-value_final.pdf. Accessed 9 May 2025

Saggi MK, Jain S (2018) A survey towards an integration of big data analytics to big insights for value-creation. Info Proc Man 54(5):758–790

Samulat P (2017) Die Digitalisierung der Welt. Wie das Industrielle Internet der Dinge aus Produkten Services macht. Springer Fachmedien, Wiesbaden

Schneider W, Grieser F (2016) Früherkennung und Intuition. Controlling—Zeitschrift für erfolgsorientierte Unternehmensführung 28(3):181–188

Schön D (2016) Planung und Reporting: Grundlagen, business intelligence, mobile BI und big-data-analytics. Springer Gabler, Wiesbaden

Seele P, Dierksmeier C, Hofstetter R, Schultz MD (2021) Mapping the ethicality of algorithmic pricing: a review of dynamic and personalized pricing. J Bus Ethics 170(4):697–719

Sivarajah U, Karnal M, Irani Z, Weerakkody V (2017) Critical analysis of big data challenges and analytical methods. J Bus Res 70:263–286

Steinberg E (2019) Big data and personalized pricing. Bus Ethics Q 30(1):97–117

Tiefenbacher K, Olbrich S (2018) Wie Big Data die Kundenbeziehungen beeinflusst—mit zusätzlichen Informationen vom Segmentierungs-zum Erlebnismanagement. In: von Keuper F, Schomann M, Sikora L (Hrsg) Homo Connectus. Einblicke in die Post-Solo-Ära des Kunden. Springer, Wiesbaden, pp 121–140

Tröbs M, Mengen A (2018) Big data im controlling—Chancen und Risiken. In: Wissenschaftliche Schriften des Fachbereichs Wirtschaftswissenschaften, Hochschule Koblenz—University of Applied Sciences (26)

van Boom WH, van der Rest JPI, van den Bos K, Dechesne M (2020) Consumers beware: online personalized pricing in action! How the framing of a mandated discriminatory pricing disclosure influences intention to purchase. Soc Justice Res 33(3):331–351

Vasarhelyi M, Kogan A, Tuttle B (2015) Big data in accounting: an overview. Account Horiz 29(2):381–396

Werani T, Schauberger A, Martinek-Kuchinka P, Freiseisen B (2017) Wertdisziplinen und digitale Transformation von Geschäftsmodellen. In: Schallmo D, Rusnjak A, Anzengruber J, Werani T, Jünger M (eds) Digitale Transformation von Geschäftsmodellen. Springer Gabler, Wiesbaden, pp 237–263

The Cornerstones of Customer Value-Centered Management: Benefits, Price and Costs

Core Function—Customer Benefits: What Are the Actual Customer Needs?

4

4.1 Customer Benefits and Relevant Performance Facets

4.1.1 Customer Benefits and Feature Attributes

"Some people say, 'Give the customers what they want'. But that's not my approach. Our job is to figure out what they're going to want before they do. I think Henry Ford once said, 'if I'd asked customers what they wanted, they would have told me, 'A faster horse! People don't know what they want until you show it to them. That's why I never rely on market research. Our task is to read things that are not yet on the page."—Steve Jobs

For marketing practice, a deep understanding of customer needs is an essential starting point that plays a role at different levels of consideration. The above quote from Steve Jobs underlines how difficult it is to assess the possibilities for satisfying needs, especially for highly innovative products, when relying on traditional methods (in this case, customer surveys) (Isaacson 2011). Customer needs can be the basis for segmenting the market and one's own customers. Ultimately, every company must ask itself which needs it wants to satisfy with its products and services. The descriptions of this vary. Collis and Rukstad (2008) describe this as the "strategic sweet spot," i.e., the point at which a company meets a customer need in a way that the competition cannot.

However, the problem often arises that the needs structure is not homogeneous: needs-oriented segmentation approaches are therefore a classic area of application. Customer segmentation can be used to develop pricing models—if clear customer groups with a high or low willingness to pay can be identified—or to evaluate the effectiveness of different sales strategies. Another area of application is strategic brand or company positioning, which often involves identifying differentiation criteria compared to the competition and highlighting USPs (Unique Selling Propositions). The more a product stands out from the competition in key performance facets, the better the chances of achieving a long-term competitive advantage (Raynor and Christensen 2003). This applies to existing and new companies

© The Author(s), under exclusive license to Springer Nature Switzerland AG 2025
A. Krämer et al., *Customer Value-centered Management*, Future of Business and Finance, https://doi.org/10.1007/978-3-031-90497-4_4

(start-ups) as well as existing and new products. When developing new products, one of the core tasks of innovation management is to ensure the economic viability of the new product. In addition to achieving a sufficiently high price, it is necessary to clarify which customer benefits are to be generated. At the same time, there are dependencies between the perceived product quality, customer satisfaction, and ultimately the success of the company (Huber et al. 2000). Knowledge of customer needs is a prerequisite for improving the design of new products and the management and optimization of product portfolios (Eppinger et al. 2011).

These introductory remarks indicate that there is hardly any dissent on the importance of customer needs as the basis of marketing, but there are different assessments of how it is possible, firstly, to fully understand customer needs—with his quote, Steve Jobs expresses that he considers classic forms of market research to be unsuitable—and, secondly, to convert them efficiently into product and service changes (i.e., performance features or attributes). The first aspect involves a knowledge problem, the second an implementation problem.

The conceptual differences between customer needs and product attributes should be briefly discussed. Customer benefits address a basic need of potential customers; a problem that needs to be solved. Product attributes, on the other hand, represent the means to satisfy customer needs (Griffin et al. 2009; Brown and Eisenhardt 1995). For example, when customers describe their use of and requirements for mouthwash, they may express the need to 'just know how much mouthwash to use.' This customer need can be satisfied by various product attributes (solutions), such as textual descriptions or visual markings on the bottle. Notably, the redesigned Sensodyne mouthwash bottle features an easy-to-see measuring cap, enhancing dosing accuracy and user convenience.

4.1.2 Customer Information: But Which Ones and for What Purpose?

The relevance of recognizing customer needs underlines the increased provision of customer information in recent years. The more diverse, varied, complete, and voluminous customer data is provided, the greater the chance of either understanding customer problems better or even being able to anticipate them. In their empirical studies on the central challenges of a digitalized world, Leeflang et al. (2014) point to four key points, namely, (1) the use of customer insights and data; (2) the threatening power of social media for brands and customer relationships; (3) the omnipresence of new digital metrics and the subsequent evaluation of the effectiveness of (digital) marketing activities; and (4) the increasing talent gap in analytical skills in companies. The topic of customer information is rightly the first priority. In combination with the fourth point, the challenges for big data become clear: it is not just about collecting and merging as much and as comprehensive data as possible, but also about the ability to support management decisions based on analytics.

Ultimately, customer information can then be used for the following measures:

- Development of new products
- Specific expansion of range
- Ensuring a continuous innovation process
- Immediate elimination of product/service weaknesses and deficits in service provision
- Change in business models.

Despite attempts to approach innovation processes in companies in a more structured and systematic way and to incorporate controlling measures (Eppinger et al. 2011) in the hope of avoiding inefficiencies and using the high budgets for research and development in a more targeted manner, the flop rates for new product launches remain high. "We know that 80 to 90 % of all new products fail with customers. They are never heard of again after a short time," explains Samuel West, Head of the Museum of Failures in Helsingborg (Sweden). The list of exhibits on display is long: It ranges from Crystal Pepsi (transparent cola, offered in Switzerland from 1992, advertised as pure and healthy; however, consumers were confused as Crystal Pepsi looked like a mineral water and yet tasted like Pepsi) to the green ketchup from Heinz to the Newton, one of the biggest Apple flops (presented in 1993 by then Apple boss John Sculley as a personal, digital assistant at the luxury price of US$700, discontinued in 1998 after Steve Jobs returned to Apple; Wietlisbach 2017). The stories about famous product flops fill entire books (McMath and Forbes 1998). Reading them sometimes makes the reader smile, but they are always bitter from the managers' point of view. After all, these stories have one thing in common: an enormous waste of resources.

The correlation between the provision of information and the ultimate failure of product innovations (see Fig. 4.1, left-hand side) needs to be examined more closely to derive insights into any potential risks. In the specific example case, based on

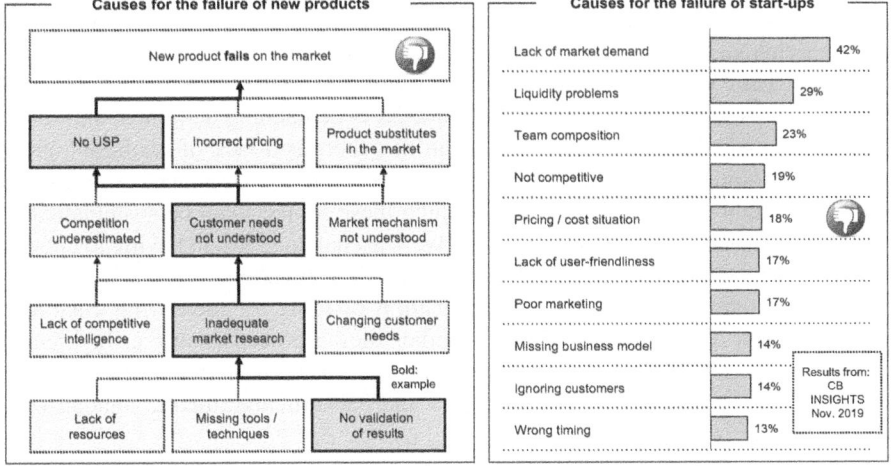

Fig. 4.1 Reasons for the failure of new products and companies

Goffin and Koners (2011), which is highlighted visually, an attempt is made to estimate key data factors regarding market acceptance, such as customer needs. However, this is done with weaknesses (there is no sufficient validation of the study results). A classic example in a concept test concerns the use of the purchase intention expressed in the interview as a real sales forecast. If, for example, the empirically measured values are not attenuated, the possible sales effects appear inflated, with far-reaching consequences for the next planning phase. In essence, the actual degree of need satisfaction is overestimated. One reason for this is that the consumer has different information in the real purchasing environment than in an interview situation. It is possible that the objectively apparent advantages of the product do not manifest themselves sufficiently in the perception of the potential buyer. In the end, the innovative product does not achieve the set goals and has failed. However, this is only one potential cause. Other correlations are also conceivable, e.g., that the market research leads to plausible sales figures, but the general conditions in the market have developed unfavorably since the study was conducted (new products from the competition, changed consumer preferences; Phagare 2025).

The causes of the failure of innovative ideas and concepts can also be viewed retrospectively. Figure 4.1 (right-hand side) shows the ranking of causes for the failure of start-ups. The aspect of a lack of or insufficient understanding of customer needs does not play a role in every case, but for several of the causes noted, the connection between the causes listed above seems obvious (lack of market needs, lack of user-friendliness, ignoring customers, etc.).

4.1.3 Recognizable and Hidden Customer Needs

There are many reasons why it is often not possible to develop products that are optimally tailored to customer needs. There are also several steps in the innovation process that need to be successfully completed. In the first step, it is important to recognize customer needs as completely as possible. In the second step, attributes and their characteristics must be defined (as a kind of translation process). The third step is to ensure that the product in its holistic form is understood by the customer as a genuine solution to a problem. This process is demanding, complex, and often fails in the first phase. This does not mean that there is a lack of methodological approaches, quite the opposite. Herstatt et al. (2007) state that management has an arsenal of methods at its disposal with which these projects can be systematically planned, controlled, and monitored. However, the challenge lies in having to choose the right method or a mix of instruments in a specific situation.

An important aid in the basic classification of tools for measuring customer needs is based on the assessment of whether they are needs that can be clearly named and described by the consumer or whether they are unarticulated needs. If consumers are aware of their basic needs and can articulate them, standardized descriptive market research methods can be used. If the needs are "hidden" and the consumer is not aware of them or finds it difficult to articulate them in a specific interview situation, qualitative methods or indirect methods of measuring needs are recommended.

4.2 Overview of Methods for Measuring Customer Needs and Selected Approaches

4.2.1 Method Overview

The relationships described are illustrated in Fig. 4.2 based on Bayus and Shane (2008, p. 127), whereby three instruments are listed as examples for the case of articulated and non-articulated needs, respectively (without claiming to be exhaustive), which represent common and particularly widespread procedures in practice.

The approach of drawing conclusions about product design based on customer needs can be found in relatively old concepts, such as Quality Function Deployment (QFD), which was frequently discussed in the 1980s and 1990s. Griffin and Hauser (1993, p. 9) state: "QFD is a total-quality-management process in which the 'voice of the customer' is deployed throughout the R&D, engineering, and manufacturing stages of product development. For example, in the first 'house' of QFD, customer needs are linked to design attributes thus encouraging the joint consideration of marketing issues and engineering issues. In the identification stage, we address the questions of 1) how many customers need to be interviewed, 2) how many analysts need to read the transcripts, 3) how many customer needs do we miss, and 4) are focus groups or one-on-one interviews superior? In the structuring stage the customer needs are arrayed into a hierarchy of primary, secondary, and tertiary

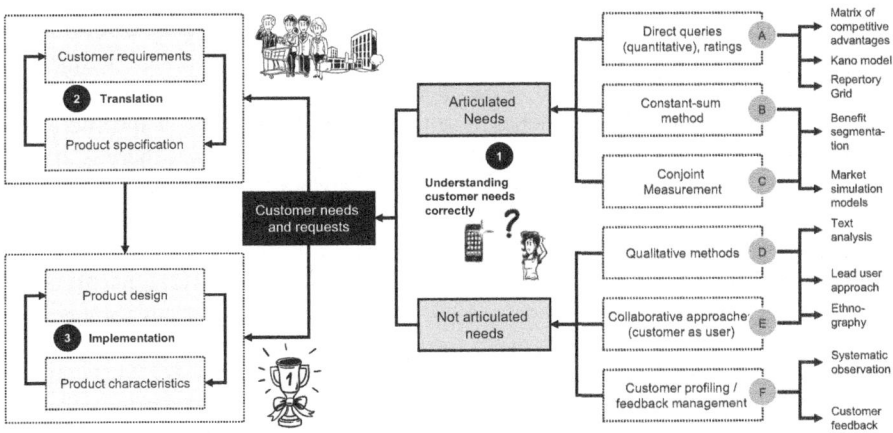

Fig. 4.2 Customer needs as a starting point for product and service optimization and possible measurement methods

needs." The following are the most important methods for determining customer needs.

4.2.2 Direct Query of Attribute Weights

If a list of theoretically important features from the customer's point of view is available, the customer benefit can be determined as part of a direct, quantitative (standardized) survey. Customers are asked directly about the importance of certain features of a product (example: "How important are the following features for you? Please rate quality, delivery service, price and brand on a scale from 1 = very important to 6 = not at all important"). This approach, which is also referred to as a compositional method (first the benefits of the individual attributes are measured and then aggregated into an overall benefit), is simple but raises several questions at the same time. For example, it must be questioned whether the characteristics presented (e.g., 10 service components) include all facets customers themselves see as relevant. An additional potential problem is that customers may be neither willing nor able to provide clearly differentiated answers to the benefit questions.

The main problem is therefore the reliability of such an approach. A major weakness is the lack of a trade-off: in a real decision, consumers or buyers are forced to make certain compromises (e.g., the highest quality level is usually not available at the lowest price). As a result, decisions are made based on a weighing-up process that results in a ranking of criteria (at least in the case of purchases that are not made spontaneously, without reflection, "on the spur of the moment"). The survey question form does not reflect this common situational reality. In market research practice, results are problematic if the average importance for several characteristics is at a high level and differentiates only insignificantly or not at all. For the project managers responsible, this is problematic in several respects, including with regard to the frustrating lack of clarity in terms of what to prioritize.

Clearly distinguishable characteristics are desirable in terms of their relevance, yet research results may show five or six positions in the ranking of the criteria with minimal differences (for example in the mean value). It is therefore not surprising that the validity of these approaches is often critically assessed in the literature (Homburg and Beutin 2000; Hartmann and Sattler 2004). However, there is agreement, at least in the world of market research, that attribute importance can be measured better and more validly in the manner described above than using other designs, such as statement ratings (Menold and Bogner 2015, p. 8).

Despite their inherent challenges, direct approaches should not be hastily consigned to the "problematic methods" pile. Even relatively simple tools can be used to point out to the interviewee the need for prioritization (as the result of a weighing-up process according to the logic "I can't have everything at the same time"). The questioning technique can also be helpful. For example, the study participants could be asked to first look at the list of all features and then start with the most important criterion from the customer's point of view. This form of conditioning can support the prioritization and focusing process. This makes it clear that if the features are complete and comprehensible and do not leave too much room for interpretation, if the decisions are largely rational and reflective, and if it is possible to convey the feeling of a real decision-making situation to the respondent, then results can be produced on the basis of directly determined feature weights, on which further project steps can be based.

Apart from multivariate methods such as regression, factor-, or cluster-analysis, which are also based on data from direct queries, there are at least a few tools that incorporate directly measured characteristics. Examples include the competitive advantage matrix, the repertory grid approach, and the Kano model.

The competitive advantage matrix is based on the considerations of Trux et al. (1984). When analyzing the competitive situation, two dimensions must be considered: firstly, the size of the advantage that can be built up over the competitor and secondly, the number of different factors upon which an advantage can be developed. The combination of the two axes creates the framework in the competitive advantage matrix in which the long-term value and the basic strategic conditions are determined. This approach can be further detailed by evaluating the most important purchase decision factors of a product in terms of importance. This corresponds to the procedure described above based on a rating scale. In addition, it is necessary to record how well a specific supplier is rated for each individual feature. In the simplest case, the combination of both dimensions results in four fields: Features with above average or low importance and features in which the provider performs better or worse than the best competitor. Strategic competitive advantages exist when suppliers are better or worse than their competitors in the most important performance features (Simon and Von der Gathen 2010). This approach is also used in strategic analysis under the term Resources and Capabilities Matrix (see Grant 2016, p. 134 for the example of Ducati).

The repertory grid approach is a cognitive mapping tool that is used in a structured interview to elicit and evaluate people's mental models regarding a subject of analysis, with the special feature that the advantages of qualitative and quantitative methods are inherently combined. The procedure distinguishes between four iterative phases that lead to a graphically condensed representation of benefit drivers (Goffin et al. 2010; Clauss and Döppe 2016).

The Kano model (Kano et al. 1984) is a widely used special form of compositional methods. It deduces the resulting satisfaction from the presence of certain product attributes that fulfill the requirements of customers and users (Rashid et al. 2011). The model not only supports the measurement of needs, but also groups requirements into several requirement groups. These are referred to as basic, performance, and enthusiasm requirements:

- Basic requirements (M: must-be requirements): These are properties that are generally assumed by customers. They are taken for granted and are therefore not explicitly demanded. As a result, the provision of services and the fulfillment of needs does not lead to customer satisfaction. However, if these requirements are not met, dissatisfaction arises. In this context, we can also speak of hygiene characteristics.

- One-dimensional requirements (O): These can generate satisfaction or dissatisfaction depending on their degree of fulfillment. If the degree of fulfillment increases, customer satisfaction increases and vice versa. In simplified terms, a linear relationship between the fulfillment of performance requirements and customer satisfaction can be assumed.
- Attractive requirements (A): In contrast to basic and performance requirements, there is no dissatisfaction if these are not met. The performance is not expected by the consumer. However, customer satisfaction arises when they are fulfilled (positive surprise effect). This group of performance features is of interest in that they can contribute to differentiation from other products in highly competitive and saturated markets but cannot be used to compensate for other requirement categories.

While the Kano model is well known in management circles, the specific procedure is probably only known to a much smaller group. The concrete recording of characteristic judgments is particularly important here. Also, the Kano approach requires an empirical survey. The questionnaire used formulates a functional and dysfunctional question for each relevant product requirement. Respondents are presented with an identical set of answer options for each feature for evaluation:

- Dysfunctional question: Assuming the product **does not** have feature X, what would you think? Answer options in five steps from "I would be very happy about that" to "I assume that" to "That would bother me a lot."
- Functional question: Assuming the product has feature X, what would you think? Answer options in five steps from "I would be very happy about that" to "I assume that" to "That would bother me a lot."

The characteristics are then assigned to one of the three groups in various steps (Roth and Bernardy 2019). For example, characteristics that determine the answer to the functional question can be assigned as basic requirements.

"I take that for granted" and receive the answer "That would bother me" for the dysfunctional question.

As can be seen, it is possible to provide concrete indications for strategic and operational marketing by means of direct assessments of attributes. However, these always require a differentiated assessment of features and individual feature characteristics.

4.2.3   Constant-Sum Method

If it is an essential condition to present results on the importance of characteristics in a sufficiently differentiated way (i.e., as in reality), it must be clarified how it can be ensured in the question design that a weighing decision is made. One form of question design that is under-appreciated in market research practice is the constant sum scale (Homburg and Beutin 2000). In contrast to the rating scale (e.g., scale with the values 1–6 according to school grades or importance), the study participants are asked to allocate, for example, 100 points of the overall importance to individual characteristics. In individual cases, the result could be as follows: 50 points for quality, 25 points for delivery service, 10 points for price, and 15 points for brand (for four characteristics). The interview situation is more strenuous for the interviewee, as it is first necessary to gain an overview of the features (in the example with 4 features this is easy, with 8–10 features it is more difficult), then the weighing decision is made.

It is questionable in the approaches described whether a certain feature such as price or delivery service is sufficiently specified in a specific survey situation. If it is assumed that decisions are made in relative terms and different characteristics are compared, the deficits become clear. But even these, weaknesses can be reduced. It is therefore conceivable to distribute 100 points not to absolute characteristics, but to relative references. In the specific example, this means that it is not the price feature that is evaluated, but a change (specific attributes are named), such as "a reduction in price by 10%, i.e., from EUR 100 to EUR 90." In relation to the delivery service, this could be an "improvement in delivery time from 7 days (today) to 3 days." This makes the question more understandable and easier to grasp for the respondent in the interview, but ultimately also more realistic and therefore more valid.

This approach was used by the authors in various sectors, including digital learning (optimization of the design of learning videos; Krämer and Böhrs 2016a) or mobility decisions (motives for using the train; Bongaerts and Krämer 2014).

4.2.4 Conjoint Measurement

Conjoint analysis is an experimental form of survey in which customers weigh up the advantages and disadvantages of alternative product profiles ("consider jointly"). It assumes that consumers evaluate the benefits of a real or hypothetical product or service by combining the partial benefits of individual characteristics of products or services. Therefore, factors such as quality, delivery service, price, and brand should not be considered in isolation, but rather in combination with specific characteristics. In the survey—as in reality—the customers questioned only state which product alternatives they would buy or prefer; they are not asked directly about the importance of features. However, based on the selection of different combinations, their benefit structure can be inferred from the customers' answers.

The following steps must be distinguished in the procedure:

- Determination of the characteristics to be included: This may sound trivial, but in practice it is not. Ultimately, the aim is to identify the actual main drivers for the purchase decision. In this respect, preliminary work can be helpful, such as qualitative research or surveys with direct approaches to measuring the importance of characteristics or the evaluation of secondary data. It is crucial that this information underpins a clear picture of the most important criteria.

- Defining the characteristics for each feature: This not only concerns the number of attributes, but also the more precise description. When it comes to price, this still seems comparatively simple if, for example, different prices are presented for each product (e.g., €80, €100, and €120). Here, it must be ensured that the specified price range is relevant in the market, i.e., it also covers the prices realized in the market. It is not so easy to define different performance levels for other features. Just think of different product quality levels, for example, for an office chair (low, medium, and high quality). Problems arise in the survey (and then later in the analysis, interpretation, etc.) if the respondents do not have a uniform understanding of certain characteristics. When describing "high product quality," a strong, subjective component is to be expected because different people have different ideas and experiences regarding the characteristics. The challenge is therefore to present this attribute transparently and objectively for all study participants to reduce the scope for individual interpretation.

- Designing the questionnaire and determining the survey design as well as conducting the field phase: Figure 4.3 (left section) shows different queries for a conjoint model. This step does not only concern aspects such as the choice of conjoint model (full profile vs. trade-off method; use of ACA or CBC or other methods), which are often the focus of textbooks. In concrete implementation, the trade-off is different in each case and ranges from the formation of a preference ranking to concrete selection decisions to the naming of preferences. In practical use, it must be ensured that the target persons (e.g., potential customers) are able to participate in the study or provide valid answers during the survey. This not only places high demands on knowledge of the relevant market, but also on skills in questionnaire design. Finally, a typical study that includes conjoint measurement consists of other topics that are important for the overall concept. Therefore, the actual conjoint measurement part of an interview must also be

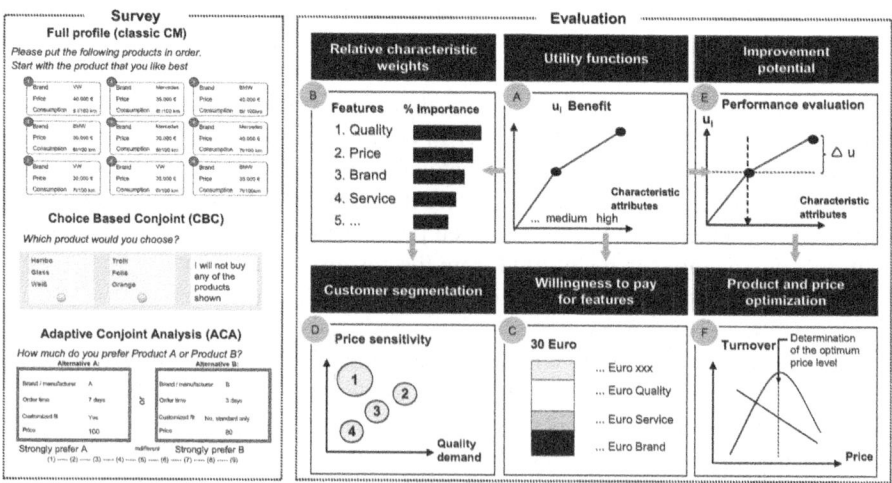

Fig. 4.3 Survey design and evaluation options for conjoint measurement (examples)

professionally prepared. This includes sufficient conditioning of the interviewees, but also, for example, the provision of information material. It may be necessary to provide preliminary information ("We will now present some aspects that may be important when deciding to buy office chairs... The following levels of product quality should be distinguished here... High product quality means the following... List with definitions") for the test person.

- Calculation of the preference function/partial benefit values: Based on the selection decisions
- To make decisions, utility functions are calculated that are ideally available at the individual level. The exact course of the utility function indicates how strong the changes in utility are between two or more values (e.g., product quality medium vs. product quality high). This is illustrated in Fig. 4.3 (right-hand side) with field A. The utility function has a non-linear progression.
- Further analyses: These can go in different directions, see Fig. 4.3 (right-hand side, boxes B to F). The relative attribute weights can be calculated from the ranges of the individual partial benefit functions (individual range of the attribute in relation to the sum of all attribute ranges). It is also possible to derive the price sales function or calculate individual willingness to pay as well as segment customers based on the relative feature weights. In addition, the utility values are a data basis for simulation models.

Conjoint analyses are very popular and widely used today as a tool for measuring customer benefits. The range of applications is very broad, whereby the use of concept development is usually in the foreground and only secondarily the estimation of price-sales effects plays a role (Steiner 2007). It took some time for the method to become established. The methodological foundations date back to the 1970s (Wittink and Gattin 1989); the development of the Internet and the processing power of PCs as well as the further development of special software offerings later led to broad acceptance in science and practice. Based on holistic utility judgments, individual utility functions are ultimately determined, whereby the utility of a product is composed additively of the partial utility values for the characteristics of individual product features or variables. The characteristic weights provide important information for marketing (Green and Srinivasan 1990). For example, the ranking of the most important criteria shows the priority of features from the customer's point of view. Individual feature weights can be used as a basis for customer benefit-based segmentation (Alibrandi and Giacalone 2008).

The utility functions provided in the result can be used in purchasing decision models to explain real purchasing behavior. This requires a high estimation accuracy of the partial utility values that determine the utility function. Software providers (e.g., Sawtooth) have long been offering simulation tools in addition to the survey tools. This makes it possible to consider different market scenarios and thus, in addition to the price-sales effects, also to play through facets such as increased competition or new suppliers (Frohmann 2018; Simon and Fassnacht 2016). This reinforces the advantage of conjoint analysis already emphasized by Teichert (1997) that the instrument provides both direct and indirect recommendations for action that can be derived for marketing. The direct analysis of the partial benefit values provides indications of the relative benefit contribution of individual product features and thus, for example, design suggestions for new products. However, there are also risks if incorrect relative weightings lead to the danger of setting the wrong priorities in product design. Unfortunately, very few scientific contributions address the limitations of the methodology in detail, such as Lohrke et al. (2010). Despite all the improvements made in recent decades, these relate to the hypothetical nature of the survey. However, there are also numerous sources of systematic errors in the design of the conjoint measurement (selection of attributes and determination of characteristic values).

Another point of discussion concerns the provision of information that was basically intended as "support," but can ultimately lead to over-conditioning of the test subjects. This is not only about the amount of information, but also about the way in which subjects can access it, i.e., the degree of interaction (Ariely 2000). Researchers therefore repeatedly find themselves in a dilemma. If too little information is provided in the study, there is an increased risk that the characteristics and attributes cannot be understood uniformly. If the provision of information is overloaded, this may result in cognitive overload or over-conditioning (the subject shows preferences that do not match those under real conditions because of dealing with the test object).

Systematic errors, distortions in the perception of test persons, etc. are present in all further steps of the analysis: this applies to the calculation of partial utility functions and extends to market simulations. Netzer et al. (2008) point out that while technological changes improve the use of computerized methods such as conjoint measurement (lower costs for collection in online studies, etc.), they also increase the challenges of maintaining the attention of the study participants during the demanding tasks (some studies contain more than 50 different features). The number of tasks is another source of bias. In the worst-case scenario, subjects are cognitively overwhelmed after a few minutes and lose the required level of attention. While the development of new software offerings (such as Sawtooth's ACBC) is becoming increasingly complex and time-consuming, market requirements are moving in a different direction. The willingness to participate in market research decreases with the length of the interview and the increasingly perceived monotony during the survey. Overloading conjoint analyses with many characteristics is also problematic from a statistical point of view because the estimation of partial utility values is no longer well secured. Although users should be aware of the recommendation not to include more than 5–6 attributes in the design, in the review by Hartmann and Sattler (2002) the number of attributes was higher than the limit value of 6 in almost two thirds of the studies examined (48% of the studies even used more than 10 attributes).

An interim conclusion can be drawn: Due to its wide range of possible applications, conjoint measurement will remain an important tool in customer benefit research. However, the idea that conjoint analysis is the only way to measure valid customer requirements seems inappropriate. The method has undeniably revolutionized research into preference analysis over the last 30 years. However, in keeping with the motto "The king is dead, long live the king," the question arises as to what comes "after conjoint analysis." In the meantime, technological possibilities have opened a wide range of alternative approaches to preference research. More than a decade ago, Netzer et al. (2008) called for: "Moving forward, we encourage researchers to go beyond conjoint analysis and explore new problems and applications of preference measurement."

4.2.5   Qualitative Methods

The instruments described in more detail so far (direct questioning, constant sum questions, conjoint measurement) can be used if, firstly, a clear set of relevant characteristics can be inferred (in the case of direct questioning of characteristic weights, e.g., 10 criteria, it must be ensured that all essential criteria are "in the room" with the discussed characteristics and that no relevant criteria are left out—in conjoint measurement, only the most relevant criteria should be included) and, secondly, stable preferences of the customers/decision-makers exist (Bühren 2010). However, if the preferences are not robust, i.e., if they are easily changed by situational influences or if they are not stable over time, classic approaches to preference measurement lose confidence and resilience.

The first question to ask is how uncertainties regarding a sufficiently comprehensive set of features can be eliminated. This is relatively easy if customers have a clear idea of their wishes, needs, and problems and can articulate them. The situation is more difficult if these aspects lie in the unconscious, quasi "below the surface." In this case, qualitative instruments can be used. The aim of projective methods is for respondents to shift unconscious feelings (unpleasant and pleasant) and desires onto other people or objects. ("Suppose company XY were an animal, which animal would it be and why?"). In this case, open and unadulterated results are more likely to be expected because internal conflicts can be avoided. After all, the background to the assignment is usually not apparent to them. Thus, stimuli are triggered by sentence completion tests ("Please complete the following sentence: When I currently think about using public transport..."). The portfolio of approaches also includes the use of visual material (e.g., advertisements) ("What story is told in the picture? To what extent does this image affect you personally? Have you experienced something similar or do you know someone who has?"). An overview of the methods can be found in Gröppel-Klein and Königstorfer (2009). Despite all the creativity and openness, there is one restriction that applies to all methods. It is almost impossible to make reliable statements about the validity of the various projective methods.

4.2.6   Collaborative Approaches: Involving Customers and Users

The previous quantitative or qualitative approaches are classic forms of survey that have been established in market research for years. The customer is questioned on specific topics in a study. This only looks at a very small part of an increasingly large portfolio of information sources. This perspective can be step-by-step expanded. For example, customer centricity could be understood as an approach that uses targeted input from customers as a starting point for the design and implementation of all marketing strategies to gain their satisfaction and loyalty. This goes far beyond the understanding of classic market research. As part of customer integration, the entire product development process can be covered (Hofbauer 2013), including in the phase of

- idea generation and pre-selection when customers are actively involved in relatively early discussions on product development (customers contribute their own ideas, evaluate concepts, provide suggestions for improvement)
- product conception and selection, when clients act as consultants for concept evaluation and selection as well as co-creators for concept refinement (they provide support in the selection process of product variants, etc.)
- product development, when customers are involved as development partners and consultants for the evaluation and selection of design variants
- test procedures and market trials when customers serve as potential buyers to assess the potential for success and market potential and provide early indications of functionality and assessment of market potential.

If existing customers can be involved in the process of co-creating products and/or services, an important step toward customer centricity has been taken. There are advantages in several respects. Primarily, the collaboration helps the company to deliver products and services that are not produced without the market in mind, but that specifically meet the needs of customers. In addition, there are opportunities to increase customer engagement if the customer appreciates this form of interaction. Overall, this can result in a sustainable competitive advantage. However, this is not a one-way street. After all, it requires a special attitude on both sides: on the one hand, the openness of the company to talk to customers at eye level and discuss projects and on the other hand, the interest of the customer to actively participate as a discussion partner. Against this background, failures in co-creation are to be expected.

In contrast to conducting descriptive studies, which focus on aspects such as representativeness and validity, companies are increasingly focusing on working with particularly qualified, advanced customers (lead users). These are described by Lin and Seepersad (2007) as "customers who push a product to its limits, experience needs prior to the general population, and benefit significantly from having those needs fulfilled." These are not necessarily representative approaches, because the aim is not to meet a market average (Herstatt et al. 2007). Instead, the focus is on customers who are above average in terms of their innovation motivation and qualifications. A variation is the "empathic design," in which observations and interviews are conducted in the customer's environment. This also addresses the ethnographic research approach. Customers and users should be observed or interviewed about their behavior in real situations to obtain the most concrete and relevant information possible for product design. Due to technological changes and the increasing use of videos, there are now cost-effective options, e.g., video technology (Schmidt 2008).

The combination of lead users and empathic design results in the target group of the "empathic lead user" (Lin and Seepersad 2007), defined as a group of ordinary customers (or designers) who become lead users by experiencing the product in a radically new way because they provide insights into extraordinary user experiences.

4.2.7 Customer Profiling and Incorporation of Customer Feedback

The methods discussed so far for identifying customer needs are based on traditional instruments that involve (human) interaction with customers, such as experience interviews and focus groups. The disadvantage of such approaches is that they are generally expensive and time-consuming. The time required proves to be a weakness when quick decisions and actions are required. Timoshenko and Hauser (2019) propose an approach based on user-generated content (UGC) as a promising alternative source for identifying customer needs. A machine learning approach is proposed that facilitates qualitative analysis by selecting content for efficient verification. The authors show that (1) UGC is at least as valuable as traditional methods as a source of customer needs for product development and that (2) machine learning methods improve the efficiency of identifying customer needs from UGC. This approach is not new. Lee (2007) already modeled the knowledge base of online customer reviews as a matrix of reviews that relate customer needs to product attributes. Procedures are required that are capable of not only structuring largely unstructured texts, but also qualifying them (i.e., determining a positive or negative direction).

After discussing the possibilities for identifying customer needs in this chapter and noting that there is no shortage of tools, but that a feeling and expertise is required for the selection of tools depending on the question, the following chapter will shed light on how customer insights can be used as a basis for decision-making in the company and what requirements arise in the process.

4.3 Customer Insights as the Basis for Decision-Making in the Company

4.3.1 Customer Insights: Different Ways to Build Proximity to the Customer

If the attempt is made to capture customer needs both continuously and as completely and authentically as possible, proximity to the customer is an essential success factor. Schmidt (2008, p. 41) states: "It can be observed time and again that it is of central importance for decision-makers in marketing and company management to gain an intuitive understanding of their potential customers." Some companies have geared their entire business model toward building proximity to the customer. When manufacturers of security cameras, providers of wet shavers, or car manufacturers offer subscription-based services today, then building proximity to the customer also plays a role in addition to the direct profit effects.

An intuitive understanding of the customer implies the ability to play through certain situations and experiences from the customer's perspective. The closer the company is to the customer, the better this empathy should be. But how can the process of building customer proximity be achieved in concrete terms? Goffin and Koners (2011) present the following instruments in a ranking according to frequency of use:

- Customer visits
- Surveys and focus groups
- Systematic observation and context interviews
- Repertory grid
- Ethnography
- Other approaches.

However, even these approaches only represent a small—albeit important—selection from a larger portfolio of instruments. It is also important to recognize the necessity of a cross-divisional and cross-functional approach (Kotler et al. 2006). For this reason alone, methods of identifying customer needs should not only be discussed in the context of market research. This is already clear from the fact that customer visits, which are in first place in the abovementioned ranking, generally do not relate to a classic market research function. The sales team plays a central role in the implementation of the required "approach to the customer." After all, the sales team not only has the core function of sales but is usually the central interface to the customer, has the closest customer contact, and receives the most up-to-date information.

This also underlines the need to move away from divisional thinking and make important customer, market, and competitor information available within the company. Krämer and Burgartz (2020), for example, emphasize the strategic importance of the sales team within the pricing process. In addition to the aspect of information distribution, information procurement is also important. In order to structure the sources of information, a more holistic approach is recommended, which first evaluates which measures the company actively uses to obtain information from customers (surveys, lead user discussions, etc.) and which information customers provide (more or less specifically) on their own initiative (service requests, complaints, product reviews on the Internet, reporting in public media).

4.3.2   A New Understanding of Corporate Market Research

The aspect of information dissemination is closely linked to the organization of functional areas such as market research, marketing, business analytics, or sales. The key question here is how essential information on customer insights (as a modern term for customer-related market research) can be incorporated into corporate decision-making processes in a structured and transparent manner.

Against this backdrop, Barton et al. (2016) classify companies according to the importance of customer insight and how concrete decisions are derived from customer information:

1. Traditional market research provider: At this stage, Customer Insight (CI) functions are mostly tactical and research-oriented, focusing on uncovering sales trends for existing products and services, primarily in existing channels and geographies. Market research is more focused on descriptive analysis to produce data in response to line manager requests. The market research unit has a limited budget, a limited number of employees, and a limited sphere of influence within the organization and receives only limited support from senior management. It is not untypical for this level to have a rather critical view of the market research unit (e.g., the lack of up-to-date data or a lack of implementation maturity of the conclusions).
2. Business Contributor: In a CI function at this stage, research usually focuses on short-term innovations such as packaging, shape and taste enhancements, pricing, and promotions. The group focuses on translating customer insights into business recommendations. A CI unit that is at this stage usually has the active support of the highest-ranking marketing or sales manager in the company as well as better access to managers and division heads. In general, however, the company managers set the priorities. Typically, ad hoc studies are used to clarify uncertainties in selective decisions.
3. Strategic insight partner: At this stage, executives have internalized that customer insights should guide most commercial business decisions. The CI function is a strategic partner and trusted advisor to the line. In addition to specialized research skills, CI team members demonstrate critical thinking, a willingness to challenge ideas, commercial and strategic understanding, and business judgment. The function's strategic or real-time research focuses on product and service improvements and short-term innovation but also includes experimentation with new data sources and research methods. This can include developing new data sources in an overarching project team (e.g., in data consolidation activities) or coordinating specific methods such as A/B tests. At this stage of development, study results are communicated throughout the organization, not just to the client.
4. CI as a source of competitive advantage: This level remains elusive for almost all companies. At this highest level, a CI function focuses on novel innovations, foresight, and predictive research. CI is applied to business decisions and core processes beyond market decisions, including research priorities, new product development, strategic planning, M&A and portfolio strategy, employee engagement, and corporate branding. A CI function at this level provides feedback on relevant trends, offers an independent perspective on high-priority topics and customer groups, and specializes in innovative methods. Market research units, or whatever the corresponding units are called, enjoy broad acceptance within the company. The team leader of the CI unit takes on management tasks, e.g., as head of strategy, analytics or marketing, and communicates closely with top management.

The typical development stages provide a clear illustration of how market research can develop from a shadowy existence into a strategic unit. However, they offer no more than a blueprint and contain a possible error in thinking. In many cases, it is not enough to simply make organizational changes, rename market research teams as "Special Customer Insight Units," and give the managers access to decision-making bodies. As a rule, development along the steps outlined above is likely to fail because other prerequisites are missing. For example, this requires a fundamental interest on the part of management in the "voice of the customer" and not just an expression of intent. In order to ensure appropriate sensitivity in this regard, companies take up programs in which managers work at the "company base." Activities can consist of top managers taking on the role of a simple clerk or salesperson with customer contact for a limited period or processing customer complaints at regular intervals and thus also making personal contact with customers and dealing with a specific concern (customer problem).

Another prerequisite is that market research is uniformly understood as the provision of objective and validated market and customer information to support decisions, and not as a tool to discredit employees or colleagues or to draw attention to errors and grievances in a one-sided manner.

The third prerequisite is sufficient competence in the interpretation of the data obtained, in the validation of results and in ensuring clear results. This also includes skills in the preparation of study results through to the formulation of concrete recommendations for implementation. Advances in artificial intelligence have significantly improved companies' ability to uncover hidden relationships in customer preferences, predict trends in new markets, and assess public sentiment in real time, transforming the landscape of customer insights and strategic decision-making, for example in e-commerce (Wu 2025).

4.3.3   Customer Experience Management as a Problem Solver

In addition to the methodological approaches discussed for determining customer needs, the appropriate collection of this information and the creation of organizational prerequisites, the customer insight aspect also includes the facets of the level of detail and speed of information provision. Particularly in the area of services, a closer look reveals that there are not just one but several points of contact between companies and customers. In this context, the concept of customer experience management is becoming increasingly important in corporate management. However, the basic idea is not new: along the individual "touchpoints" (contact points) in the customer process, the aim is to evaluate the expectations of buyers or users, the degree to which needs are met and how additional customer benefits can be generated (Verhoef et al. 2009). Focusing on the customer's service experience is particularly important when, as Frow and Payne (2007) point out, less than 10% of customers are enthusiastic about the service they perceive, while 80% of service providers would assume the same. The challenge is therefore not only to establish a status quo, but also to formulate target figures in the evaluation of customer contact as a basis for continuous research.

Using the tourism industry as an example, Yachin (2018) refers to the different interactions that need to be considered as part of the "customer journey." The phases of planning (pre-trip period phase), the use of services (active tourism experience), and the experiences and perceptions after the trip (reflective post-trip phase) can be roughly differentiated. In concrete terms, using the example of an overnight stay in a hotel (Stickdorn and Zehrer 2009), this can mean that customers who return to the hotel several times are asked about their satisfaction with partial services repeatedly (hotel website in search queries, through check-in to the hotel's rating on a review site).

However, what can theoretically lead to a detailed inventory of individual touch-points may prove to be a source of customer frustration, namely, if the survey on individual partial satisfactions is carried out directly after the touchpoint experiences, and this is perceived as tedious by the customers. One way to avoid these problems is to ask customers about particularly good or bad experiences after they have used the service. This is possible, for example, if the transaction data can be assigned to a specific customer and this customer can be contacted by email, for example. Telephone service providers or airlines use these instruments and carry out CRM-supported monitoring studies in which satisfaction with a specific service is recorded (e.g., satisfaction with a flight from Cologne to Munich 3 days ago). However, researchers are moving away from the traditional market research approach, which is characterized by anonymized data collection (Krämer 2018). The advantages of this approach are obvious: the results are available promptly (albeit not in real time) and can be assigned to a specific contact situation (specific flight, specific inquiry, specific customer relationship, etc.) and can therefore be used directly for operational marketing. Customer Experience Management (CXM) serves as a strategic approach to identifying and solving customer problems, thereby increasing customer satisfaction and loyalty. For further study, the framework by Meierhofer et al. (2024) is recommended.

In the next section, the interrelationships discussed will be dealt with using the example of the company simpleshow. simpleshow not only makes it possible to illustrate the opportunities of interaction with the customer and also co-creation in the network economy using a case study. A software-as-a-service (SaaS) application developed by simpleshow also makes it possible to present complex topics in an understandable way, an aspect that was already emphasized in Chap. 1.

4.4 Recognizing and Managing Customer Needs: The simpleshow Case Study

4.4.1 Videos as a Central Communication Medium

4.4.1.1 Changed Communication Structures

The reach of video content on the Internet is constantly increasing. According to the ARD/ZDF online study (2019), 83% of the German population watch moving images online at least occasionally, the majority of whom use online videos at least weekly and around a third daily (usage remains on a similar level in more recent studies). The increased use of video affects almost all types of content, with YouTube, media libraries, and video streaming services also increasing the frequency of use. Explainer videos are a special video format that are characterized by the following key points: Firstly, the basis for the creation is a script that often uses storytelling approaches while highlighting the most important key messages. The trick is to create a "good" story to inspire and convince an audience (Wright 2004). As a result, communication is extremely focused. Secondly, the length of the videos is reduced: According to Bonk (2008), "short videos of 1 to 4 min are ideal." The current trend is toward further shortening. Thirdly, the use of metaphorical elements in the video contextualizes the key points of an explanation, making the core message easier to understand and connect with the audience (Schmelzle 2014). In a world described by the terms volatility, uncertainty, complexity, and ambiguity (VUCA, see Chap. 1) (Bennett and Lemoine 2014), explanatory videos offer the opportunity to get to the heart of complex content in a targeted, concise, and efficient manner in a form that appears simple (Krämer and Böhrs 2017a).

In recent years, these short online videos have become a preferred content medium for business-to-business (B2B) marketers (Krämer and Böhrs 2016a, b). To increase sales effectiveness and efficiency, companies use appealing videos in all phases of the sales cycle to educate, entertain, inspire, and retain potential customers (Litt 2014). However, explainer videos are also used for internal communication. This can range from training employees in customer service to presenting new product ideas. The area of application (compliance, strategic topics, processes in sales and production, IT, new programs, etc.) is extremely broad (Krämer and Böhrs 2018). Another area of application is education (Laaser and Toloza 2017; Krämer and Böhrs 2016a, b).

The constantly changing framework conditions and related drivers such as digitalization, acceleration, and agility in management and teaching not only lead to an intensified use of explainer videos, but also change the way in which explainer videos are produced.

4.4.1.2 Drivers for Greater Use of DIY Tools

Platform providers are gaining increasing acceptance not only in the B2C sector but also in the B2B sector, as services that have to be purchased by companies are being offered as an alternative to conventional offerings as part of new business models. This applies, for example, to the use of market research, the use of external consultants or legal advisors, and even the purchase of agency services. As a rule, the benefit argument is because there are either cost advantages, the service can be provided more quickly or better quality is expected. For the example of SurveyMonkey (do-it-yourself (DIY) market research), this means several combined benefits: The platform offers a tool for conducting market research independently (Zakharov et al. 2017). Even if companies opt for a paid version with professional features, there are considerable cost-cutting opportunities compared to purchasing the service. The standardized support enables a very quick processing of an online survey, whereby the company's employees design the questionnaire themselves and carry out the survey independently (Krämer et al. 2017). Purchasing an external service provider can be replaced by an internal DIY market research team. Similar services are also offered for legal or consulting services such as COMATCH (Hardt 2018).

While the provision of standards, e.g., the specification of certain question formulations and answer categories, can be a great support in the case of market research, a high degree of creativity is usually required for other services such as communication services. This is illustrated by the example of the "simpleshow video maker" product (Hanke and Holländer 2019). Registered users are given the opportunity to create an explanatory video themselves. This appeals not only to users in the private segment but also to users with a business background. While the company simpleshow, for example, provides videos as an agency service and therefore as a highly professional service (production takes several weeks and costs around €8000–€10,000), video platforms now enable independent production in less time and at lower costs. With simpleshow video maker, simpleshow also offers a corresponding option. The business model is based on the SaaS approach.

The background to the increased use of DIY video platforms by companies is, on the one hand, that companies have to deal with a larger number of topics and, on the other, that the demand for speed is increasing and budgets are limited. This is because hypercompetition, digitalization, and a VUCA-market environment are leading to an acceleration of processes and changes in communication requirements. For example, the minimum viable product (MVP) is a key focus of business and product development activities at software start-ups. This is not just about speed per se, but about a high level of agility in product development (Duc and Abrahamsson 2016). A scenario that is now not uncommon: customers expect a video to be delivered in 15 h, e.g., because they are under time pressure due to rapid interaction with customers or discussions on social media. This is where so-called DIY platforms come into play, which help companies to create their own explainer videos in just a few hours.

4.4.2   Explanatory Videos (simpleshow): Customer Segmentation and Customer Feedback

4.4.2.1 The Special Features of Explainer Videos

A key requirement for an explainer video is that it must be highly effective and efficient in conveying information or knowledge. In an experimental study, Krämer and Böhrs (2017b) examined different video formats in two target regions (Germany and the USA). As part of a knowledge transfer test, the level of knowledge (topic: presidential elections in the USA) was measured before and after watching an explanatory video on the topic. The improvement in the objective level of knowledge is negatively correlated with the subjective level of knowledge, i.e., the lower the target persons' knowledge of the topic, the greater the observable improvements in the level of knowledge. As expected, respondents in Germany had a lower level of knowledge on the topic of the study than study participants from the USA, and the relative improvement in knowledge was greater here than in the USA. Among the video formats, a video created using the DIY tool mysimpleshow only achieved a slightly weaker result than a fully professional video created by simpleshow (with a longer video duration). However, it should be noted that in both cases a professional team was involved in the creation of the videos. In principle, the study results demonstrate the opportunities for increasing efficiency with DIY video platforms.

Other studies in the university environment also confirm the high effectiveness of explanatory videos as a learning tool (Ifenthaler 2015). A very high customer benefit arises when the goal of increasing effectiveness (condensed knowledge transfer) goes hand in hand with efficiency advantages (cost-effective provision). At the same time, this opens up the opportunity to exploit economies of scale by setting up video production portals and to offer services to a broad range of users at a low price or free of charge.

4.4.2.2 The Competition for the Leading Explainer Video Platform

In recent years, many providers have established themselves that enable the independent online creation of videos, with explanatory videos representing only one aspect of this. One particularly prominent example is the US platform Powtoon (Graham 2015). From a market perspective, the range of video platforms can be classified according to the area of application (focus on explanation, promotion, or entertainment) and the style of presentation. While Powtoon, the video portal with the most users worldwide, has historically focused primarily on the B2C segment and therefore has an extremely large reach/number of videos created, simpleshow is a provider that operates in the B2B environment. In addition to the agency service, a DIY video platform has recently been launched (simpleshow video maker). Here, the video creation process is text-based, just like the agency video, but the visualization service is supported by artificial intelligence (AI) in the tool. Like simpleshow, the provider Vyond pursues a B2B approach. The tool appeals to a more professional target audience in the company, with high creative demands on the user.

4.4.2.3 Customer Requirements Using the Example of the User simpleshow Video Maker

As already explained, self-produced explanatory videos are gaining in popularity both for private users (including schools/universities) and for users in companies. interest. This is also reflected in the user structure of simpleshow video maker. Figure 4.4 shows a simplified distribution of registered customers regarding the area of use (business/private) on the one hand and the form of payment (with/without payment model) on the other, as well as exemplary evaluations of the user experience. First, the characteristics of platform models with a freemium revenue model can be seen (Krämer and Kalka 2017). Most users do not have a payment option (Seufert 2013; Holm and Günzel-Jensen 2017). This is also the case in the business segment, which is generally characterized by a higher willingness to pay. Only 22.5% of all simpleshow customers use the application for business purposes and only 1.0% of these are on a paid subscription. As the production of a video is a complex process (from the user's point of view), the evaluation of the process from the user's perspective is essential. Only if a perceived "ease" of the production

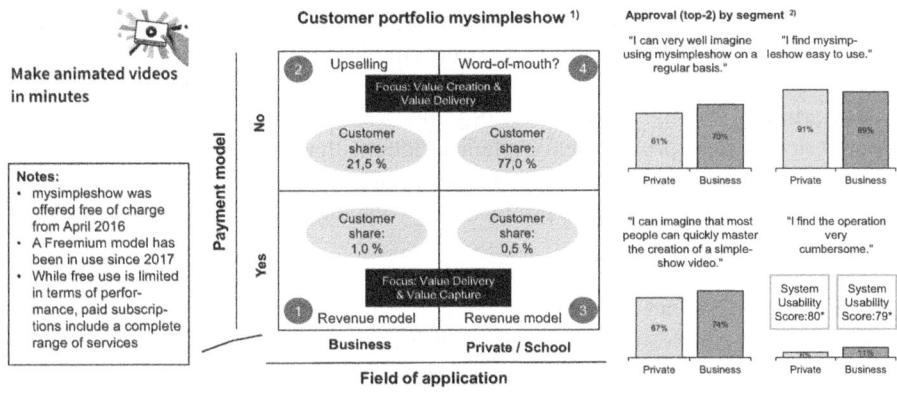

Fig. 4.4 Customer segmentation at the platform provider simpleshow (Krämer and Böhrs 2017a)

process is achieved by means of system support is there an opportunity to intensify the customer relationship from the user's perspective. To this end, individual facets of the customer experience are recorded as part of continuous user surveys and summarized in a system usability score (Fig. 4.4, right-hand side).

It is therefore crucial for the successful economic growth of the platform not only to recruit new users, but also to maintain the level of user activity (Holm and Günzel-Jensen 2017). How complicated customers perceive project work at simpleshow video maker to be plays an important role here. As part of the continuous user survey, the intention to continue using the tool, the ease of use and critical experiences in using the tool are recorded. As Fig. 4.4 underlines, there are no major differences in perception depending on the private or business customer segment. The system usability score (as a summarized overall result) reaches a value of around 80 points in both segments.

It is crucial for the success of the business model if users of the platform see the creation of an explainer video as a way of communicating complex issues differently than before. A recent study showed that explanatory videos can be used to communicate market research results, for example, more effectively and efficiently than with conventional PowerPoint slides (Krämer et al. 2021).

In the following interview, the simpleshow team explains in their own words how customer needs are measured and incorporated into product design.

4.4.3   How simpleshow Recognizes Customer Needs: Interview

About simpleshow: simpleshow is a platform for digital products and services related to the medium of explainer videos. Employees in the offices in Berlin,

Luxembourg, London and Zurich, Miami, Singapore, Hong Kong, and Tokyo serve major international companies that value simpleshow as a partner for simple explanations.

The artificial intelligence of the SaaS solution simpleshow video maker supports the user in creating a professional explainer video with just a few clicks. In addition, customized videos and e-learning formats can be implemented easily, quickly, and professionally as commissioned productions by the more than 400 certified partners on the global platform.

Question: What tools does simpleshow use to measure customer needs and obtain input for product changes?

simpleshow: simpleshow sees itself as the leading quality provider when it comes to creating explanatory products. Customer benefit is therefore the central argument of our market efforts. This applies first and foremost to the quality of our products themselves, but also to all product-related services. Our more than 50 globally active sales employees advise customers on site and work with them to tailor the right package of offers to suit their needs. The aim is to be represented throughout the company, because good explanations are needed at all levels and for a wide range of topics every day. During the creation of the videos, trained Customer Success Managers are available to assist customers if they have any questions about how to use the tool, but above all how to make a really good explanatory video themselves. If the customer decides not to create a video themselves, but to place it in the hands of the more than 400 certified explainer experts on the platform, the video is created together with the customer in an iterative process. In addition to a detailed briefing, this includes various intermediate steps, such as concept creation, preliminary sections, etc., so that customers can be involved live, so to speak, at all levels of the service creation process. This also includes numerous feedback loops until our customers are satisfied.

Our Customer Success Managers in the software business keep a feature list of customer requests that come up in conversations with customers. The list also includes customer feedback, which is sent to the sales staff in the field. This is discussed with product management at regular intervals. If certain feature requests come up again and again, we add them to our product roadmap. Our partners (certified explanation experts who also work with the tool) also provide feedback on the software, which is then incorporated into product development. These interviews are conducted in the form of focus groups, with various emphases such as storytelling, scribbles, or voice over.

We conduct an anonymous survey of all our tool users once or twice a year. Among other things, we determine the Net Promoter Score (NPS = tool for determining the intention to recommend) and ask many questions regarding the assessment of the general usage of the tool or questions about new feature requests. As a rule, these are direct methods, such as ratings, but we also work with constant-sum approaches to determine relative importance for our customers in terms of to better validate possible new feature requests. For example, the direct comparison of packages such as multilingualism, new styles, and the possibility of interaction resulted in a clear vote for further styles and color choices.

Another important tool for us is the regular exchange with lead users. Large companies in particular often have specific customer requirements that can also help others. We then often implement joint projects together with the company's IT or compliance departments.

If we support our customers in the creation of a video or have the creation completely in our own hands, the customer receives a small satisfaction survey when the clip is delivered. This is about satisfaction with the clip itself, but also about the quality of service (the scale ranges from 1 to 5). Around 15% of our customers fill this out.

Question: Are there any examples of how Customer Insights has led to specific product changes?

simpleshow: For example, we developed the so-called single sign-on process together with a large automotive customer. The challenge was that employees frequently change or leave the company, especially in large, internationally active companies. We worked together with the IT and compliance department to ensure that administrators in companies with more than 100 licenses in use can manage data security and user administration conveniently and professionally.

Multilingualism of the tool was an important issue for a pharmaceutical company. In general, feature packages such as diversity and data security were also developed together with our customers.

Question: How important is customer insight in the management of simpleshow? simpleshow: CI is generally very important to us. See the examples described above. We have been working with our customers for many years and it is important to us to be able to fulfill specific wishes. Nevertheless, simpleshow is not a software company that implements customer requirements on a project-by-project basis. We see ourselves as a SaaS solution and have a clear product vision and strategy that we implement for all our customers. It goes without saying that this is sometimes a balancing act. We therefore try not to be "too agile" when it comes to the long-term product vision regarding customer requirements.

Question: How does simpleshow ensure that the customer perspective is continuously considered in management decisions?

simpleshow: Our software is a huge reservoir of customer information. We have set up comprehensive dashboards on which we evaluate customer usage behavior in real time. One example is the use of various ready-made templates that help with the creation of videos. If we find that certain templates are not being used, they are replaced by other topics.

In addition, we monitor the selection of scribbles or images uploaded by customers themselves to constantly update and improve our scribble database.

We look at how long it takes customers to create videos and where the break-off points are. We then draw conclusions from this for the user experience design. Of course, we also look at the sales success of the respective online subscription products in order to make improvements to pricing, for example. Of course, all customer data is analyzed anonymously. Data security is very important to us. We constantly review our processes and partners in order to protect the sometimes very specific information of our users 100%.

The interlocutors
Dr. Sandra Böhrs, Chief Marketing Officer.
Susanne Ilemann, Managing Director, Tech.
simpleshow gmbh.

4.5   Outlook: Customer Proximity and Understanding in a Digitalized World

If recognizing and satisfying customer needs is a—if not *the*—central function in marketing, then proximity to the customer, the ability to interact with the customer, to recognize and understand what is important to customers and what they can do without, is an essential prerequisite. It is to be expected that customer preferences will change more in VUCA times than was previously the case. It is sufficient to consider the various effects of the corona crisis in different areas of life and how, for example, consumption or mobility decisions are influenced. Changing consumer habits in turn have a direct impact on companies' business models: Just think of a stronger preference for food from the region with consequences for the business model of food retailers and supplier relationships, a stronger weighting of the sustainability factor and carbon footprint on the choice of means of transportation or the increased use of home offices on the demand for commuter offers in local transport or the value of office real estate.

The framework conditions for measuring customer needs are becoming more difficult, but not impossible. In some cases, trends also make measurement easier. However, it is important to realize that proximity to the customer must be a core objective of management. This applies to different facets of proximity (e.g., locally and regionally or within the value chain or in terms of content in the sense of understanding customer concerns). There is no shortage of instruments for measuring customer needs. However, it is important to review the performance of existing methods (which have worked in the past) regarding their future viability. In the future, it will also be important to rely on a mix of instruments that support and enable accelerated management decisions. Some companies have fundamentally aligned their business model with customer proximity, including prominent examples such as Amazon, but also less prominent examples such as Dollar Shave Club, a start-up founded in 2012 that supplies razors and grooming products directly to end customers via a previously unestablished subscription system (see Sect. 10.4.3). This subscription system was not only the central point of attack against market giants such as Gillette, but also represented the prerequisite for direct interaction with the customer and was later a key argument for the unusually high sales price agreed in 2016 (the company was acquired by Unilever). This argument can be extended to other subscription providers such as Spotify. Here is another quote from Steve Jobs, who obviously did not correctly predict later developments on this point. His approach was rather to make customers pay individually for each music track they accessed:

"Subscription models for music are finished, I don't think even a subscription model with the rebirth of Christ built in would be successful."—Steve Jobs

References

Alibrandi A, Giacalone M (2008) Overview and recent advances in conjoint analysis for customer satisfaction measures. MTISD, 2008. Meth, Mod Info Tech Decis Support Syst 1(1):119–122

ARD/ZDF (2019) ARD/ZDF-Onlinestudie 2019. https://www.ard-zdfonlinestudie.de/ardzdfonlin-estudie/videonutzung-online/. Accessed 10 Feb 2021

Ariely D (2000) Controlling the information flow: effects on consumers' decision making and preferences. J Cons Res 27(2):233–248

Barton C, Koslow L, Dhar R, Chadwick S, Reeves M (2016) Why companies can't turn customer insights into growth. The Boston Consulting Group. https://www.bcg.com/publications/2016/center-customer-insight-marketing-sales-why-companies-cant-turncustomer-insights-growth. Accessed 14 Jan 2021

Bayus BL, Shane S (2008) Understanding customer needs. In: Shane S (ed) Handbook of technology and innovation management. Wiley, Hoboken, pp 115–142

Bennett N, Lemoine GJ (2014) What a difference a word makes: understanding threats to performance in a VUCA world. Bus Horiz 57(3):311–317

Bongaerts R, Krämer A (2014) Value-to-value-Segmentierung im Vertrieb. Mark Rev St Gallen 31(4):12–21

Bonk CJ (2008) YouTube anchors and enders: the use of shared online video content as a macrocontext for learning. In: American Educational Research Association (AERA) 2008 Annual Meeting, New York

Brown SL, Eisenhardt KM (1995) Product development: past research, present findings, and future directions. Acad Manag Rev 20(2):343–378

Bühren C (2010) Präferenzmessung für Produkte mit hochinnovativen Attributen. Cuvillier, Göttingen

Clauss T, Döppe S (2016) Why do urban travelers select multimodal travel options: a repertory grid analysis. Tran Res Part A: Pol Prac 93:93–116

Collis DJ, Rukstad MG (2008) Can you say what your strategy is? Harv Bus Rev 86(4):82–90

Duc AN, Abrahamsson P (2016) Minimum viable product or multiple facet product? The role of MVP in software startups. In: International Conference on Agile Software Development. Springer, Cham, pp 118–130

Eppinger E, Braun A, Kamprath M (2011) Produktivität und Dienstleistungen-Neue Anforderungen an das Innovationscontrolling. Controlling-Zeitschrift für erfolgsorientierte Unternehmenssteuerung, Controlling 23(10):496–501

Frohmann F (2018) Digitales pricing. Springer Gabler, Wiesbaden

Frow P, Payne A (2007) Towards the 'perfect' customer experience. J Brand Manag 15(2):89–101

Goffin K, Koners U (2011) Hidden needs: versteckte Kundenbedürfnisse entdecken und in Produkte umsetzen. Schäffer-Poeschel

Goffin K, Lemke F, Koners U (2010) Repertory grid technique. In: Identifying hidden needs. Palgrave Macmillan, London, p 125–152

Graham B (2015) Power up your PowToon Studio project. Packt Publishing

Grant RM (2016) Contemporary strategy analysis: text and cases edition. Wiley

Green PE, Srinivasan V (1990) Conjoint analysis in marketing: new developments with implications for research and practice. J Mark 10:3–19

Griffin A, Hauser JR (1993) The voice of the customer. Mark Sci 12(1):1–27

Griffin A, Price RL, Maloney MM, Vojak BA, Sim EW (2009) Voices from the field: how exceptional electronic industrial innovators innovate. J Prod Innov Manag 26:222–240

Gröppel-Klein A, Königstorfer J (2009) Projektive Verfahren in der Marktforschung. Qualitative Marktforschung. Gabler, Wiesbaden, pp 537–554

Hanke, Holländer S (2019) Erkläre es doch schnell per Video Videos. In: Fühles-Ubach S, Georgy U (eds) Bibliotheken: Einsatzszenarien und Gestaltungsmöglichkeiten. Festschrift für Achim Oßwald. Bad Honnef, pp 125–140

Hardt C (2018) The best of two worlds – Digitization of matchmaking between consulting firms and independent consultants. In: Nissen V (ed) Digital transformation of the consulting industry. Springer, Cham, pp 389–399

Hartmann A, Sattler H (2002) Commercial use of conjoint analysis in Germany, Austria, and Switzerland. Univ., Fachbereich Wirtschaftswiss., Inst. für Handel und Marketing

Hartmann A, Sattler H (2004) Wie robust sind Methoden zur Präferenzmessung? Schmalenbachs Zeitschrift für betriebswirtschaftliche Forschung 56(1):3–22

Herstatt C, Lüthje C, Lettl C (2007) Fortschrittliche Kunden zu breakthrough-innovationen stimulieren. In: Herstatt C, Verworn B (eds) Management der frühen Innovationsphasen. Gabler, Wiesbaden, pp 61–75

Hofbauer G (2013) Customer Integration: Prinzipien der Kundenintegration zur Entwicklung neuer Produkte (No. 26). Arbeitsberichte-Working Papers. Technische Hochschule Ingolstadt (THI), Ingolstadt

Holm AB, Günzel-Jensen F (2017) Succeeding with freemium: strategies for implementation. J Bus Strateg 38(2):16–24

Homburg C, Beutin N (2000) Value-based marketing: die Ausrichtung der Marktbearbeitung am Kundennutzen, Bd 49. Inst. für Marktorientierte Unternehmensführung, Univ. Mannheim

Huber F, Herrmann A, Braunstein C (2000) Der Zusammenhang zwischen Produktqualität, Kundenzufriedenheit und Unternehmenserfolg. In: Hinterhuber HH, Matzler K (eds) Kundenorientierte Unternehmensführung. Gabler Verlag, Wiesbaden, pp 49–66

Ifenthaler D (2015) Learning with the Simpleshow. In: Isaías P, Spector J, Ifenthaler D, Sampson D (eds) E-learning systems, environments and approaches. Springer, Cham, pp 57–66

Isaacson W (2011) Steve Jobs, Thorndike Press, 2011 (large print edition). C. Bertelsmann Verlag, München

Kano N, Seraku N, Takahashi F, Tsuji S (1984) Attractive quality and must-be quality. Hinshitsu 14(2):39–48

Kotler P, Rackham N, Krishnaswamy S (2006) Ending the war between sales and marketing. Harv Bus Rev 84(7/8):68–71

Krämer A (2018) CRM-data-supported Interviewing: how CRM-data can make empirical research more effective and efficient. General Online Research 2018, Cologne, March 1

Krämer A, Böhrs S (2016a) Experiences and future expectations towards online courses– An empirical study of the B2C-and B2B-Segments. J Educ Train Stud 4(1):23–31

Krämer A, Böhrs S (2016b) International study on the use and effects of different explainer video formats. Berlin. https://simpleshow.com/jp/press-releases/international-study-on-the-useandeffects-of-different-explainer-video-formats-2016/

Krämer A, Böhrs S (2017a) Erklärvideos als effektives und effizientes Marketing-Instrument. Mark Rev St Gallen 34(2):54–61

Krämer A, Böhrs S (2017b) How do consumers evaluate explainer videos: an empirical study on the effectiveness and efficiency of different explainer video formats. J Edu Lear 6(1):254–266

Krämer A, Böhrs S (2018) The use of explainer videos as a learning tool: an internal and external view. On the Line. Springer, Cham, pp 189–202

Krämer A, Böhrs S, Ilemann S (2021) How to effectively and efficiently communicate research results? Experimental study on the influence of interactivity and presentation form on knowledge transfer and cognitive activity. J Edu Lear 10(4):87–103

Krämer A, Burgartz T (2020) Mehr Verhandlungserfolg in VUCA-Zeiten. Sal Exce 27(12):20–23

Krämer A, Kalka R (2017) How digital disruption changes pricing strategies and price models. In: Khare A, Schatz R, Stewart B (eds) Phantom ex machina: digital disruption's role in business model transformation. Springer, Cham, pp 87–103

Krämer A, Tachilzik T, Bongaerts R (2017) Technology and disruption: how the new customer relationship influences the corporate strategy. In: Khare A, Schatz R, Stewart B (eds) Phantom ex machina. Springer, Cham, pp 53–70

Laaser W, Toloza EA (2017) The changing role of the educational video in higher distance education. Int Rev Res Ope Dist Lear 18(2):264–276

Lee TY (2007) Needs-based analysis of online customer reviews. In: Proceedings of the ninth international conference on Electronic commerce, p 311–318

Leeflang PS, Verhoef PC, Dahlström P, Freundt T (2014) Challenges and solutions for marketing in a digital era. Eur Manag J 32(1):1–12

Lin J, Seepersad CC (2007) Empathic lead users: the effects of extraordinary user experiences on customer needs analysis and product redesign. Int Des Eng Tech Conf Comp Info Eng Conf 48043:289–296

Litt M (2014) How online video is changing the way B2B marketers engage and convert prospects. J Bra Stra 3(2):129–134

Lohrke FT, Holloway BB, Woolley TW (2010) Conjoint analysis in entrepreneurship research: a review and research agenda. Organ Res Methods 13(1):16–30

McMath R, Forbes T (1998) What were they thinking?: Marketing lessons I've learned from over 80,000 new-product innovations and idiocies. Random House International. Three Rivers Press

Menold N, Bogner K (2015) Gestaltung von Ratingskalen in Fragebögen. Mannheim, GESIS–Leibniz-Institut für Sozialwissenschaften (SDM Survey Guidelines). https://doi.org/10.15465/gesis-sg_015

Meierhofer J, Pascher N, Wulf J (2024) The Value of Solving Pains. arXiv preprint arXiv:2412.03130

Netzer O, Toubia O, Bradlow ET, Dahan E (2008) Beyond conjoint analysis: advances in preference measurement. Mark Lett 19(3):337–354

Phagare M (2025) The Limits of Market Research: When the Data Doesn't Tell the Whole Story: CognitiveMarket Research, 29.4.2025. https://www.cognitivemarketresearch.com/blog/the-limits-of-market-research-when-the-datadoesnt-tell-the-whole-story. Accessed 9 May 2025

Rashid MM, Tamaki JI, Ullah AMM, Kubo A (2011) A Kano model based linguistic application for customer needs analysis. Int J Eng Bus Manag 3(2):29–36

Raynor ME, Christensen CM (2003) Innovating for growth: now is the time. Ivey Bus J Online September–October:1–9

Roth M, Bernardy BO (2019) Vorhersage von Anforderungen durch Verknüpfung von Szenario-Technik und Kano-Modell. 15. Symposium für Vorausschau und Technologieplanung, Band 390 der Verlagsschriftenreihe des Heinz Nixdorf Instituts Berlin, S 293–312

Schmelzle J (2014) 5 Rules for explaining things simply. Simpleshow Whitepaper

Schmidt S (2008) Marktforschung ohne Realitätsausschluss: Konsumentennähe durch den innovativen Einsatz qualitativer methodischer Settings. Sozialwissenschaften und Berufspraxis 31(1):39–52

Seufert EB (2013) Freemium economics: leveraging analytics and user segmentation to drive revenue. Elsevier

Simon H, Fassnacht M (2016) Preismanagement: Strategie – Analyse – Entscheidung – Umsetzung. Springer, Berlin

Simon H, Von der Gathen A (2010) Das große Handbuch der Strategieinstrumente: Werkzeuge für eine erfolgreiche Unternehmensführung. Campus

Steiner M (2007) Nachfrageorientierte Präferenzmessung: Bestimmung zielgruppenspezifischer Eigenschaftssets auf Basis von Kundenbedürfnissen. Springer, Wiesbaden

Stickdorn M, Zehrer A (2009) Service design in tourism: customer experience driven destination management. In: First Nordic conference on service design and service innovation, Oslo, November

Teichert TA (1997) Schätzgenauigkeit von Conjoint-Analysen (No. 444). Manuskripte aus den Instituten für Betriebswirtschaftslehre der Universität Kiel

Timoshenko A, Hauser JR (2019) Identifying customer needs from user-generated content. Mark Sci 38(1):1–20

Trux W, Müller G, Kirsch W (1984) The management of strategic programs, vol 1. Materials to the state of the art

Verhoef PC, Lemon KN, Parasuraman A, Roggeveen A, Tsiros M, Schlesinger LA (2009) Customer experience creation: determinants, dynamics and management strategies. J Retail 85(1):31–41

Wietlisbach O (2017) Sie haben einfach nie den Durchbruch geschafft: Die größten Produkte-Flops der Geschichte. https://www.watson.ch/digital/wirtschaft/291290254-die-groessten-undskurrilsten-produkte-flops-der-geschichte. Accessed 28 Jan 2021

Wittink DR, Gattin P (1989) Commercial use of conjoint analysis: an update. J Mark 53(3):91–96

Wright K (2004) Screenwriting is storytelling: creating an A-list screenplay that sells! TarcherPerigee, New York

Wu Q, Xia C, Tian S (2025). AI-Driven Sentiment Analytics: Unlocking Business Value in the E-Commerce Landscape_v1. arXiv preprint arXiv:2504.08738

Yachin JM (2018) The 'customer journey': learning from customers in tourism experience encounters. Tourism Manag Perspect 28:201–210

Zakharov I, Nikulchev E, Ilin D, Ismatullina V, Fenin A (2017) Web-based platform for psychology research. In: ITM Web of Conferences (Bd 10, S 04006). EDP Sciences

Core Function—Pricing: What Is the Optimal Price and How Can It Be Determined?

5

5.1 Pricing: High Earnings Potential, Quick Effect ... But Also Dangerous!

5.1.1 Key Earnings Lever "Price Management" and the Importance of Value-Based Pricing

"The single most important decision in evaluating a business is pricing power. You've got the power to raise prices without losing business to a competitor, and you've got a very good business. And if you have to have a prayer session before raising the price by a tenth of a cent (laughs), then you got a terrible business."—Warren Buffet (2010)

In order to illustrate the importance of price for the economic success of a company, rough calculations are often used in which a 1% price increase is simulated for well-known companies, e.g., the DAX companies or the largest US companies, resulting in profit increases of 10% or more (Simon and Fassnacht 2016; Baker et al. 2010). This is also described by Warren Buffet as term "pricing power." Against this backdrop, it is not surprising that the primary focus from a company's perspective is on enforcing higher prices. Price as an element in the marketing mix involves the following key considerations (Simon and Fassnacht 2016):

- Strong direct influence on sales and market share (price elasticity significantly higher than advertising elasticity)
- Quick applicability of the instrument (e.g., in comparison to innovations, advertising campaigns or cost savings)
- Direct effect of the price on consumers
- No requirement for upfront expenditure/investment.

The advantages of using price as an instrument are not limited to individual companies but are available to all market participants. This is associated with a central

© The Author(s), under exclusive license to Springer Nature Switzerland AG 2025
A. Krämer et al., *Customer Value-centered Management*, Future of Business and Finance, https://doi.org/10.1007/978-3-031-90497-4_5

risk, namely, the triggering or intensification of price competition through rapid (downward) price adjustments by market participants. The more intensively and aggressively the instrument is used, the greater the risk of a price war (Krämer et al. 2016). In addition, even innovative pricing models may make it difficult to achieve sustainable competitive advantages.

Academics who specialize in price research often complain about a gap between an approach to professional price determination on the one hand and the practice of price management on the other. Bergers and Fassnacht (2017, p. 51) cite the "unmeasured use" of cost-plus pricing in this context. Other authors point to the problems of purely competitive pricing (Fisher and Gallino 2017; Kossmann 2008). Although academia and consulting firms predominantly describe cost- or competition-oriented pricing as suboptimal and instead offer value-based pricing as a solution (Hinterhuber 2008; Liozu et al. 2015; Töytäri et al. 2015), practice seems to be "catching up" only with a delay and with great persistence. This is surprising given that practitioners and researchers agree that value-based pricing (VBP) generally achieves higher profits than cost- or competition-based pricing (Michel and Pfäffli 2009) given that customer groups with specific needs often assess a product or service differently than others and consequently attribute different benefits to these services.

This results in a differentiated willingness to pay. Value-based pricing, in contrast to cost- or competition-based variants, attempts to exploit this fact by determining willingness to pay and largely skimming it off through differentiated pricing that leads to profit increases. Despite this fundamental superiority of VBP, various cross-industry and cross-national studies show that cost- and competition-based approaches are still widely used in practice. As the analysis by Hinterhuber and Liozu (2012) underlines, although most companies strive to set prices in such a way as to create value for the customer, very few companies make the transition from cost-based pricing to value-based pricing. The problem is therefore not so much one of awareness as one of implementation.

5.1.2   In Search of the "Right" Price Elasticity

The example cited above of a 1% price increase and the resulting profit contains an obvious error in reasoning or at least an improper simplification. As a rule, demand reacts to price changes: It increases when the price is lowered, it decreases when the price is raised—at least this is the common way of thinking in microeconomics. This gives the concept of price elasticity a central role in price management. For example, when deciding on a planned price increase, the question arises as to what percentage of sales volume is at risk of being lost as a result. For a one-product company, knowledge of price elasticity (percentage change in sales volume with a 1% price change) in relation to the current market price is therefore an essential basis for decision-making. Price increases make economic sense if the price increase effect on sales is stronger than the demand displacement effect. However, the concept of price elasticity can also be applied to customer segments or sales channels. Some studies conclude that the Internet channel has a higher price elasticity than traditional channels (Granados et al. 2009). This may be due, for example, to increased access to information about competing offers via the Internet or greater price involvement (Granados et al. 2009; Lynch and Ariely 2000).

As easy as it is to use price elasticity to calculate at least maximum sales prices, it is difficult to determine it precisely. An unreflective look at the textbook is not recommended for practical use given the different value ranges for price elasticities of individual products or product categories.

Demand fluctuations depend on very specific framework conditions that vary from company to company. The desire for a more precise understanding of the dependencies between price and sales leads to the question of how the price-sales function works. This also includes information on price elasticity. Before going into the specific course of the price-sales function, however, a series of questions of pricing strategy must be clarified. These relate to aspects of corporate strategy, regulatory and legal frameworks, as well as which phase of the product life cycle individual products are in and how the product portfolio is to be evaluated. These points alone convey how complex the dependencies and interactions in pricing are. Frohmann (2018) has made an initial attempt to model price management as an extended process, which Kalka and Krämer (2020) have further extended. Krämer and Burgartz (2020) illustrate the process using the so-called 9-C model (see Fig. 5.1).

This 9-C model has been developed to take account of the changed VUCA (volatility-uncertainty-complexity-ambiguity) conditions on the one hand and the advantages of different methods on the other. A VUCA environment has far-reaching consequences for the estimation of willingness to pay. For example, it is already questionable whether the assumption of robust consumer preferences and customer needs can be maintained (Krämer 2015). This in turn has implications for the choice of a suitable instrument for determining the price-sales function. In a scenario characterized by stable willingness to pay on the part of potential buyers, acceptance of

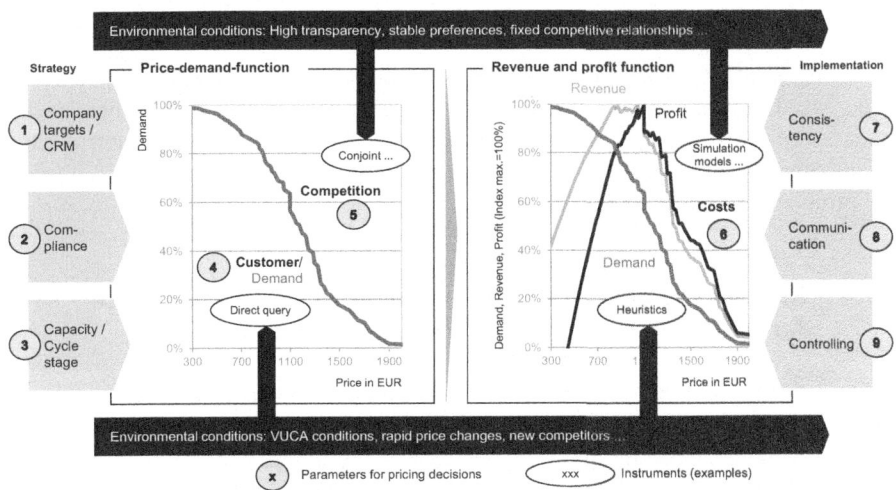

Fig. 5.1 Price management as a process—the 9-C model

the use of complex instruments is many times higher than in a VUCA scenario, which gives priority to simple, transparent, and less costly approaches (Krämer 2015). For example, although conjoint measurement is an established tool in price research, it is usually time-consuming to collect and analyze (Chap. 4). In addition, the analysis and interpretation require a great deal of expertise, assuming stable customer preferences.

5.1.3   Price-Sales Function: The Ideal Image of the Pricing Manager

A large part of the work on the way to price determination is achieved if it is possible to obtain as detailed an idea as possible of the price-sales relationships. If estimates of potential customers' individual willingness to pay are available, these can be transformed into a demand function (possibly by including purchase quantities). To do this, it is necessary to determine the maximum willingness to pay (e.g., via an empirical study) and to present these values (individual values at the maximum accepted price) cumulatively in descending order as a graph. This is shown in the middle section of Fig. 5.1.

Once a validated price-sales function has been developed, the path to determining sales or profit-maximizing price points is not far away. First, the sales function can be determined by calculating the sales (price * sales volume) for each price point. In the next step, the directly attributable costs can be included in the analysis so that the contribution margin-optimal price point can be determined. For each price point, the unit contribution margin (price minus variable unit costs) is multiplied by the sales volume. By including the fixed costs, it is possible to calculate the profit effects for each price point.

In Fig. 5.1, the sales and profit functions are shown indexed to make the graph as clear and meaningful as possible. The index points with a value of 100% are the maximum levels achieved in each case.

At this point, it becomes clear that the idea, sometimes associated with the term value-based pricing, that pricing should be centrally geared toward customers' willingness to pay is too simplistic. After all, costs are a key input factor for determining the maximum profit price. This becomes clear because of the drifting apart of sales and profit-maximum price points.

5.1.4   Knowledge of Willingness to Pay: A Key Factor for Price Automation, Dynamic Pricing, and Offers "For Free"

The central importance of knowing the price elasticity—at least for the relevant price range—has already been discussed. The basis for this is again a price-sales function, which is made up of the maximum price willingness of potential customers. In this context, two questions need to be discussed in more detail. The first question relates to how stable the consumers' or customers' willingness to pay is:

The more stable the preferences and therefore the more robust the willingness to pay, the more detailed and longer they can be used for marketing and the more effort for data generation can be justified in terms of research economics to determine the willingness to pay based on individual customers or customer segments. The second question is based on trends in price management, e.g., common revenue models such as freemium or "For Free" or instruments such as dynamic pricing and price and offer automation processes. It remains to be seen whether knowledge of individual customers' willingness to pay is still relevant for pricing or companies' business models.

5.1.4.1 Robustness of Maximum Willingness to Pay

Academic price research in recent decades has primarily focused on investigating the differences in consumers' willingness to pay based on different measurement approaches and, on this basis, making recommendations for the most undistorted determination possible. However, an at least equally relevant question concerns the facet of which factors influence the maximum willingness to pay. Some aspects will be briefly outlined here:

- Involvement of the respondent: Behavioral science in particular states that value judgments are influenced, for example, by the context in which the consumer decision takes place. It has been found that values differ between product types, individuals, and circumstances (over time and in different environments) (Lowe et al. 2013). For example, Bosenick (2014) was able to empirically prove that the preference for an iPad among test subjects differs depending on whether the device is only described as a concept with a picture (preference lower) or whether the product is experienced haptically. Actual use shifts the customer preference: the iPad preference share in the concept test increases from approximately 25% to 31% in the usability test. At the same time, the Samsung tablet, which was also part of the evaluation as a competitor product, becomes less attractive.
- Concrete context of the survey: In case there are new or adapted price anchors in the market, the willingness to pay can consequently be altered. The use of long-distance buses in Germany can be taken as an example (the market was liberalized in 2013). The offer of low prices for coach travel has led to travelers also perceiving rail prices more critically. As a result, the perceived threshold for low prices is falling. Similar effects have also been demonstrated for hotel bookings (Viglia et al. 2016). This argument can be extended to include other aspects of contextual influence. Even the question design can be a relevant context factor. For example, it can be shown that in an open question about the willingness to pay for a train ticket, an influence on the results can arise if another price point, such as the price considered to be cheap, is recorded before the actual question about maximum willingness to pay. The average willingness to pay is increased by roughly 5% in the test group with a "preceding" question on affordability (Krämer 2019). This effect can be explained by the fact that the perception of and engagement with the topic of low-ticket prices also influences the willingness to pay.

- "Over-involvement": The question of the extent to which conditioning of the test person must be generated in a specific survey situation (e.g., in an online survey) and the point at which this turns negative and can become a bias is an important but rarely discussed issue, even in specialist circles.

If too much emphasis is placed on the topic of price in surveys, price sensitivity can be exaggerated during the interview. In addition, purchase intentions can be overstated. There is also a risk of over-involvement. For the study participant, the facets discussed in the survey then take on a significance in the worst-case scenario that bears no relation to a real purchasing or decision-making situation.

This list of factors affecting willingness to pay can certainly be extended further, even to the question of the ownership perspective. Numerous studies have examined whether people who own a certain product have a higher willingness to pay (also described as a willingness to accept) than people who do not own the product. The results are relatively clear, as Horowitz and McConnell (2002) state: "Willingness to accept (WTA) is usually substantially higher than willingness to pay (WTP)." In a new paper, Sunstein (2025) emphasizes the overarching meaning of WTA and WTP.

Against this backdrop, the suggestions that willingness to pay should not be based on a fixed value seem perfectly understandable. In specialist circles, this is discussed under the heading "Willingsness-to-Pay (WTP) as a range" (Dost and Wilken 2012).

5.1.4.2 Relevance of Information on Maximum Willingness to Pay

At a time when numerous products are offered to end users at a price of zero (e.g., Google or WhatsApp and in the basic version of freemium business models), it is debatable what relevance knowledge of the maximum willingness to pay has at all if the usage price is effectively zero. This issue is exacerbated by the strong trend toward dynamic pricing, which now extends far beyond e-commerce.

Even in the extreme situation where a company offers the use of a service free of charge (the price paid by users is the provision of personal data), a company may have a considerable interest in knowing how highly users value it. After all, this information is a very good indicator of the degree of customer loyalty. For freemium providers, for example, it is relevant how many users switch to a paid service (subscription) when the price falls below a certain threshold, i.e., when they migrate from a free service to a higher-value paid service. Finally, in addition to the size of the platform, the ratio between paying and non-paying users is one of the most important indicators for evaluating the business model. But even the public has an interest in the willingness to pay, as the example of digital offerings shows. Gross domestic product (GDP) and derived metrics such as productivity are of central importance for understanding economic progress and prosperity. It is measured in prices for the products and services produced. This approach becomes skewed when a significant proportion of the services used is available as a free service but at the same time is still highly valued by users.

Brynjolfsson et al. (2019) conclude that the willingness to pay for the use of Facebook is USD48 per month. The added value generated by the platform is not priced out. Other companies have taken this as an opportunity to change their pricing model: After initially offering WhatsApp for free, the company introduced a subscription pricing model in 2013 (not for smartphones with IOS operating systems). In 2016 the messenger service became free again. As the new owner, Facebook was apparently primarily interested in exceeding the target of 1 billion users and only later focusing on monetizing the Messenger service. Currently, the focus is less on B2C customers and more on B2B customers.

5.2   Determination of Willingness to Pay

5.2.1   Overview of the Methodological Approaches

In view of the relevance of knowledge of willingness to pay for price determination (and beyond), the question arises as to which data sources and instruments (some of which have already been mentioned in Chap. 4) are both theoretically possible and practically useful. A brief overview is provided below (see Fig. 5.2):

- Purchase data: This includes historical data on the one hand and experimental studies on the other. Econometric models for estimating demand functions are possible if large amounts of data and sufficient variation in market prices are available. This approach has the advantage of being cost-effective. However, it is often impossible to measure the price effect in isolation if several disturbance variables have had an effect on the market at the same time, which cannot be

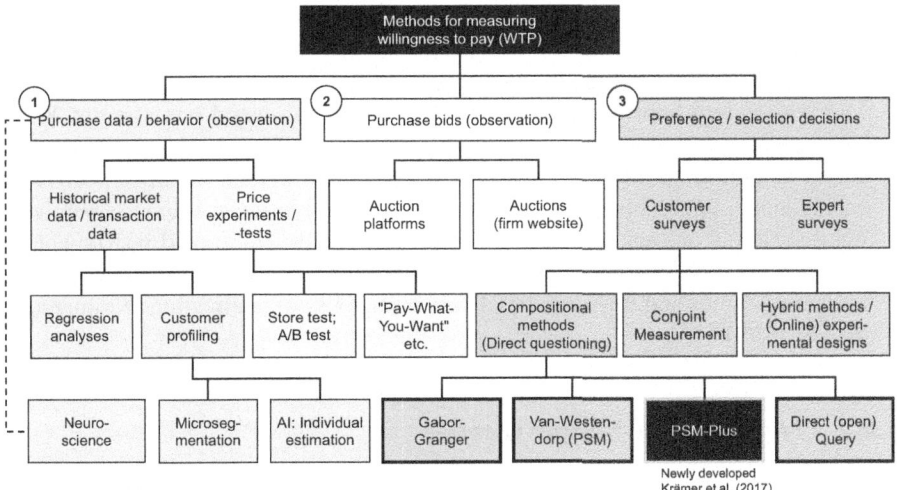

Fig. 5.2 Different approaches to measuring willingness to pay

neutralized retrospectively. Existing data is also used in customer profiling to draw conclusions about price sensitivity on the basis of characteristics assigned to individual persons or customer segments. A/B tests are becoming increasingly popular, as online sales have increased significantly in many areas, providing a good technical framework. Alternative prices, e.g., on online portals or sales portals, are tested with regard to customer reaction (purchase quantity, purchase frequency, etc.). However, the complete mapping of a price-sales function is only possible with a great deal of effort (several sequential tests are required). However, the procedure is usually sufficient for evaluating a planned price measure.

- Purchase offers: As a result of increasing digitalization, the possibilities for monitoring purchase bids has increased rapidly. Auction platforms such as eBay are used, but also the online portals of companies themselves (e.g., Lufthansa: Bid for your upgrade). The bidding process allows data to be collected not only on the purchase, but also on the bids that were not successful.
- Preference and selection decisions: If these are based on surveys, customers can be motivated to take part in an interview, while the survey can also involve experts. According to Frohmann (2018), the method is based on subjective estimates by internal company market and sales experts regarding sales potential at different prices. After recording the experts' individual estimates at various price points (own sales, competitors' sales, competitors' price reaction), an aggregated price-sales function is derived. This approach is suitable if it is not possible or too costly to address buyers or potential buyers directly. Customer surveys are used particularly frequently when the data situation does not otherwise allow for decision support. In terms of concrete implementation, a distinction must be made between direct and indirect methods of estimating willingness to pay. The direct price survey is a simple method for determining willingness to pay as part of a customer interview. In the simplest variant, study participants are asked directly how they react to certain prices or price changes or what maximum price they accept for a product or service (open entry). Variations include asking about purchase probabilities for different preset price points (Garbor-Granger) or the Van Westendorp approach, which openly asks about several price points. With indirect methods, the willingness to pay is determined by considering the price not in isolation, but always in relation to the value drivers. This perspective is catchy and comprehensible because it comes closest to the consumer's purchasing decision. Conjoint measurement is a particularly widespread instrument in this area, whereby it can be used not only for pricing topics, but also for other marketing topics and therefore has a very broad field of application (Krämer and Wilger 1999).

5.2.2   Trend Toward Simple Queries

In the academic world and in the community of pricing consultants, indirect methods for measuring preferences and willingness to pay are clearly preferred to simple, direct approaches. Conjoint measurement does not ask direct questions about maximum willingness to pay but calculates willingness to pay via choice-based conjoint (CBC), adaptive conjoint analysis (ACA), or ranking of options using multivariate analyses. The literature that emphasizes the superiority of conjoint measurement over direct approaches is now almost unmanageable (Balderjahn 1994; Simon and Fassnacht 2016). For example, Breidert et al. (2006) describe the different methods in a review article and state: "Because of its practical relevance, special focus will be put on indirect surveying techniques and, in particular, conjoint-based applications will be discussed in more detail." This suggests that indirect methods should be given priority in the practice of price research. Schindler (2011) goes one step further and asserts: "Perhaps the most commonly used of the survey methods is conjoint analysis." However, the description "Discrete choice conjoint is the gold standard of pricing research" by Jensen (2013) reaches a level that can ultimately be described as unbalanced and one-sided.

There are only isolated indications of the effectiveness of direct approaches to measuring willingness to pay. Löffler (2015) draws the conclusion: "The empirical results clearly support the application of indirect methods, as direct methods are prone to country-specific artefacts and reveal only close to optimal prices." Unfortunately, there is no consideration of how much effort is required to achieve unbiased results compared to direct queries with slightly suboptimal results. More recent research comes to further relativizing conclusions, such as those of Schmidt and Bijmolt (2019), which are based on a meta-analysis: "In contrast with conventional wisdom, indirect methods actually overestimate real WTP significantly stronger than direct methods." This is noteworthy because the valid representation of price willingness has often been seen as an important advantage of conjoint studies, while direct questions are suspected of being biased (mostly in the sense of "for tactical reasons the real price willingness of the test persons is underestimated").

Academic research is primarily focused on distortions that arise when a willingness to pay is recorded directly. The weaknesses identified are understandable. However, the argument regarding the validity of the measured willingness to pay falls far too short. After all, it is only one facet in the selection of the "right" method for determining willingness to pay. Finally, the question arises as to the extent to which differences and distortions in the measurement of willingness to pay come into play when simulations of the optimal price are carried out based on the data in the next step. In this context, Miller et al. (2011) state the following:

> Even when the OE (the open-ended) format and Choice-Based Conjoint (CBC) analysis generate hypothetical bias, they may still lead to the right demand curves and right pricing decisions.

There appears to be a discrepancy between the approaches to price research favored by academics and the methods used in practice. This is indicated on the one hand by surveys on which instruments are increasingly used by market research institutes and on the other hand by studies on price research from a company perspective. For example, the survey results of Steiner and Hendus (2012) show that direct approaches to measuring willingness to pay are predominantly used in market research practice, with the authors explaining that this is probably due to less costly application. They also argue that researchers should therefore focus more on the further development of direct methods and/or indirect approaches that require less interview time to save costs. Miller and Hofstetter (2009) examine the company perspective and confirm the great importance of direct approaches for measuring willingness to pay. To round off the picture: The study results shown refer to measurements of willingness to pay that have been made. The complete picture also includes the fact that many companies—especially in the B2B sector—suffer from an information deficit that does not allow for a textbook pricing process. Based on expert interviews with price managers, Schmutz and Reinecke (2020) point to exogenous information deficits (cannot be directly influenced by companies or pricing managers, e.g., legal or methodological restrictions) and endogenous information deficits (structural, process-related or personnel-related and can therefore be directly influenced by the company or pricing managers). In conclusion, it should be noted: By no means every company has information on its customers' willingness to pay; many, for example, do not survey their customers and see no opportunities to obtain decision support from existing data.

5.2.3   Direct Approaches to Measuring Willingness to Pay

Price determination and optimization is one of the most challenging tasks for marketing decision-makers. In addition to market tests and observations or the use of scanner and purchase data, in which the preferences and willingness to pay of consumers are derived from real behavior, consumer surveys are a frequently used option for determining optimal prices. A distinction is usually made between direct and indirect methods. Direct methods focus on the explicit inquiry of willingness to pay or price thresholds. Indirect methods such as conjoint measurement determine preferences and willingness to pay "in a roundabout way" by evaluating product alternatives with different prices. Despite the approaches preferred in research for the indirect measurement of willingness to pay, it can be observed that direct measurement approaches are very popular with market research institutes and with price decision-makers in companies. The current framework conditions underline this. From a list of different influencing factors (Krämer 2017), only the most important ones are listed here:

- Marketing decision-makers prefer methods of price determination that are transparent and comprehensible.
- Due to increased competitive pressure and a dynamic market environment, pricing decisions are being made more quickly. As a result, tools that are more complex (and therefore generally more time-consuming) to collect and evaluate are becoming less important.
- Complex data collection methods such as direct preference measurements or conjoint measurement are being critically scrutinized regarding their practical

applicability when the study design of online research is increasingly moving towards mobile research (data collection via mobile devices). At the same time it is stated that open questions regarding the WTP can be effective under certain market conditions (Schmidt et al. 2023).

- A secondary condition is that behavior-based and psychological pricing (low prices, price thresholds, etc.) has received significantly more attention in recent years.

Direct methods for measuring willingness to pay include methods such as the open query, the Gabor-Granger approach with the specification of price points, and query of purchase probabilities and the Price Sensitivity Meter (PSM, Van Westendorp approach). The latter focuses comparatively less on pure willingness to pay and determines an optimal price and an acceptable price range based on the query of four price points (see Fig. 5.3). Van Westendorp's PSM has been a cornerstone of price sensitivity analysis for decades and has proven to be an effective tool for assessing consumers' price perception. The approach has also found at least partial acceptance in the scientific community (Reinecke et al. 2009).

After more than 40 years of practical application, a wide range of research literature is now available, both on the classic PSM approach and on various extensions of PSM.

The advantages of the classic Van Westendorp approach lie on the one hand in the simplicity of the query and on the other hand in the simple preparation of the results. The simple query implies a low expenditure of time for the respondent, also because no additional information (e.g., via information sheet or concept presentation) has to be provided. At the same time, the method can also be used in unfavorable interview situations (e.g., when time is very limited or when using mobile

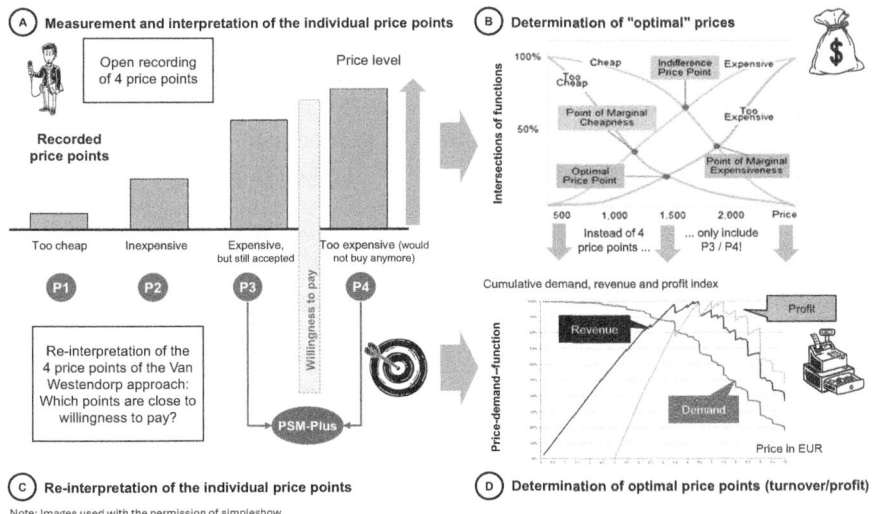

Fig. 5.3 PSM-Plus approach as an alternative to Van Westendorp (PSM). Note: Images used with the permission of simpleshow

devices). The preparation of the results is largely standardized (the derivation of the intersection points is predefined) and is visually supported.

The general interpretation of the overlapping cumulative price functions varies. One frequently used interpretation is that the intersection of the functions of the price points "too cheap" (inverse) and "expensive" represents the lower limit of an acceptable price range (see Fig. 5.3, Part II). This is sometimes described as the "point of marginal cheapness" (PMC). Similarly, the intersection of the functions "too expensive" and "cheap" (inverse) can be regarded as the upper limit of an acceptable price range (point of marginal expensiveness). Finally, the intersection of the functions "too cheap" (inverse) and "too expensive" represents an "optimal price point" (OPP) (Chhabra 2015). This is the point at which an equal number of respondents describe the price that either exceeds their upper limit or falls below their lower limit. Optimal in this sense refers to the fact that equal proportions of extreme perceptions and sensitivities to price exist at both ends of the price spectrum.

5.2.4   PSM-Plus: Reinterpretation of the Van Westendorp Approach

In addition to the strengths of the methodology, there are limitations in the use of the tools, which have led to the classic PSM approach being expanded to include additional questions and perspectives, ultimately leading to a more valid result. The principles of the classic approach and PSM extensions are first briefly explained (see Fig. 5.3):

- Approach A (classic PSM): The classic PSM approach described above includes all four price points in the analysis, but the optimal price point (OPP) is derived from the intersection points of the functions "too cheap" and "too expensive." In this case, the proportion of consumers who do not buy because they fear a lack of quality is as high as the proportion of decision-makers who no longer buy because the price is too high. Points of criticism here relate to the substantive argumentation. It is not comprehensible why the company's view is that the optimum price should exist in this case. The interpretation ignores the facet of the price-sales function.
- Approach B: Extended approaches attempt to increase the robustness of the estimate by asking additional questions. For example, in addition to the four price points, it is proposed to ask about the purchase intention for the two middle price points. On this basis, distributions of the most preferred price points can be determined. Liebermann (2015) comes to the following conclusion: "Demand for the product almost always drops off at the point of marginal expensiveness. This is where the tested item should be priced." However, this also highlights the fact that the "Optimal Price Point (OPP)" derived from the PSM is lower than the optimal price for the company. This problem is discussed in detail below.
- Approach C: Approaches to extend the PSM approach go in the same direction, in which an additional behavioral analysis is carried out or the respondents are

classified into different decision types. On this basis, the individual price points in the data set are validated, but the derivation of the optimal price point remains the same (Drewes et al. 2010). Here too, empirical testing shows that the corrected optimal price points are higher than those of the classic PSM approach.

• Approach D: A fundamentally different approach is based on the consideration of which surveyed price points come closest to the actual willingness to pay. The approach presented below by Krämer (2017) is based on the criticism of Roll et al. (2010a, b). They argue that a PSM offers neither mathematical nor theoretical arguments as to why the intersections of distribution functions can be interpreted as price barriers and price recommendations. Furthermore, the intersections are not linked to a company's target system (sales or profit targets). However, as Krämer et al. (2017) explain, the relevant price-sales function can be formed by approximation from the two upper price points ("expensive but acceptable" and "too expensive"). This can be explained as follows: With the price point "expensive but acceptable," the willingness to pay is not met (underestimated). On the one hand, the consumer sees a high price, but on the other hand also a considerable value (whose benefit is higher than the loss of benefit due to the price). In other words, a consumer surplus remains at this price. The maximum willingness to pay, on the other hand, means a consumer surplus of zero. At the price point "too expensive," no more purchases are made, i.e., the price is above the consumer's maximum willingness to pay (Krämer 2024b).

5.2.5   PSM-Plus: The Practical Application

On the basis of three project examples, Krämer et al. (2017) first determined the acceptable price range, expressed as a classic PSM approach according to the range between the point of marginal cheapness (PMC) and the point of marginal expensiveness (PME), as well as the optimum price point (OPP).

Different markets and products were included (organic muesli at a discount store, seat reservations on the train, and a complete menu from a system catering provider). The studies were conducted as online surveys in Germany (2015–2017) with case numbers ranging from 300 to around 3500 test subjects. As a result, in all three project examples, the optimal price point (OPP) shown according to the classic PSM was below the market price (it is assumed that the market price was deliberately chosen and optimized by the supplier companies). This is less surprising than the magnitude of the deviation. To make the results comparable, the prices were indexed (market price = 100). The optimum prices according to the classic PSM are in the range of 58–78 index points, i.e., at least 20 points below the real market price. The Price of Marginal Expensiveness recommended by Liebermann (2015) as a reference point for the optimal market price is only within the range of the market price in one of three examples.

A price determination based on a modified PSM approach ("PSM-Plus") was carried out using the identical data material. The mean value from the recorded price points "expensive but acceptable" and "too expensive" serves as an approximation of the individual willingness to pay.

The cumulative descending distribution represents the estimate of the price-sales function. Based on the aggregated price-sales function, the sales function can be determined as a function of the price level. In addition, information on the costs of service provision can be included. These vary depending on the product, industry, and time perspective. Turnover and profit functions can be indexed (maximum value = 100) (see Fig. 5.3, bottom right).

Krämer (2018b), based on an experimental test arrangement (see Fig. 5.4), illustrates the efficiency of different direct methods for measuring willingness to pay and ultimately also for determining an optimal price level via simulation. Four groups were randomly formed as part of an online study and asked about their willingness to pay for an iPhone 6s. The PSM-Plus approach was used in the first and second groups. The estimate was made using price points P3 and P4; only the total number of price points recorded varied. In the third test group, an open query of willingness to pay was used, which was supplemented in the fourth test group by a hint intended to neutralize the hypothetical bias ("If the price you specify is above a randomly determined price, you will be given the opportunity to buy this product at the specified price"). As a result, the approaches arrive at a profit-optimal price in the range of €525–549 (at the time of the survey, the market price for the device was €519). The price recommendations based on the open price quotation come to a total price level of less than €500. Incidentally, the price recommended in the Van Westendorp approach the optimal price point (OPP) determined by the classic PSM approach is less than €300, which underlines the suboptimality of this method.

In principle, the experiment presented confirms the results that Miller and Hofstetter (2009, p. 4) describe as follows: "We conclude, that even though the

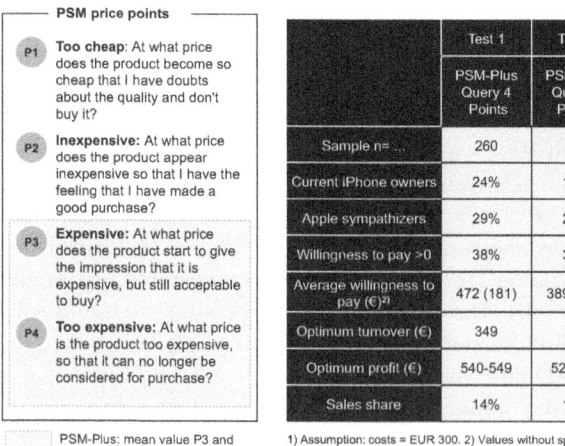

	Test 1	Test 2	Test 3	Test 4
	PSM-Plus Query 4 Points	PSM-Plus Query 2 Points	WTP open Query	WTP open query + incentive
Sample n= ..	260	259	266	260
Current iPhone owners	24%	16%	26%	20%
Apple sympathizers	29%	22%	29%	30%
Willingness to pay >0	38%	38%	30%	42%
Average willingness to pay (€)²⁾	472 (181)	389 (149)	392 (120)	358 (154)
Optimum turnover (€)	349	349	349	299
Optimum profit (€)	540-549	525-549	450	499
Sales share	14%	10%	13%	12%

PSM price points

P1 **Too cheap**: At what price does the product become so cheap that I have doubts about the quality and don't buy it?

P2 **Inexpensive**: At what price does the product appear inexpensive so that I have the feeling that I have made a good purchase?

P3 **Expensive**: At what price does the product start to give the impression that it is expensive, but still acceptable to buy?

P4 **Too expensive**: At what price is the product too expensive, so that it can no longer be considered for purchase?

PSM-Plus: mean value P3 and P4 as estimated values for WTP

1) Assumption: costs = EUR 300. 2) Values without specification = EUR 0 (values for all respondents). 3) Optimal price point according to the classic Van Westendorp approach (Price Sensitivity Measurement). WTP=Willingness-to-Pay=Willingness to pay

Fig. 5.4 PSM-Plus approach and other methods for measuring willingness to pay in the test (iPhone 6s)

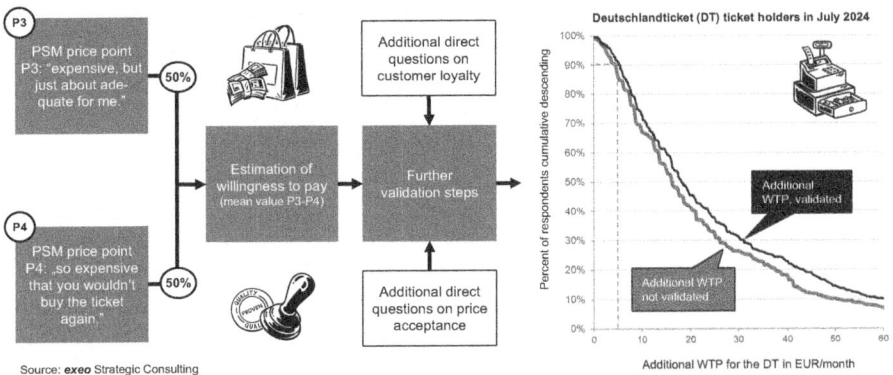

Source: *exeo* Strategic Consulting

Fig. 5.5 Using the "PSM-Plus" approach to determine the price-demand-relationship (example Deutschlandticket). Note: Images used with the permission of simpleshow

direct approach shows statistically biased results, it is able to guide the marketing manager to good business decisions." At the same time, however, it should also be noted that the problem of hypothetical bias, namely, the generation of an answer without sufficient concrete reference to the purchase decision, is not an invariable variable. It is therefore possible to use a suitable set of questions to put a study participant in a situation that promotes a realistic and therefore also valid indication of a maximum willingness to pay (Mahieu et al. 2012; Lusk 2003).

At this point, we would also like to make a note on the PSM-Plus methodology's claim to accuracy: it is illusory to want to hit the market price exactly with the modified PSM approach ("PSM-Plus"). However, the derived optimal price points for sales and profit are closer to the market price than the recommendations of the classic PSM. The authors have also succeeded in proving this in examples other than those discussed. Both approaches (classic PSM and modified "PSM-Plus" approach) are based on the same data material. In principle, no further queries are required for the modified PSM-Plus approach, which distinguishes it from previous PSM modifications. In this respect, this methodology results in an improvement in the quality of the results provided, without any additional expense or complexity. At the same time, however, it is also possible to link this validation with other extensions to the PSM method. The modified PSM approach is a way of determining prices quickly and cost-effectively, particularly considering the changed framework conditions described above, both in terms of the business practice of price decisions and the trends in online surveys. It is possible to reduce the interview duration if, for example, the "too cheap" price point is not queried. At the same time, the inclusion of costs is essential for price optimization. This also makes it clear that professional interaction between market research, controlling, and pricing decision-makers is required for a meaningful interpretation of the data.

Section 5.4 provides a further example of the application of PSM-Plus in the context of the price adjustment of the so-called Deutschlandticket (price increase from 49 euros to 58 euros from January 1, 2025). Figure 5.5 illustrates the PSM-Plus-process as well as the result (price-demand-function).

5.3   Price Optics: Identical Prices Displayed Differently

5.3.1   Rational and Emotional Decision-Making Models

For more than 20 years, research into price management—and in recent years also practical pricing in companies—has been increasingly determined by behavioral pricing.

Behavioral pricing is based on the understanding that consumers' decisions are irrational (or at least not completely rational) and can be influenced. The consumer's perception of the price is therefore not only determined by the price level, but also by a variety of elements, such as the price presentation, the reference point of the price, the color contrast and anchor information, etc. The main challenge is to combine microeconomic and behavioral science perspectives. The major challenge is to combine microeconomic and behavioral science perspectives. This is particularly challenging in pricing: Traditionally, companies set prices based on customer, competitor, and cost analyses, while the presentation of prices has tended to be classified as a sales or communicative function with little relevance. This is different with behavior-based pricing, where the type and context of the price presentation play a decisive role (e.g., related to number, size, color, additional information). The basic assumption of behavioral economics is that cognitive biases prevent people from making rational decisions despite their best efforts. Ariely (2008) uses the following metaphor: "If people were cartoon characters, we would be more closely related to Homer Simpson than to Superman." In addition, it is not only noted that people do not deal with the prize rationally, but also "make predictable mistakes" (Bauer 2014). The awarding of the 2017 Nobel Prize in Economics to behavioral economist Richard Thaler underscores this perspective (Krämer 2018a).

However, it is not really news that human perception is (extremely) subjective; after all, it selects certain stimuli and blocks out others, and it accentuates, colors objective relationships based on subjective expectations, and coarsens perceptions through simplification processes. As a result, several people may see the same product but perceive it differently. Price is no different. In the context of behavioral economics, this has been increasingly discussed in recent years, whereby it is assumed that people make no or hardly any rational decisions despite their best efforts. Other researchers go one step further and state that consumer decisions are not only irrational, but that the suboptimal decisions for the consumer are even predictable. The question therefore arises as to whether and to what extent the perception of prices can be controlled by the supplier. Some of the current literature cites extraordinary effects, which other authors often adopt uncritically in their articles. However, to what extent these are generalizable effects from which marketing decision-makers can draw clear conclusions or whether "if-then rules" can be derived remains open in many cases (Krämer 2018b).

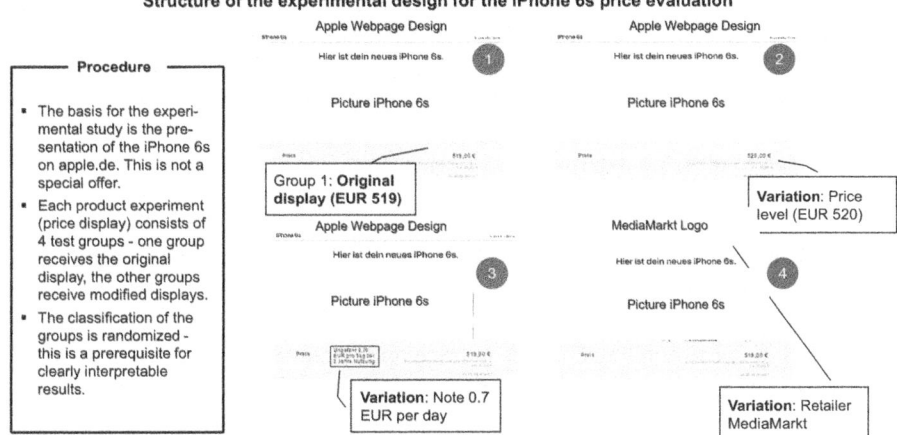

Fig. 5.6 Structure of the experimental design for the iPhone 6s price evaluation

5.3.2 Basic Considerations on the Use of Price Psychology Instruments

From the multitude of possibilities for changing the price appearance—several dozen individual effects have now been described in the literature, with Larson (2014) mentioning more than 50 effects in his review article—three instruments are examined in more detail here. To illustrate these effects, they are first presented using the iPhone 6s as an example product (see Fig. 5.6):

- The first example shows the presentation of the product on the manufacturer's website. This representation serves as a comparison group.
- Suppliers often use prices ending in 9 because this is associated with the idea that a price that is lower than the objectively shown price will manifest itself in cognitive processing. In the second example, the price of €519 is deliberately contrasted with a slightly higher price of €520. One would expect poorer results in the price assessment here.
- In order to influence the price perception of consumers, some providers of generally fixed-term products have started to communicate a price per (smaller) usage unit, generally per day, i.e., a significantly lower price ("pennies-a-day" strategy), rather than the total price. In relation to the iPhone example, this means that the product price of €519 is allocated over a period of, for example, 2 years, resulting in a penny amount of €0.7 per day (example 3). This should lead to improved results in the price assessment.
- Since the iPhone is not only sold directly via apple.de, but also through specialist retailers, the question also arises as to whether the price of €519 in connection with a specialist retailer (in the example 4 MediaMarkt) is evaluated differently by the consumer.

This only covers a small section of possible modified price displays. A visually larger display not only makes it easier for potential buyers to recognize the displayed price but could also give the price a different weight in information processing, making it appear more relevant. This effect can be further influenced by changing the color contrast. Frequently, strike prices (previously €599, now €519) are also used to place an external anchor price (Fig. 5.6).

5.3.3   Empirical Results: Influencing Price Perception Through Price Optics

The effects of corresponding changes in price optics can be verified based on experimental studies (see Fig. 5.7). In the following, selected results of the "Pricing Lab" study, which is being conducted in cooperation with exeo Strategic Consulting AG and Rogator AG, are presented. The study is based on a representative survey of German consumers aged 18 and over (online, with a sample size of n = 500–1000). A total of six survey waves have been conducted since 2015 and more than 50 individual effects have been examined (Krämer and Hercher 2016). As a rule, each survey wave comprises three different price experiments, with three changes being tested in addition to the original advertisement. During the interview, the test subjects are presented with an offer in the experiment. This is followed by an evaluation of different price image facets. At the end of the survey, the results of the test group can be compared with those of the control group (original advertisement).

The presumed advantages of a price of 9 are not evident in the experiment. In fact, the opposite is the case. The evaluation of the "value for money" facet is improved in test group 2 (comparison of group 2 vs. 1). The differences are

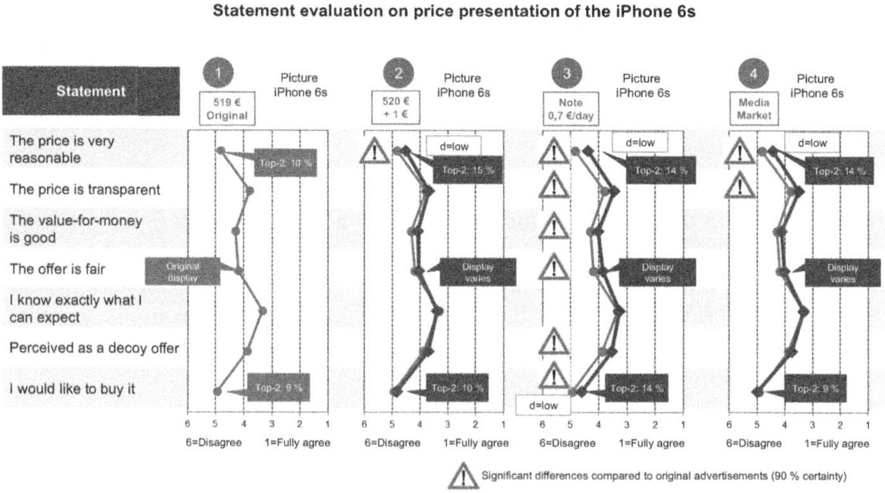

Fig. 5.7 Experimental results on the changed price appearance using the iPhone 6s as an example

statistically significantly different. The effect size (Cohen's d) indicates that there is a (small) relevant difference. There are no significant differences in the other price image facets.

A changed retailer framing (the identical offer is presented in the context of a different retailer; group 4 vs. 1) can also have an influence on price perception. In the specific test, the presentation with the frame "MediaMarkt" scored better in terms of value for money and price transparency. This effect was confirmed in the study for various products and sectors (food, travel, mobile phone contracts). There are thus reciprocal effects between the product/manufacturer image on the one hand and the image of the retail company on the other. This must also be taken into account when determining the price optics.

Consumers' price perception can be partially influenced if the focus is not on the total price, but instead the provider offers a price per (smaller) usage unit, usually per day, i.e., a significantly lower price. This temporal reframing was also described by Gourville (1998) as the "pennies-a-day" strategy. For example, VRR, the largest German transport association, offered the subscription for the "BärenTicket" in 2021 at a monthly price of €91.35 (price level D) and is emphasized the price of €3.00 per day. The insurance company Europa offers household contents insurance from €2.79 per month instead of quoting the annual price. This type of price reduction, in which the price level is not reduced but the total price is related to a new basis for comparison (and thus reduced), aims to make a price that is high in absolute terms appear relatively attractive.

In the specific case of the iPhone 6s, the price reduction leads to a better price rating. In six out of seven image dimensions, the results are statistically better (group 3 vs. 1). An attempt at an explanation: Apple's products are considered expensive, which is also confirmed by the study (only 10% of consumers rate the range as reasonably priced). However, if the price is seen in relation to a useful life of 2 years, the benefit-price ratio is significantly more favorable for the consumer. Despite identical prices, the price of €1 times €519 is perceived as less favorable than €730 (days) times €0.71 (2-year term). In times when the smartphone has become a constant companion that is in constant use, this seems understandable. Similar effects can also be observed with other products, although some tests also show more negative effects. This makes it clear that it is not possible to generalize the effects—no matter how desirable this might be from a management perspective.

Other price visualization instruments that were not the subject of the abovementioned experiment but were examined as part of the Pricing Lab test series also had some astonishing effects (Krämer 2018a). For example, an increase in the price shown can lead to an improved price assessment but does not necessarily have to. Corresponding studies were carried out on the basis of current advertisements for coffee offers (Dallmayr Prodomo) and sports shoes, which were manipulated in the price display. The results showed that the price image evaluation can be influenced (to a limited extent) by identical price levels—both positively and negatively. However, the observed effects are usually small. The possibilities of controlling price perception in the context of price communication are available, but in most cases are limited overall. Price optics is therefore certainly not a "magic bullet."

However, it still makes business sense to explore the existing possibilities of price-optical variation. It may be possible to achieve similar effects on consumer perception through a change in price communication as with a (slight) price reduction. The difference is that even slight price reductions (e.g., of 5%) usually require significant increases in demand to at least keep profits stable (Krämer 2020).

The examples shown are intended to illustrate how heterogeneous the facets of pricing optics can be. Used correctly and consciously, these can improve sales success. In addition to A/B tests, the online experimental design can provide important information for an optimized offer presentation. Equally important is the integration of sales staff to pick up important impulses before the go-live of marketing campaigns.

Against this background, what are the main learning effects? Three aspects should be noted as follows:

- Not only the amount of the product price influences the purchase decision, but also the type of price presentation (e.g., additional information, color change, size of the price display, etc.).
- The strength and direction of effect of the change in price optics are context-dependent. This makes it almost impossible to generalize effects.
- In order to determine the optimal price presentation, tests should be carried out before implementation in the market. Simple rules of thumb (if ..., then) cannot usually be used.

The following section deals with a case in which both aspects discussed so far play a fundamental role; Firstly, the question of how an optimal price for a product can be determined (target: maximizing sales) and, secondly, which psychological pricing factors play a pivotal role in the purchase decision. The Deutschlandticket is a nationwide, monthly cancelable ticket for local public transport in Germany. It was introduced in May 2023 and costs €49 per month (from January 1, 2025, €58).

The aim of this ticket is to facilitate access to local public transport, promote the use of public transport, and at the same time support transport and climate policy. The ticket is valid nationwide on all local public transport such as buses, trams, subways, S-Bahns, and regional trains (second class). It is not valid on long-distance trains (e.g., ICE, IC, EC) or with private providers such as FlixTrain.

It is available digitally or as a chip card and can be canceled monthly. The Deutschlandticket has important psychological effects on users and society. One effect is increased mobility and freedom. The ticket offers the opportunity to travel anywhere and at any time without worrying about the cost of individual journeys. This promotes a feeling of independence. This is also described as a non-use benefit (the ticket holder benefits not only when using the ticket, but also when not using it). A related effect is reduced mental strain, an effect that is often observed with flat-rate offers (Krämer 2024a [1]). If, for example, the effort of buying tickets is eliminated, the cognitive load associated with travel planning is reduced. In a positive case, the offer can lead to people leaving their cars at home more often and using public transport instead. This increases environmentally friendly behavior. Studies that have examined the influence of the ticket on the choice of means of transport confirm a positive shift in demand from cars to local transport in the range of 10–15% of the trips made with the ticket (Krämer and Korbutt 2023 [1]). This effect occurs primarily among new subscription customers (this customer segment accounts for around 50% of Deutschlandticket holders). The precarious financial situation of the local transport industry in 2024 has led to a discussion about how much the price of the Deutschlandticket must be increased in order to cover the industry's financial needs. After all, the income from regional tariffs will be reduced by the cheap Deutschlandticket. The federal and state governments compensate for the losses financially, which is a complex distribution issue. However, this loss compensation was limited to 3 billion euros annually (Krämer and Mietzsch 2024 [2]).

5.4   Interview Hamburger Verkehrsverbund (hvv), Carsten Dürselen

Could you briefly explain the background to the introduction of the Deutschlandticket and describe the specific situation in the Hamburger Verkehrsverbund (hvv) before the Deutschlandticket was introduced?

Carsten Dürselen: In March 2022, the federal government decided to offer a 9-euro ticket for the months of June, July, and August as part of the relief program. This ticket enabled nationwide use of local transport in one calendar month. This idea was initially viewed very critically, but the sales figures then far exceeded expectations. Up to 27 million tickets were used nationwide each month—almost 2 million tickets were used in the hvv. The experience with the 9-euro ticket led to a rethink in politics and society, as it became clear that a much larger proportion of the population could be won over as users for buses and trains than experts had thought possible. Based on this extremely positive public response, the decision was made to launch a successor service on the market. In order to ensure long-term financial viability, a significantly higher price of EUR 49 was set, although it remains extremely attractive compared to the existing offer. In addition, the product was set up as an automatically renewing subscription with a high digital claim compared to the EUR 9 ticket.

It should be noted that the 9-euro ticket was introduced at a time of greatly increased inflation (the official inflation rate reached the 10% mark in autumn 2022), the climate targets set by the German government were not met, demand for public transport was around 80% of the 2019 level at the end of the coronavirus pandemic, and the number of people with public transport season tickets had fallen dramatically due to the coronavirus pandemic. Since the coronavirus pandemic, the financing of local public transport has therefore been secured solely on the basis of a bailout mechanism. Even in 2023, with the introduction of the Deutschlandticket, the pre-coronavirus revenue level had not yet been reached.

Public transport in the hvv was very well developed in a nationwide comparison before the coronavirus crisis. With a 62% share of total revenue, the majority of demand was for season tickets. The price level was above the national average. In 2022, the number of season ticket subscriptions in the hvv was around 670,000, around 30% lower than before the coronavirus crisis.

What impact did the introduction of the Deutschlandticket have on the hvv, specifically on the number of customers, customer loyalty and passenger numbers?

Carsten Dürselen: It was foreseeable that the sales figures of the 9-euro ticket would not be achievable due to the different structure and the higher price—but this was never the goal. Nevertheless, the hvv set itself ambitious targets for market penetration with the new product and clearly aligned its own fare and product structure with the Deutschlandticket. This was one of the reasons why around 700,000 Deutschlandtickets were already sold via the company's own sales channels in the month of the market launch. Less than a year later, the threshold of 1 million Deutschlandtickets was exceeded—1.2 million Deutschlandtickets have now been reached. The proportion of respondents with a Deutschlandticket rose to 35% in our continuous survey (population of the hvv catchment area, aged 18+). Looking at the past 12 months, 47% of the study participants stated that they had owned a Deutschlandticket (DT) in at least 1 month since May 2023. In the city of Hamburg itself, the proportion of current holders of the Deutschlandticket is as high as 50%. This means that the proportion of owners in relation to the population in this federal state is higher than in any other. At the same time, the number of passengers in the hvv has returned to pre-crisis levels with the introduction of the Deutschlandticket.

In our view, the sales success of the Deutschlandticket in the hvv is due not only to the attractive core product but also to our early strategic anticipation of the product. The product range, consisting of over 120 season ticket fare levels, was clearly simplified with the Deutschlandticket to 3 season ticket fares around the Deutschlandticket (weekly ticket, Deutschlandticket, monthly ticket). In the sales channels, the Deutschlandticket was not simply incorporated into the old structures, but the hvv switch app was reprogrammed so that the purchase of the nationwide season ticket feels more like a simple one-way ticket than filling out complicated forms. In addition, subsidy programs based on the Deutschlandticket were developed together with the public sector for certain target groups, such as school pupils, trainees, or people receiving benefits.

In the fall of 2023, it seemed as if a price increase for the Deutschlandticket was virtually inevitable. New price points of 59–89 euros were discussed. In the end, however, there was no price increase. Was this not a missed opportunity?

Carsten Dürselen: A price increase always has two facets: At best, it increases the revenue level in public transport and thus strengthens the customer share in the financing of the transport companies—but at the same time it also reduces the price attractiveness of the product and thus its demand. The discussions within our industry are strongly influenced by the market situation before the coronavirus pandemic, in which price elasticities of demand were extremely low (empirical values of around −0.2 in each case). Price increases were therefore quickly used as a possible solution to minimize the financing risk of the federal and state governments (providing funds of EUR 3 billion per year for the Deutschlandticket). However, our continuous market studies suggested that we are now in a very different market situation. The Deutschlandticket is no longer a traditional public transport subscription with an annual commitment, which involves a long-term, well-considered purchase decision. Instead, we see a high proportion of new subscription customers who greatly appreciate the attractive price level and the flexibility mentioned—and who have increased their local transport journeys and often also their level of spending on public transport as a result. In particular, with unprecedented price increases of 10%+ compared to public transport in the past, we saw the risk of major customer migration. In our view, this could not only lead to a drop in passenger numbers, but also to a drop in revenue if prices are not adjusted correctly.

In order to estimate the effects of a price increase on the number of customers, journeys on local transport, and revenue from the Deutschlandticket, it is therefore necessary to have a concrete idea of the price-sales relationship. At hvv, we expanded our own market survey to include a block of topics on the willingness to pay for the ticket and were thus able to provide our stakeholders with a database for decision-making.

What was the concrete result of this research approach and how was this data used for the specialist discussion?

Carsten Dürselen: At the end of 2023, we decided to use the PSM-Plus toolkit in our study and thus gave preference to non-traditional approaches such as the Van Westendorp approach or direct measurements of willingness to pay. In this novel approach, two measurement points of the Van Westendorp approach are used in a survey (price point P3 "Expensive, but just reasonable" and P4 "So expensive that I would no longer buy the ticket"), but interpreted in a new way. The mean value from both price points is interpreted as an estimated value for the individual maximum willingness to pay (Fig. 5.5). Different validation steps are used here.

When looking at the price-sales function developed in this way, it becomes clear that the risks of losing customers when raising the ticket price from EUR 49 to EUR 59 or EUR 69 are considerable. This indicates that the price elasticities in the specific example can be 1 or higher, depending on the strength of the price adjustment. On this basis, the hvv has derived the following positions:

- High price increases will inevitably lead to a clearly noticeable decline in customers. The empirical values from price scenarios before the coronavirus pandemic are no longer applicable. This loss of customers particularly affects segments that have previously used public transport less and are more price-sensitive. These factors must also be critically integrated into the pricing and financing discourse because the customer group in question makes a major contribution to achieving the strategic objectives (climate and relief targets) of the Deutschlandticket.

- Individual initiative price increases purely to close the acute financing delta will only further increase uncertainty in the market ("If the price is increased this much now, how much will the price increase be next year"). Instead, the fastest possible implementation of a stable price mechanism, based on existing indexation mechanisms (e.g., pension adjustment formula), is recommended. This will not only lead to better predictability for customers, but also for public transport authorities and companies.
- Different estimates of sales potential point to considerable untapped opportunities that are not sufficiently recognized in the discussion about price increases. In addition to the potential in the basic product and job ticket, new potential can also be tapped through greater customer orientation.

Against this backdrop, the decision of the political bodies in favor of price stability (at least until the end of 2024) is a good decision compared to the alternatives discussed. I am also pleased that the Conference of Transport Ministers has called for a long-term price mechanism to be set up for the Deutschlandticket. The nationwide surveys also show a considerable ramp-up in the months following the introduction of the Deutschlandticket. Even 12 months later, there is still no sign of market saturation. The PSM-Plus instrument was later also used to determine the effects on demand and revenue of an increased price for the Deutschlandticket (Krämer 2024b).

The interview partner: Carsten Dürselen studied business administration at the Vienna University of Economics and Business (WU). He currently works as Head of Sales & Digital at Hamburger Verkehrsverbund GmbH (hvv). Previously, he worked for various companies in the mobility and logistics sector, including the Austrian Federal Railways (ÖBB). Since summer 2024, he has also been co-head of the sub-working group "Forecast, price and scenarios" of the Deutschlandticket Coordination Council of the federal and state governments.

5.5   Core Function Pricing: Take-Aways

The previous explanations should have made clear the particular importance of price as a driver of corporate success. In the next step, the dependencies of different key points in the pricing process were pointed out to shed more light on the basics for estimating the price-sales effects against this background. Based on microeconomic theory, an attempt can be made to concretize ideas about the demand function to secure management decisions in this way. The central aspect here is the measurement of potential customers' willingness to pay. From a wealth of methodological approaches, direct forms are examined in more detail, which have so far been regarded as less acceptable from an academic point of view—because they tend to be distorted and therefore invalid. However, as has been shown, sufficiently accurate basic data for modeling price-sales relationships can also be provided with simplified approaches such as direct questions on willingness to pay or price thresholds. In this context, the PSM-Plus approach presents a methodology that combines the advantages of the Van Westendorp method (querying 4 price points) and direct open-ended information on willingness to pay without requiring additional effort in the survey. This approach is also particularly sustainable under changing market conditions, which demand quick results and simple surveys. For example, the PSM-Plus approach has been used to simulate different price scenarios for the Deutschlandticket (Krämer et al. 2025).

In a further step, possibilities were discussed that would make it possible to achieve significant changes in the price perception and purchase intention of customers with minimally adjusted or completely unchanged price levels. These approaches to price presentation have a not inconsiderable profit potential, but their concrete effect must be examined more closely in each individual case.

The influence of changing market conditions (VUCA) on price management in companies, which calls for new pricing methods, integrated and dynamic approaches, and rapid decision support in practice, may be overlooked or underestimated by academics (Krämer and Schmutz 2020; Krämer 2015).

For pricing managers, both simple methods for measuring price willingness and experimental test set-ups for measuring price-optical effects will become more important because they can be easily adapted to the conditions of a VUCA environment (Mack et al. 2016). These correlations must be taken into account, even if the pricing community is increasingly discussing dynamic pricing, price automation, and artificial intelligence. In this context, the "PSM-Plus" methodology is explained. It enables the estimation of individual willingness to pay and can serve as a basis for price optimization (e.g., with the aim of determining prices that maximize sales). Different use cases are described. A current example is the price adjustment for the Deutschlandticket in 2025.

This chapter has primarily dealt with the question of how profit-optimal prices can be formed on the basis of reliable data and what possibilities exist to positively influence price perception through suitable price optics. The next step must be to evaluate the effects of these measures as part of the implementation process. After all, it can be a long way from the target prices that a company imagines to the prices that are ultimately effectively realized in the market. This applies to the B2C sector (pricing across several stages of the value chain) as well as the B2B sector, where (historically evolved) condition systems are often used.

References

Ariely D (2008) Predictably irrational. HarperCollins, New York
Baker WL, Marn MV, Zawada CC (2010) The price advantage, 2. Aufl. Wiley, Hoboken
Balderjahn I (1994) Der Einsatz der Conjoint-Analyse zur empirischen Bestimmung von Preisresponsefunktionen. Marketing ZFP 16:12–20
Bauer F (2014) Behavioral Pricing – Die Kunst nicht am Kunden vorbei zu bepreisen. Planung & Analyse 2:27–30
Bergers D, Fassnacht M (2017) Debiasing Strategies in the Price Management Process. Mark Rev St Gallen 34(6):50–58

Bosenick T (2014) Messen, was zählt – User Experience Tool untersucht ganzheitliches Produkterlebnis. Planung & Analyse 2014(5):26

Breidert C, Hahsler M, Reutterer T (2006) A review of methods for measuring willingness-to-pay. Innov Mark 2(4):8–32

Brynjolfsson E, Collis A, Eggers F (2019) Using massive online choice experiments to measure changes in well-being. Proc Natl Acad Sci 116(15):7250–7255

Buffet W (2010) Financial Crisis Inquiry Commission Staff Audiotape of Interview with Warren Buffett, Berkshire Hathaway, May 26, 2010. https://healthywealthywiseproject.com/2011/06/warren-buffett-the-single-most-important-decision-in-evaluating-a-business. Accessed 8 Jan 2020

Chhabra S (2015) Determining the optimal price point: using Van Westendorp's price sensitivity meter. Managing in recovering markets. Springer, India, pp 257–270

Dost F, Wilken R (2012) Measuring willingness to pay as a range, revisited: when should we care? Int J Res Mark 29(2):148–166

Drewes F, Keck C, Pale C (2010) Zahlungsbereitschaften realistisch messen. Planung & Analyse 37(2):40–43

Fisher M, Gallino LJ (2017) Competition-based dynamic pricing in online retailing: a methodology validated with field experiments. Manage Sci 64(6):2496–2514

Frohmann F (2018) Digitales pricing. Springer Gabler, Wiesbaden

Gourville JT (1998) Pennies-a-day: the effect of temporal reframing on transaction evaluation. J Cons Res 24(4):395–408

Granados N, Gupta A, Kauffman RJ (2009) Online and offline demand and price elasticities: evidence from the air travel industry. Inf Syst Res 23(1):1–10

Hinterhuber A (2008) Customer value-based pricing strategies: why companies resist. J Bus Strateg 29(4):41–50

Hinterhuber A, Liozu S (2012) Is it time to rethink your pricing strategy. MIT Sloan Manag Rev 53(4):69–77

Horowitz JK, McConnell KE (2002) A review of WTA/WTP studies. J Environ Econ Manag 44(3):426–447

Jensen M (2013) Setting profitable prices: a step-by-step guide to pricing strategy – without hiring a consultant. Wiley

Kalka R, Krämer A (2020) Einordnung, Aufgaben und Rahmenbedingungen der Preiskommunikation. In: Preiskommunikation. Springer Gabler, Wiesbaden, pp 3–25

Kossmann J (2008) Die Implementierung der Preispolitik in Business-to-Business-Unternehmen: Eine prozessorientierte Konzeption, vol 18. WiGIM ev, Nürnberg

Krämer A (2024a) New Mobility – Vom 9-Euro-Ticket zur Verkehrswende? Springer Gabler, Wiesbaden

Krämer A (2024b) "PSM-Plus": Eine neue Methode zur Messung von Zahlungsbereitschaften. VARI Forschungsbericht Nr. 7, Iserlohn, Nov. 2024

Krämer A, Korbutt A (2023) Das Deutschlandticket aus Sicht des hvv und in der bundesweiten Betrachtung. Internationales Verkehrswesen 75(4):10–14

Krämer A, Mietzsch O (2024) Zukunft Deutschlandticket: Verkehrswende, Finanzierung und wohlfahrtsökonomische Wirkung. Wirtschaftsdienst 104(9):636–643

Krämer A (2015) Pricing in a VUCA world – how to optimize prices, if the economic, social and legal framework changes rapidly. In: Mack O, Khare A, Krämer A, Burgartz T (eds) Managing in a VUCA world. Springer, New York, pp 115–128

Krämer A (2017) Van Westendorp Reloaded: Wie sich auf Basis des PSM-Ansatzes (doch) gute Preisentscheidungen treffen lassen. Vortrag auf der Research & Results Messe, 25.10.2017, München

Krämer A (2018a) Bounded Irrationality – Chancen und Grenzen beim verhaltensbasierten Pricing. Marketing Rev St Gallen 35(2):102–110

Krämer A (2018b) Identische Preise anders dargestellt. Identische Preise anders dargestellt. Sales Excellence 1(5):42–45

Krämer A (2019) Price setting in a VUCA world: a simple approach to re-interpret the van-Westendorp-approach (PSM). GOR Conference, Cologne, March 7, 2019

Krämer A (2025) Preiskommunikation in Zeiten des "Behavioral Pricing". In: Preiskommunikation. Springer Gabler, Wiesbaden, pp 29–53

Krämer A, Burgartz T (2020) Mehr Verhandlungserfolg in VUCA-Zeiten. Sales Excellence 27(12):20–23

Krämer A, Hercher J (2016) Die Grenzen der Irrationalität – Robustheit der Preiswahrnehmung bei Verbrauchern. Res Results 5:46–47

Krämer A, Schmutz I (2020) Mythos value-based pricing: Der Versuch einer (wertfreien) Einordnung. Mark Rev St Gallen 37(2):44–53

Krämer A, Wilger G (1999) Messung von vielschichtigen Kundenpräferenzen mittels Conjoint Measurement. Planung & Analyse 18(5):50–56

Krämer A, Jung M, Burgartz T (2016) A small step from price competition to price war – Understanding causes, effects and possible countermeasures. Int Bus Res 9(3):1–13

Krämer A, Dethlefsen H, Baigger J (2017) Auf der Suche nach dem optimalen Preis: Der PSM-Ansatz neu überdacht – von der von der Preispunktanalyse zur Zahlungsbereitschaft. Planung & Analyse 6:54–56

Krämer A, Wilger G, Bongaerts R (2025) Deutschlandticket zum Preis von 29 Euro – Ticketbestand, Einnahmenwirkung und Verkehrsverlagerung. Eine Studie der exeo Strategic Consulting AG, im Auftrag von Greenpeace, Hamburg, Jan. 2025

Larson RB (2014) Psychological pricing principles for organizations with market power. J Appl Bus Econ 16(1):11–25

Liebermann M (2015) Pricing research: a new take on the Van Westendorp model. Quirks Media, June 2015. Verfügbar online at: https://www.quirks.com/articles/pricing-research-a-new-takeon-the-van-westendorp-model. Accessed 8 Jan 2021

Liozu S, Boland D, Hinterhuber A, Perelli S (2015) Mindful pricing: transforming organizations through value based pricing. Marketing dynamism & sustainability: things change, things stay the same. Springer, Cham, pp 412–421

Löffler M (2015) Measuring willingness to pay: do direct methods work for premium durables? Mark Lett 26(4):535–548

Lowe B, Lowe J, Lynch D (2013) Behavioral aspects of pricing. In: Innovation in pricing. Routledge, Abingdon, pp 357–375

Lusk JL (2003) Effects of cheap talk on consumer willingness-to-pay for golden rice. Am J Agr Econ 85(4):840–856

Lynch JG, Ariely D (2000) Wine online: search cost affect competition on price, quality and distribution. Mark Sci 19(1):83–103

Mack O, Khare A, Krämer A, Burgartz T (2016) Managing in a VUCA world. Springer, New York

Mahieu PA, Riera P, Giergiczny M (2012) The influence of cheap talk on willingness-to-pay ranges: some empirical evidence from a contingent valuation study. J Environ Planning Manage 55(6):753–763

Michel S, Pfäffli P (2009) Implementierungshürden des Value Based Pricing. Mark Rev St Gallen 26(5):26–31

Miller KM, Hofstetter R, Krohmer H, Zhang ZJ (2011) How should consumers' willingness to pay be measured? An empirical comparison of state-of-the-art approaches. J Mark Res 48(1):172–184

Miller KM, Hofstetter R (2009) Precision pricing: measuring consumers' willingness to pay accurately. BoD–Books on Demand

Reinecke S, Mühlmeier S, Fischer PM (2009) Die van Westendorp-Methode: Ein zu Unrecht vernachlässigtes Verfahren zur Ermittlung der Zahlungsbereitschaft? Wirtschaftswissenschaftliches Studium 38(2):97–100

Roll O, Achterberg LH, Herbert KG (2010a) Innovative approaches to analyzing the price sensitivity meter. Results of an international comparative study. COM-BI2010 Conference Proceedings, p 181–193

Roll O, Achterberg LH, Herbert KG (2010b) Innovative approaches to analyzing the price sensitivity meter. Planung & Analyse 2:27–30

Schindler RM (2011) Pricing strategies: a marketing approach. Sage, Los Angeles

Schmidt J, Bijmolt TH (2019) Accurately measuring willingness to pay for consumer goods: a meta-analysis of the hypothetical bias. J Acad Mark Sci:1–20

Schmidt J, Steiner M, Krafft M, Eckel N, Dahl DW (2023) Hitting the bullseye: accurately measuring willingness to pay for innovations with open and closed direct questions. Int J Res Market 41(2):383–402

Schmutz I, Reinecke S (2020) Gibt's nicht, geht nicht! Eine Konzeptionalisierung von Informationsdefiziten im Preisprozess. Mark Rev St Gallen 37(6):64–73

Simon H, Fassnacht M (2016) Preismanagement: Strategie – Analyse – Entscheidung – Umsetzung. Springer, Berlin

Steiner M, Hendus J (2012) How consumers' willingness to pay is measured in practice: an empirical analysis of common approaches' relevance. Available at SSRN 2025618

Sunstein CR (2025) Willingness To Pay: An Interrogation. Harvard Public Law Working Paper Forthcoming. Available at SSRN 5145225.

Töytäri P, Rajala R, Alejandro TB (2015) Organizational and institutional barriers to value-based pricing in industrial relationships. Ind Mark Manage 47(2015):53–64

Viglia G, Mauri A, Carricano M (2016) The exploration of hotel reference prices under dynamic pricing scenarios and different forms of competition. Int J Hosp Manag 52:46–55

Core Function—Costs: Which Costs Are Relevant for Decision-Making?

6

6.1 Cost Management: Understanding Costs Correctly

"If you think about costs too late, you ruin your company. If you always think about costs too early, you kill creativity."—Philip Rosenthal

6.1.1 Shaping Function of Cost Management

In order to understand costs as the cause or effect of business decisions, it is certainly necessary to think holistically beyond the purely quantitative aspects. If costs are to be adequately included in the pricing mechanism, it is important to find the right balance: No exclusive focus on costs, but also no negation of costs, as is often the case under the assumption of "Marginal costs = 0" happens. Philip Rosenthal (1916–2001), known for transforming the porcelain company Rosenthal AG into an internationally recognized brand, points out the necessary sensitivity with the passage quoted at the beginning. To ensure an analysis and evaluation of cost causation and generation and to take on a formative, active role, various approaches and framework conditions are proposed in the broad-based discussion on cost management. In the scientific discussion, a uniform understanding can be recognized that influencing costs with regard to cost level, structure, and development serves significantly to improve efficiency and profitability (Ewert and Wagenhofer 2014; Männel 2005; Coenenberg et al. 2016; Kilger 2012; Weber and Weißenberger 2015). In practical application, too, cost management is often an overarching instrument that aims to consciously influence costs and can therefore react to market changes, changes in customer behavior, and changes in raw material prices at any time (Kremin-Buch 2007). For customer value-centered cost management, it is also crucial that there is a mutual exchange between controlling (orientation toward "hard" economic data as a basis for decision-making) and marketing or

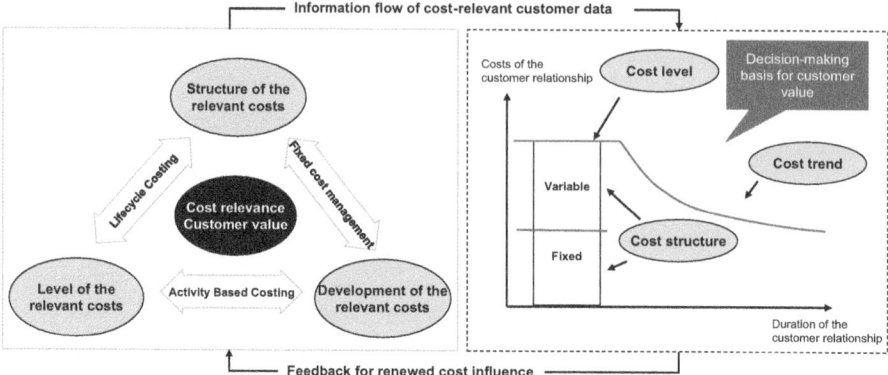

Fig. 6.1 Between influencing costs and focusing on customer value

CRM (possibly strong orientation towards behavioral science explanatory approaches). With the right balance, it is both sensible and advantageous to make more qualitative decisions based on quantitative information (Burgartz 2018). In addition to the findings from customer satisfaction or purchasing behavior research, for example, the findings on the amount, structure, and development of the relevant costs in particular form the basis for determining and assessing customer value. The information flow of the relevant cost data is shown in Fig. 6.1. The filtering and subsequent preparation of the decision-relevant costs (left side) lead to a transparent presentation of the customer-related costs as a basis for the decision to classify the customer value.

6.1.2   Cost Management and Customer Value Centricity: Creating Transparency

From a holistic perspective, the first step in designing transparent, comprehensible cost management is to interlink certain dimensions (Ulrich 2001; Stibbe 2009). Active cost management requires a comprehensible cost logic and knowledge of how costs are caused and incurred. Depending on the intention, urgency, and timing of the decisions or influence, certain tools are then used, each of which pursues a different objective.

The focus of cost level management is the level of costs, which generally needs to be reduced or at least stabilized. From a value-oriented perspective, influencing the cost level is about optimizing profitability (Graumann 2017), where there are interdependencies and interactions with the other dimensions of cost structure and cost behavior. It is important to bear in mind that a change in costs is often accompanied by a change in services. In particular, this shows the dependence and importance of a value-to-value approach (cost reduction with accompanying devaluation of benefits by the customer). Cost structure management serves to optimize cost distribution. Influencing cost structures therefore aims to achieve a targeted change in the composition of costs, i.e., a change in the various cost blocks, categories, or types. The aim here is to achieve an ideal structure of fixed and variable cost ratios. Companies with a very broad product range and a strong customer focus often have a disproportionately high share of overheads due to the permanent provision of product variations and a resource-intensive customer service. The competition between combustion and electric drives in cars is older than some people think. Initially, it was electricvehicles that came out on top. The Scotsman Robert Anderson produced the first battery-powered electric vehicle between 1832 and 1839. In the 1920s, the triumphant advance of gasoline-powered vehicles began (Anderson 2024), which was also driven by considerable economies of scale. To make automobiles more accessible, costs had to be reduced. To reduce costs, production had to be standardized and simplified. If the unit costs could be reduced, Ford lowered the price, with corresponding positive effects on sales. His reasoning: people don't value better seats and more color choices (Laird and Sherratt 2010). His words: "Choose any color you want as long as it's black". In 16 years, Henry Ford managed to: increase production by a factor of 20 and reduce costs by 70%.

As part of cost trend management, the responsiveness of costs should be optimized or made more flexible. When influencing cost behavior, the time at which costs are incurred is analyzed. The costs of individual processes or life cycles are examined on the basis of their development over time in order to initially recognize their occurrence and adjust them if necessary. In addition, any cost dependency on other influencing variables (e.g., personnel resources) is determined and assessed (Götze 2010). In the case of a long-term customer relationship, the cost trend can be an indicator of how the service intensity changes over time, how different customer segments develop, and what indications this provides for pricing.

Tried and tested controlling and cost management tools can be assigned to each of the three areas, which meet the objectives presented in one or more areas. The focus here is on three typical tools that have proven to be extremely helpful and easy to implement.

The essence of activity-based costing is the allocation of overhead costs according to actual utilization (cost-by-cause principle). To determine costs, it is first necessary to determine main processes as well as sub-processes and cost drivers and to ensure a clear allocation of a cost driver to a cost center. Activity-based costing (ABC) allows the company's overheads to be allocated to the products according to causation and can be used in all areas of cost management via the direct customer and product reference.

The constantly increasing costs of the indirect service areas (customer management, marketing, sales) lead to rising overhead rates and a correspondingly increasing risk that disproportionately high costs are allocated to products in the direct service area with the consequence of low revenue transparency, for example, in the case of discount campaigns (Lücke 1997; Hansen et al. 2007).

In target costing, a company determines the allowable costs of a product or service on the basis of the customer's willingness to pay. The target costs (standard costs) are determined on the basis of a target price that can theoretically be achieved on the market and a target profit. In this context, it should be noted that target pricing in conjunction with target costing is the most consistent form of customer value-based pricing.

Based on customer needs, a product concept is developed for which the accepted price is determined (target price). In the internal way of thinking, the target costs represent the budget available for the development and production of a product or service. This means that compliance with the target costs must already be realized during the development process (Reichmann et al. 2017). However, a pure focus on costs should be viewed critically, especially in innovation-intensive industries (Davila and Wouters 2004).

Life cycle costing refers to the consideration of all costs incurred over all periods of a lifecycle. Life cycle costing is also a component of target costing and provides the cost-relevant information for the respective reference object to be analyzed (Raubenheimer 2010). It is used to minimize life cycle costs and determine ongoing profitability and is primarily applied to products, projects, processes, and resources (or production factors) by making statements about product profitability, amortization time, product cost development, and medium- to long-term value development. The economic relevance has recently increased due to shorter product life cycles and the proportionate increase in up-front and follow-up costs compared to the total costs of a product. Life cycle costing is mainly used to influence customer and product-related cost levels and structures.

Fixed cost management refers to the target-oriented planning, management, and control of fixed costs with the aim of increasing the company's responsiveness to market fluctuations and, accordingly, its flexibility (Steger 2010; Stelling 2005; Oecking 1997). The fixed costs influenced by this are costs "that are independent of the influencing variable or decision under consideration, i.e. costs that do not change with the influencing variable under consideration. The decisive factor is not the behavior of the quantity component, but the influence on the amount of expenditure or payments" (Weber and Steven 2014). Fixed cost management provides a holistic view of a company's fixed costs with the aim of influencing their structure and behavior. The use of fixed cost management is particularly useful in the case of customer-related, fixed direct costs, as it results in significantly greater transparency for certain customer segments.

6.1.3   Selected Tools with Particular Relevance for Cost Control and Customer Value

All of the cost management approaches outlined above offer the fundamental possibility of supporting profitability and investment decisions in customer value management. A more in-depth examination of their applicability shows that each of these tools has a special ability to provide cost management and controlling with decision-relevant information for certain industries, markets, market participants,   products,   or   services.   The   three   instruments   described above—Activity-Based Costing (ABC), Lifecycle Costing and Fixed Cost Management—are particularly suitable for a more transparent analysis and ultimately a focused influence on cost-oriented customer value development. These tools help value-oriented customer management to identify basic cost levels and to influence the cost structure of certain customer segments by means of a classic target/actual comparison.

ABC identifies the key cost drivers along the process chain and costs initiated by customers (customer journey) and, in conjunction with target costing, for example, shows recommendations for action for an optimal alignment of customer expectations of a product with the company's own possibilities. The question to be answered is whether these benefit expectations can be mapped cost-efficiently by identifying the necessary cost reductions for ideal target pricing using ABC, for example, by highlighting redundant customer processes or cumbersome process sequences such as excessively long waiting, ordering, and delivery times. These findings can be used to set new prices for unprofitable customer relationships, improve production processes for faster delivery, develop more cost-effective products, or align product variety more closely with customer benefits.

The analysis of the cost composition holds optimization potential for the development, maintenance, and expansion of certain customer segments and flows into a needs-based adjustment of limited budgets while maximizing profitability in customer management. The perception of costs from both the customer's and the company's perspective is decisive for the possibly necessary correction of customer value-related costs while maintaining profitability targets and at the same time maintaining existing customer benefit expectations. Both perspectives must be understood in the sense of a value-to-value approach.

6.2 Cost Perception from the Company's Perspective

6.2.1 Fixed Costs and Short-Term Marketing Decisions

Economists usually refer to the relevance of marginal costs, not full costs, when describing rational decision-making in a company for short-term decisions. For example, for most database marketing decisions, Blattberg et al. (2008) suggest calculating customer lifetime value (CLV) using only variable costs, without considering the costs associated with customer acquisition. In a more recent article, Bendle and Bagga (2016) support this view. When pricing a product, the variable costs per product unit are also considered as a reference point for the lowest possible price from the supplier's perspective (Guilding et al. 2005). Taking fixed costs into account, on the other hand, is seen as irrelevant to the decision because they cannot be changed in the short term. Not taking this principle into account is a particular focus of research in behavioral science. When people allow themselves to be influenced by sunk costs when making decisions, this is referred to as the "sunk cost fallacy." This could also be described with the phrase "throwing good money after bad."

Hammond et al. (1998) describe this effect as "making decisions in a way that justifies past, erroneous decisions" and explain this using the example of a banker who grants problem loans and advances more and more money to borrowers to protect and justify his previous decisions, even though the loans still default.

According to Arkes and Blumer (1985), the sunk cost fallacy is the "tendency to continue an endeavor once an investment in money, effort or time has been made." The term sunk cost can easily be transferred to the field of production management. Fixed costs of a plant that were made as an investment in the past and that continue to exist over a longer period of time even when the plant is shut down are also "sunk." Sunk costs quantify the cost value of the resource consumption of an investment or project. However, they are not relevant to the decision to continue an investment project. They should not be considered.

At this point, we will first critically question whether an apodictic negation of fixed costs in short-term decisions makes sense in practical corporate management. This will be done using the areas of customer value management and pricing as examples:

- Calculating the CLV without considering the costs of customer acquisition may seem obvious at first glance. At second glance, questions arise, for example, as to whether the information regarding the amount of the initial investment in the customer relationship is not a relevant aspect. If, for example, two customers are considered that have an identical customer value, while the acquisition costs (not included) differ greatly, then important information is missing for the management of direct marketing. If a company focuses on customer acquisition channels that turn out to be inefficient, this problem cannot be openly discussed (and remedied) because only an incremental perspective, rather than a holistic view of costs, should be allowed. In this case, not only is there a lack of transparency, but the lack of an overall view of the costs of the customer relationship can lead to wrong decisions.
- In the pricing community, the inclusion of fixed costs in pricing is usually regarded as a "deadly sin," the worst possible way of pricing. Management guru Peter Drucker (1993) is often quoted as follows: "The third deadly sin is cost-driven pricing. The only thing that works is price-driven costing. Most American and practically all European companies arrive at their prices by adding up costs and then putting a profit margin on top. And then, as soon as they have introduced the product, they must start cutting the price, have to redesign the product at enormous expense, have to take losses—and, often, have to drop a perfectly good product because it is priced incorrectly. Their argument? We have to recover our costs and make a profit." The negation of fixed costs in pricing not only poses some risks in a world full of digital business models, but also in traditional business areas. Unfortunately, the argumentation results in a primary focus on the short-term price floor (in which the variable unit costs are covered) at the expense of the long-term price floor (in which the total unit costs are covered).

This can have negative dynamic effects if the need to cover fixed as well as variable costs in the medium term is no longer considered or is no longer given sufficient weight, in the mindset of decision-makers, potentially leading—at worst—to a destructive price war (Wilger and Krämer 2025).

6.2.2   Competitive Strength, Price Enforcement, and Cost Perspective

The relationships between the factors of competitive strength, the ability to enforce target prices, and the perception of costs by management will be illustrated using a brief example. Here are some basic assumptions:

- Total capacity: 1 million units (100% capacity utilization)
- Fixed production costs: €10 million
- Variable costs: €10 per piece
- Short-term price floor: €10 (to cover variable costs)
- Oligopolitical market structures: Only four customers
- Planning period: 12 months, starting in January.

Scenario 1 is intended to describe a market environment in which the company is in a strong starting position: Strategic competitive advantages exist in several service facets. In addition, the number of customers is low. The company manages to secure orders from customer A at the beginning of the planning period, which already cover 40% of production capacity. At an average price of €25, revenue of around €10 million is secured. Customers B and C follow at a later stage and, although they demand a lower price, they enable a cumulative revenue volume of €21.3 million at the end of the first quarter. Capacity is therefore already 90% utilized. In addition, the fixed costs of €10 million are covered. Customer D does not order until much later in the planning year and is prepared to pay a maximum of €15 per unit. The company accepts this price because, firstly, the fixed costs are already covered at the time of the decision and, secondly, the price of €15 is higher than the variable costs of €10 per unit (Fig. 6.2). In total, the revenue amounts to €22.8 million per year. After deducting the fixed and variable costs (€10 million each), the company generates a profit of €2.8 million (revenue of €22.8 million minus costs of €20.0 million).

In this scenario, a possible medium-term risk remains, namely, that customers exchange the prices actually paid and thus obtain transparency on pricing and price differentiation. However, if the company uses a condition system that does not take into account the effective prices, e.g., by granting various discount elements and benefits "opaque," this risk can be limited (Krämer and Beger 2017).

In Scenario 2, the market conditions for the example company are relatively unfavorable. Significant competitive advantages no longer exist. The planning phase in the first quarter proves to be extremely difficult. Rumors of overcapacity in the market spread, resulting in increasing price sensitivity on the part of customers. Customer A demands significant price concessions for its large purchase volume, while negotiations drag on. Ultimately, the final negotiated price of €18

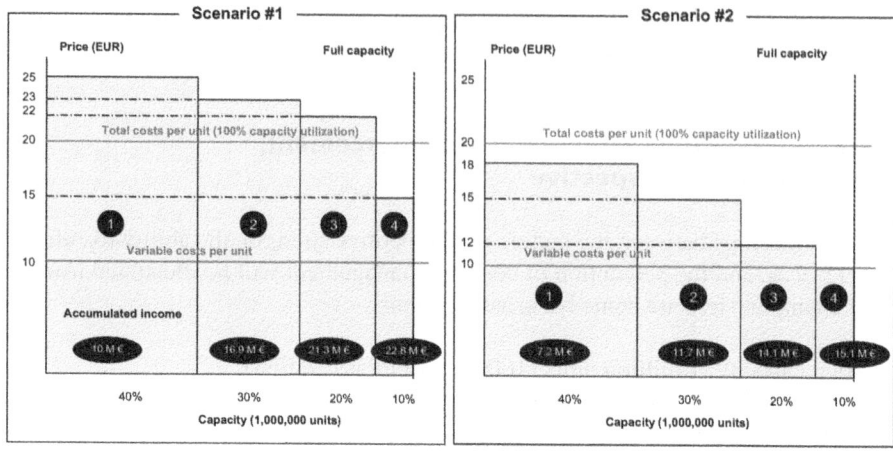

Fig. 6.2 Realized prices, revenues, and profits for the model company

reaches a level that does not guarantee full cost coverage (at 100% capacity utilization). The situation worsens for customer B, with management's focus increasingly shifting toward a short-term price floor. Customer B's demand to accept a maximum price of €15 is conceded on the grounds that this price still yields a marginal profit: "Better to accept this price and be in a position to at least partially cover the fixed costs than to lose the customer," argue the negotiators from the sales team. After the negotiation with customer C intensifies further (negotiation result €12 unit price), the following overall perspective emerges. After 90% of the production capacity has again been planned, the cumulative revenue is only €14.1 million. Customer D then only accepts a price of €10. The management's reasoning: "At €10, we have at least covered the variable costs. The year will be difficult anyway. It can certainly help if we at least achieve full capacity utilization." Ultimately, the revenue volume of €15.1 million is not enough to cover the costs. The loss amounts to €4.9 million.

Based on this simple simulation, it should become clear how the competitive situation and market situation, as well as the perception of costs within the company, influence pricing. In fact, the question arises as to whether the focus on the short-term price floor does not give the false impression that "there is always room to go down in price." Rather, dynamic effects need to be discussed more:

- To what extent do high discount concessions in this planning period lead to corresponding customer expectations in the next planning periods?
- How can willingness to pay be prevented from successively moving downward (over time)? How can excessive price transparency about the effective product price be prevented?
- How are price concessions interpreted by competitors if they receive this information?

6.3   Cost Perception from the Consumer's Perspective

6.3.1   Do Fixed Costs Influence Consumer Decisions?

The apodictic statement that "fixed costs should not affect short-term decisions, only variable costs should be taken into account" is not only relevant for business decisions, but also for consumer decisions.

For more than three decades, behavioral economists have explained that consumer perception biases often lead to poor decisions that companies can exploit to their advantage. As Grubb (2015) describes, consumers often fail to choose the best price because they spend too little time searching, they become confused when comparing prices, and/or they bring excessive inertia by deviating too little from previous decisions or default options. Despite a plethora of papers dedicated to getting people to make better decisions (Thaler and Sunstein 2009), many factors can be found that successfully discourage consumers from the aforementioned rational decision-making (Houdek 2016). For example, there is extensive evidence that decision-makers in the real world violate the predictions of standard economic theory. The so-called sunk cost bias is particularly prominent in this context (Al-Najjar et al. 2005). The origin of this theory goes back to Thaler (1980), who states that "... only incremental costs and benefits should affect decisions. Historical costs should be irrelevant. But do (non-economist) consumers ignore sunk costs in their everyday decisions? ... I do not believe that they do." The simple logic in the argument is that consumers are influenced in their decisions by fixed costs so that they end up making choices to their own disadvantage.

The sunk cost fallacy is not limited to consumer behavior or economic decisions but extends to many others, including political decisions. Nevertheless, the next section will initially focus on consumer cost perception and decision-making. The challenge here is to further investigate and understand the core elements of the sunk cost fallacy. This is summarized by Kelly (2004) as the combination of two conditions: (1) Individuals take historical costs (past investments) into account when making decisions, and (2) it is irrational to do so.

6.3.2   Cost Perception When Using a Private Car

In order to describe as broad a range of applications as possible, car ownership is used as an example below. The results of the Mobility TRENDS 2016 study can be used to analyze the perception of the costs of car use (Krämer 2016). This is a study to identify and evaluate trends in the mobility market. It is carried out in cooperation with exeo Strategic Consulting AG and Rogator AG. The study is based on a representative survey of around 4500 people aged 18 and over (German-speaking population in the DACH region). Within the study, drivers were asked about the costs of a car journey of varying distances. Three groups were formed randomly, namely, (a) with a total distance of 200 km, (b) 600 km total distance, and (c) 1000 km total distance. A total of five cost items were asked for support (respondents were asked to indicate which costs they included in a calculation). The items fuel costs (fuel) and other variable costs (e.g., for oil) can be described as out-of-pocket costs. Just under two thirds of drivers in Germany only state these variable costs as part of their estimate. More than a third include other cost items. Fifty-five percent of respondents named only one item, and 8% of study participants named all the cost items asked about. In Germany, costs of around €53 are estimated for a short car journey (200 km) (average distance of 600 km: €110 and longer distance of 1000 km: €174). Converted to the kilometer, the costs decrease non-linearly from the short distance (€0.27/km) to the medium distance (€0.18/km) to the longer distance (€0.17/km). The mean value of around €0.20/km is already an indicator that it is not only the out-of-pocket costs of the car journey—depending on consumption and fuel, these are between €0.07 and €0.11/km—that determine the perception of car drivers but that other cost elements are also taken into account. However, the value is also significantly below the full cost level. According to calculations by the ADAC, these are, for example, for a VW Golf VII at around 43 cents per km.

The interim result is as follows: Car users perceive costs that generally go well beyond the variable costs but are nowhere near the full costs.

The structure of the perceived costs is again dependent on the route length. For shorter journeys, the average number of cost items mentioned (2.3) is significantly higher than for longer journeys. The proportion of drivers who include depreciation costs or replacement costs in their calculations is 25% for shorter journeys of 200 km and falls to 6% for longer journeys (1000 km).

As the study is designed as a multi-country study, country-specific features can also be identified in the cross-comparison. There are relatively clear differences between Switzerland on the one hand and Germany and Austria on the other regarding the amount of the cost estimate and the structure of the cost components mentioned for car trips. As Fig. 6.3 (right-hand side) shows, the cost estimate in Switzerland is around twice as high in CHF as in Germany and Austria, which are relatively similar in terms of the cost function. However, in addition to the higher

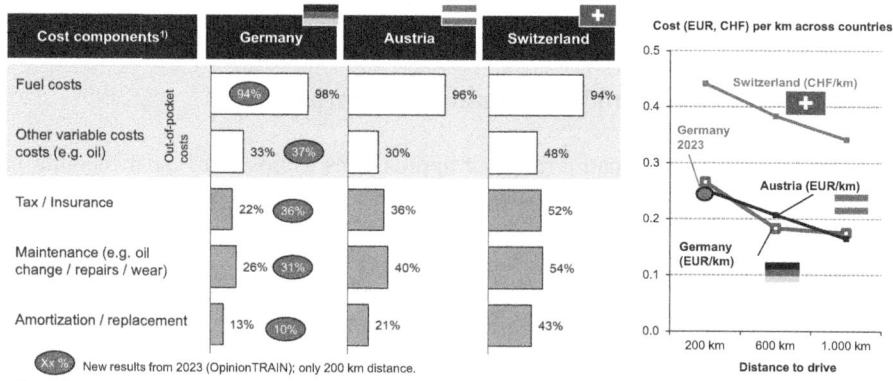

Fig. 6.3 Consideration of different car cost components according to route length (D-A-CH-region, 2017 and 2023)

price level in Switzerland, the differences are mainly due to the different perception of cost elements (Fig. 6.3, left section). Swiss drivers integrate more fixed cost components into their cost estimates.

As the empirical study shows, although the cost of a car journey is a relevant decision criterion alongside other facets such as convenience, travel time, etc., it is difficult to quantify. The estimated cost of a car journey in Germany averages around 20 ct/km, with a very wide variation. The first thing to note here is that, as a rule, neither the out-of-pocket costs nor the full costs are used to estimate the costs. The pure fuel costs are estimated at approximately 6.5 ct/km (diesel) to 9 ct/km (petrol). If the estimated average costs of car use are compared with earlier surveys (e.g., values of approximately 18 cents/km were calculated for 2002; cf. Wilger 2004), there are only slight increases in the level, even in the longer term.

While this study deals with the question of whether fixed costs are also taken into account in addition to variable costs when deciding to use a car, the study by Andor et al. (2020) approaches the topic from a different angle, namely, the question of whether German consumers calculate all the costs of car ownership. The authors come to the conclusion that there is a considerable underestimation of the total costs. The average costs stated in their survey amount to €221 per month, which corresponds to 52% of the actual costs (full costs according to ADAC). While the costs for fuel were estimated correctly on average, the discrepancy between customer perception and actual costs is greatest for the cost component of depreciation. With an average performance of approximately 12,800 km, i.e., 1073 km per month, costs of 20.6 cents/km are calculated. Despite the different perspectives, the two studies resulted in similar costs per kilometer.

Firstly, it is important for the further discussion that consumers go well beyond the variable costs per kilometer in their cost perception and sometimes also include fixed costs in their calculations. However, this should not be equated with "unreasonable" behavior in the sense of the "sunk cost fallacy" (Krämer 2017). If 43% of car drivers in Switzerland include fixed costs for depreciation and replacement in their cost estimates, compared to just 13% in Germany, this is less an expression of the irrationality of Swiss consumers and more an expression of a more long-term view of car use. This is neither distorted nor irrational.

6.3.3   Cost Perception and Choice of Transportation with the BahnCard

The way the BahnCard works has long been explained by means of the sunk cost effect using the following narrative: Customers invest in the card, and these card fees are "sunk." They are no longer included in the choice of means of transportation. Consequently, only the reduced ticket price (e.g., 50% reduction) is relevant for the choice of means of transport, which is competitive with the costs of alternative means of transport. To explain the success of the BahnCard, Firner and Tacke (1993) describe that this brings rail pricing closer to that of the car (assumption: sunk costs, i.e., fixed costs, are not taken into account here either; however, this is refuted in the last Sect. 6.3.2). If the flex price is a known quantity, this means planning security for the customer with regard to the final price of the ticket, but not necessarily for the total expenditure for rail travel (Ding et al. 2005).

In the case of an isolated decision regarding the BahnCard 50, it can be estimated that the break-even point of the card is reached at around €458 annual revenue in flex price (second class, price 2021). In this case, the expenditure with BahnCard 50 (€229 for the card and €229 for tickets) is as high as the expenditure for non-discounted tickets at the flex price (€458). Assuming a price per km of €0.20 (flex price second class), this point is reached at 2290 km (or assuming an average distance of 350 km one way for approximately 3.3 trips). In reality, the calculation of the break-even point is not only made more difficult by the fact that instead of linear kilometer prices for DB long-distance transport, there are in fact relative prices (in addition, in recent years the flex price has varied depending on the day of travel) but also that the inclusion of the BahnCard 25 as an alternative to the BahnCard 50 means that the break-even point is reached later than in the isolated consideration of flex price without BahnCard 50 vs. possession of the BahnCard 50 and 50% discount on the flex price (Schmale et al. 2013).

By holding a BahnCard, rail customers have an incentive to shift journeys from other modes of transport to rail. Tacke formulates this as follows:

"... The ticket price is considered 'sunk costs'—they are gone. They no longer influence the customer's decision as to whether to travel by train or car.... each of these decisions is based on the 50% discount" (Tacke 2015). The success of the German Rail is therefore explained by the fact that the BahnCard mimics the cost structure of the car (Simon and Butscher 2001). The perceived prices (50% of the flex price in the case of the BahnCard 50) are at or below the variable costs of using a car and lead to a choice of means of transport in favor of rail. In fact, however, this "textbook" consumer behavior cannot be empirically proven in this form, on the contrary: Both BahnCard 50 are not the only ones to include the reduced ticket prices in their decision and price assessment; this is also the case for car users with regard to variable costs. From the decision-makers' perspective, fixed and quasi-fixed costs are partly included in the choice of means of transport and cost perception (Krämer 2016). And here, too, the question arises as to whether this can be equated with irrationality.

Obviously, other mechanisms such as pre-commitment, simplification processes, and the affinity to rail or the desire to use rail more in the future, which are rationally justifiable, or rather non-rational factors such as the overestimation of one's own travel volume and the desire not to have to pay the full flex price (DellaVigna and Malmendier 2006).

Having a BahnCard simplifies the choice of means of transport. This significantly reduces the number of perceived alternatives to rail, i.e., there is a stronger focus on rail as a means of transportation. The resulting shift in demand in turn leads to a higher rail modal share. The more trips the BahnCard holder shifts to rail, the sooner the BahnCard break-even point is reached and exceeded. In this case, the effective discount on the Bahn-Flexpreis increases with each rail journey. In the end, the BahnCard holder therefore undertakes significantly more journeys by rail

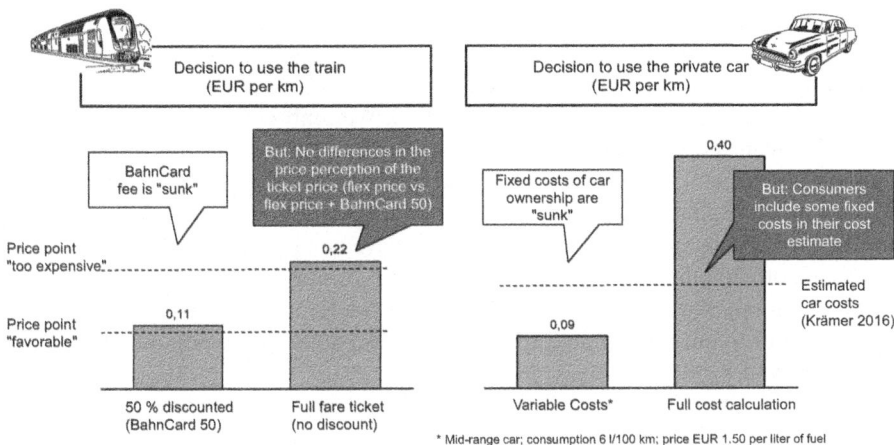

Fig. 6.4 Decision to use the train or your own car (Germany, 2021)

than in a situation without a BahnCard offer, albeit at a significantly lower price. By discounting the flex price, the ticket price in the case of the BahnCard 50 is around 10 cents/km and thus reaches a level at which consumers consider rail travel to be reasonably priced. Even if the card fees are included on a pro rata basis, rail fares appear more cost-effective than car travel (Fig. 6.4). This does not include other benefits such as better use of travel time and comfort aspects. There is indirect evidence that the BahnCard basic fee is taken into account in travelers' decision-making. If a BahnCard 50 holder is offered a ticket at €55 for a 500 km train journey (50% discount, 0.11 cents * 500 km), while a customer without a BahnCard pays €110 in the flex price (no discount, 0.22 cents * 500 km), it would be expected that the price assessment by the BahnCard 50 customer would be significantly better than for the traveler without a BahnCard (who is offered the undiscounted price and pays twice as high a price) without taking the sunk costs (card fee) into account. According to empirical studies, however, the price assessment is relatively similar in both cases (Krämer 2017). BahnCard ownership is associated with a kind of self-commitment, the desire to transfer a certain volume of mobility to rail.

Taking the card fees into account leads to an additional shift in demand in favor of rail, which at the same time has the effect that the costs per rail kilometer decrease with increasing mileage, meaning that the customer is better off than in a situation without BahnCard ownership.

In the case of the BahnCard 50, the additional demand generated in this way (additional traffic) can amount to between 30% and 35% of the rail travel volume. Corresponding rates were measured in the Mobility TRENDS 2018 study not only for the BahnCard 50, but also for the "sister products" of ÖBB (VORTEILSCARD, Austria) and SBB (Half-Fare travelcard, Switzerland) (Krämer 2018).

The survey results lead to the assumption that the willingness to commit plays a decisive role in explaining consumers' decisions. Axhausen et al. (2001) conclude that a model that includes the pre-commitments of travelers should be an essential part of any modeling. There are product or service categories—such as ordering online, using the train or owning and driving a car—where consumers want to pre-commit to a certain level of usage (Nunes 2000; Wertenbroch 1998).

As Fleischer (2001) states when explaining the decision-making process for a BahnCard, travelers cannot see far into the future at any time, so their decision on when to buy a BahnCard is made with a high degree of uncertainty. This can also explain why, on the one hand, sunk costs often have an influence on short-term decisions and, on the other, why this is not necessarily irrational.

The high popularity of research findings on behavioral economics leads to the impression in science and practice that human decisions are predominantly irrational (Bauer and Koth 2014).

This means that decision-making is strongly determined by heuristics and bias, which leads to misjudgments and inaccurate decisions. In this context, it is not intended to refute that there are situations in which poor (irrational) decisions are made due to the consideration of fixed costs. However, there are reasonable doubts that this should always be the case (Gigerenzer 2024).

As has been shown, situations are conceivable in which the consideration of previous investment decisions does not necessarily lead to irrational decisions. As McAfee et al. (2010) stated: "Although responding to sunk costs is rational in many situations, ignoring sunk costs is rational in other situations. According to our models, ignoring sunk costs is rational in any situation in which past investments are uninformative, reputational concerns are unimportant, and budget constraints do not matter." Based on our own empirical findings, the bounded rationality approach seems to be a good way of explaining decisions under uncertainty. It is important to emphasize that bounded rationality is not an inferior form of rationality, as Gigerenzer and Selten (2001) point out: "Theories of bounded rationality should not be confused with theories of irrational decision making."

6.4   Practical Example: The Cost Perspective in the Freemium Model Using the Example of Spotify

As the business models developed in the last 10 years in particular are characterized by a high level of fixed costs, the prominent example of Spotify will be examined in more detail below.

The history of Spotify is often told as a "rescue story" of how the music industry was rescued from a deep crisis that lasted almost a decade—a narrative that soon became part of the company's own storytelling. Back in 2009, 1 year after the company was founded, Spotify CEO Daniel Ek explained in an interview: "From the very beginning, our vision was to offer a legal music service that is as good or better than the pirate sites and gives users access to all the music in the world—for free."

In June 2016, Spotify was described as the "largest streaming platform in the world," with more than 100 million active monthly users. A year later, this figure had risen by a further 40 million; with more than 50 million subscribers, the company also overtook its closest rival Apple Music (Vonderau 2019). Spotify's enterprise value was valued at US$13 billion in 2017. This made Spotify the most highly valued venture capital-funded company in Europe. In May 2021, the market capitalization of the now listed company was around €35 billion (by Feb. 2022, it had fallen to around €29 billion, as of May 11, 2025, market capitalization is approximately $133 billion USD).

Spotify is not a pioneer in this respect. The very first music streaming service, Rhapsody, was launched back in late 2001, followed by a newly legitimized Napster in 2003, both of which had the same features that Spotify adopted 7 years later, namely, a flat monthly fee for unlimited access to streamed music, personalized playlists, and tailored recommendation mechanisms. In fact, at the time of Spotify's launch, Rhapsody's catalog was much larger than Spotify's, as it had distribution agreements with all five major music labels (Rayna and Striukova 2016). However, Rhapsody and Spotify's other predecessors lacked a decisive additional advantage, namely, the simple and mobile use of the streaming service. This was only made possible by the triumph of mobile devices.

Spotify's business model is based on the freemium revenue model, which provides a free service (limited) and a premium service that can be used as a subscription. In 2021, there were be around 365 million users compared to around 165 million subscribers (ntv 2021, rising to approximately 600 million in QI 2024, see Fig. 6.5). Maintaining the free offering is costly for the company, as it represents an investment to obtain future paid subscribers. The group of free users is the "breeding ground" for the recruitment of paid customers. The "for free" service is financed by advertising customers. A special service therefore consists of separating the attractiveness of the free and paid service in a way that is sufficiently noticeable for users. Finally, the free offer may also reduce users' willingness to pay for the

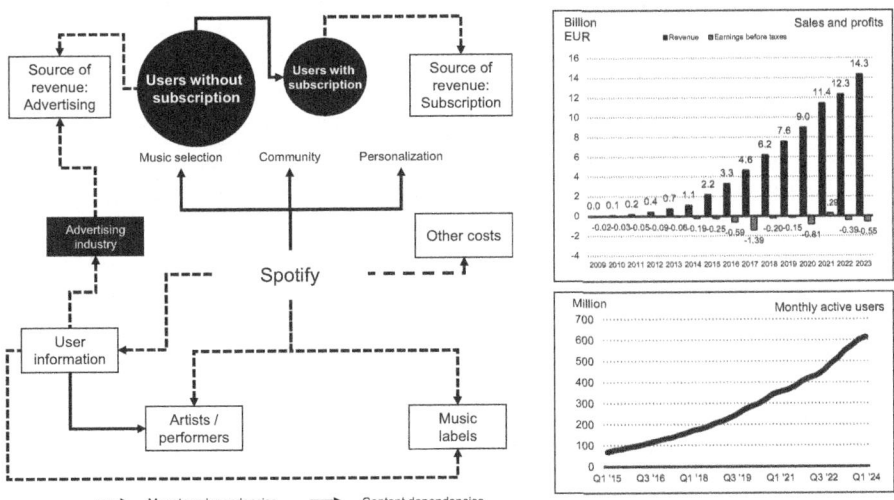

Fig. 6.5 Spotify's business model, profitability and user numbers

service if users find that the service satisfies their immediate needs and decide to choose the free offer (or to start further free trials in the future) instead of becoming paying subscribers. The subscription price must therefore not be set too high but must meet the willingness to pay for higher quality streams, more simultaneous streams, offline consumption, etc. Content owners (record labels, artists) usually have a large share of the revenue from distribution, which is their main source of profit. Ultimately, the various revenues must be sufficient in total to cover the costs of providing the service to paying and non-paying customers. Since Spotify does not control the rights to the music it provides on its platform, it must compensate copyright holders—including major and independent record labels—for each stream of each track. If music publishers are included, around 70% of Spotify's revenue goes directly to the rights holders (Fig. 6.5). Since, according to Prey (2020), it is unlikely that these rates will ever be significantly reduced through negotiations, it is imperative that Spotify reduces its dependence on content providers.

Although Spotify is often mentioned in the context of Netflix—Aversa et al. (2019) call them the best-known and most advanced digital distribution services to emerge in the last decade—there are significant differences between the companies and their strategies. One particularly relevant difference is pointed out by Fleischer (2021): Netflix never had the ambition to offer "everything," as is the case with Spotify with music.

In addition, Netflix began commissioning its own exclusive content early on, starting with "House of Cards" in 2013. Netflix also began putting a lot of effort into developing recommendation algorithms even before the launch of its streaming service in 2007, when the company was still distributing DVDs by post. Spotify did not do this until its "curatorial turnaround" in the mid-2010s. In the context of the topic of cost structure, it should be emphasized that, despite all similarities, Spotify remunerates its suppliers on a per-view basis, while Netflix either pays fixed fees for third-party series or produces its own series, the costs of which represent one-off expenses.

The fact that Spotify was unable to generate profits until 2024 despite its size and steady growth (Fig. 6.5) is often explained by the "Get Big Fast" business model (Crain 2014), which initially requires a strong focus on growth and economies of scale in order to shift the focus to generating profits once the market position has been secured (Prey 2020). This seems doubtful in the case of Spotify: the pay-per-stream approach means that license fees increase in line with revenue and, unlike other prominent platform operators such as Amazon or Netflix, no sufficient economies of scale can be achieved (Frohmann 2018). In order to ensure that the platform functions properly, the incentives for use must not only be sufficiently high for demand (users), but also for providers (musicians, labels).

Graf (2021) explains: "Anyone who is not signed to a label can expect to receive US\$0.0038 for a single stream. To earn the US minimum wage of US\$1472 per month, around 380,000 streams are required. The problem, however, is that the payouts to artists are very unevenly distributed. A very small proportion of artists account for 90 percent or more of the streams and therefore of Spotify's payouts." Nevertheless, Spotify achieved its first full year of profitability in 2024, reporting a net income of €1.14 billion, driven by a substantial growth in premium subscribers (reaching 263 million).

Companies in the rail transport sector have to deal with a different form of network effect, but one that is similar to digital platforms. In addition to some large state-owned companies, there are also private companies in Europe that offer their services. A precise understanding of the level of costs and their structure is of fundamental importance here. The Austrian-based company WESTbahn is one example.

The company Westbahn (full company name WESTbahn Management GmbH) is a railway company operating long-distance passenger transport between Vienna, Salzburg, and Munich or Bregenz. The company has been active on the market since December 2011, when it started operating on the route of the same name between Vienna and Salzburg.

A market entrant competing against a dominant company initially has a difficult time, as established companies often have enormous resources, brand awareness, and customer loyalty. Nevertheless, there are various strategies and opportunities that a newcomer can use to successfully assert itself. The example of Westbahn in Austria shows some important lessons for such market entrants.

Westbahn differentiated itself from the state-owned ÖBB (Austrian Federal Railways) by (1) offering new services and an improved customer experience (convenience, free Wi-Fi access, direct and regular connections, and a clear and user-friendly fare system); (2) pursuing a competitive pricing strategy and often offering cheaper tickets compared to ÖBB, especially at market launch; (3) responding more flexibly to market needs and being able to implement new ideas more quickly (e.g., the boarding procedure without traditional ticket controls, where passengers simply show their ticket to the on-board staff, or the cost-efficient focus on online sales); and (4) it implemented a clear differentiation strategy by positioning itself in Austria as a modern, citizen-oriented, and customer-friendly alternative to ÖBB, while at the same time focusing on profitable routes and foregoing less profitable routes.

In February 2024, WESTbahn management published data on the 2023 financial year (WESTbahn 2024), which is described as Rail Holding AG's highest-revenue financial year. A total of around 7.7 million passengers are reported (compared to 2022, this is expected to be an increase in passengers of around 34%). The preliminary figures for 2023 show a three-digit total turnover of over 120 million euros (+35 compared to the previous year). Profit is expected to be over 10 million euros. Exact figures will be published after the annual financial statements and the Annual General Meeting. WESTbahn also had big plans for 2024 as part of its growth and expansion offensive.

6.5   Interview WESTbahn Management GmbH, Thomas Posch

Question: If you had to briefly describe the positioning of WESTbahn, which characteristics of your company do you consider to be particularly relevant?

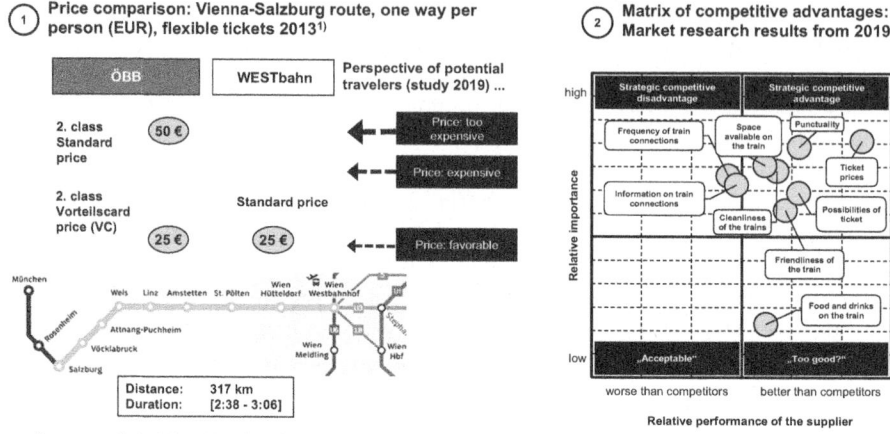

Fig. 6.6 WESTbahn: Price comparison ÖBB vs. WESTbahn for 2013 and Matrix of competitive advantages of WESTbahn (2019)

Thomas Posch: From its launch in December 2011 until spring 2022, WESTbahn operated exclusively domestic Austrian services on the Vienna–Salzburg route. In April 2022, the service was extended abroad for the first time with the line extension to Munich. In December 2022, a further service extension from Salzburg to Innsbruck was added, and in December 2023, Bregenz was added to the route network. In December 2024, the Vienna–Salzburg–Munich line will be extended to Stuttgart, marking WESTbahn's entry into the German domestic market.

In long-distance passenger rail transport, the incumbents ÖBB and DB are strong competitors. WESTbahn has a market share of around 50% on the core Vienna–Salzburg route and around 30% on the extensions to Innsbruck and Munich.

In addition to the competitors in rail transport, the car is almost exclusively relevant in intermodal competition. Only on the Vienna–Munich and, in the future, Vienna–Stuttgart routes air travel can be regarded as significant competitor.

Since its market launch, WESTbahn has tried to position itself through superior performance and low prices (Fig. 6.6). Fully flexible tickets were initially offered at around half the comparative price of ÖBB. The opportunities to achieve significant margins were limited, but the medium-term price image was consolidated in the market. At the same time, it succeeded in increasing the market (i.e., the number of train passengers). The low price appealed to price-sensitive demand that was not enthusiastic about the competitor ÖBB. A later study on the perception of WESTbahn then showed that, from the customer's point of view, we were superior to our rail competitor not only in terms of price, but also in a whole range of service facets. This was a starting point for aligning WESTbahn more strongly towards value-based pricing.

Another special feature of rail transportation in Austria is the Austrian Climate Ticket (KlimaTicket Österreich, KTÖ, introduced in 2021). The KTÖ is a discounted annual network ticket that costs €1095 per year for adults. It allows an unlimited number of journeys within a year with all transport association organizations (VVOGs) and railway companies (EVUs) in Austria, including the WESTbahn. Only tourist services are not covered by the KTÖ. The loss of revenue resulting from the subsidized KTÖ is compensated by the state on the basis of passenger kilometers traveled.

Question: What impact does the cost structure of a rail company have on pricing? Could you start by describing the basic cost structure in your company?

Thomas Posch: In order to be able to operate economically, a privately organized railway company must cover not only the variable costs, but also the fixed costs in the medium term. The variable costs are mainly made up of track access charges, energy costs, mileage-dependent maintenance costs, and personnel expenses. There are also vehicle costs and other operating expenses as (leap) fixed costs. The relative shares of the total costs vary depending on the network served, which is due to the significant difference in the level of the train path usage charge in Austria and Germany. While the charge in Austria is only around EUR 1.50 per train kilometer, this cost block is significantly higher in Germany on the routes served by WESTbahn, averaging EUR 10 per kilometer.

As capacities cannot be changed in the short term, they must be regarded as a fixed factor. In such a case, instruments such as revenue management play an important role. Partially dynamized pricing is intended to generate additional demand in phases with relatively low capacity utilization (for this purpose, discounted tickets with fare conditions such as train binding are offered), while in phases with very high capacity utilization, the sale of discounted tickets is restricted or completely prohibited. Instead, flexible-use tickets are then offered. However, by including seat reservations with every ticket (as long as seats are still available), even with flexible tickets a "voluntary" commitment of travelers to a specific train was indirectly achieved.

Question: What dependencies do you see in your business model between the parameters of price and fixed costs?

Thomas Posch: In pricing, it is often argued that variable costs alone are relevant for setting prices in the short term. It is understandable to assume that high fixed costs, e.g., for buildings or networks (such as rail or telecommunications), are irrelevant for decision-making ("sunk costs") because they cannot be influenced in the short term. In practice, however, there are dependencies between price and fixed costs in the following way. I would like to differentiate between two points in time:

- Situation A: The decision on future capacities is open: If timetables are defined or investment decisions in train material are made, then not only demand and capacity play a role, but also the understanding of the interactions between price, demand, and capacity utilization. The assumption regarding a certain realizable price level clearly also influences the decision regarding the planned capacity and even the fundamental question of whether a new service should be started at all or not.

- Situation B: Decisions on future capacities have been made: In this case, the question arises as to how well the capacity offered and the actual market demand can be reconciled. If the volume of demand for non-discounted tickets has been overestimated, an attempt can be made to stimulate demand via the price factor. In the past, WESTbahn has primarily relied on time-limited promotions without quotas and train commitments. In the meantime, however, it is mainly working with existing yield management products in order to minimize the risk of cannibalizing full-fare passengers.

Question: Is there a development path from cost- or competition-driven pricing to pricing in the sense of value-based pricing?

Thomas Posch: This is exactly the path that WESTbahn has taken in recent years: Especially after the end of the corona pandemic and the resulting recovery in demand, WESTbahn was able to use its superiority in terms of reliability and service orientation in its pricing. While competitors ÖBB and DB struggled with weaknesses in the areas of rolling stock, punctuality and staff availability, and vehicle capacities were sometimes massively exceeded, especially in Austria due to the KTÖ, WESTbahn's forward-looking capacity planning and the resulting vehicle fleet, which grew in line with the market, guaranteed that the high quality of the travel experience was maintained despite highly dynamic growth in demand. This in turn was the basis for a gradual increase in prices, whereby today the price level of competitors is even slightly exceeded in nominal terms on most routes (in each case on the basis of comparable discount options). However, due to the seat reservation included with every WESTbahn ticket, there is still a marginal price advantage for WESTbahn passengers when considering all price components of the competitors.

About the person:

DI Thomas Posch

Managing Director, WESTbahn Management GmbH

Spokesman of the Board Rail Holding AG

After studying spatial planning at the Vienna University of Technology, Thomas Posch held various positions within the ÖBB Group from 1997, where he was responsible for the design of ÖBB's national and international long-distance transport services for several years. He then worked as Head of Services and Network Development at the international rail alliance Railteam in Amsterdam before taking over the sales and marketing agendas at WESTbahn as Chief Commercial Officer in June 2013. He has been Managing Director of WESTbahn and Spokesman of the Board of Rail Holding since March 2022.

6.6   Outlook

The relevant costs of customer value orientation are decision-relevant costs that form a business cost category. These are costs that arise during a realized alternative course of action (building, maintaining, winning back a customer relationship). Relevant costs cannot be defined in absolute terms, as they are determined by the respective context in which the decision is made. Understanding costs correctly and classifying the perception of costs from the perspective of consumers and companies is an essential cornerstone of customer value-oriented cost management. In economics textbooks, there is a paradigm that only the variable costs in the sense of marginal costs should be taken into account when making short-term decisions.

If this is not observed, and fixed costs (sunk costs) are included in the decision, distortions of perception are assumed, resulting in irrational decisions.

As has been shown, examples can be found in which sunk costs by companies or consumers can be considered relevant to decision-making. Mc Afee et al. state: "Contrary to conventional wisdom, we argue that, in a broad range of situations, it is rational for people to condition behavior on sunk costs, because of informational content, reputational concerns, or financial and time constraints. Once all the elements of the decision-making environment are taken into account, reacting to sunk costs can often be understood as rational behavior." Unfortunately, corresponding states are hardly ever included in the discussion on behavioral economics.

Taking fixed costs into account when making marketing decisions is not only recommended from a long-term perspective. Consideration is also often useful for short-term decisions; however, recognizing this requires a dynamic analysis of the interactions between price, costs, and customer value. One aspect of this is the need for management to understand its own cost situation as well as possibly to arrive at an optimal pricing model on this basis. As the example of Spotify shows, the freemium revenue model is attractive from the user's point of view. The limited revenue per month due to the subscription is problematic if the costs cannot be controlled (the perceived value for the customer increases with the number of music tracks accessed). Active cost management therefore becomes a critical success factor in the Spotify case study discussed.

References

Al-Najjar NI, Baliga S, Besanko D (2005) The sunk cost bias and managerial pricing practices. CSIO Working Paper, No. 0076, Northwestern University, Center for the Study of Industrial Organization (CSIO), Evanston

Andor MA, Gerster A, Gillingham KT, Horvath M (2020) Running a car costs much more than people think – stalling the uptake of green travel. Nature 580:453–455

Arkes H, Blumer C (1985) The psychology of sunk cost. Organ Behav Hum Decis Process 35:124–140

Aversa P, Hervas-Drane A, Evenou M (2019) Business model responses to digital piracy. Calif Manage Rev 61(2):30–58

Axhausen KW, Simma A, Golob T (2001) Pre-commitment and usage: season tickets, cars and travel. European Research in Regional Science 11:101–110

Anderson PL (2024) Cars, costs and cognitive dissonance. Business Economics 59(4):258-274

Bauer F, Koth H (2014) Der unvernünftige Kunde: mit Behavioral Economics irrationale Entscheidungen verstehen und beeinflussen. Redline Wirtschaft

Bendle NT, Bagga CK (2016) The metrics that marketers muddle. MIT Sloan Manag Rev 57(3):73–82

Blattberg RC, Kim BD, Neslin SA (2008) Issues in computing customer lifetime value. Database marketing: analyzing and managing customers, p 133–159

Burgartz T (2018) Kennzahlengestütztes Customer Value Controlling. In: von Wiesehahn A, Kißler M (eds) Erfolgreiches Controlling Theorie Praxis und Perspektiven. Nomos, Baden-Baden, pp 235–248

Coenenberg A, Fischer T, Günther T (2016) Kostenrechnung und Kostenanalyse, 9. Aufl. Schäffer-Poeschel, Stuttgart

Crain M (2014) Financial markets and online advertising: reevaluating the dotcom investment bubble. Inf Commun Soc 17(3):371–384

Davila A, Wouters M (2004) Designing cost-competitive technology products through cost management. Account Horiz 18(1):13–26

DellaVigna S, Malmendier U (2006) Paying not to go to the gym. Amer Econ Rev 96(3):694–719

Ding L, Xin C, Chen J (2005) A risk-reward competitive analysis of the Bahncard problem. In: van der Aalst WMP et al (eds) International Conference on Algorithmic Applications in Management. Springer, Berlin, pp 37–45. June

Drucker P (1993) The five deadly business sins. Wall Street J 21:A18

Ewert R, Wagenhofer A (2014) Interne Unternehmensrechnung, 8. Aufl. Springer, Berlin

Firner H, Tacke G (1993) BahnCard: Kreative Preisstruktur. Absatzwirtschaft 36(5):66–70

Fleischer R (2001) On the BahnCard problem. Theoret Comput Sci 268(1):161–174

Fleischer R (2021) Universal Spotification? The shifting meanings of "Spotify" as a model for the media industries. Pop Commun 19(1):14–25

Frohmann F (2018) Digitales pricing. Springer Gabler, Wiesbaden

Gigerenzer G, Selten R (2001) Rethinking rationality. Bounded rationality: the adaptive toolbox 1:1–12

Götze U (2010) Kostenrechnung und Kostenmanagement, 5. Aufl. Springer, Berlin Heidelberg

Graf RLY (2021) Streamingdienste und Umbrüche in der Musikindustrie, Universität Leipzig

Graumann M (2017) Kostenrechnung und Kostenmanagement, 6. Aufl. nwb, Verlag Neue Wirtschafts-Briefe, Wiesbaden

Grubb M (2015) Failing to choose the best price: theory, evidence, and policy. Rev Industrial Organ 47:303–340

Guilding C, Drury C, Tayles M (2005) An empirical investigation of the importance of cost-plus pricing. Manag Audit J 20(2):125–137

Gigerenzer G (2024) The rationality wars: a personal reflection. Behavioural Public Policy :1–21

Hammond JS, Keeney RL, Raiffa H (1998) The hidden traps in decision making. Harv Bus Rev 76(5):47–58

Hansen DR, Mowen MM, Guan L (2007) Cost management – accounting & control, 6. Aufl. South-Western Cengage Learning, Mason, MI

Houdek P (2016) A perspective on consumers 3.0: they are not better decision-makers than previous generations. Front Psyc 7:848

Kelly T (2004) Sunk costs, rationality, and acting for the sake of the past. Noûs 38(1):60–85

Kilger W (2012) Einführung in die Kostenrechnung. Springer, Wiesbaden

Krämer A (2016) Kostenwahrnehmung bei PKW-Reisen – Empirische Analyse zur Schätzung der PKW-Kosten und der wahrgenommenen Kostenkomponenten bei Autofahrern im DACHGebiet. Internationales Verkehrswesen 68(4):16–19

Krämer A (2017) Demystifying the "Sunk Cost Fallacy": when considering fixed costs in decision-making is reasonable. J Res Mark 7(1):510–517

Krämer A (2018) Wirkungsweise der BahnCard aus Kunden- und Unternehmenssicht. Internationales Verkehrswesen 70(3):16–19

Krämer A, Beger F (2017) Die Rolle des Vertriebsteams bei der Umsetzung von Konditionensystemen. Sales Excell 26(6):78–85

Kremin-Buch B (2007) Strategisches Kostenmanagement: Grundlagen und moderne Instrumente. Gabler, Wiesbaden

Lücke W (1997) Einheitskalkulation, Einflußgrößenrechnung und Prozeßkostenrechnung. In: Freidank CC, Götze U, Huch B, Weber J (eds) Kostenmanagement – Aktuelle Konzepte und Anwendungen, Berlin, pp 121–140

Laird RA, Sherratt TN. (2010) The economics of evolution: Henry Ford and the Model T. Oikos 119(1):3-9

Männel W (2005) Kostencontrolling und Kostenmanagement. Lauf an der Pegnitz. Verl. der GAB, Ges. für Angewandte Betriebswirtschaft

McAfee RP, Mialon HM, Mialon SH (2010) Do sunk costs matter? Econ Inq 48(2):323–336

Nunes J (2000) A cognitive model of people's usage estimations. J Mark Res 37(November):397–409

Ntv (2021) Spotifys Europachef im Interview "Empfehlungen sind ein Luxusgut". https://www.n-tv.de/wirtschaft/Empfehlungen-sind-ein-Luxusgut-article22810636.html. Accessed 5 Oct 2021

Oecking G (1997) Fixkostenmanagement bei wechselnden Marktverhältnissen. In: Freidank CC, Götze U, Huch B, Weber J (eds) Kostenmanagement – Aktuelle Konzepte und Anwendungen. Springer, Berlin, pp 175–194

Prey R (2020) Locating power in platformization: music streaming playlists and curatorial power. Soc Med + Soc 6(2):1–11

Raubenheimer H (2010) Kostenmanagement im Outsourcing von Logistikleistungen. Gabler Verlag, Wiesbaden

Rayna T, Striukova L (2016) 360°Business model innovation: toward an integrated view of business model innovation: an integrated, value-based view of a business model can provide insight into potential areas for business model innovation. Res Technol Manag 59(3):21–28

Reichmann T, Kißler M, Baumöl U (2017) Controlling mit Kennzahlen – Die systemgestützte Controlling-Konzeption, 9. Aufl. München

Schmale H, Ehrmann T, Dilger A (2013) Buying without using–biases of German BahnCard buyers. Appl Econ 45(7):933–941

Simon H, Butscher SA (2001) Individualized pricing: boosting profitability with the higher art of power pricing. Eur Manag J 19(2):109–114

Steger J (2010) Kosten- und Leistungsrechnung: Einführung in das betriebliche Rechnungswesen, Grundlagen der Vollkosten-, Teilkosten-, Plankosten- und Prozesskostenrechnung. Oldenbourg, München

Stelling JN (2005) Kostenmanagement und Controlling, 2. Aufl. Oldenbourg, München

Stibbe R (2009) Kostenmanagement: Methoden und Instrumente, 3. Aufl. München

Tacke G (2015) "Durch Zwei teilen kann jeder", Interview in der TAZ, 13.3.2015. http://www.taz.de/!5017032/

Thaler R (1980) Toward a positive theory of consumer choice. J Econ Behav Organ 1(1):39–60

Thaler RH, Sunstein CR (2009) Nudge: improving decisions about health, wealth, and happiness. Penguin, London

Ulrich H (2001) Anleitung zum ganzheitlichen Denken und Handeln: Ein Brevier für Führungskräfte, 3. Aufl, Bern

Vonderau P (2019) The spotify effect: digital distribution and financial growth. Television & New Media 20(1):3–19

Weber J, Steven M (2014) Fixe Kosten, in Springer Gabler Verlag (Hrsg.): Gabler Wirtschaftslexikon. http://wirtschaftslexikon.gabler.de/Archiv/1288/fixe-kosten-v9.html. Accessed 19 Mar 2014

Weber J, Weißenberger BE (2015) Einführung in das Rechnungswesen: Bilanzierung und Kostenrechnung, 9. Aufl. Schäffer-Poeschel, Stuttgart

Wertenbroch K (1998) Consumption self-control via purchase quantity rationing. Mark Sci 18(4):317–337

WESTbahn (2024) Umsatzstärkstes Jahr in der Geschichte der WESTbahn. Nahverkehrspraxis
    v. 1.2.2024, https://www.nahverkehrspraxis.de/umsatzstaerkstes-jahr-in-der-geschichte-der-
    westbahn/. Accessed 2 June 2024
Wilger G (2004) Mehrpersonenpreisdifferenzierung. Diss. DUV, Wiesbaden
Wilger G, Krämer A (2025) Signaling gegenüber Wettbewerbern–Erkennen und Verhindern von
    Preiswettbewerb und „Preiskrieg ". In: Preiskommunikation: Strategische Herausforderungen
    und innovative Anwendungsfelder, Springer Fachmedien Wiesbaden, p. 141–163

Part III

The Value-to-Value Perspective (Networked Value Perspectives)

Customer Value: From ABC Analysis to Customer Lifetime Value (CLV)

7

7.1 The Different Aspects of Customer Value from the Company's Perspective

Customer value can have different meanings to different firms. Therefore, it is worth taking a moment to clarify its usage here.

7.1.1 Customer Value as a Central Parameter for Sales and Corporate Management

"There are three kinds of lies: lies, damned lies and statistics."—Mark Twain

Numbers and statistics can always be used in an improper, manipulative, or deliberately false way in a certain context. Mark Twain exaggerates this connection when he equates lies and statistics. Ultimately, it is important to interpret existing statistics correctly and include them in a balanced context with other decision-relevant considerations. The fundamental criticism of statistics also applies to the assessment of customer value. Two perspectives are anchored in the concept of customer value, both of which deeply impact company success.

Firstly, it is the value that the provision of products and services generates for customers. In this context, the term "value-to-the-customer" is also used, calculated as the value perceived by the customer minus the price paid. When making a rational decision, the customer selects the option that offers the best ratio of value and price in comparison to an alternative offer, i.e., the option with the greatest net benefit for the buyer (Dolan and Gourville 2009).

Secondly, customer value includes the perspective of value generation for the company, also referred to as "value of the customer." The focus here is on how much value the individual customer generates for the organization. The idea that marketing and corporate management should be concerned with the profitability of

© The Author(s), under exclusive license to Springer Nature Switzerland AG 2025   153
A. Krämer et al., *Customer Value-centered Management*, Future of Business and
Finance, https://doi.org/10.1007/978-3-031-90497-4_7

individual customers is not new. As early as the mid-1940s, Sevin (1947) presented a method for calculating the profitability of an individual customer by assigning functional cost groups to specific customers and deducting them from the customer's annual turnover. The reason given for this was, as the Pareto Principal points out, the unequal distribution of sales and profits per customer:

> In many businesses a large number of customers... may bring in only a minor proportion of the sales.

Recently, however, the topic has been taken up with renewed vigor, as advances in data collection and database technology make it possible to record and analyze not only the accounts of individual large corporate customers, but also the purchase history of households, i.e., a large number of individual customers. The prerequisite for this is a customer-centric approach on the part of the company. In the most modern understanding, individual customer analysis goes beyond the calculation of the profitability of a single year and includes the forecast of the profit stream attributable to the customer and the calculation of a discounted present value. The value that a customer generates for a company is considered over the entire lifetime of the customer relationship. In this case, the term Customer Lifetime Value (CLV) is also used. What at first glance appears to be a rather academic exercise ultimately leads to a view of the individual customer relationship that can have lasting impact on corporate decisions. In extreme cases, this can lead to a firm actively seeking to terminate the customer relationship. For example, Shin et al. (2012) propose customer cost-based pricing in order to eliminate unprofitable customers. Managers who, over the past 30 years, have adopted the maxim "Zero Customer Defection," i.e., doing everything possible to prevent customer churn (Reichheld and Sasser 1990), may seem counterintuitive at first.

However, in a specific situation it seems rational to terminate a customer relationship if (1) the CLV is negative and (2) there is no chance to improve economically and (3) the customer has no strategic value for the company.

7.1.2   Customer Value: Claim and Reality

Since the beginning of the millennium, companies have been paying increasing attention to customer value management (CVM). In their seminal article in the Harvard Business Review, Rust et al. (2004b) suggest that companies should abandon the conventional wisdom of investing in brand equity in the hope that sales will follow. Instead, they should focus on customer equity ("the net profit a company accrues from transactions with a given customer during the time that the customer has a relationship with the company"). Through customer-centric management systems, companies seek to maximize customer value and, ultimately, company value. This can happen under particular conditions, namely, if:

1. Value orientation is used to improve company performance.
2. Management processes are customer-driven rather than IT-driven.
3. Customer Lifetime Value is a key performance indicator.
4. Companies invest in analytical skills.
5. The key factors of customer acquisition, customer retention, and customer expansion are understood.
6. Companies manage sales channels in such a way that added value is created for the customer (Verhoef and Lemon 2013).

Malthouse and Mulhern (2008) establish the following causal chain in this context:

Customer Loyalty → Buying Behavior → Customer Value → Firm Performance

The starting point of the connection is customer loyalty. Loyalty can refer to a company or a brand but equally means the loyalty of a consumer. The term brand loyalty is used more in the consumer goods industry or in sectors in which purchases are made over a longer period of time as relatively independent transactions. Customer loyalty tends to be used in sectors such as services (travel or credit cards) and in contractual purchasing situations, such as telecommunications or fitness studios.

Calculating customer value requires a considerable amount of information, especially when companies have a broad product portfolio and many customers. To obtain a truly comprehensive picture of customer-relevant data, the specialist departments of marketing, sales, controlling, and market research must be involved. This may explain the gap between the importance of customer value calculation from a scientific perspective and its practical application. In a study on the marketing controlling methods used in the early 2000s, only 7% of companies stated that they regularly carried out such (customer value) analyses (Reinecke and Tomczak 2001).

Almost three quarters of the larger companies surveyed did not use customer value analysis at all. At the same time, marketing science describes this study as particularly important. This early assessment was confirmed a decade later by Bruhn (2013) and Mengen (2011). In conclusion, in corporate practice, the measurement of customer value is not prioritized as much as value-based management requires. Even more recent surveys, for example, from the insurance industry, one a wide range of market and customer information, show far-reaching deficits with regard to customer value calculations. Zur Horst (2021) explains: "Many insurers are currently unable to really answer the question of customer value. However, this is a key to managing sales and use discounts in a more targeted manner, for example. Instead, high base discounts are often granted on the tariff prices—these thwart intelligent pricing."

If customer value management is placed at the center of corporate action in the following, several questions arise, starting with what customer value means and how it can be operationalized.

7.2   Prioritizing Customers and Sales Activities: Theory and Practice

7.2.1   Forms of Determining Customer Value from the Company's Perspective

As shown, a key figure such as customer value has a right to exist if it supports management decisions and can therefore increase the value of the company. To manage sales activities, for example, different structures and classifications are available, each of which entails a graduated degree of complexity (see Fig. 7.1). The following primarily discusses instruments that are based on quantitative variables such as turnover and profit:

- In the simplest case, customers should be classified according to their sales class and designated as A, B, or C customers. This classification is easy to carry out, whereby the class boundaries can be set on a company-specific basis. This procedure is not only easy to determine, but also simple to understand, intuitively appealing, and communicable for all parties involved.
- The contribution margin or profit calculation per customer is more complex. In this case, not only all revenues from the customer relationship must be determined over time, but also the costs. The more detailed the cost allocation, the more meaningful the target value will be. At the same time, the more heterogeneous the customer's cost structure, the more likely it is that a pure revenue perspective will reach its limits or lose its informative value.

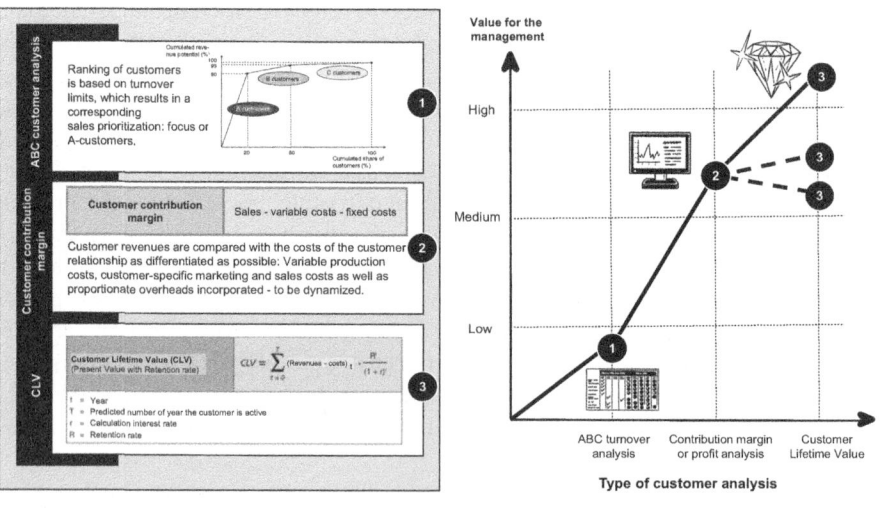

Note: Images used with the permission of simpleshow

Fig. 7.1 Selected approaches for determining customer value and value for management

- The preferred method in science and literature is the CLV. This involves dynamizing the contribution margin calculation and applying it to a "lifetime of the customer." The individual annual values of the revenue surpluses are discounted or compounded to 1 year so that they are comparable. In addition, a customer-specific shelf life can be taken into account by including a churn rate.

ABC analysis, the customer contribution margin calculation and the Customer Lifetime Value method are characterized by close integration with operational accounting. In addition, further estimates are required for the CLV (e.g., determination of the observation period, forecast of churn rates, determination of the internal rate of return). At this point, it should be noted that the literature sometimes distinguishes between customer equity and CLV. Jasek et al. (2018), for example, cite what they consider to be the generally accepted definition of CLV: "CLV is the present value of future net cash flows associated with a particular customer" and refer to Fader (2012). Customer equity is understood to be the sum of the CLV of existing and potential customers on the one hand and in some cases the average CLV less customer acquisition costs on the other (Estrella-Ramón et al. 2013). In the further discussion, it is strongly recommended that the costs attributable to the customer relationship are always considered. For the sake of completeness, it should be noted that there are other methods of determining customer value that are not discussed in detail here. These can be RFM methods (the letters stand for Recency of Last Purchase, Frequency of Purchases, Monetary Value) or scoring methods (Mengen 2009). Non-monetary aspects such as strategic importance (dependency, joint innovation management, etc.) or customer loyalty (satisfaction, commitment) can also be integrated into scoring methods (Tewes 2013).

In the literature, CLV is discussed as one—if not the most important—customer-oriented key figure. It usually considers the net present value of all future profits that can be generated by a customer over their lifetime with the company. It is also argued that the customer value can replace the product-oriented key figures frequently used by companies, such as market share, which is normally defined at product-market level. The focus on market share is determined by the desire to gain a large slice of the overall "pie." The assumption here is that larger market shares can lead to economies of scale, greater market power, and higher profits (Szymanski et al. 1993). However, this approach can have a fundamental disadvantage and lead to inefficiencies if product-oriented key figures are incorrectly optimized. If managers are encouraged to achieve sales targets in a specific product or service category, this can be achieved through the use of sales promotions or price reductions, with corresponding temporary shifts in sales.

In the medium term, however, sales promotions can increase consumers' price sensitivity and undermine customer loyalty. The development of the US automotive industry from 2005 onward is a good example of this: Although sales increased in the short term because several US car manufacturers carried out aggressive sales promotions, the continuation of these measures led to ruin (Pauwels et al. 2009). Another example is the sales promotions of the German DIY store Praktiker ("20% off everything ..."), which initially achieved positive sales successes, but the transfer of temporary discounts (promotions) to regular operations later led to extreme margin problems and ultimately to the company's insolvency.

The strong and clear scientific preference for the CLV approach is initially plausible and understandable, as all important parameters that influence the value of the customer relationship are taken into account in the calculation. The claim of completeness or a 360-degree perspective is fulfilled. As a consequence, this results in a key figure that not only illustrates the efficiency and effectiveness of the company in aggregated form, but also the operational management of the company, e.g., sales and marketing activities. However, the CLV concept has not yet established itself as a standard approach in practice. Empirical studies even show that many companies do not use the CLV concept when categorizing sales, having remained stagnant at the A, B, and C customer categorization stage. If more complex approaches are implemented, this generally results in better control options for management but also increases the complexity of the calculation and thus the internal effort. This is particularly the case with CLV. For example, Krämer and Bongaerts (2023) show in their empirical analysis that CLV does not play an important role in the ranking of customer-related key figures for German companies. The analysts at ZETA (2024) come to similar conclusions: "While most organizations collect data around CLV, it isn't being shared and used in strategic decision-making".

At this point, the importance of customer data and the ability of companies to accurately map internal and external data to a customer cannot be emphasized enough. Even in a world in which the possibilities of big data (Chap. 3), sales automation, and personalization of products and services (and prices) are being discussed (Chap. 8), many companies still have a—sometimes extreme—need for information. For example, Leeflang et al. (2014) find that data-driven customer insights are gaining the most traction in subscription businesses such as financial, high-tech, and telecommunications companies. They note that over 80% of companies in their survey (777 marketing managers worldwide) still do not have granular customer data. According to the managers surveyed, this only applies to 18% of companies. These companies are in a position to combine different data in such a way that a clear customer view is possible ("single customer view"). Only when this challenge has been mastered do the potential benefits of information coding become apparent. The most important benefits that companies hope to gain from analyzing customer data include (1) that this data will enable them to increase sales (43% of all companies), (2) that it will lead to more active management of innovations, and (3) that it will enable them to improve the quality of their products and services (28%) and stronger customer loyalty can be achieved—also by greater brand loyalty (42%).

The use of customer data will therefore not only become a bottleneck factor for companies at the interface to the customer in the future, but also in the management of the company or company management.

7.2.2   Hurdles in Implementing the CLV Approach

While textbooks consistently emphasize the superiority of the CLV approach to measuring customer value, implementation in corporate practice faces several hurdles:

- Providing different customer data at an individual level and calculating it using a complex formula is still the smallest challenge. However, this information also needs to be converted into a consistent, complete, and up-to-date form. A distinction must be made between different types of data (Reimer and Becker 2011). Basic information, such as age, gender, income, and level of education, is relatively easy to collect and therefore readily available to many companies and is mainly used by companies to segment the customer base or as control variables and not as descriptive variables. Information about customer behavior is more meaningful. For example, purchase data, i.e., information about purchase times (recency), purchase frequency, and turnover (monetary value), often significantly influence the target figures in all phases of the customer life cycle. It is advisable to differentiate between existing customers (at least one purchase in a defined period) and potential customers. Purchase data can only be collected for existing customers. Action and reaction data can also be recorded for potential customers and interested parties.
- While all the information required for the purchase is available directly to firms, the situation is different for their customers' transactions with competing firms.
- Empirical studies show a considerable information deficit in this respect (Du et al. 2007). To ensure a complete understanding of the customer, a 360-degree view is required. Firstly, the volume that customers transact within a company correlates poorly with the volume they transact with the company's competitors (i.e., actual sales are a poor indicator of potential sales) and secondly, a small percentage of customers often account for a large proportion of all external transactions (equating to significant potential to increase sales). Against this backdrop, the effectiveness of a targeted customer management depends on being able to estimate the "share of wallet" of your own customers accurately.
- It is therefore advisable to take an outward-looking approach to customer relationship management in order to supplement companies' internal records and databases with insights into their customers' relationships with competing companies. This requires, for example, the active involvement of the sales team and external information (Krämer and Burgartz 2020).
- If the CLV are calculated for a longer period, assumptions or forecasts about future income and costs per company are required. In times of VUCA market conditions (Volatility, Uncertainty, Complexity, and Ambiguity), this approach easily reaches its limits (Mack et al. 2015). It is all too easy for the impression of "fictitious accuracy" to become entrenched, which is often the beginning of declining acceptance among employees and managers. Mengen (2009) explains: "The models for calculating future cash inflows and outflows in particular can become very complex. Then the comprehensibility for the user is limited."

However, a lack of comprehensibility is the first step toward a lack of acceptance. If employees do not understand how a customer value parameter is calculated, this leads to a loss of confidence in the significance of the performance indicator. This sets off a "vicious circle," at the end of which customer value no longer plays a role as a point of orientation and guiding principle.

- The challenges for the operational and organizational departments are even greater. Implementation: In accordance with the requirement "Maximize (Don't Just Measure) CLV," the parameter becomes the central control variable in the company, in all areas (Bell et al. 2002). The individual operational decisions are ultimately measured by the extent to which they contribute to an increase in the CLV of individual customers or customer segments. The customer value, calculated as CLV, therefore not only contains an information value, but also concrete instructions for action and becomes the central control parameter for value-oriented sales management, among other things. However, this must firstly be achievable with reasonable means and secondly be intentional.

Figure 7.2 shows the areas in which customer value plays a role in the company and also defines the step sequences in order to limit complexity. Within the "House of CRM," customer value plays an important role in the corporate strategy and the orientation of customer management. In the strategic guidelines, a decision must be made as to which customer value model should be used. This can be the CLV, for example. Customer intelligence is responsible for providing up-to-date information on the customer relationship (including information on customer value). The CLV can be used both in transaction management (customers are directed at the company) and in loyalty management (the company is directed at specific or all customers).

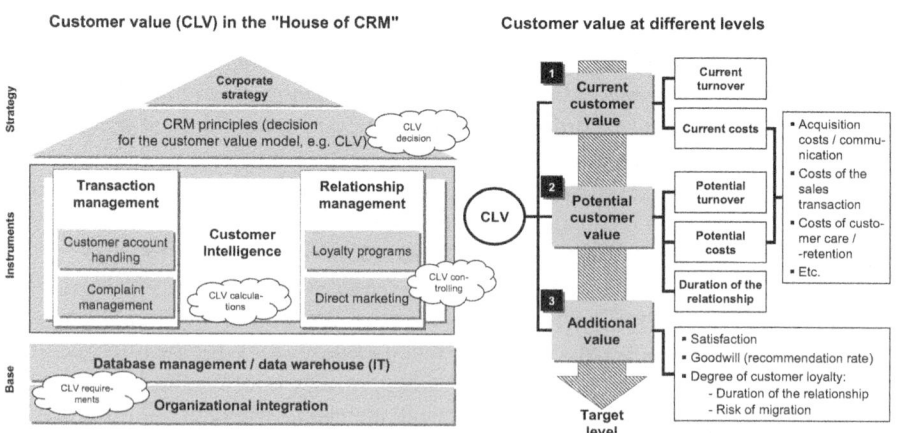

Fig. 7.2 Customer value: anchoring in the organization and modeling steps

In addition to these organizational aspects, it must be ensured that the customer value can be validly and currently determined as a control parameter. Therefore, the necessary prerequisites must be created, e.g., for efficient data management. In addition, the modeling of customer value should not be understood as a static "one-off action," but as a continuous process.

7.2.3   Customer Contribution Margin as a "Must-Have"

However, the major implementation challenges should not lead to a situation where, in the event of the perceived unfeasibility of CLV measurement, a "relapse" to revenue-based customer categorization occurs. The transition from a sales perspective to a profit perspective is a "must" for strategic and operational customer management. The background to this is that a pure sales perspective often obscures the relevance of individual customers for the company's success. An example of this is illustrated in Fig. 7.3. Since, for example, sales, service, and marketing costs are highly dispersed or the sales prices realized per unit sold are distributed unevenly and inconsistently across customers, the customer profit and loss account show very profitable cases outside the group of A customers on the one hand and customers whose costs are not covered by revenues on the other.

In the case of prioritization according to turnover, the management's attention would be focused primarily on the A customers. The five customers with the highest turnover account for 40% of total turnover. Only the consistent and stringent allocation of costs to the level of individual customers creates sufficient transparency and forms the basis for prioritizing customers and alternative courses of action. It is also important to recognize that individual customers are negative in terms of their customer value (Blattberg and Deighton 1996). The consequence: the cumulative profit

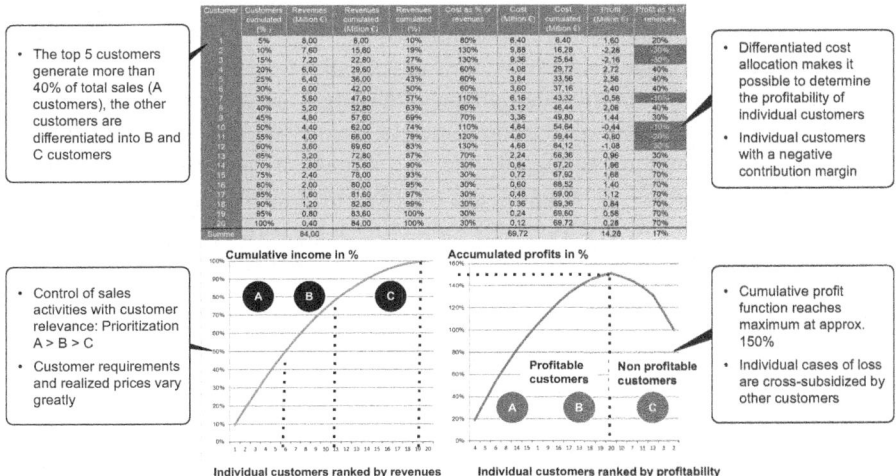

Fig. 7.3 Example calculation of cumulative sales and profits by customer

function first increases, reaches a maximum at more than 100% of the current profit level, and then decreases again (if customers with negative profitability are included).

Overall, a profit is made, but negative contributions are subsidized by positive contributions from other customers. By concentrating on profitable customers, not only can profit be increased, but expenses can also be reduced. The entire customer service could be geared more toward needs and value at the same time. However, these relationships can only be presented transparently if a customer-specific income statement is available.

7.2.4 High Fixed Costs: When Are Costs Actually "Sunk Costs"?

The company's overheads and fixed costs present a particular challenge when allocating costs. In simplified terms, it is often assumed that high fixed costs, for example, costs for buildings or networks (such as rail or telecommunications) are irrelevant to decisions ("sunk costs") because they cannot be influenced in the short term. The connection is particularly serious in the so-called sunk cost fallacy, which is frequently addressed in the context of behavioral science. In a nutshell, this states that when making decisions, people include investments that have already been made as a point of reference in further decisions (although these should not be relevant to the decision) and this then leads to wrong decisions (Krämer 2017). Caution is required with this interpretation, as the example of building costs for hotels shows: While real estate costs are "sunk" for short-term decisions, they take on a variable character over a horizon that enables real estate franchising and leasing. Other authors even go so far as to completely ignore the costs of customer acquisition when calculating the CLV. This is also justified with supposed "sunk costs" (Bendle and Bagga 2016). On closer inspection, these arguments turn out to be grossly negligent. This procedure leads to a fragmented customer-cost perspective. In contrast, the aim should be to allocate all costs incurred to existing customer relationships as comprehensively as possible.

If the costs and complexity of providing and calculating data appear too high for the individual company or the uncertainties in the future are great that the CLV cannot be calculated, there are still opportunities to identify and prioritize the options for action for sales and marketing. To this end, it makes sense not only to classify the individual customers in terms of their current profitability, but also to assess whether an improvement in customer profitability is possible with adequate measures (i.e., from a cost-benefit perspective). Both perspectives can be summarized in a customer development portfolio (Fig. 7.4).

On the one hand, short-term negative profitability is not necessarily a problem if this situation can be improved through targeted measures. However, if this is not the case, it is time to consider terminating the business relationship. On the other hand, the need for action is low if customer relationships are robustly profitable but there are no clear indications of an increase in customer value (increase in customer

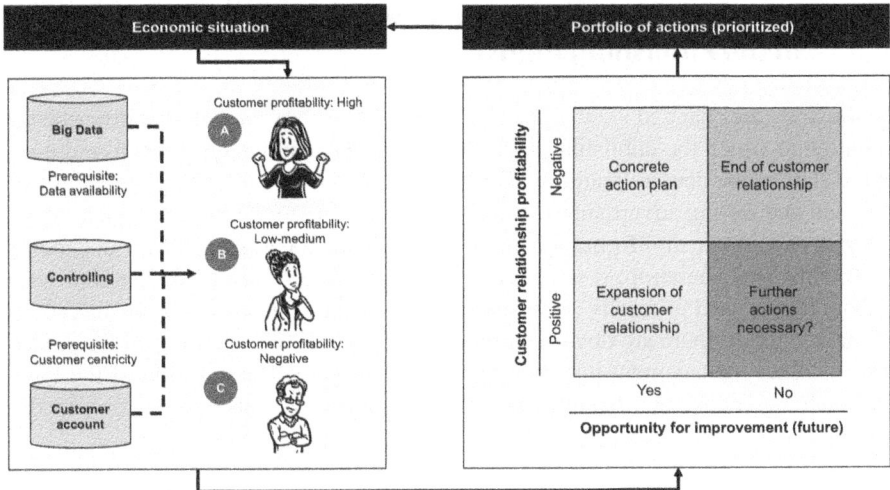

Note: Images used with the permission of simpleshow

Fig. 7.4 View of the profitability of customer relationships as a continuous process

loyalty, reduction in costs, increase in revenue, etc.) The portfolio of actions derived from this classification in turn has consequences for the perceived value of the service offered from the customer's perspective. For example, if companies generate a high perceived value from the customer's perspective by offering low prices, this is usually at the expense of profit and therefore customer value or shareholder value. If, for example, a decision is made to raise prices due to a problematic earnings situation in individual customer segments or to increase specific costs in sales, marketing, or service, the net benefit for the customer changes.

In addition, a decision-oriented assessment of customer value from the company's perspective must take into account the phase a customer relationship is in and when the acquisition costs are amortized. For example, a transparent picture of the earning power of individual customers (groups) only emerges with falling (support) costs and simultaneously increasing profitability due to decreasing price sensitivity.

As has been shown, the transitions from a sales-based to a profit-oriented classification of customers and, in turn, to the measurement of Customer Lifetime Value involve different expenses and complexities. The economic principle also applies here: A transition makes sense if the costs are more than offset by the resulting benefits. In some cases, a simplification of the customer value approach makes sense in practice. However, determining customer value based solely on turnover is generally an oversimplification and carries the risk of ineffective customer value management.

7.3   Practical Example: Customer Value in the Publishing Industry

To illustrate the changed view of the customer relationship, we will first describe the situation in which the publishing industry (newspapers and magazines) found itself at the start of the new millennium. This was already characterized by declining circulation and falling advertising revenues, not least due to the increasing use of the Internet as a source of information and a change in media usage behavior in general.

Against this backdrop, it is understandable that the business models that were previously focused primarily on the advertising business had to be reconsidered. At the same time, if there are obvious limits to the acquisition of new customers, existing customer management inevitably comes to the fore. The question of the long-term value of a customer from the publisher's perspective must also be answered.

7.3.1   Initial Situation for Publishers: Problematic Declines in Circulation and Advertising Sales at the Beginning of the 2000s

The tense economic situation of German publishers was mainly due to the circulation trend, which had already been declining for several years. For example, while the paid circulation of German daily and Sunday newspapers amounted to around 30.2 million copies until 1995, 10 years later it was only 25 million copies. The decline continued thereafter, with only around 50% of the 1995 peak level being reported for 2019 at 14.9 million copies. The main reason for this development was the weak economy and the generally restrictive propensity to consume:

- From the consumer's point of view, daily newspapers were an option when it came to saving money. The result of the AWA 2003 (German media analysis) was that 29% of consumers were considering canceling their newspaper subscriptions in response to the poor economic situation.
- In this situation, price increases were critical even if the average price increases over several years were only moderate.
- Another problem was the change in reading behavior ("aging readership of daily newspapers") and the reduced loyalty of customers. Around 76% of the German population stated that they regularly read a daily newspaper, with this figure standing at 83% in the over-70s segment. The 14- to 19-year-old segment only reached 54%.

These conditions led to previous business models in the publishing industry being increasingly called into question. As a result, advertising revenues fell along with circulation figures—both revenue levers were affected. In the first half of 2004, gross advertising revenues for newspapers amounted to €2.2 billion, around 44% below the comparable figure for 2000. While growing circulations also had a positive effect on the advertising business in a boom phase, the existence of publishing houses was under threat in the 2000–2005 phase. Two aspects came to the fore here: firstly, the focus of activities on "economic circulation" (revenue per unit) and secondly, a stronger customer orientation.

While marketing has so far been heavily focused on acquiring new customers (the high expenditure is reflected in the exorbitant increase in "Costs per order"), existing customer management became more important.

At the same time, analyzing current trends revealed that subscriptions were losing importance both in absolute and relative terms. The situation was even more problematic due to a reduction in customer retention rates. This called into question the conventional assessment of the profitability of subscriptions compared to individual sales in the publishing industry, as well as the high premiums for acquiring new subscribers. The American direct marketing guru A.M. Hughes (2003) stated: "Discounts do not buy loyalty. They reduce loyalty. They reduce margin." Although low prices can attract interested and less interested trial subscribers, it is hardly possible to create loyalty to the product.

7.3.2 Measurement of Customer Value in Different Phases of Customer Development

As a result of changing consumer behavior as well as economic pressure, the publishing industry is also increasingly discussing the use of customer value as a performance indicator. If, for example, the CLV is used as a measure of customer value, the customer-specific income and expenditure must be netted for a defined period. Discounting the annual amounts to the first year results in an indicator that shows the contribution a customer makes to the overall contribution margin of the property. This provides operational marketing with an indicator that allows sales activities to be controlled. Individual measures can be compared with each other in terms of whether a positive customer value is generated (i.e., whether the actions create value) and how strong the effect is (Rust et al. 2004b).

To make the complexity manageable, an aggregated calculation of the value added for 1 year is recommended (Kling et al. 2004). As Fig. 7.5 shows as an example, the contribution margin for new customers becomes negative in the first year if high premiums are spent on acquisition. These investments can only be justified if the "customers remain loyal to the product for a sufficiently long time."

In the second step, this analysis can be dynamized by relating the calculation to a specific period. Even a differentiated calculation on a segment basis (e.g., new customers vs. existing customers) often provides important information about how the publisher earns money. Up to this step, the individual customer view has been ignored. In a further step, the previous calculations can be broken down to individual customers. This is possible if the modeling of customer value is transferred to individual readers in the subscription portfolio. Often this data may only be available in rudimentary form, but it can be supplemented with non-system data.

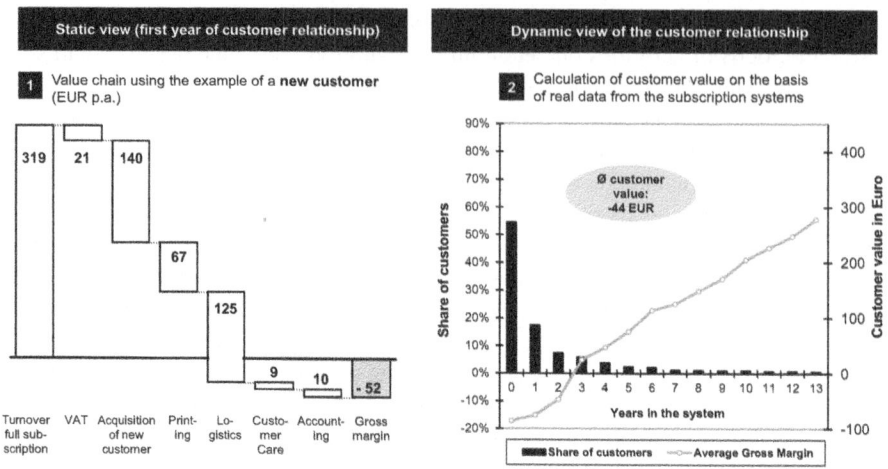

Fig. 7.5 From the static to the dynamic calculation of customer value (publishing industry)

Important information can be derived from the distribution of customer values by customer lifetime. Figure 7.5 (right-hand side) shows the average customer values by year in the subscription portfolio.

The example given shows that:

- New customers generate a negative contribution margin and are therefore "value-destroying" if they do not remain subscription customers for at least 2 years on average.
- Existing customers who have been with the system for more than 10 years have customer values of €200 and more. In addition to these mean values, the scatter must also be considered. Overall, 70–75% of the customers in the portfolio are value-destroying (not including revenues from advertisements). They do not achieve a positive contribution margin for the publisher through the sale of newspapers. It is also to be feared that they will account for a large proportion of marketing resources.

Only with this step is a calculation completed at customer level. If an individual customer value is available for individual customers, this information can also be used as a control parameter for direct marketing and customer care. It is perfectly understandable that a customer who has been a regular reader for 10 years and complains should be treated differently from a customer with a negative contribution margin. In addition to the operational management of call centers through differentiated customer care, customer loyalty measures can also be assessed on this basis with regard to the value contribution for the company.

This results in close cooperation between those responsible for CRM in the company and market research/analysis: The construction of the customer value model allows the key levers for increasing customer value creation to be identified. The market research/analysis provides clues as to how effective individual instruments can be, e.g., what leeway exists in pricing (primary lever for increasing customer value) and what measures can be used to increase the durability of subscription customers. This requires cost-benefit calculations for different concepts (Krämer et al. 2001).

Even if it is not at all clear to the customer that he is a customer of several titles or properties of a publishing house, the overarching customer value has an impact on the internal treatment of the customer.

The overarching customer view not only has implications for marketing, but also for the publisher's IT strategy. The question of whether it makes economic sense to consolidate different customer databases within a publishing house essentially depends on the synergy potential of a uniform customer view. Secondary evaluations—such as the consumer analysis study—can be used to identify the affinity of different reader groups. One way to do so is to consider "hit rate": The incidence of core reader of a specific magazine (out of a portfolio of magazines of a publishing company) is sometimes 40 times higher in existing address databases of neighboring magazines than in addresses purchased on the market for campaign implementation without special selection characteristics.

7.3.3   Marketing Decisions Based on Customer Value

Against the backdrop of increased efficiency requirements for new customer acquisition and customer retention in the publishing industry, customer value analysis offers a solution. Customer value analyses make sense:

*   To examine the value chain within individual properties and filter out customers with long-term profitability and provide them with appropriately differentiated support
*   To utilize the synergy potential within a publishing house and at the same time to identify and treat the particularly profitable customers as such across all properties
*   And as a conceptual framework for a structured approach to rethinking the business model and focusing on sales revenue

Customer value is not only used to identify revenue and loss customers at the top level, it can also be used to evaluate and manage individual marketing and advertising channels. If the individual customer value is combined with the respective cost blocks and customer retention rates of individual advertising channels, a differentiated (customer value) picture of the various marketing channels emerges as an example. While, for example, existing customers acquired via stand advertising have a below-average customer value, existing customers acquired via mailings or "readers recruit readers" campaigns are characterized by above-average customer values (Wilger and Krämer 2005). In this case, the customer value analysis reveals a ranking in relation to the contribution margin share of individual advertising channels. On the new customer side, the customer value analysis serves to identify unprofitable advertising channels. For example, it has been shown that new customers acquired via "Readers recruit readers" have a positive customer value (due to their relatively high customer retention rates, they justify the use of high-quality premiums for customer acquisition). In contrast, new customers acquired via stand advertising or mailings have a negative customer value; in this case, money is C because customers acquired via these channels cancel their contracts so quickly that the marketing expenses for customer acquisition are not justified under any circumstances. The consideration of customer value therefore not only reveals the efficiency of individual advertising channels, but in extreme cases even calls them into question entirely (effectiveness) and thus helps to minimize wasted budgetary resources in marketing.

Customer value therefore plays a central role in the optimization of new customer management, as it can be used to determine how much money customer acquisition may cost (Malthouse and Mulhern 2008). Market research and analyses have an important function here because they expand the internal data with additional customer information relevant to decision-making. This also includes predictive analytics: The ability to determine customer retention rates for the future is becoming a core competence.

A further dimension of complexity is added when determining customer values, especially in the publishing industry. Publishers serve different market segments with different products or properties, often within the framework of organizational and economic independence. Customer value analyses not only help to target customers in individual properties but also show that numerous customers are readers of several properties of a publishing house at the same time. One person can therefore represent several customer relationships (with possibly different customer values).

Publishers have since been able to partially compensate for the losses in the offline business. The momentum in digital marketing has increased noticeably in recent years. Here is just one key figure: the e-paper circulation of newspapers sold in Germany was 0.8 million in 2015 and increased to 2.1 million in 2020. Publishers took a relatively long time to adapt their business and revenue models to the changed conditions. The view of the individual customer relationship has helped to open up new revenue models in times of digitalization.

7.3.4   Looking Back and Looking Forward: Profitability of the Customer Relationship

It is comparatively easy to make digitization a demand, but it is quite another to implement it consistently. When Mathias Döpfner became CEO of Axel Springer AG in 2001, the problems in the industry had long been apparent: considerable margin problems, declining sales figures, and little contact with end customers. The lack of end-customer contact resulted from the comparatively low subscription circulation of Springer-Verlag. The Bild newspaper, by far the product with the highest circulation, was primarily sold offline in individual sales. However, in the years that followed, Döpfner set clear priorities in the direction of digitalization (Jaekel 2016). It took the industry almost two decades to develop a stringent offer and pricing policy. Today, most newspapers in the digital version offer the option of consumption with the consent of advertising presence or access by subscription. This was different at the beginning of the millennium. With the aim of positioning their own sites as information portals and generating traffic to become interesting for the advertising industry, media content was predominantly offered free of charge.

Axel Springer Verlag took that step in 2001 when Bild and T-Online signed a cooperation agreement. "*bild.t-online.de* is more than just a website. It is the multimedia extension of the BILD brand," described Bild management (Hansen 2001). Frohmann (2018, p. 57) explains: "The more users a portal has, the more attractive the internet platform is for advertisers due to the network effect." However, this did not only have advantages: Once consumers had become accustomed to consuming free digital media reports, an elementary problem in customer value became apparent. The willingness to pay for information fell to almost zero in large sections of the public. In specialist circles, this connection has also been described as the "financing crisis of journalism" (Müller 2015).

Reversing this process will take years. Reporting in times of the coronavirus crisis became a point of discussion in 2020. There was a demand that important information should be provided free of charge during the crisis. Döpfner clearly opposes this demand, as the BDZV (2020) explains:

"That there are not, on the one hand, the stupid ones who create content for a lot of money and, on the other, the smart ones who take it for free and market it very successfully." The "advertising only" revenue model is over, summarized Döpfner: "The great future lies in paid content and digital subscriptions, because more and more people are realizing how important trustworthy, truthful authorship is—and how willing they are to pay for it."

This postulates an important connection: At least some segments of the population have a high appreciation for high-quality journalism. This is associated with a willingness to pay for this consumption. If publishers succeed in siphoning off this willingness to pay through suitable pricing models, customer value will increase. At the same time, digital subscriptions, which are currently being marketed more intensively, are leading to expansions of business models that not only generate additional income, but also enable the development of customer proximity. With its digital Bild subscription, Axel Springer Verlag is closer to its customers than ever before due to the direct and interactive connection to the end consumer. For a company, it is crucial to understand which customers generate the most profits and why. This applies to the B2C-industries, but is at least as important for the B2B segment, as the following interview highlights.

7.3.5 Customer Lifetime Value: Interview with Cosimo Franco, CEO of Certiquality Srl

This chapter of the book deals with the aspect of customer value, i.e., the question of what value individual customers or a customer company have for the company. What different experiences have you had with the concept of customer value? Have you specifically used customer value as a target value?

Cosimo Franco: In principle and in theory, customer value as a performance indicator is associated with various advantages for companies. The instrument I am referring to here is Customer Lifetime value (CLV): This starts with the aspect of segmenting and prioritizing customers (on closer inspection, customers are usually fragmented in terms of their value). Ultimately, customers with a high CLV can be prioritized in order to develop targeted marketing measures and customer retention strategies. Customers with a low CLV can receive less cost-intensive offers. The basic idea is to allocate marketing and sales budgets in such a way that they achieve the greatest return on investment (ROI). If companies have an idea of what the customer value from a new or existing customer relationship will be in the future, the CLV can be used to determine how much they can spend on acquiring a new customer without making a loss. At the same time, customer retention can be optimized to maximize the value of existing customers because we do not have to forget that an existing, good customer is also the best target to sell additional products or services. Based on my knowledge, many suppliers do a lot of efforts to search for new customers forgetting to develop the existing one whose development costs are much less in comparison with the amount necessary to develop a new one. So much for the theory: In practice, there are often problems with implementation. This often starts with a lack of high-quality data. Companies often only have incomplete, inaccurate, and inconsistent data. Added to this is the effort involved in the complexity of the calculation: Scientific approaches require complex statistical or machine learning methods that are difficult for many companies to implement or understand.

Companies often only use a classification of customers according to A, B, and C customers (especially in the B2B sector). Is this enough to manage the company correctly?

Cosimo Franco: The ABC analysis is a simple method of customer differentiation, for example, according to turnover. It separates customers with high turnover from customers with low turnover. In certain situations, ABC analysis can be a viable alternative or supplement to Customer Lifetime Value (CLV); in individual cases, its suitability depends heavily on the specific objectives, resources, and complexity of the business model.

ABC analysis for sure helps to figure out in an easy manner the relation between the amount of turnover generated by a segment of clients (A or B or C or D) and the number of clients within the specific segment. Most of the time there is no perception by the sales department that to generate a relatively small amount of turnover (usually segment D) a large number of clients must be managed. Inevitably this means costs with no other benefits for the company. Usually, this happens in any business regardless it is B2B or B2C. In my opinion segment D is always an area to put under the magnifying glass in order to optimize costs and to increase CLV.

The advantages of ABC analysis are that it is intuitive and very easy to understand and implement, especially for small companies or teams with limited analytical expertise. It can provide guidance when it comes to prioritizing existing customers or products based on sales. If the focus is on the short term, the concept can help. For example, there are markets with high customer turnover (e.g., retail or fast-moving consumer goods) in which a long-term view is often less relevant.

It is problematic when using the ABC analysis if the sales and profit situation of individual customers differs greatly. It may be the case that customers generate a considerable turnover, but this was generated by heavy discounts and the customer is very service-intensive at the same time, resulting in high costs. Then a pure ABC analysis can then lead to wrong decisions.

My own experience relates more to B2B markets. The framework conditions are very different here. It starts with the fact that several people or departments (e.g., purchasing, technology, management) are often involved in the decision-making process in B2B markets. The CLV must take into account the dynamics of these groups, the so-called buying center. In addition, there are individual contract structures in which prices, payment terms, and contract terms often vary greatly. One particularly important aspect is that relationships between suppliers and customers are often long-term and strategic. In addition, the power positions between the parties can vary greatly.

According to my experience, to analyze a customer, I usually combine ABC analysis with a simple 2×2 matrix where customer's potential growth and margin generated by the customers are plotted. By doing such segmentations, it is possible to divide all clients in four categories which can be managed according to four different commercial strategies. Of course, and here I go back to the first questions, to apply this more sophisticated strategy high-quality data are needed. A good and well-managed company usually owns these data.

Some people argue that it is firstly not possible to truly quantify customer value and secondly that it does not make sense (e.g., because the strategic value of a customer cannot be expressed in euros). What is your personal perspective?

Cosimo Franco: Even if it is not possible to calculate the Customer Lifetime Value (CLV)— whether due to a lack of data, resources or suitable methods—there are still approaches that managers can use to prioritize the value of customers and make strategic decisions. I strongly think that a manager can take decision facts based by mean on quantitative KPIs but also based on semiquantitative information which are not 100% facts based; therefore, in my view, one can measure in euros the strategic value of a customer anyhow.

For instance, one step is to reduce complexity to the point where it becomes actionable for your team without disregarding crucial information. For example, it makes sense to expand the classic historical sales view to include contribution margin data in order to identify valuable customers. It is also conceivable to calculate the costs of acquiring a customer and to set these in relation to the revenue generated. Simple customer segmentation based on simple criteria, e.g., sales volume, purchase frequency, product categories, or geographical markets, can also be helpful. Scoring models are somewhat more complex.

Qualitative data such as customer feedback and satisfaction should also be included—these can be customer surveys or Net Promoter Score (NPS), but not only monetary aspects, i.e., factors such as brand impact, recommendation rate, or market position. The strategic value of the customer relationship is easily identified here.

What experience have you personally had with customers who have a high strategic value but do not generate any significant profit? What advice would you give companies in such cases?

Cosimo Franco: In theory, a customer is considered strategically important if it is crucial to the long-term success and competitiveness of a company. Importance can include various aspects: (1) direct economic importance, such as a high share of sales; (2) the conclusion of long-term contracts that lead to stable business relationships with high recurring revenues; (3) high growth potential; (4) influence on the market or industry, for example, if it is particularly prestigious and reference value; (5) the customer enables access to new markets or target groups; or (6) it brings indirect benefits by generating new contacts, partnerships, or recommendations.

In a particularly extreme case, if the customer has a dominant position in an industry, but the profit is not significant I would suggest to ponder whether it is useful to maintain such a customer or not. Here, there are other and more complex, intangible considerations which must be considered. Questions like "does this customer contribute to my company image and reputation?" or "is this customer important to collaborate with because my company improve its technological knowledge?" are crucial and add to the complexity of decision-making in such cases.

Let's assume that the customer value is negative (i.e., the cash flow is negative over time) and at the same time the strategic value is low. Is it consistent to terminate the customer relationship unilaterally?

Cosimo Franco: If the customer consistently generates more costs than revenue and there is no prospect of improvement, then the business relationship is problematic. After all, this customer is cross-subsidizing other customers who are profitable. By abandoning unprofitable customers, companies can better focus their resources on more lucrative customers. Therefore, it is always important to keep customer value in mind, regardless of how it is calculated.

However, there are also arguments for reconsidering the customer relationship and taking other considerations into account. If the customer is unprofitable in the current situation but could become significant in the future, for example, through growth, cross-selling, or up-selling, then it may make sense to accept a temporarily unprofitable customer relationship. The customer contributes indirectly to the company's success, e.g., through recommendations, prestige, or market opening. The situation is similar if it would be difficult or expensive to replace the customer. In this case, it may make more sense to optimize the relationship.

It is important to have an open discussion with customers in order to improve cooperation and minimize unproductive aspects.

In conclusion, when margin with a certain customer is negative over the time, I wonder why such situations occur. The only explanation I have is that there is no appropriate management control of the business. In my opinion customer value or even better customer experience works well when both supplier and customer have a win-win situation. Such conclusion might seem as obvious but it isn't because all other possible combinations (win-lose, lose-win, lose-lose) destroy value for everyone. The difficult task is to find out the right equilibrium of the infinity game of the business.

Cosimo Franco

Dr. Cosimo Franco is the CEO of Certiquality Srl, an Italian leading company specialized in the field of certifications which also is a notified body for Medical Devices. He has a degree in Organic Chemistry at University of Florence and a MBA at High School Enrico Mattei—ENI in Milan. He started his career as researcher at the university and then moved as researcher to the chemical industry. He worked for four multinational chemical companies and for an Italian family-owned chemical company covering different positions as Innovation manager, Sales & Marketing manager, Business manager up to top positions as CEO. He wrote some articles for Italian specialized magazines regarding strategy, management, innovation, and sustainability. He was board member of Federchimica (Italian Association of Chemical Industry) and chair of an American task force dealing with EPA.

7.4   Outlook: No Basis for a Joint Partnership Between Companies and Customers Without Profitability

If, firstly, managers pursue the objective of generating profits with their company and, secondly, if the customer relationship represents the lowest common denominator for generating profits, then a focus on the individual customer value from the company's perspective is a necessary consequence. In this respect, companies should be able to recognize which customers generate a significant profit contribution and which customers do not.

If this perspective is expanded to include opportunities to improve customer value, the portfolio of actions shown in Fig. 7.4 emerges. An increase in customer value is possible by increasing customer retention, reducing customer-specific costs, increasing the effective price level, or generating additional income for extended services. Determining the appropriate instruments requires the integration of customer preference into the considerations: Which services are customers willing to spend additional money on? Which product features can be dispensed with (so that costs can be reduced) without generating a significant loss of customer benefit?

The relationship between customer benefits and customer value has only been empirically investigated to a limited extent to date. Almost two decades ago, Rust et al. (2004a) investigated the extent to which the increase in benefits triggered by quality improvements is reflected in an increase in Customer Lifetime Value (CLV). For airlines, for example, their analysis shows that an increase in benefits of 0.2 index points results in an average CLV increase of 1.39% across the 355 respondents. Similarly, Pan and Luo (2006) analyze the relationship between perceived service benefit and the level of price premium achieved as well as the size of the customer base. They show that a considerable proportion of service investments is not reflected by a corresponding price premium. However, both studies only consider an average correlation for the entire sample of customers of one organization or a large number of firms from different sectors. These studies therefore assume a homogeneity across customers and companies with regard to the transformation of customer benefits into customer value, which is probably unrealistic (Burgartz and Krämer 2014). It can be assumed that different benefit segments exist whose customer value differs considerably. The success of the company then depends heavily on the allocation of marketing resources to the market segments with high customer value.

References

BDZV (2020) "Corona-Krise ist für digitale journalistische Nachrichtenangebote eine riesige Chance", Presseinformation v. 27.5.2020. https://www.presseportal.de/pm/6936/4607692. Accessed 21 Feb 2021

Bell D, Deighton J, Reinartz WJ, Rust RT, Swartz G (2002) Seven barriers to customer equity management. J Serv Res 5(1):77–85

Bendle NT, Bagga CK (2016) The metrics that marketers muddle. MIT Sloan Manag Rev 57(3):73–78

Blattberg RC, Deighton J (1996) Manage marketing by the customer equity test. Harv Bus Rev 74(4):136–144

Bruhn M (2013) Relationship Marketing. Das Management von Kundenbeziehungen. 3. Aufl. München

Burgartz T, Krämer A (2014) Customer relationship controlling – IT-gestütztes customer value management. Controlling 26(4/5):264–271

Dolan RJ, Gourville JT (2009) Principles of pricing. Harvard Business School, Boston

Du RY, Kamakura WA, Mela CF (2007) Size and share of customer wallet. J Mark 71(2):94–113

Estrella-Ramón AM, Sánchez-Pérez M, Swinnen G, VanHoof K (2013) A marketing view of the customer value: Customer lifetime value and customer equity. South African Journal of Business Management, ISSN 2078–5976, African Online Scientific Information Systems (AOSIS). Cape Town 44(4):47–64

Fader PS (2012) Customer centricity: Focus on the right customers for strategic advantage. Wharton Digital Press, Philadelphia, PA

Frohmann F (2018) Digitales pricing. Springer Gabler, Wiesbaden

Hansen S (2001) T-Online holt Springers BILD mit ins Boot, heise online News v. 04.04.2001. https://www.heise.de/newsticker/meldung/T-Online-holt-Springers-BILD-mit-ins-Boot-42299.html. Zugriff am 24. Febr. 2021

Hughes AM (2003) The customer loyalty solution. McGraw-Hill, New York

Jaekel M (2016) Die Anatomie digitaler Geschäftsmodelle. Springer, Wiesbaden

Jasek P, Vrana L, Sperkova L, Smutny Z, Kobulsky M (2018) Modeling and application of customer lifetime value in online retail. Informatics 5(1):2. (online), Multidisciplinary Digital Publishing Institute

Kling O, Wilger G, Krämer A (2004) Kundenwert-Analysen für Verlage – Wie wertvoll ist ein Kunde für einen Verlag? Planung & Analyse 5:50–53

Krämer A (2017) Demystifying the "Sunk Cost Fallacy": when considering fixed costs in decision-making is reasonable. J Res Mark 7(1):510–517

Krämer A, Burgartz T (2020) Mehr Verhandlungserfolg in VUCA-Zeiten. Sal Excel 27(12):20–23

Krämer A, Keck C, Tien M (2001) Preisreduktion oder Serviceverbesserung? Planung & Analyse 2:56–62

Krämer A, Bongaerts R (2023) Kundenwertzentrierte Unternehmenssteuerung als Maßgabe für das Marketing von morgen. In: Stammkundenbindung versus Neukundengewinnung: Marketing und Vertrieb im Spannungsfeld von Hunting und Farming, Springer Fachmedien, Wiesbaden, p 211–230

Leeflang PS, Verhoef PC, Dahlström P, Freundt T (2014) Challenges and solutions for marketing in a digital era. Eur Manag J 32(1):1–12

Mack O, Khare A, Krämer A, Burgartz T (2015) Managing in a VUCA world. Springer, New York

Malthouse E, Mulhern F (2008) Understanding and using customer loyalty and customer value. J Relat Mark 6(3/4):59–86

Mengen A (2009) Verfahren der Kundenwertermittlung: Darstellung und Bewertung der Kundenwertmessung als Bestandteil des Marketing-Controlling (No. 1–2009). Wissenschaftliche Schriften des Fachbereichs Betriebswirtschaft

Mengen A (2011) Mit Kundenwert-Controlling zu mehr Erfolg in Marketing und Vertrieb. Controlling 23(1):55–63

Müller P (2015) Gib mir Orientierung, gib mir Redestoff! Wie sich die Wahrnehmung des Medienwandels auf die Zahlungsbereitschaft für journalistische Inhalte auswirkt. In: Schnittstellen (in) der Medienökonomie, Oktober, Nomos Verlagsgesellschaft mbH & Co. KG, S 361–378

Pan X, Luo X (2006) Service capabilities in value appropriation: a conceptualization and investigation of internet retailers, Working Paper, Indiana University, Bloomington

Pauwels K, Ambler T, Clark BH, LaPointe P, Reibstein D, Skiera B, Wierenga B, Wiesel T (2009) Dashboards as a service: why, what, how, and what research is needed. J Serv Res 12(2):175–189

Reichheld FF, Sasser WE (1990) Zero defections: quality comes to services. Harv Bus Rev 68(5):105–111

Reimer K, Becker JU (2011) Revisiting the use of customer information for CRM. Neue Medien und Marketing, Institut für Betriebswirtschaftslehre, Universität Kiel, Arbeitspapiere des Lehrstuhls für Innovation

Reinecke S, Tomczak T (2001) Einsatz von Instrumenten und Verfahren des Marketingcontrolling in der Praxis. In: Reinecke S, Tomczak T (Hrsg) Handbuch Marketing Controlling. Gabler Thexis, St. Gallen, S 76–89

Rust RT, Lemon KN, Zeithaml VA (2004a) Return on marketing: using customer equity to focus marketing strategy. J Mark 68(1):109–127

Rust RT, Zeithaml VA, Lemon KN (2004b) Customer-centered brand management. Harv Bus Rev 82(9):110–118

Sevin CH (1947) Some aspects of distribution cost analysis. J Mark 12(1):92–98

Shin J, Sudhir K, Yoon DH (2012) When to "fire" customers: customer cost-based pricing. Manage Sci 58(5):932–947

Szymanski DM, Bharadwaj SG, Varadarajan PR (1993) Standardization versus adaptation of international marketing strategy: an empirical investigation. J Mark 57(4):1–17

Tewes M (2013) Der Kundenwert im Marketing: Theoretische Hintergründe und Umsetzungsmöglichkeiten einer wert- und marktorientierten Unternehmensführung, Bd 45. Springer, Wiesbaden

Verhoef PC, Lemon KN (2013) Successful customer value management: key lessons and emerging trends. Eur Manag J 31(1):1–15

Wilger G, Krämer A (2005) Wie wertvoll ist der Leser wirklich? Res & Results 3:64–65

Zur Horst S (2021) Warum Versicherungen trotz Digitalisierung beim Smart Pricing hinterherhinken; it-finanzmagazin.de v. 17.3.2021. https://www.it-finanzmagazin.de/warumversicherungen-trotz-digitalisierung-beim-smart-pricing-hinterherhinken-118652/. Accessed 20 Mar 2021

ZETA (2024) The Strategic Gap: How Companies Underutilize Customer Lifetime Value. June 11, 2024, https://zetaglobal.com/resource-center/companies-underutilize-customer-lifetime-value/?utm_source=chatgpt.com. Accessed 12 May 2025

Customer Centricity: Focusing on Customer Needs and Touchpoints

8

8.1 The Strategic Direction: From Product-Centricity to Customer-Centricity

"The most important single thing is to focus obsessively on the customer. Our goal is to be earth's most customer-centric company."—Jeff Bezos

8.1.1 "Share of Wallet" Instead of Market Share: A Change of Perspective

One of the basic building blocks of modern customer management is the realization that a change in perspective from product-centric to customer-centric is necessary. Like no other, Amazon founder Jeff Bezos stands for the company's total focus on the customer. At first glance, this exaggerated focus on the customer relationship is becoming the central cornerstone for Amazon to generate strategic competitive advantages. While other companies focus on creating loyalty based on contractual relationship, Amazon primarily addresses the aspect of loyalty with a focus on giving multiple options on pricing and quality as well as recommendations and excellent customer service (B2C).

With the previous focus on transactions as a whole, sales, the actual price achieved and market share, etc. are at the center of corporate management. Key questions are then, for example: What turnover has been achieved in a product category? What is the potential for price increases? Or: How much can the market share of a product be increased? The customer potential view focuses on other questions, namely: To what extent is the customer's purchasing potential already covered? What measures are required to exploit the full potential? Against this background, customer centricity is seen in the literature in particular as a counter-movement to product centricity (Galbraith 2005; Shah et al. 2006). The underlying assumption of a product-centric approach sees the company as a supplier of resources and competencies that can be used to develop products or services. The products and services are the central value proposition, whereby the company strives to satisfy as many customers as possible. In contrast, customer centricity describes a process in which customers become the focus of attention. This involves determining what turnover could be achieved with these customers (and what measures are required to do so) and then linking this to existing turnover. This opens up a view of the "share of wallet" (defined as the share of your own product in all customer spending on the product category) as a counterpoint to the "share of market" (market share). This may seem logical, but it is challenging to implement. After all, the approach not only requires a change of perspective, but also, for example, a completely different depth of data. Simply looking at the market is no longer enough. At the very least, detailed information on the most important customers must be collected and made available—a sometimes enormous effort, depending on the industry and customer structure. Faced with this challenge, managers have often looked for a "shortcut." Instead of spending a lot of energy collecting and evaluating customer-specific information and using it to make decisions, the focus has been on simple customer indicators: Global satisfaction or the Net Promoter Score (the latter in particular is associated with the hope of being provided with a condensed indicator of growth opportunities).

However, a simplistic focus on improving customer satisfaction for all customers does not seem to be the best management approach if the goal is to maximize the overall profitability of the company. Keiningham et al. (2005) come to the conclusion that this one-sided focus on one parameter could even lead to a negative return on investment. In their study, they found that customer turnover is negatively correlated with customer profitability in the case of unprofitable customers, but positively correlated with profitable customers. The conclusion: customers should first be segmented according to their profitability for the company before resources are used to improve customer satisfaction and the "share of wallet."

What options are available if traditional loyalty metrics are not related to "Share of Wallet"? A two-year longitudinal study (Keiningham et al. 2005, 2011) with more than 17,000 consumers examined purchasing behavior in more than a dozen industries and in nine countries. One of the subjects of the study was the relationship between the preference ranking of a brand (relative to the other brands used) and the "share of wallet." The so-called wallet allocation rule was derived from the findings. This can be described as a rule because the correlation between the value of a brand's wallet allocation rule and its share of wallet was relatively consistent from company to company and from sector to sector (on average, the correlation was over 0.9). The procedure is as follows: The first step is to determine the number of brands (or stores or companies) that customers use in the product category. In the second step, customers are asked about their satisfaction or loyalty for each brand. The collected ratings are then converted into rank positions. In case of a tie, the average value is used, e.g., if two brands are ranked first, a rank of 1.5 is assigned. In the third step, the brand share of wallet is calculated. The higher this is, the more strongly the brand is manifested in the customer's purchasing process.

As shown, the change in perspective from product-centricity to customer-centricity is easy to articulate, but its implementation is often more complex and challenging than expected. The next step is therefore to develop a model that integrates the key cornerstones on the path from strategy development to the operational implementation of customer centricity.

8.1.2   A Model for Understanding and Implementing Customer Centricity

Once the change in perspective towards customer centricity has taken place at a strategic level, the next step is to create the conditions for implementation to ensure that customer orientation is lived and becomes a central element of the company's DNA at the operational level. These relate to the management of the company, the organization, communication and processes in which customers are directly or indirectly involved, as well as efficient data management, which extends to control based on KPIs. Once these prerequisites have been created, the question of how customer centricity manifests itself in operational marketing must be clarified. These different phases are illustrated based on Shah et al. (2006) (see Fig. 8.1). In the following chapters, the key areas of "Creating prerequisites" and "operational customer orientation" are presented in more detail.

Also shown is the importance of customer data, which plays an important role in the development of CRM and ultimately customer centricity, albeit one that changes over time (Saarijärvi et al. 2013): While the first phase focuses on the realization of systematically collecting available customer data and developing corresponding technologies, later phases focus on the strategic relevance of customer data as well as on the distribution of data, which extends to the provision of data for the customer (e.g., maintenance of own master data or customer profile).

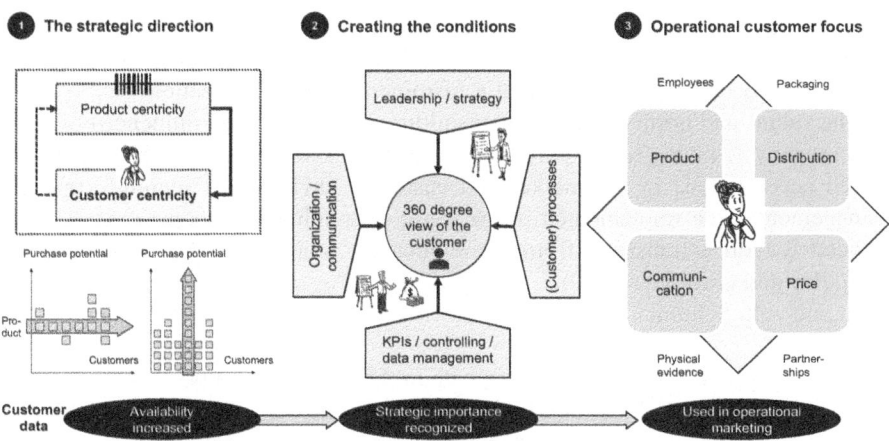

Fig. 8.1 Model for understanding and implementing customer centricity

The phases shown for implementing customer centricity also coincide with the directions and areas of action that are associated with customer centricity in literature and practice (Lamberti 2013). Firstly, this includes the company's ability to generate a better understanding of the customer, i.e., to collect and process data and information in order to build up comprehensive databases on the interactions between the customer and the company. This is not an end in itself, but ultimately serves to support decision-making. Secondly, the aim is to shift the focus from the product or service offered to the entire customer experience. This requires transparency about the points at which the company interacts with the customer. As a result of this approach, the research direction of customer experience management has developed considerably in recent years. A third line of action attempts to actively involve customers in marketing and innovation processes and to create value together with them. The focus here is on the term co-creation.

8.2 Creating the Conditions for Customer Centricity

8.2.1 The Role of Leadership and Strategy

Corporate cultures have many levels and facets that can make them resistant to change. Customer-centric organizations, on the other hand, are held together by the central viewpoint that every decision begins with the customer and the expected benefits for the buyer. It is therefore essential for decision-makers in the company to view all points of contact with customers from the customer's perspective and to examine how they can be improved.

Other components of corporate culture are norms that represent shared convictions about appropriate or expected behavior. Translated for a customer-oriented organization, this means that employees see themselves as customer advocates. Another characteristic norm is the willingness of individual employees to share information with their colleagues so that the entire company is better able to meet customer needs. At the same time, a destructive norm that can be found in many companies is that sales "owns the customer," a classic form of silo thinking that fundamentally contradicts the idea of a customer-centric organization.

The values and norms of a corporate culture are significantly influenced by how the company is managed. In particular, uncertain framework conditions and perceived accelerations in the market and customer environment require corporate management to be implemented in the sense of a culture of cooperation. This is associated with a transition from hierarchical to more networked organizations (Moodley and Govender 2020).

In line with Schuman (2006), the following key points should be considered:

1. Give employees a reason to participate in the collaboration process.
2. Involve all stakeholders who have a significant interest in the issues concerned.
3. Giving interested people the chance to participate voluntarily.
4. Ensure that the stakeholders involved shape the processes.

5. Plan sufficient flexibility into the processes.
6. Enable equal access to information for all stakeholders.
7. Recognizing and appreciating diversity: Values, interests, and knowledge.
8. Define individual and joint responsibility for contributions and the process.
9. Realistically assess what is to be achieved within the given schedule and what is actually possible.
10. Ensure that solution approaches are followed up and, if implemented, accompanied by monitoring/controlling.

In this section, we first looked at the areas of strategy and management in order to initiate change processes towards a rethink in the direction of customer centricity. This has consequences for the organization and communication within the company.

8.2.2   Organization and Communication

Customer centricity anchored in the corporate culture manifests itself in organization and communication. Two core elements that characterize a customer-centric organization are, on the one hand, improvements to products and services based on proximity to the customer and, on the other, customer loyalty as a key to long-term profitability. This is also associated with a special view of marketing and the question of whether marketing activities represent a cost item, which must be implicitly reduced, or should be seen as an investment. A customer-centric culture is evident when the time spent with customers is given special importance. Overall, the corporate culture can be either an important facilitator or a major obstacle on the path to customer centricity.

In an ideal customer-centric organization, all functional activities are integrated and geared towards delivering greater customer value. This orientation is the exact opposite of a typical product-oriented company. This tends to be organized in functional silos and defined by product categories or product types. In a world that focuses primarily on transactions and products, a product-specific allocation of responsibilities to product and/or sales managers is almost inevitable. The transition to a customer-centric organization therefore requires a change in role formation.

Informal coordination activities are particularly important when customer information is a relevant basis for company decisions and is available in a rather fragmented form within the company. They should aim to overcome the known deficits of product or functional silos. Well-trained and well-incentivized product managers can take on this role. Integrating functions, such as key account managers or segment task forces, can help to coordinate existing customer contact activities.

Installing a special area of responsibility in top management can also be a measure to overcome barriers on the way to becoming a customer-centric company. Shah et al. (2006) point out that there has been a lot of movement on this point since the beginning of the millennium, which can be seen in the increasing number of functions such as CMO (Chief Marketing Officer) or CCO (Chief Customer Officer). In the years that followed, a fierce debate broke out in practice and research as to whether companies with such functions actually perform better than companies that do not have them. For example, Nath and Mahajan (2011) report that the presence of a Chief Marketing Officer in the top management team (TMT) has neither a positive nor a negative impact on company performance. The analysis by Germann et al. (2015) comes to the opposite conclusion: "The key finding of our study is that firms seem to benefit from having a CMO among the Top Management Team." Too strong a focus on the position of CMO.

Appears unsuitable in this context insofar as the interaction between managers is certainly also important. The results of studies that show, for example, that CEOs generally have a high level of trust in the position of CFO, while this is not the case for the position of CMO, are therefore worrying (Fournaise 2012). This could also be the reason why CMO positions are replaced much more frequently than other top management positions (Whitler et al. 2020).

The communicative aspects of customer centricity discussed so far deal with communication between the employees of a company, i.e., the purely internal view. However, customer centricity also has implications for communication between companies and customers. This also raises the question of whether companies and customers have the same understanding of customer centricity. From a customer's perspective, customer centricity could be linked to questions such as "How interested is the provider really in my opinion as a customer?", "Am I treated fairly as a customer, e.g. by the provider providing me with all the important information that is relevant to my decision?" or "As a customer, do I accept it if I observe that the provider treats its customers differently and I perceive this as unfair?"

As part of a separate study, the customer relationship of people with mobile phone providers in Germany was examined. The statement "My mobile phone provider offers products and services that meet my needs" achieved 50% agreement (9% disagreement). In the subgroup of people planning to switch providers, only 25% agreed with the statement. The statement "With my provider, new customers are treated better than regular customers" was also evaluated. More than one in three mobile customers agrees with the statement; in the group of customers planning to switch providers, the preference for new customers over existing customers is seen as above average (52% agree, 17% disagree). The detailed results are shown in Fig. 8.2 (for further information see Krämer 2023).

Correspondingly differentiated customer treatment is not uncommon. From the company's point of view, it may seem sensible to target new customers with particularly attractive offers and large discounts. However, the fact that communicative fencing of new and existing customers is hardly possible is overlooked. If customers who see themselves as loyal regulars realize that new customers are treated better than themselves, disappointment can easily arise on the customer side. After all, customers expect a reward or consideration for loyalty, not an indirect punishment.

The example of electricity contracts also reveals that it is ideal for customers to switch providers every year. According to a report by the news portal ntv (2021), which sums up the key finding of a price comparison analysis as follows: "Loyal customers are still penalized by providers. As a long-standing customer who has never switched, you usually pay the highest price. But even those willing to switch

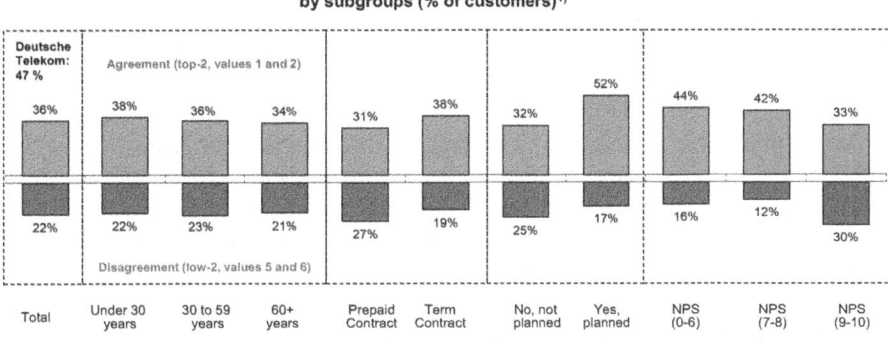

Fig. 8.2 Perceived prioritization of customer segments by customers in the area of telecommunication

can be lured into a trap: Tariffs for new customers often include high bonus payments that lead to a very attractive price in the first year.

It becomes much more expensive in the second year, as the bonus only applies in the first." For customers, this can lead to a far-reaching loss of trust in their provider if it becomes apparent that customers who were previously unknown to the company are being offered better prices than customers who, for example, have accepted price increases in recent years without complaining. The correlations described address an important point in marketing and, at the same time, in customer value-centered management: it can rightly be questioned whether activities in the area of new customer acquisition and customer retention are actually independent of each other, as previous observations in practice and science would suggest. Recent research in this field has uncovered interesting correlations, e.g., between the organization of new and existing customer care and the financial performance of companies (Dong et al. 2011).

8.2.3 Customer Processes and Customer Information Systems

In the context of transaction management, it is important to design the existing customer contact points and customer processes in such a way that a "perfect customer experience" is created. Based on their empirical analysis, Payne and Frow (2005) come up with five different generic processes that are essential for a company to become customer-centric:

1. Strategy development process that includes not only a business strategy but also a customer strategy.
2. Dual value creation process at the heart of the exchange process.
3. Multi-channel integration process that covers all customer contact points.

4. information management process, which includes the functions of data collection and analysis, and,

5. Performance evaluation process that links the measures at the interface to the customer with the company's performance.

At this point, it is important to note that the different process levels involve the individual customer to varying degrees. As part of the strategy development process, the customer relationship is usually addressed when analyzing market conditions, whereby aspects such as customer segments, customer structure or sales potential can play a role. In this context, it is also possible to speak of customer data at an aggregated meta-level. For individual customer contact processes, however, customer-specific information must be available. According to Liang and Tanniru (2006), we can speak of a customer-centric information system if the four main components—customer, process, technology and product/service—can be configured to meet a customer need. The customer is the core and the driving force behind the system. At the same time, the reality often looks different when, for example, customers have to explain their concerns several times during the complaints process, when service employees work with out-of-date customer data during customer contact, when customer care centers are not available or, even more extreme, when an online contact form is provided as the only way to make contact but cannot be activated due to technical defects.

8.2.4 Customer Key Figures, Controlling, and Data Management

A VUCA (Volatility, Uncertainty, Complexity, Ambiguity) environment, described as a rapidly changing, highly turbulent and almost unpredictable environment for companies, presents them with additional challenges (see Burgartz and Krämer 2014, p. 265f.). The socio-cultural environment includes demographic developments and consumer-relevant social trends. They manifest themselves in heterogeneous customer behaviors that are difficult to assess and are based on differentiated expectations and different levels of knowledge; sustainability, striving for climate neutrality and electrification of mobility are just a few key points. Furthermore, fast-moving trends have an impact on companies' product range policies. Therefore, a well-founded risk identification using suitable tools (e.g., market research, especially on customer needs and trend developments, etc.) is required in order to ultimately derive targeted measures with regard to customer approach, product policy and product range design. If the focus is on the value of a customer relationship, the customer can be regarded as the smallest unit of risk (customer equity) and must be allocated when identifying risks (Burgartz and Krämer 2020). Companies are therefore faced with the challenge of obtaining transparency about how stable customer relationships are and what economic effects emanate from customer management. The formulation of impact chains can help here.

The sequence of the chain of effects or the strength of the relationships between the individual constructs/phases of the success chain is influenced to a significant extent by moderating factors, such as the competitive environment, supplier activities or product characteristics, either negatively or positively, whereby the functional relationship cannot be traced exactly. As a result, the change in one upstream variable does not influence another variable one hundred percent. Various studies address the conditions under which the assumed impact relationships do not apply or only apply to a limited extent. A high degree of heterogeneity in customer expectations, for example, can lead to a large number of customers not being satisfied despite high service quality, as not all expectations are considered. It is also conceivable that a satisfied customer will not buy the service again, e.g., due to convenience. Furthermore, even the successful retention of a customer does not necessarily lead to greater economic success if, for example, there is no need for the service or there is a lack of willingness to pay the corresponding price. Furthermore, based on plausibility considerations and empirical results, it can be assumed that the postulated relationships are non-linear. Figure 8.3 shows the causal chain, starting with customer proximity and ending with customer value, based on Burgartz (2008). At this point, it is important to note that the entire causal chain must be taken into account. The strong focus on the parameter of customer satisfaction—especially in the 1990s—was based on the fundamental idea that it was sufficient to concentrate on maximizing customer satisfaction, as increasing the satisfaction level was the decisive driver for customer growth (Jones and Sasser 1995). Other authors, e.g., Malthouse and Mulhern (2008), only examine partial aspects of the chain of effects (Customer Loyalty → Buying Behavior → Customer Value → Firm Performance).

The impact chain in itself only contains added value for companies if recommendations for management action can be derived from it. Today, it is no longer sufficient for management to obtain information about the status of the customer relationship based on individual key figures. Accordingly, approaches such as the Net Promoter Score are increasingly being criticized. More promising are indicator

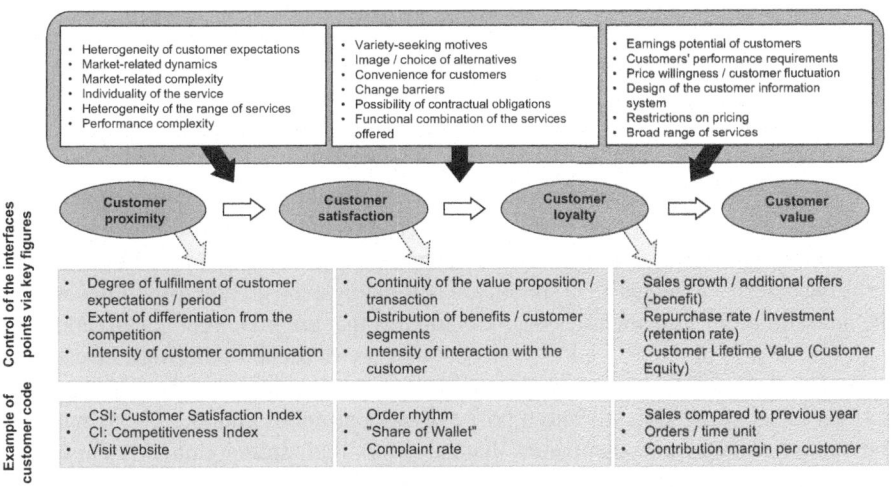

Fig. 8.3 Risky interfaces of a customer relationship and derivation of customer key figures

systems that map the risk of the customer relationship over the individual phases. On the one hand, the respective phases, e.g., the degree of fulfillment or achievement of customer loyalty via the customer's actual behavior (repurchase, cross-buying, recommendation, price increase acceptance) and the customer's behavioral intentions (repurchase, cross-buying and recommendation intentions, price increase tolerance), are the point of orientation. On the other hand, however, it is particularly important to control the transitions and interfaces between the phases using key figures.

Because it is these moderating factors that enable the holistic management of a customer relationship and the conscious addition of which can help to build market share or increase sales, the interfaces must be analyzed and evaluated in a sustainable and transparent manner in the form of risk-oriented measures.

Clear structures in the underlying, data-generating customer processes are the basis for such a complex system of key figures. With the help of new technologies, data is available in a much shorter time and it is important to be able to generate internal data and access external data. Increasing data volumes and growing computer capacities form the basis for modern, customer-oriented risk management. Big data and predictive analytics methods are not the only tools to be used for optimized risk management; artificial intelligence also offers the opportunity to carry out competitor and customer portfolio analyses (real-time analyses) and thus support sales in a targeted manner.

8.3   Customer Centricity in Retail: More Theory than Practice—Interview with Prof. Dr. Wolfgang Merkle

Question: Why is it important for retail companies to rethink or think more about customer centricity, especially in times of coronavirus?

Wolfgang Merkle: Hardly a week goes by without reports of new insolvencies of formerly well-known brands and companies, the streamlining of major store networks and staff redundancies. A development that is taking place in almost all sectors—in fashion, sports and shoe retail, perfumeries, bakeries and restaurants. The German economy is suffering one of the most severe structural crises in its history, with more and more companies being forced to close down.

It seems as if the various crisis which are actually taking place have triggered an enormous, exogenous shock; a game-changer with massive transformative power. As a result, companies that were already considered to be struggling before coronavirus the external changes have started are still facing even greater difficulties within the new situation: This includes business models that are no longer able to compete with online providers, as well as concepts that are burdened with high investment backlogs and no longer present themselves in a contemporary enough way. The various crisis plunged us all into a phase of discontinuous change. The winners in the market will be those companies that can adapt their strategy quickly enough to the new situation and to the new behavioral patterns and expectations of consumers.

This challenge for traditional business models is likely to be exacerbated by the fact that, after being forced to learn a new way to behave, many have not returned to old consumer behaviors but rather continued along the new situation they are confronted with.

Even customers in the second half of life are learning to appreciate the alternative business models of the internet with all their advantages—the convenient selection, easy ordering and fast delivery has altered their expectations. It is therefore understandable that companies are facing a new reality post-crisis: Instead of returning to the old norms, companies are having to find their way in a new reality.

For this reason, the following applies more than ever: if retailers want to continue to inspire consumers, they must align their entire thinking and actions even more strongly and consistently with the wishes and needs of their customers.

Question: Why is the term customer centricity in retail often just a buzzword that is brought into the discussion from time to time?

Wolfgang Merkle: For some time now, customer centricity has been referred to as the "Customer centricity" is being discussed as a fashionable term for an even more consistent focus of all processes on the needs and wishes of customers. However, the current corporate failures show that in many sectors, customer centricity is used more as a buzzword to generate applause than as a holistic corporate concept—in order to inspire consumers in the long term, lip service must be turned into a consistent, holistic corporate approach across all contact points, and there are still too many managers, particularly in the retail sector, who cling to old standards and processes that serve to further rationalize their own processes rather than provide genuine customer benefits.

Question: How can the retail sector improve—what should it focus on in future?

Wolfgang Merkle: When it comes to customer orientation, traditional business models can learn from their competitors on the Internet. This is because business models based there have a comprehensive customer focus across all design aspects. When designing the shopping experience, the respective providers are not content with a product range tailored to the customer, but include all operating and handling processes down to the smallest detail: In the case of online providers, individual products are provided with even more information through the integration of exciting tutorials, lively moving image sequences or helpful experiences from other customers. Most traditional providers usually display their product ranges on the shelves without commentary or emotion, and where the actual product range is supplemented with meaningful accompanying articles on the Internet, in many traditional models you stumble across obviously margin-driven specials and items. While the click effort in the checkout and check-out process is constantly being further optimized in terms of programming to enhance the customer experience in online retail, consumers in supermarkets feel driven at the checkout to put their purchases away as quickly as possible to make room for the next customer.

Some managers may object to such a comparison by saying that the design standards of the internet are hardly valid for traditional business models; however, it should not be forgotten that consumers experience the design quality of processes there in detail daily and obviously also value them. This kind of conditioning also raises expectations and the level of expectations of all other companies—and traditional providers must adapt to this. In the past, analyses were carried out via 'mystery shopping' to make one's own processes even more efficient; today, they should evaluate the entire purchasing process in all its facets from a customer perspective—a relentless assessment of the entire customer experience.

Question: How can you tell that a company really lives customer orientation?

Wolfgang Merkle: The systematic observation, evaluation and resulting optimization of individual process steps is carried out by online providers under the heading of "user experience"—a concept that is still too little known in many traditional business models, but offers a lot of design potential for traditional providers. Customer centricity and user experience require a new perspective in the evaluation of all business processes. The focus must not be solely on cost and efficiency-driven considerations from the singular perspective of the company. Rather, the customer's perspective must become the benchmark for evaluation. The founder of Amazon, Jeff Bezos, is quoted in this context as saying that he always designs all business processes backwards; the customer always comes first and only then is planning carried out. As a consequence, all concepts and processes must be rethought, especially in traditional business models—in order to inspire today's consumers, procedural bureaucracy and emotionless controlling thinking must be systematically eliminated.

This makes it clear that retailers in today's world should no longer talk about the point of sale—they need to move from thinking and acting as a whole to consciously designing a point of experience: Holistically from the customer's perspective across all design and process levels down to the smallest detail. This is the only way for customers to directly experience customer centricity.

The interview partner:

Prof. Dr. Wolfgang Merkle.

Marketing and Management Consultant in retail and related industries and Professor of Marketing & Management at the University of Europe for Applied Sciences.

Email: mail@merkle-consulting.com.

8.4   Customer Centricity in Operational Marketing

While the previous sections have dealt with the change in perspective from product to customer orientation and then with the prerequisites for implementing customer centricity in companies, the next step is to ask how operational market development can be changed in the direction of customer centricity. This ranges from the outgoing question of product and service adaptation, to the sales facets of customer centricity (how must sales activities be coordinated in order to increase customer value), to the communicative challenges of addressing customers as individuals with specific needs. Customer centricity is in play when not only the product/service but also the entire marketing process is adapted (Wind and Rangaswamy 2001). The range of checkpoints also includes the question of whether and how pricing should be customer-centric. The latter aspect represents a relatively young branch of research, but one that is experiencing a great deal of momentum in the context of customer centricity and customer engagement and will be given special attention below.

8.4.1   Development of Products and Services Tailored to the Customer's Needs

Within marketing, the approach of offering customers products or services that are tailored to their needs as much as possible is a top priority. On the one hand, this is because consumer preferences are becoming increasingly fragmented; on the other hand, the changed technological framework also offers more opportunities for individualized product design. The aim of this is to increase customer loyalty to the company, but also to create scope for pricing. Selden and MacMillan (2006) explain "By offering increasingly tempting value propositions, firms avoid the trap of having to compete on price."

In categories ranging from luxury automobiles to breakfast cereals, marketers are offering consumers the opportunity to tailor products to their own preferences. Recent research shows how marketers can increase the value of customized products for both the consumer and the company. The study by Burghartz et al. (2020) uses a series of field and laboratory studies to investigate a robust effect of customized product design on the customer relationship using the example of muesli mixes. The authors worked with a large European company that offers consumers the opportunity to create their own muesli mixes. Customers selected their favorite muesli ingredients (muesli base, fruits, nuts, chocolates) on the website. After finalizing their mix, half of the customers were randomly selected to receive a pop-up message. This test group was informed that they were the first to create this special muesli mix. The other half of the customers did not receive such a message. Ultimately, the additional information led to a 2.24% increase in the conversion rate. For the company, this means an additional annual turnover of more than one million euros. Obviously, the customer's perception of having put together a truly unique product leads to an increased appreciation and thus to an increased willingness to pay.

While the example of product configuration is a highly individualized product variant, other providers try to create the perception of an individualized product by offering customers a modularized product configuration. Examples can be found in vehicle configuration for cars. The airline industry also has largely adopted the ancillary pricing approach, which originated from the low-cost airline business model (Garrow et al. 2012). In addition to the option of booking a flight without special services, customers are offered a range of additional offers during the purchase process, which enable them to put together a complete service to suit their personal needs. This method of modular product composition has advantages for the customer (if he appreciates that he only puts together services that are of benefit to him), but also for the provider. The revenue generated from the sale of additional services amounted to around USD 60 billion worldwide in 2015 (Shukla et al.

2019). In this context, it is important to point out the special features of the airline industry, in particular the perishable nature of the service. Other providers rely on a strategy of offering prefabricated service bundles (e.g., in the sense of "Good, Better, Best").

Some providers involve the user in the creation of the product. For example, the simpleshow video maker platform (see Chap. 4) offers the option of creating a customized explainer video based on text input. Tools such as SurveyMonkey enable individuals as well as companies to conduct their own surveys.

The interrelationships and effects of customerization described could give the impression that only advantages are associated with the individualization of product design. However, this is not necessarily the case. Ultimately, the costs and benefits of individualization must be examined in each case. Secondary marketing represents an additional facet. While consumers are willing to pay a premium for customized products at the time of manufacture, Fuchs and Schreier (2020) point out that the same consumers also have to accept monetary disadvantages when they offer them for sale on the second-hand market. The authors analyzed a data set of 500,000 cars on the resale market. Result: The uniqueness of a product can be a disadvantage (i.e., poorer sales results), especially if the vehicles have paint finishes that are in low demand.

8.4.2 Involvement of the Customer in Price Determination

Compared to the question of how product variations or customized products are created on the basis of consumer wishes, the aspect of consumer involvement in pricing has not played an important role to date. At this point, a distinction should first be made to avoid possible misunderstandings. Customer-centric pricing is partly understood as pricing that places the customer and his willingness to pay at the center of the consideration and pursues the goal of exploiting the willingness to pay as much as possible and thus monetizing value-to-the-customer for the company (Cross and Dixit 2005, p. 487). In this case, the term value-based pricing can also be used directly (Krämer and Schmutz 2020). However, this approach will not be explicitly dealt with in this subchapter (see Chap. 5). The focus is less on the passive involvement of customers in pricing and more on an active approach in which customers themselves can influence the price.

As has been shown, technological changes are enabling greater customer involvement in product design. It remains to be seen whether this can and should also be the case in pricing. In recent years, so-called participatory pricing models have indeed been increasingly discussed, in which the buyer helps to determine the final price at which the transaction takes place. In auctions, for example, the final price is set by the buyer based on the bids. The seller's options for exerting influence relate to determining the auction rules in advance (e.g., eBay). A less well-known alternative model is "Name-Your-Own-Price" (NYOP) or reverse pricing. In the first step, the buyer states his asking price (maximum price willingness) for a product or service. If this bid is equal to or higher than a minimum price set in advance by the seller, a binding purchase is made. In contrast to auctions, it is not the highest bid that wins, but the bid that reaches or exceeds the internal minimum price (e.g., priceline.com). A particularly strong form of consumer involvement in pricing is the "Pay-What-You-Want" (PWYW) model. In this case, the consumer decides whether and, if so, how much to pay for a product or service. Kunter (2015) sees a use case here in cultural goods, but also in the increasingly relevant area of digital products (for a current overview see Güzel et al. 2025).

While innovation processes were seen less in price management in the past, innovative pricing models are currently being discussed more in professional circles and are at least being tried out in practice. Hinterhuber and Liozu (2013) point out that the "pay-what-you-want" model can be beneficial for both consumers and suppliers and expect a growing range of applications in the consumer goods sector and in industrial markets. Bertini and Koenigsberg (2014) and Lu et al. (2021) also refer to practical applications. These include, for example, Wikipedia, by far the best-known online encyclopedia since its foundation in 2001, the marketing of the new album "In Rainbows" by the British rock band Radiohead in 2007, in which interested parties were offered a download and then left to pay for the songs, and through to services such as banking (GoBank allows customers to make a monthly contribution of between US$0 and US$9) or legal advice (Summit Law Group in Seattle). The rise of PWYW is perhaps most visible across YouTube, where it has become standard across channels to include an invitation in every segment for viewers to sponsor them with donations via, for example, Buymeacoffee.com or Patreon.

The case of the rock band Radiohead is special in that the application of "Pay-What-You-Want" generated broad media coverage for the first time and proved that the business model, which at first glance seems to contradict all economic logic, can actually lead to positive earnings effects. However, the special framework conditions must be taken into account. For example, the band's existing label contract with EMI/Capitol had expired. A new contract with a music label was open (Tyrangiel 2007) and the album "In Rainbows" had already been completed. While the rock band's new marketing channel was initially viewed critically by experts and colleagues, an overall view reveals positive correlations. Firstly, the direct effects: The proportion of paying users was an impressive 38%, with the average payment amounting to around US$2.30 (Mak et al. 2010). The number of downloads was over two million. As there were hardly any additional costs associated with the distribution campaign, almost all of the proceeds remained with the band. This meant that all of the band's previous revenue effects from earlier albums were exceeded. There were also indirect effects from the marketing campaign. The high level of awareness and the increase in popularity ensured better capacity utilization at the concerts. One aspect that is often overlooked was that pop legend Prince had already initiated a precursor campaign in July 2007 and offered his album "Planet Earth" for free in the UK. This led to a sell-out of all concerts in London. It was therefore known: Including the effects on complementary goods, such as concerts, an increasingly important source of income for musicians, giving away the product, in this case a music album can therefore also make economic sense. To be able to fully assess the effects of the price model, the entire revenue model must therefore be examined.

In addition to zoos (for example Lincoln Park Zoo, Chicago) and museums (for example Tate Gallery, London) PWYW is also used in the media sector. While competitors such as "Die Welt" or "FAZ" now offer fixed payment models for online use (free use is limited to a few free articles), TAZ takes a different approach. It offers a 3-tiered price for the electronic subscription: With the ePaper subscription, customers can choose between a standard price (€29.90), a reduced price (€19.90) and a political price (€35.90) (as of Apr. 2022). The content is offered online free of charge. This price scale already includes the mechanism of readers choosing their own price according to their financial capabilities and solidarity. In addition to the classic print offering, almost all print content and other content is also offered free of charge via TAZ.de. Customers are encouraged to pay a voluntary amount. In 2016, for example, the homepage showed that 6979 users (as of 01.02.2016) were already willing to pay voluntarily for the TAZ. The editorial team's considerations were as follows: A total of 20,000 paying users (minimum payment €5) were required to make TAZ content freely accessible (the total cost was estimated at around €780,000). With a readership of 1.3 to 1.5 million unique users of TAZ.de, the rate of paying customers was around 0.5% (Krämer and Burgartz 2016). Nine years later, the homepage has around 44,000 paying customers (May 2025).

In contrast to the assumption of rational consumer behavior (homo oeconomicus), in which consumers maximize their customer benefit by setting a price of zero, empirical results show that a significant proportion of users also pay for the service provided (Kim et al. 2009). However, the average prices are around two thirds of the previous price level. Theoretically, the "pay-what-you-want" pricing model includes the possibility of perfect price discrimination, namely when consumers pay exactly the maximum price they are willing to pay. This can be justified by considerations of fairness and fear of violating social norms (Kunter 2015). In addition to the internal perspective of the company regarding the cost situation, a key question in the customer relationship is therefore whether the price paid corresponds to the individual willingness to pay. It is also sometimes argued that with low price transparency, prices are even achieved that are higher than the previous price (e.g., unit price). This effect is compensated for by the case that some consumers consume the service and pay nothing at all. This results in two levels of decision-making: Firstly, the realization to pay a price for using a service and secondly, to quantify the exact amount of the price.

In a separate study (Krämer and Burgartz 2016), the interview partners (approx. 1000 consumers, aged 18+, Germany) were asked about their willingness to pay in the case of "pay-what-you-want" (see Fig. 8.4).

As many as 42% of respondents agree with the statement "I would actually be prepared to pay voluntarily for a service" (25% disagree). In contrast, the statement "Most customers would not be prepared to pay voluntarily for a service" achieved an approval rate of 61%. Only 11% reject the statement and thus support the view that consumers are also predominantly willing to pay (see Fig. 8.4). It can also be seen that most respondents are rather indifferent to the fairness concept of this pricing model. Only one in four consumers welcomes the pricing model because it is seen as fair. Participatory pricing approaches are therefore not necessarily

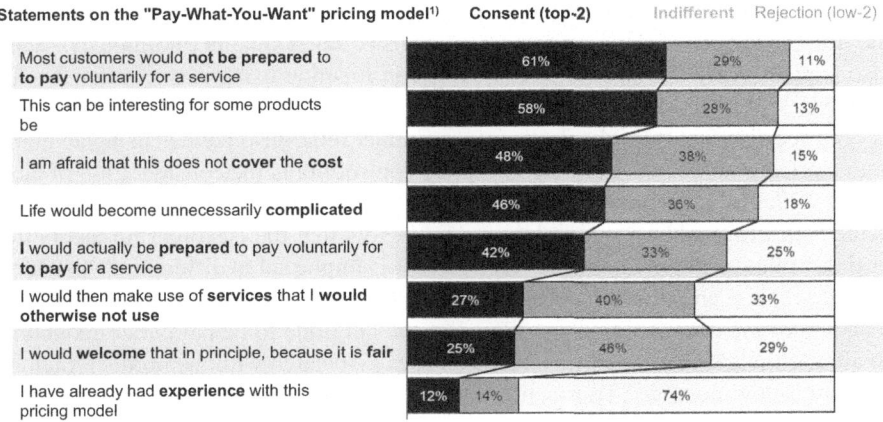

Statements on the "Pay-What-You-Want" pricing model[1])   Consent (top-2)   Indifferent   Rejection (low-2)

Statement	Consent (top-2)	Indifferent	Rejection (low-2)
Most customers would **not be prepared** to to pay voluntarily for a service	61%	29%	11%
This can be interesting for some products be	58%	29%	13%
I am afraid that this does not **cover** the **cost**	48%	38%	15%
Life would become unnecessarily **complicated**	46%	36%	18%
I would actually be **prepared** to pay voluntarily for to pay for a service	42%	33%	25%
I would then make use of **services** that I **would** otherwise not use	27%	40%	33%
I would **welcome** that in principle, because it is **fair**	25%	46%	29%
I have already had **experience** with this pricing model	12%	14%	74%

1) Recently, price models have also been discussed in which the customer decides how much they pay for the product or service (e.g. for online newspapers or music downloads) or a donation is requested. How would you rate the following statements? 6-point scale from 1="Completely true" to 6="Not true at all".

Fig. 8.4   Statement evaluation of the "Pay-What-You-Want" pricing model

synonymous with high customer acceptance or preference. The study results of Sulser's field experiment (2021) are also consistent with this: "Participants prefer fixed pricing over pay-what-you-want pricing, and pay-what-you-want over pay-per-minute pricing."

From the consumer's point of view, there are therefore also predominantly doubts as to whether the price model can cover the provider's costs. However, the empirical analysis also highlights another problem from the consumer's point of view. Respondents' experience to date with this model is very limited and rather selective.

If the "pay-what-you-want" model were to become more widespread, this would also have an impact on consumer behavior and decision-making processes as a whole. After all, the model not only represents an opportunity for the consumer (to be involved in the company's pricing), but also an expense, in that they may have to deal with the issue of payment options several times a day when making purchasing decisions. Almost one in two consumers in our own survey is of the opinion that life would become unnecessarily complicated if the pricing model were to prevail (18% disagree). This confirms previously expressed fears that consumers could be deterred from consuming due to the complexity (Bertini and Koenigsberg 2014). This may also explain why subscription models have become increasingly popular in recent years and are now even described as pioneering in sectors such as the automotive and food retail industries: Customers are offered convenience with the subscription, which in turn is very advantageous from the customer's point of view and can therefore be interpreted as customer-centric.

A key objective of innovative pricing models is to mobilize latent demand. The offer of possibly paying nothing for a service appears to be particularly effective in attracting new customers. From a behavioral economics perspective, disproportionately high increases in benefits are often observed when switching to a zero-price offer ("for free"). Ariely (2010) describes this as follows: "Zero is virtually a different world. The difference between two cents and one cent is small, whereas the difference between one cent and zero cents is much smaller enormously." This also explains why one in four respondents can imagine using services that would otherwise not be used.

The decisive factor for the design of a customer relationship when using an innovative pricing model and therefore for price controlling is the consideration of customer value. In addition to customer-related benefit aspects, the level of customer value is determined by value-reducing cost factors that the customer invests in the business relationship with the provider. Here it is important to differentiate between product-related and transaction-related cost components. Product-related costs are made up of the consideration sacrifice, i.e., the net price to be paid after deduction of all discounts and the total financial expenses associated with the product, including any follow-up costs. Transaction costs include the resources required to carry out a transaction as well as overcoming the risks inherent in the purchase, which essentially include search and information costs, control and adjustment costs as well as negotiation costs (Burgartz 2008). Taking these and other aspects into account, an innovative pricing model must be integrated.

Analogous to the optimization of customer value as part of a customer's purchasing decision, a value-oriented provider is also interested in optimizing value accordingly. The costs incurred by a provider to create high customer value are generally offset by monetary returns, for example in the form of sales achieved, but also by non-monetary returns, for example in the form of information.

When evaluating whether the "pay-what-you-want" pricing model makes sense for your own company, it is not only necessary to weigh up the advantages and disadvantages of a specific pricing model against each other, but also in contrast to the respective alternatives. In this respect, price models must be presented from the perspective of the consumer (acceptance) on the one hand and from the perspective of the company on the other, particularly with a focus on the economic risk. This corresponds to the value-to-value approach, which combines the value perspectives of the customer and the company.

8.5 Outlook: Customer Proximity and Understanding in a Digitalized World

When the CEO of Levi's, Chip Bergh, announced in 2019 that general clothing sizes would disappear within the next 10 years and be replaced by custom-fit garments, this was just one indication of how much companies were trying to better understand consumers' wishes and implement them in product design. However, movement in this direction has been limited. In fact, the fashion industry has garnered significant attention for the opposite—controversy surrounding the rise of brands like Brandy Melville that produce clothing with "One Size Fits All" or "One Size Fits Most" labels that eliminate rather than increase size differences in the clothing offered, yet technological advances may soon affect sectors in which customized production was not previously possible. They may even lead to a complete change in business models: body scanning using augmented reality now makes customized clothing production feasible, if not yet the norm. The challenge will be to design a new business model not based on traditional economies of scale that factors in evolving technological possibilities.

But there are also opportunities for competitive differentiation in product and service improvement. IKEA, for example, set new standards by offering its customers a new shopping experience featuring immersive design Other providers are improving the customer experience by displaying the availability of products online (e.g., Hornbach or MediaMarkt).

Customer centricity focuses its attention on the buyer and the buying experience: as a result, it should be possible to build a mutually satisfactory customer relationship (Day 2003). Customers consciously or unconsciously articulate needs and specific requirements, which in the next step lead to the activation of the company's resources, which in turn develop solutions that can satisfy these customer needs. However, doubts exist as to whether sustainable improvements in the competitive position are possible through a complete focus on the customer. Gummesson (2008) points out that a monolithic focus on customer centricity is inferior to an approach in which a balance is sought between customer centricity on the one hand and resource focus on the other. This challenge is discussed in more detail in Chap. 9.

References

Ariely D (2010) Predictably irrational, revised and expanded. The hidden forces that shape our decisions. Harper, New York

Bertini M, Koenigsberg O (2014) When customers help set prices. Sloan Manag Rev 2014:57–66

Burgartz T (2008) Kennzahlengestütztes Kundenbeziehungs-Controlling. Ein konzeptioneller Ansatz zur entscheidungsorientierten Planung und Kontrolle von Kundenbeziehungen. Peter Lang, Frankfurt a M

Burgartz T, Krämer A (2014) Customer relationship controlling – IT-gestütztes customer value management controlling 26(4/5):264–271

Burgartz T, Krämer A (2020) Risikoorientiertes Kundenbeziehungsmanagement – Fokus auf die Kausalkette im Kundenbeziehungsmanagement. Controlling 32(4):38–45

Burghartz P, de Bellis E, Krause F, Franke N, Klanner IM, Häubl G (2020) You're one in a million: strict uniqueness of mass-customized products marketing science institute working paper series report No. 20–145

Cross RG, Dixit A (2005) Customer-centric pricing: the surprising secret for profitability. Bus Horiz 48(6):483–491

Day GS (2003) Creating a superior customer-relating capability. MIT Sloan Manag Rev 44:77–82

Dong Y, Yao Y, Cui TH (2011) When acquisition spoils retention: Direct selling vs. Delegation under CRM. Manag Sci 57(7):1288–1299

Fournaise (2012) "80% of CEOs do not Really Trust Marketers (Except if they are ROI Marketers)". http://www.fournaisegroup.com/CEOs-Do-Not-Trust-Marketers.asp. Accessed 26 Mar 2021

Fuchs M, Schreier M (2020) Paying twice to have it your way? The backfiring effect of mass customization on a product's resale value. MIT Working Paper

Galbraith JR (2005) Designing the customer-centric organization: a guide to strategy, structure, and process. Jossey-Bass, San Francisco

Garrow L, Hotle S, Mumbower S (2012) Assessment of product debundling trends in the US airline industry: customer service and public policy implications. Transp Res A 46(2):255–268

Germann F, Ebbes P, Grewal R (2015) The chief marketing officer matters! J Mark 79(3):1–22

Gummesson E (2008) Extending the service-dominant logic: from customer centricity to balanced centricity. J Acad Mark Sci 36:15–17

Güzel O, Vizuete-Luciano E, Merigó-Lindahl JM (2025) A systematic literature review of the Pay-What-You-Want pricing underPRISMA protocol. European Research on Management and Business Economics 31(1):100266

Hinterhuber A, Liozu S (2013) Innovation in pricing – introduction. In: Hinterhuber A, Liozu S (eds) Innovation in pricing. Harper-Collins, New York, pp 4–23

Jones TO, Sasser WE (1995) Why satisfied customers defect. Harv Bus Rev 73(6):88–91

Keiningham TL, Perkins-Munn T, Aksoy L, Estrin D (2005) Does customer satisfaction lead to profitability? The mediating role of share-of-wallet. Manag Serv Qual 15(2):172–181

Keiningham TL, Aksoy L, Buoye A, Cooil B (2011) Customer loyalty isn't enough. Grow your share of wallet. Harv Bus Rev 89(10):29–31

Kim JY, Natter M, Spann M (2009) Pay what you want: a new participative pricing mechanism. J Mark 73(1):44–58

Krämer A (2023) Mobilfunkverträge–Kundenbeziehungsrisiken und kundenspezifische Preisgestaltung. In: Stammkundenbindung versus Neukundengewinnung: Marketing und Vertrieb im Spannungsfeld von Hunting und Farming,Springer Fachmedien, Wiesbaden, p 167–185

Krämer A, Burgartz T (2016) Controlling von innovativen Preismodellen – Status Quo, Anforderungen und praktische Umsetzung am Beispiel "Pay-What-You-Want". Controlling 28(6):325–337

Krämer A, Schmutz I (2020) Mythos value-based pricing: Der Versuch einer (wertfreien) Einordnung. Mark Rev St Gallen 37(2):44–53

Kunter M (2015) Exploring the pay-what-you-want payment motivation. J Bus Res 68(11):2347–2357

Lamberti L (2013) Customer centricity: the construct and the operational antecedents. J Strateg Mark 21(7):588–612

Liang TP, Tanniru M (2006) Customer-centric information systems. J Manag Inf Syst 23(3):9–1

Lu S, Yao D, Chen X, Grewal R (2021) Do larger audiences generate greater revenues under pay what you want? Evidence from a live streaming platform. Marketing Science

Mak V, Zwick R, Rao, A R (2010) "Pay what you want" as a profitable pricing strategy: theory and experimental evidence, University of Cambridge, Cambridge, UK. http://rady.ucsd.edu/faculty/seminars/2010/papers/zwick.pdf

Malthouse E, Mulhern F (2008) Understanding and using customer loyalty and customer value. J Relat Market 6(3–4):59–86

Moodley T, Govender KK (2020) Collaborative leadership and customer-centricity: the case of an insurance service provider. J Pub Val Admin Insig 3(3):66–81

Nath P, Mahajan V (2011) Marketing in the C-suite: a study of chief marketing officer power in firms' top management teams. J Mark 75(1):60–77

Ntv (2021) Wahrheit oder Bluff? Diese 3 Tricks verschweigt Ihr Stromanbieter, 14. März 2021. https://www.n-tv.de/ratgeber/Diese-3-Tricks-verschweigt-Ihr-Stromanbieter-article22418175.html. Accessed 25 Mar 2021

Payne A, Frow P (2005) A strategic framework for customer relationship management. J Mark 69(4):167–176

Saarijärvi H, Karjaluoto H, Kuusela H (2013) Customer relationship management: the evolving role of customer data. Mark Intell Plan 31(6):584–600

Schuman S (2006) Creating a culture of collaboration: the international association of facilitators handbook. Jossey-Bass, San Francisco

Selden L, MacMillan IC (2006) Manage customer-centric innovation-systematically. Harv Bus Rev 84(4):108

Shah D, Rust RT, Parasuraman A, Staelin R, Day GS (2006) The path to customer centricity. J Serv Res 9(2):113–124

Shukla N, Kolbeinsson A, Otwell K, Marla L, Yellepeddi K (2019) Dynamic pricing for airline ancillaries with customer context. In: Proceedings of the 25th ACM SIGKDD international conference on knowledge discovery & data mining, S 2174–2182

Sulser PA (2021) Pay-per-minute pricing: a field experiment comparing traditional and participative pricing mechanisms. J Behav Exper Econ 92:101684. https://doi.org/10.1016/j.socec.2021.101684

Tyrangiel J (2007) Radiohead says: pay what you want, TIME Magazine Online, Monday, Oct 01, 2007

Whitler KA, Morgan NA, Rego L (2020) The impact of chief marketing officer role variance on marketing capability. Marketing Science Institute 20–112

Wind J, Rangaswamy A (2001) Customerization: the next revolution in mass customization. J Interact Mark 15:13–32

Combining Value Perspectives: Value-to-Value Segmentation in Practice

9

9.1 Introduction: The Simultaneous Consideration of Customer Benefit and Customer Value

"There is only one boss. The customer. And he can fire everybody in the company from the chairman on down, simply by spending his money somewhere else."—Sam Walton

In the course of increasing customer orientation, concepts for creating customer satisfaction and customer loyalty have moved to the forefront of entrepreneurial activity (Anderson 1996; Stauss 1994). In this context, the quote from Sam Walton, who sees the customer as the ultimate decision-maker and the nucleus for the economic success of the company. However, this suggests that increasing customer satisfaction and strengthening customer loyalty can be equated with the economic success of the company, but maximizing customer satisfaction does not necessarily lead to maximizing shareholder value. In reality, the correlations are often even more complex.

Such a corporate policy of customer centricity can be achieved first and foremost through a sustainable and consistent alignment of the range of services with the wishes and requirements of customers. The creation of preference-creating benefits for customers is therefore the focus of marketing activities. Chapter 4 deals with this aspect in detail. In addition to pure product benefits, many companies invest in increasing relationship benefits through additional customer service and customer retention activities, such as customer clubs and loyalty programs. From a strategic point of view, offering additional services is often considered more sensible than simply increasing the net benefit by granting discounts. Empirical findings confirm that a price reduction, which is intended to achieve the same increase in benefit or increase the probability of purchase as a non-price instrument (additional service, additional equipment, etc.), would have to be significantly higher than the costs of these "discount alternatives" (Diamond 1992). The strategies mentioned so far in the context of CRM are primarily oriented towards the criterion of marketing effectiveness (cf. Schnäbele 1997, p. 38). The focus of interest is usually on the effectiveness of marketing instruments in satisfying customer needs to achieve the goal of selling products and services on the market at the desired prices (Karlöf 1999). In recent years, the approach of customer centricity, i.e., the ultimate customer centricity of the company, has been propagated (Chap. 8). However, such a one-sided target orientation without taking into account the resources used for this involves the risk of "supply inflation" and therefore also profitability problems in the sense of unsatisfactory efficiency (Meyer-Waarden 2007).

Due to increasing cost pressure and limited marketing and sales budgets, marketing is increasingly faced with the challenge of concentrating not only on increasing effectiveness, but also on the efficient design of the service offering. Companies are therefore well advised not to always launch the product that promises the greatest benefit and therefore the largest market share. In contrast to the performance-related aspect of effectiveness, efficiency puts the result achieved in relation to the resources used and thus provides a measure of the profitability of the company's actions. The customer value can serve as a measure for checking the economic efficiency of the use of resources (Chap. 7).

Simultaneous consideration of efficiency and effectiveness criteria represents an attempt at double optimization, which often results in conflicting objectives. The improvement of the efficiency of measures, e.g., a more cost-effective production process or use of materials can lead to a reduction in effectiveness in the form of lower product quality—i.e., customer benefit (Budäus and Buchholtz 1997). The objective, therefore, must be to consider both the effectiveness and efficiency of customer engagement within the framework of customer management. This can be achieved by integrating the two value perspectives—"Value-to-the-customer" and "Value-of-the-customer"—into a unified "value-to-value approach" (Krämer et al. 2005; Böhrs et al. 2009):

- Value-to-the-customer: Sufficient customer benefit is the basic prerequisite for a lasting business relationship. For this reason, companies should pay particular attention to the question of what customer benefits the company generates and what competitive advantage arises from this. The real challenge here lies in measuring the customer benefit of your own products and services and then offering the target customer exactly the level of service that meets their requirements as precisely as possible.
- Value-of-the-customer: The generation of customer benefit must also lead to a genuine contribution to the company's earnings by the customer, the amount of which must be quantified. The analysis goes beyond the individual transaction and requires the cost-benefit assessment of each business relationship over the customer life cycle. This enables a strategic decision to be made as to which customer relationship should be prioritized and which customer relationship should be terminated or worked on less intensively (Venkatesan et al. 2007). The basis for this is an information management system that collects and consolidates relevant customer data and transfers it into management knowledge.

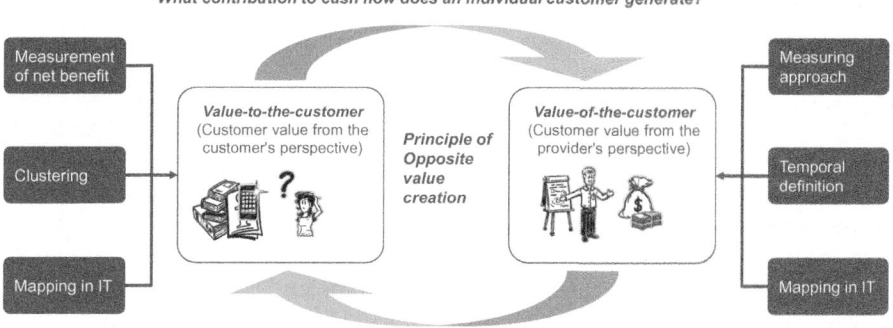

Fig. 9.1 Dependencies between "value-to-the-customer" and "value-of-the-customer"

The customer value management approach presented here attempts to integrate two essential components of the CRM concept, namely the creation of sustainable customer benefit and the achievement of lasting customer value, into the analysis and to use this to develop a framework for strategic and operational marketing management (see Fig. 9.1). The first step is therefore to operationalize the underlying constructs of customer benefit and customer value and then to combine them into an overall model. Customer benefit ("value-to-the-customer") is a core variable in marketing. The aim is to understand and address customer needs. Customer value ("value-of-the-customer") is a core value in value management. Both dimensions require a centralized and objective measurement approach as well as the consolidation of this information. In companies with many customers, mapping in the IT system is also necessary.

Both value perspectives are independent, but affected by each other.

9.2   Implementation of Customer Value Management

Customer benefits and customer value are the central constructs for successful customer relationship controlling. The constructs can only be measured and evaluated if meaningful and valid customer information can be provided as a basis.

The constructs mentioned in the previous chapter can be examined and determined using traditional market research, for example. However, this is too time-consuming in the long term, meaning that an IT-supported approach is required for operationalization. In order to establish IT-supported customer value management, various prerequisites must be created. These begin with the provision of customer-specific information. Based on this information, it must be possible to operationalize both value axes.

9.2.1 Customer Information and Its Mapping in IT Systems

Awareness of the importance of customer information as a competitive factor has grown steadily and with it the realization that the performance and value creation of all areas of the company depend to a considerable extent on the quality of the information supply to the operational units and departments (Gerth 2001). Customer-oriented information systems (CIS), such as database marketing, computer-aided selling and online marketing, have to ensure increased coordination and cooperation between the functional areas of marketing, sales and customer relationship controlling and thus all customer data available in the company in the sense of decision-oriented customer relationship controlling. If, in addition to customer information, marketing-relevant basic data including regarding sector, company size, socio-demographic data and risk data are available, acquisition efforts can be organized more efficiently.

Technological progress enables companies to have a high degree of transparency in the purchasing behavior of different customer segments. This applies to online sales as well as offline sales channels. As soon as credit cards or loyalty cards are used in a purchase process, for example, a dynamic data flow is set in motion. While the generation of customer data is not a particular problem, the challenge lies in the meaningful utilization of customer information. The most successful business models of recent years—Amazon, eBay and Google—have responded to this challenge and developed complex systems for analyzing customer data (Murray 2013). Today, these represent a decisive strategic competitive advantage.

9.2.2 Operationalization of the Customer Benefit (Value-to-the-Customer)

Customer benefit (value-to-the-customer) is the net benefit that results from the balance of the positive benefit components (benefits) of an offer—as a measure of the satisfaction of a customer's needs—and its negative benefit components in the form of the costs of purchasing and using the service (price, time required, etc.). When purchasing a service, customers will choose the alternative with the highest customer benefit, i.e., the one with the best benefit-cost difference (Menon et al. 2005). Measuring benefit requirements is therefore essential for the successful design of the first sub-process of customer relationship management (benefit generation). Based on this, customer segments must be defined for operative marketing, unless actual 1:1 marketing is realized.

It is possible to derive the preference structure of individual customers if the provider has a complete view of customer behavior and decisions. In this case, e.g., with online retailers, conclusions can be drawn about the customer preference structure from the actual behavior of the customers. This is much more difficult if there is no or only fragmentary information about the customers and their transactions. In this case, for example, empirical studies can be used if the data situation is otherwise insufficient. For example, a direct method, i.e., an assessment of the benefit weightings of the service features by the respondents themselves, should be used to measure benefits. Tools such as a constant sum approach or conjoint measurement can be used to ensure trade-offs between the benefit requirements and therefore realistic information (Chap. 4). Regardless of the method, it is crucial to divide benefit and cost components into individual building blocks as a first step. The second step involves identifying the drivers of net benefit and clustering them by customer group level.

Allocating marketing resources to activities that generate benefits for customers is just one important process for creating sustainable competitive advantages. To reflect the second process of capitalizing on customer value in the market, customer value must be measured.

9.2.3   Operationalization of Customer Value (Value of the Customer)

The successful design of the second sub-process—benefit capitalization—requires the measurement of customer value. In our understanding, customer value is a monetary, profitability-oriented variable. It therefore includes an assessment of the sales and customer-specific costs of a business relationship over the customer life cycle (Reinartz and Krafft 2001). Customer value is usually conceptualized through two dimensions ("partial values"), namely the base value and the growth value (upselling, cross-selling and reference potential).

The first question that arises here is the period to which the determination of the base value should relate. The base value is usually operationalized by the customer's last-period contribution margin, which can easily be taken from the accounting system. According to numerous empirical findings, the past contribution margin is a very good predictor of the future contribution margin and thus of the value potential that can be expected with relative certainty. However, this is not a universally valid approach. Depending on the business model and the purchase cycles in the market, it may make sense to base the customer value on an observation period of more than five years. In the case of growth value, a distinction must be made between direct additional revenue from the sale of higher-value services (upselling) or extended services (cross-selling) and indirect revenue effects from recommendations. Product reviews and recommendations are becoming increasingly important due to technological changes on the internet and social media.

The operationalization of the two value axes discussed can be illustrated using the example of a mobility service, for example rail travel (Krämer and Schmutz 2020). Figure 9.2 shows an example of the procedure. From a value-to-the-customer perspective, the first step is to understand the individual needs of each (potential customer. This can be done methodically using traditional survey techniques or through observation via search queries, bookings, purchase history, etc. As a rule, it is then at least possible to separate people with a high relevance of the ticket price from those who use the train more for reasons of convenience or travel time advantages (Bongaerts and Krämer 2014). The value-of-the-customer perspective focuses

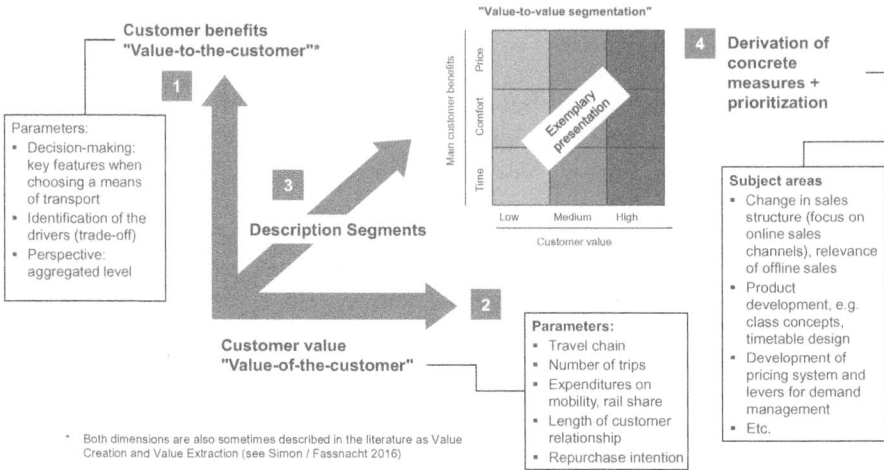

Fig. 9.2 Operationalization of the dimensions "value-to-the-customer" and "value-of-the-customer" using the example of rail users

on the cash flow generated for the rail company over the duration of the customer relationship. Important parameters in this context include the price paid, the number of rail journeys and the duration of the customer relationship. Combining both dimensions results in a matrix (value-to-value segmentation) that can be used to support decision-making (Bongaerts and Krämer 2014; Burgartz and Krämer 2015).

The effects of positive communication through customer recommendations described above can also be an important driver of customer value in the mobility sector. Krämer et al. (2020) use the example of the provider WESTbahn to show that a large proportion of new customers used the provider due to personal recommendations. Market studies show that WESTbahn achieves a significantly better price-performance ratio as a competitor of ÖBB on the Vienna-Salzburg route: The significantly lower price level of WESTbahn is perceived by rail users in Austria and is responsible for the positive word-of-mouth effect (see Sect. 6.5).

9.3   Merging the "Value-to-the-Customer" and "Value-of-the-Customer" Dimensions

Studies show that companies are successful in different ways despite providing similar services to customers (Slotegraaf et al. 2003; Pan and Luo 2006). Apparently, companies differ with regard to the second fundamental process for creating competitive advantages, which reflects the profitable utilization of the generated benefits on the market. One explanation for this could be that the relationship between customer benefit and customer value varies greatly across customer segments and that companies differ in their ability and willingness to align their service offerings specifically with the benefit requirements of valuable customer segments, i.e., to prioritize these segments.

In an exchange relationship, realizable value gains can be increased through the cooperative behavior of customers and suppliers. It is therefore entirely plausible and theoretically justifiable to link the two constructs back together (Cornelsen 2000). However, situations are conceivable in which the customer establishes or maintains a business relationship with the supplier even if the customer value is only slightly positive or negative due to barriers to switching set up by the supplier or individual inertia. It is therefore crucial for the provider to assess the customer-specific and market-specific circumstances.

In this context, it seems understandable that both perspectives are legitimized (see Fig. 9.1): In addition to the process of creating benefits or value for customers ("value creation"), attention must also be paid to the process that capitalizes investments in customer benefits in the form of an increase in company value ("value appropriation").

Due to rising marketing and sales costs combined with shrinking budgets, marketing is increasingly faced with the challenge of focusing on both processes— effective benefit generation and efficient benefit capitalization. For example, companies that offer products with high customer value may be outperformed by companies that offer a lower level of value but are better able to capitalize on this in the form of high customer value. Companies are therefore well advised not to always launch the product that promises the highest benefit and thus the largest market share. This can be illustrated with a simple example: Assuming a company lowers the effective price level in the market across the board, this has two consequences. Firstly, the net benefit is increased while performance remains the same. The "value-to-the-customer" (in economic terms, the "consumer surplus") increases. Secondly, whether the price reduction leads to a higher customer value depends on how elastically the market reacts to the price reduction, i.e., whether this results in a corresponding increase in consumption. If this reaction is inelastic, the result is a reduction in cumulative customer value.

The relationship between customer benefits and customer value has so far only been empirically investigated to a limited extent. Rust et al. (2004) investigate the extent to which the increase in benefits triggered by quality improvements is reflected in an increase in customer lifetime value (CLV). Some companies, such as Deutsche Bahn, are currently using elaborate models to investigate the causality between the level of customer satisfaction and the resulting impact on sales. Similarly, Pan and Luo (2006) analyze the relationship between perceived service benefits and the level of the price premium achieved as well as the size of the customer base. The example of flat price offers shows that very different value assessments are made depending on individual use. For example, a customer who uses the provider's service extremely intensively has the maximum perceived value, but is to be assessed critically from the provider's point of view (depending on the cost situation) (cf. Spotify or BahnCard 100). These studies therefore assume a homogeneity between customers and companies with regard to the transformation of customer benefits into customer value, which is probably unrealistic (Hahn et al. 2002).

Rather, it can be assumed that different benefit segments exist whose customer value differs considerably. The company's success then depends heavily on the allocation of marketing resources to the market segments with high customer value. Customer segmentation is therefore necessary to take account of the heterogeneity of the customer base, ideally including both value perspectives. This approach, first published by Krämer et al. (2005), is presented below as the "value-to-value approach."

As part of the value-to-value segmentation, the two value axes are combined to form a matrix. This is illustrated schematically in Fig. 9.2. The procedure is illustrated below using specific examples.

9.4   The Value-to-Value Approach (V2V) in Business Practice

The derived link between the two value perspectives in the context of a value-to-value segmentation in different markets is discussed with a view to the question of which strategic and operational aspects arise for market development. Due to the differences in market conditions, B2B and B2C business models must be presented separately.

9.4.1   V2V View in a Company in the Mobility Sector (B2C Relationship)

A key difference between B2C markets and B2B markets is the generally higher number of customers. This leads to a relatively uncertain customer image, especially if no transaction data is recorded for the purchase. The following scenario from the mobility sector is not an isolated case: with the aim of constantly optimizing customer processing, the company developed various segmentations in the past including product-oriented, demographic, customer value-oriented and psychographic approaches, but without lasting success. In order to increase value-oriented marketing, the CRM strategy was revised and completed with the implementation of value-to-value customer segmentation.

Determining the user drivers is one of the main challenges for mapping the V2V approach. If behavioral and preference information, usually in the existing CRM systems, is available/, it can be used directly. This is the case, for example, in the telecommunications or banking sector (Bayer 2010). In the specific project example, however, it was necessary to carry out an empirical study, as the corresponding basic data on customer use was not available in the IT systems. In terms of methodological approaches, various instruments were evaluated, including conjoint measurement, stated preference methods and a simple query with a weighing constraint (Kalt et al. 2013). A multi-stage trade-off question was used to determine the primary benefit in the travel decision.

When determining customer value, a balance must also be struck between maximum accuracy (with high resource input) and a focus on the key drivers (justifiable in terms of research economics). The challenge is to break down the company's financial flows into individual customers or segments. This requires close cooperation between various specialist departments, including Strategy, Marketing/Sales, IT, and Controlling.

The project focused on deriving the most important revenue and cost components, as revenue calculations vary greatly depending on the product segment. The cost calculation was based on the production costs attributable to the customer.

On this basis, a static customer value was quantifiable (contribution margin of the transport company), which could be dynamized by an additional query on the duration of the customer relationship (subscribers) (a 5-year view was taken in the project).

In a further step, the two value perspectives were merged (see Fig. 9.3, left-hand side). This requires a clear customer (data) view. The determination of the number of segments to be processed must meet the basic requirements (sufficient size, responsiveness). In the present case, the target dimensions are each subdivided threefold, resulting in nine sub-segments. The importance of the segments with regard to the dimensions of number of customers, revenue, and costs varies.

In addition to V2V segmentation, particular emphasis was placed on change processes in customer care. This required not only describing the individual segments, but also mapping them in the CRM system. When describing the relationship status of the V2V segments, it was examined, among other things, whether and which subscription the customers have (see Fig. 9.3, right-hand side), how high the degree of customer loyalty is (number of subscriptions in the last 5 years) and how high the satisfaction and repurchase intention is with regard to the subscription. From the perspective of customer development opportunities, the main questions were how high the "share of wallet" is and whether it is possible to mobilize latent demand.

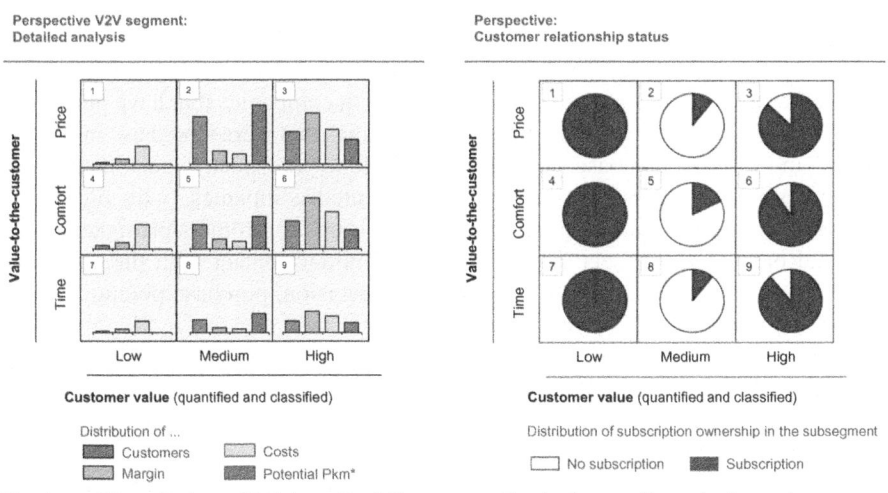

Fig. 9.3 Example of V2V segmentation in the mobility sector

A segment-specific approach is essential here, as the following considerations will make clear. In this specific case, negative customer value always exists in combination with a subscription. Negative contribution margins are possible in long-distance rail travel, for example, if flat-price offers are made that are extremely popular with individual customer groups (in Germany, for example, Deutsche Bahn offers the BahnCard 100, while the General Abonnement, or GA for short, is very popular in Switzerland). In the case of extreme use, the revenue per kilometer for time tickets with a flat price can be lower than the costs of providing the service (Merz and Krämer 2013).

There are similar correlations in local public transport. For example, season tickets account for more than two-thirds of all bus and train journeys. This mobility sector was also affected by the outbreak of the corona pandemic, with a significant drop in demand. As part of a study for the city of Frankfurt am Main, for example, a collapse in demand was measured in Sep. 2020 compared to Sep. 2019, i.e., before the Covid-19 crisis, and assigned to different customer segments (Krämer et al. 2021a). As the crisis progressed, it became apparent that the regular customer segment of season ticket holders remained loyal to their transport companies for a long time, even when mobility decreased significantly due to the crisis. This has also led to a change in the industry's view of this customer group (Krämer et al. 2021b). After the 9-euro ticket was introduced for three months in 2022, the Deutschlandticket replaced it. It has been available in Germany since May 2023. It excludes the high-speed InterCity Express trains but includes the use of local and regional trains and buses throughout the country at a monthly cost of 58 euros at the time of writing (Krämer 2024).

9.4.2 V2V View in a Multimedia Company (B2B Relationship)

As part of the development of an internationalization strategy, an inventory of previous customer relationships was carried out for a multimedia company (see Fig. 9.4). The marketing activities have so far focused less on companies that have purchased products in the last two years and more on companies that were stored as "interested parties" in the CRM database. The designation alone "Prospective customer" gives the impression that these are very product-oriented companies (with high sales potential). As part of an empirical study, both groups (customers/prospects) were surveyed on various aspects (including type of initial contact with the company, frequency of purchase, drivers for the purchase decision, purchase potential, satisfaction and intention to recommend).

Figure 9.4 shows the result of the most important condensed information using V2V segmentation. From a strategic point of view, it can be deduced that segment 2 (high quality requirements coupled with high coverage potential) is particularly important for the orientation of marketing activities and is given high priority. On the other hand, it can also be seen that around half of the contacts maintained in the CRM system represent companies that are relatively price-sensitive. This is reflected

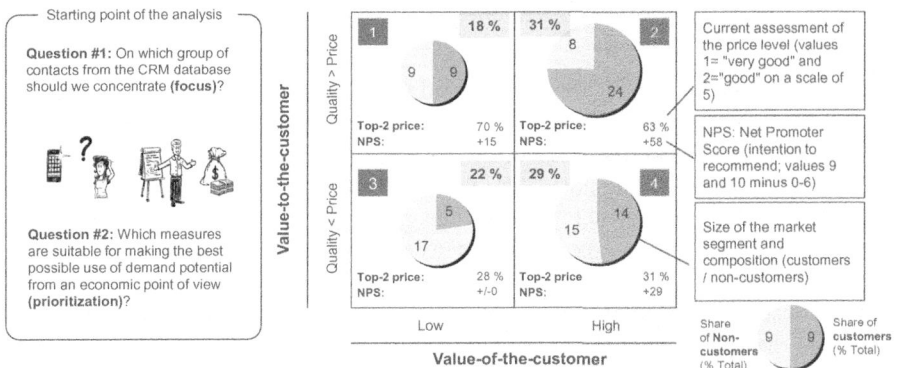

Fig. 9.4 Example of a V2V segmentation in the multimedia sector

in the assessment of the relevance of quality criteria in relation to price importance as well as in the assessment of the current price level.

Contrary to the assumption of those involved in the project that the initial contacts that lead to customer relationships are mainly generated by online presences, the results of the study show that recommendations from colleagues or private contacts are very important for current customers in the group. The analysis of the intention to recommend leads to a consistent picture: While the Net Promoter Score of the companies surveyed reaches a medium level on average, there are significant differences between customers (average NPS 58 points) and non-customers (average NPS -8). This also resulted in a paradigm shift in operational marketing, with the promotion of recommendation marketing becoming more important.

At the same time, as a "side effect" of the survey, a number of weaknesses in the setup and use of the company's own CRM data became apparent. The implementation of the V2V approach requires that the two value dimensions are also mapped in the system. This requires a unified customer view when determining the "value of the customer" including central customer account, consolidation of all transactions and sales activities, etc. With regard to the drivers of the purchase decision or "value-to-the-customer," better maintenance of customer data and an expansion with regard to expressed customer expectations such as performance evaluation, customer satisfaction, evaluation of the price level, etc. is required.

9.4.3   V2V View in the Household Electricity Sector (Industry Study)

The third project example concerns a different initial situation. The German electricity market was liberalized at the end of the 1990s. Since then, electricity providers have been competing for private customers. Electricity providers who want to survive on the market must develop the ability to attract and retain customers. In this context, Henseler (2006) develops an approach that examines four determinants of supplier switching, namely.

- Customer satisfaction with its existing provider.
- The attractiveness of the alternatives, i.e., how much additional benefit is expected from switching providers.
- The perceived switching costs, i.e., the consumer's assessment of the effort and risks associated with switching providers.
- Involvement, i.e., the degree of interest in and involvement with the power supply.

For households intending to change their electricity provider, price is the most important reason (Stöhr et al. 2020). As a result, competition for customers in traditional electricity sales nowadays largely takes place on comparison platforms such as Verivox and Check24. After all, this is where the majority of consumers obtain information about providers and prices. Other customer segments are less price sensitive. Topics such as perceived security of supply, preference for the local electricity provider, or sustainability can be important points of orientation. In these segments, there is also considerable inertia in terms of creating transparency regarding alternative providers (ntv 2021).

The scope of application of this linked value perspective will be demonstrated using an empirical study on the electricity market in eastern Germany. A customer segmentation logic was used for the "value-to-the-customer" dimension, which categorizes the respondents into six different subgroups based on roughly a dozen statements. For reasons of simplification, only two benefit segments are distinguished below, namely a) the "price-sensitive" (price plays a fundamental role in the choice of provider) and b) the "performance-oriented" (performance elements are more important than price). The "value-of-the-customer" dimension is mapped by quantifying the income of electricity customers (Krämer and Bongaerts 2015). To this end, household expenditure on electricity was estimated and multiplied by the years of the customer relationship. Households were then divided into "low" and "high" groups according to the median value. Customer-specific cost information was not utilized but could potentially be expanded and detailed further.

Once customer benefit and customer value have been determined, the dimensions can be combined into a V2V customer segment matrix. This is shown in Fig. 9.5 using the example of the regionally analyzed electricity market, divided into two parts so that four customer segments can be distinguished. For the market as a whole, for example, a total of 45% of electricity consumers are classified as price-sensitive, of which 29 percentage points can be described as belonging to a low value customer segment and 16 percentage points to a high value customer segment. The largest single segment is made up of performance-oriented customers with high customer value.

In addition to the holistic view, it is also possible to look at customers of municipal utilities separately from customers of other companies, for example (see Fig. 9.5). Here it becomes clear that the structures in the submarkets differ considerably. For example, the customers of municipal utilities are characterized on the one

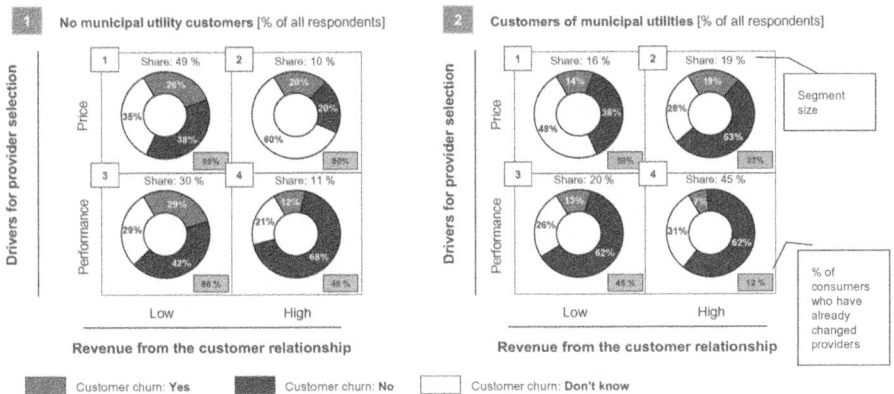

Fig. 9.5 Example of V2V segmentation in the household electricity sector

hand by a comparatively low proportion of price-sensitive customers (35%) and on the other hand by a very high proportion of customers with high customer value.

This results in very different framework conditions for strategic and operational marketing depending on the company. The following are examples of how to increase efficiency in terms of customer approach, customer loyalty, pricing, and product development.

- Once the segments have been defined, the question arises as to whether and in what form they can be identified and addressed for targeted market development. This is the
- This is a prerequisite for using V2V segmentation to improve efficiency in marketing and sales. To this end, the segments must be described as accurately as possible using internal/external data. Depending on the company and industry, the focus is on different characteristics. A generally important aspect for identifying the need for action is the state of the relationship with the company (duration and type of relationship, level of loyalty/satisfaction/intention to repurchase, etc.). The ideal data source for this is a CRM database, in which the relevant customer information/data including customer service should be available in a customer-centric manner.
- Figure 9.5 shows customer loyalty in the form of relationship duration in the municipal utilities and other energy supply companies submarkets. Structural differences can also be seen here. In particular, municipal utility customers with a high customer value have a very high level of loyalty: The duration of the customer relationship is longer than 4 years for almost 96% of customers in the segment. This is in stark contrast to customers of other companies. Here, too, customer value is correlated with the duration of the customer relationship, although the duration of the customer relationship is at a significantly lower level overall.
- Together with the benefit preferences, these findings can be used for targeted new customer acquisition, for example, but also for customer retention. A key indica-

tor in the energy market is the customer's intention to switch. Consistent with the duration of the customer relationship, high-value customers of municipal utilities are also characterized by a low intention to switch. In general, the intention to switch is rather low in the performance-oriented segments. The price-sensitive segments are particularly at risk. More efficient market development can start here: Municipal utilities have a recognizable competitive advantage, which is based on the relatively low intention to switch among high-value customers.

- In customer contact, energy suppliers are regularly faced with the challenge of having to communicate difficult messages (tariff increases, annual financial statements with additional payments, etc.)—this becomes particularly clear at the beginning of 2022, when electricity and gas prices reach peak levels. This is where V2V segmentation can be used to set the right tone depending on the segment or to proactively initiate measures that make such communication at least partially superfluous. In general, the V2V approach optimizes marketing communication (Belz 2009).
- The segment view can also help with pricing: Price-sensitive customers are more at risk of churning than performance-oriented customers. They can be addressed particularly well through discount and bonus campaigns. However, the empirical results show a comparatively low level of customer loyalty. This fundamentally calls into question new customer campaigns that primarily work via a discount.
- It may also be a good idea to review the product design in order to improve the market development of the segments and exploit additional potential. Service bundles (e.g., electricity-gas) or other service bundles are also an option here. Experience has shown that the more diverse the range of services purchased, the lower the intention to switch.
- In addition to the static view, the development of a sustainable customer relationship must also consider the development over time. To this end, it makes sense to develop customer development paths for the individual sub-segments. Depending on customer value and customer preference, these can include a set of different measures from the marketing mix in the customer life cycle.
- Optimization of marketing and sales can only become visible if the activities can be tracked in the short and medium term. The segmentation approach explicitly allows for this controlling perspective (Kalt et al. 2013).

The result shows that the networking of the value perspectives "value-to-the-customer" and "value-of-the-customer" within the framework of value-to-value segmentation is a suitable instrument for significantly optimizing marketing and sales efficiency by treating customers and potential customers in a differentiated manner and optimally allocating marketing budgets to individual measures. The SBB case study provides some details on this.

9.5 SBB's Experience with the V2V Approach—Interview with Markus Kalt Manager Planning and Performance, SBB AG, Markt Personenverkehr

Question: The Swiss Federal Railways work with the V2V segmentation approach. How can the segmentation be described in simple terms? Can you explain how this segmentation came about and how it has been further developed to date?

Markus Kalt: The starting point for the development of a new segmentation approach was the realization that different approaches were being used in product range development, marketing and sales depending on the situation. On the one hand, the distinction between commuter, business and leisure travel is an obvious approach to dividing up the market. On the other hand, the age groups, based on the fare structure, are relevant for marketing along the life cycle. With the strategic focus on value-oriented customer development, the need for an integrated approach was recognized (Fig. 9.6). With V2V segmentation, the value dimension is combined with a focus on customer needs. At the same time, known attributes such as age structures and travel activities can be mapped within the segments.

The benefit dimension (value-to-the-customer) today comprises two characteristics—price affinity and service affinity. The allocation is made clearly via a trade-off question sequence and thus shows the basic attitude of the respondents. The value-of-the-customer dimension is divided into four categories (low, medium, high, very high) and shows the contribution margin. Essentially, the frequency of use, the distances traveled and the tickets used (season tickets, one-way tickets) over the course of the year are taken into account. On the cost side, the production cost shares of the kilometers consumed are compared with the income from the tickets. This results in eight customer segments and a ninth segment of non-users, which thus cover the entire market in Switzerland.

The V2V segmentation is based on empirical surveys with periodic updates. The segmentation methodology has been greatly simplified over time. Today, the

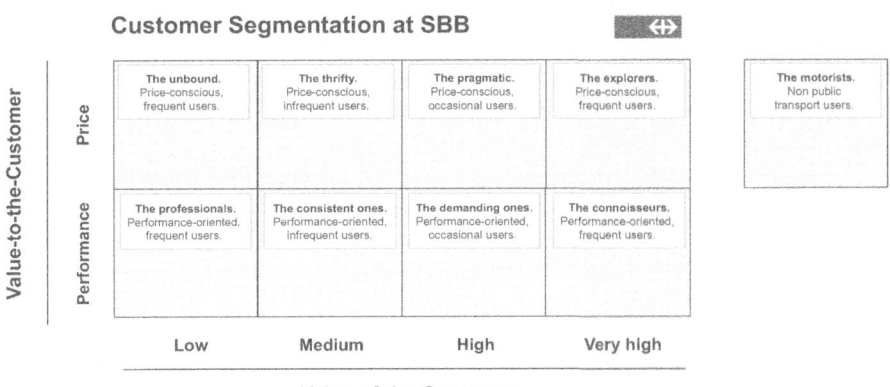

Fig. 9.6 Customer Segmentation at SBB using the Value-to-value-approach

segments are formed categorically using a decision tree. The quality of the content is largely retained, but the survey has been considerably simplified. A simple and stable set of questions makes it possible to include the segmentation in specific market research studies and thus continuously expand the content.

In addition to pure rail usage, it is crucial for marketing to understand the customer segments beyond this. How do attitudes, media use, life circumstances, interests and behavior differ in different areas of life? By synchronizing an external consumer study, we were able to enrich the customer segments with this colorful information.

Question: Can you give examples of how V2V segmentation has been used in marketing and how broad the range of applications is?

Markus Kalt: For strategic marketing planning, the customer segments are prioritized based on their influence on the objectives. The campaign concept is based on this. For example, a marketing focus is implemented with the topic of saving money among price-sensitive infrequent users to activate leisure travel. Performance-oriented segments with a higher willingness to pay form the target group for upsell offers in first class and for high-quality services, e.g., in rail catering.

For operationalization, it is essential to make the customer segments available in the customer master data. The transfer from the empirical survey to the real customer data is achieved by applying learning rules, which are continuously optimized. The hit rate is sufficiently good to use the segments as a selection attribute for direct marketing measures.

Question: How is the segmentation approach being received by employees and what measures have been/are being implemented to make segmentation more present in the company and to incorporate it into decisions?

Markus Kalt: During the introduction, the employees were given team-specific workshops to enable them to use segmentation, i.e., for conception, communication/media and implementation. Initial skepticism is completely normal. A new approach will be accepted by the organization if, on the one hand, the added value is there and, on the other hand, the management is behind it. As part of the periodic update process, it is important to actively communicate changes and new content. In order to create direct benefits for users, in-depth topics such as services, rail gastronomy, shopping behavior at the station, etc. are defined together with the teams. New study results are analyzed with the teams, measures are derived and included in the publication. This ensures that customer segmentation grows in line with needs and remains relevant.

To support the campaign management process, the customer segments are present in the briefing templates, in the planning system and in the operational CRM system. The organization thus makes an active commitment to ensure that customer segmentation is incorporated from the conception to the implementation of measures.

The main instrument for publishing customer segmentation is a publication with detailed profiles of the nine customer segments, background information and overview graphics showing the key characteristics of the segments. In addition, detailed information in tabular form on affinities and reach is prepared in such a way that relative deviations between the segments are easily recognizable. Today, customer segmentation is an established tool for marketing in passenger transportation.

Question: Are there other segmentation approaches at SBB besides V2V segmentation? How complementary are these approaches? Or what opportunities and risks exist if several customer segmentation approaches are used in the company at the same time?

Markus Kalt: In the area of customer experience and in the expansion towards journey marketing, we work with personas to define the customer journey, which are naturally formulated very specifically. They cannot always be assigned to a specific customer segment. There is potential to standardize the methods by using customer segments as the basis for personas or replacing them. The marketing management team has made a clear commitment to the primacy of customer segmentation, meaning that personas will not be used in future and only customer segmentation will be used. In terms of product and price management, the V2V approach in public transport has certain limits, as the framework conditions in the timetable and fare system are regulated. Demand in commuter, business and leisure travel and the age structures of customers dominate here. However, the V2V approach is effective in marketing the services and product ranges.

Question: What further development opportunities do you see for V2V segmentation in the future with regard to (a) the definition of segments (keyword: digitalization) and (b) the range of applications (support for decisions at SBB)?

Markus Kalt: With the development of digital information and sales channels, customer-specific interaction data is increasingly available. This means that in personalized marketing, sales and behavioral data are increasingly controlling customer communication. The importance of traditional customer segmentation will diminish in the medium term and be replaced by response- and data-based dialog. The V2V approach remains relevant in that customer benefit and value, alongside interaction data, should be key aspects for target group selection. By using advanced analytics/machine learning methods, target groups will increasingly be formed situationally via scores and thus partially replace classic, anonymous marketing communication.

The interview partner: Markus Kalt is Manager Planning and Performance, SBB AG, Market Passenger Transport Function.

9.6   The 7 Steps to Operationalizing the Value-to-Value Approach

In principle, a customer relationship can be described and reviewed at different levels. For example, perspectives such as the business model, customer strategy, and operational marketing can be related to each other. Overall, it can be stated that the combination of customer benefit and customer value analysis provides numerous starting points for understanding, managing, and controlling the customer relationship status in the layers under consideration. It is the basis for customer value-centered management. By analyzing how the alignment with the benefit requirements

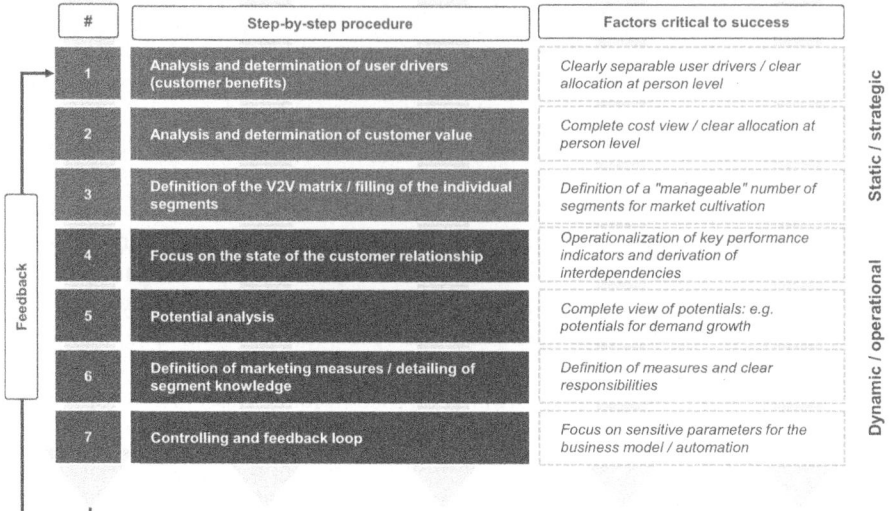

Fig. 9.7 Seven steps for operationalizing the V2V segmentation

of the respective segments is capitalized in the form of customer value, decisions on the allocation of resources to the different target groups can be improved. In a next step, the results of the benefit segmentation enable the implementation of segment-specific marketing measures to optimize the fulfillment of the benefit requirements of valuable customers and consequently to increase customer satisfaction. The V2V segmentation approach presented here considers both value perspectives, value creation for the customer and value appropriation for the supplier, and against this background enables a focus on customer needs and at the same time an analysis of the economic effects of efforts to achieve customer orientation.

A particular challenge of the approach is that the implementation fundamentally requires a specific approach that must take into account the particularities of the respective company-customer relationships and the market. Another special feature is the link between the concept of the V2V approach and operational data management. Networking is necessary to ensure success-oriented, IT-supported customer value management. This ensures that the customer segments are adapted as long as up-to-date information is available. The segment solutions can also be developed further, as described in the interview with Markus Kalt from SBB.

It is important to realize that defining the value-to-value matrix is only an intermediate step (see Fig. 9.7). In the static-strategic phase, an understanding of the benefit drivers from the customer's perspective is created. The aim is to assign each customer to a benefit segment (step 1). In the second step, the customer value is evaluated and quantified with the aim of assigning each customer to a specific customer value segment (step 2). Merging the two value axes results in the value-to-value segmentation (step 3).

The activities that follow are dynamic and operational. The aim is to establish an understanding of the customer relationship status. For the individual V2V segments, it should become transparent how convinced the customers are of the provider's performance, what level of customer satisfaction is achieved and how strong the customer loyalty or intention to switch is (step 4). In addition, the question of what potential exists in relation to specific customers with regard to improving customer value must be answered (step 5). If the information and assessments described are available, step 6 involves defining specific marketing measures within an overall plan once the following questions have been answered for each sub-segment:

- Does this segment fit our strategy?
- What are the chances of improving the segment's profitability?
- To what extent should resources be allocated to this segment?

Once the measures have been implemented, the individual changes that have occurred must be determined. This controlling loop also examines which assumptions turned out to be incorrect in retrospect (step 7). This turns the system into a learning, dynamic approach.

The examples from both B2B and B2C markets illustrate a broad range of applications (Fig. 9.7).

9.7   Outlook: From the Value-to-Value Approach to the Interfaces of Price, Costs, and Benefits

The conception and implementation of the value-to-value approach is an important, but not the final step towards customer value-centered management. The next steps include clarifying how the key points of price, costs, and benefits can be optimally coordinated and which instruments can support this.

Figure 9.8 attempts to describe these interfaces in simplified form and then assign tools to them:

- The first interface is about highlighting the dependencies between price and benefit. With the help of value-based pricing, an attempt is made to derive the price based on knowledge of the customer benefit, in that the price determination is primarily based on the customer benefit. It is based on the willingness to pay of customers, be they individuals or segments. The customer's perceived value can also be influenced by the price if customers expect a price-quality correlation. The effects of price optics can also be classified in this direction.
- The second interface deals with the dependencies between costs and price. Target costing is used to identify the target costs by calculating back from a specific target price in the market. In the opposite direction, the price can also be determined by calculating a product price based on the costs per unit using a mark-up calculation.
- In the third interface, the dependencies between benefits and costs are discussed. With the help of target pricing, marketing and product design focus on services for which there is a willingness to pay: Benefit and price deltas are therefore permanently compared. On the other hand, it also appears possible to influence customer benefits through costs, e.g., by disclosing and actively and transparently communicating production costs and margins.

These three topics are discussed separately and examined in detail in the following three chapters.

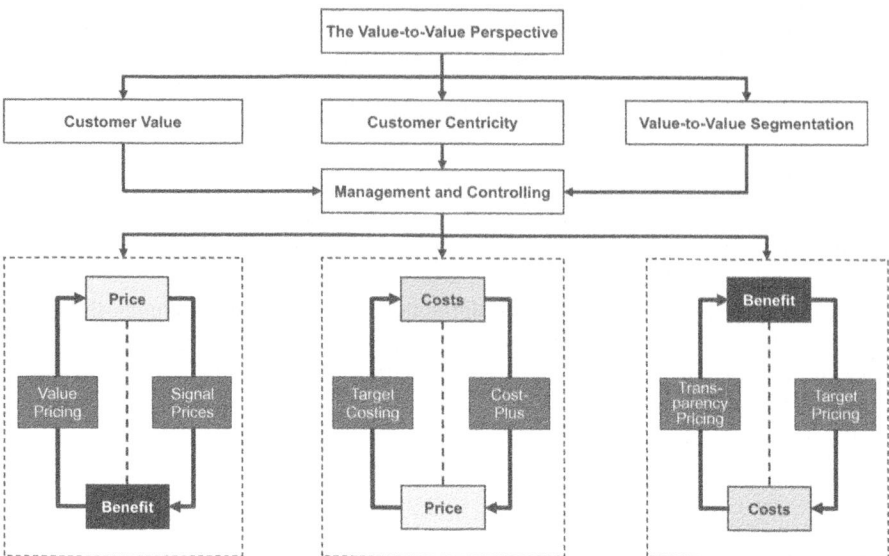

Fig. 9.8 From the value-to-value approach to the interfaces of price, costs, and benefits

References

Anderson EW (1996) Customer satisfaction and price tolerance. Mark Lett 7(3):265–274

Bayer J (2010) Customer segmentation in the telecommunications industry. Datab Mark Cust Strat Manag 17(3/4):247–256

Belz C (2009) Segmentierung – Die Kritik. marke 41(4):20–27

Böhrs S, Hammerschmidt M, Krämer A, Bauer H (2009) Wertgenerierung für Kunden und Unternehmen – Wie können Unternehmen Kundennutzen in Kundenwert transformieren? Die Unternehmung 63(3):307–326

Bongaerts R, Krämer A (2014) Value-to-Value-Segmentierung im Vertrieb. Mark Rev St Gallen 32(4):12–20

Budäus D, Buchholtz K (1997) Konzeptionelle Grundlagen des Controlling in öffentlichen Verwaltungen. Die Betriebswirtschaft 57(3):322–337

Burgartz T, Krämer A (2015) Customer value controlling – Combining different value perspectives. Bus Manag Stud 1(2):11–19

Cornelsen J (2000) Kundenwertanalysen im Beziehungsmarketing, Theoretische Grundlegung und Ergebnisse einer empirischen Studie im Automobilbereich, Schriften zum Innovativen Marketing, Nürnberg

Diamond WD (1992) Just what is a dollar's worth? Consumer reactions to price discounts vs. extra product promotions. J Retail 68(3):254–270

Gerth N (2001) Zur Bedeutung eines neuen Informationsmanagements für den CRM-Erfolg. In: Link J et al (eds) Customer relationship management: Erfolgreiche Kundenbeziehungen durch integrierte Informationssysteme. Springer, Berlin, pp 103–116

Hahn C, Johnson MD, Herrmann A, Huber F (2002) Capturing customer heterogeneity using a finite mixture PLS approach. Schmalenbach Bus Rev 54(7):243–269

Henseler J (2006) Das Wechselverhalten von Konsumenten im Strommarkt: eine empirische Untersuchung direkter und moderierender Effekte. Deutscher Universitats-Verlag, Wiesbaden

Kalt M, Bongaerts R, Krämer A (2013) Value-to-Value-Segmentierung im praktischen Einsatz. Planung und Analyse 39(6):21–24

Karlöf B (1999) Effizienz: Die Balance zwischen Kundennutzen und Produktivität. Hanser Verlag, München

Krämer A, Bongaerts R (2015) Mit der doppelten Wertperspektive zum Erfolg – Einsatz der Value-to-Value-Segmentierung im Strommarkt. ew Magazin für die Energiewirtschaft 114(9):39–42

Krämer A, Schmutz I (2020) Mythos Value-Based Pricing: Der Versuch einer (wertfreien) Einordnung. Mark Rev St Gallen 37(2):44–53

Krämer A, Wilger G, Böhrs S (2005) Value-to-Value-Segmentation – Die Integration von Kundennutzen und Kundenwert als Ansatz für das Kundenmanagement. Planung & Analyse 31(4):55–59

Krämer A, Wilger G, Posch T (2020) Monetization of customer value in the rail business: improving yield, revenues and customer relationship at the same time is possible – the case of WESTbahn in Austria, General Online Research (GOR) Video Conference, Sep. 10th 2020

Krämer A, Bongaerts R, Reinhold T (2021a) Kundenwert – die zwei Seiten einer Medaille: Valueto-Value-Segmentierung für die traffiQ Frankfurt. IVW 73(3):80–83

Krämer A, Bongaerts R, Reinhold T, Schmitz W (2021b) ÖPNV-Nutzung im Stadtgebiet Frankfurt Mobilität insgesamt und Nutzung von Bussen und Bahnen vor, während und nach der Krise. Der Nahverkehr 39(1–2):33–39

Menon A, Homburg C, Beutin N (2005) Understanding customer value in business-to business relationships. J Bus Bus Mark 12(2):1–38

Merz R, Krämer A (2013) Verknüpfung von zwei Perspektiven: Kundenwert zum Kundennutzen – ein Erfahrungsbericht der SBB. Vortrag Konferenz "Kundenmanagement 2013", Stegersbach, 6/7 Juni 2013

Meyer-Waarden L (2007) The effects of loyalty programs on customer lifetime duration and share of wallet. J Retail 83(2):223–236

Murray KB (2013) The retail value proposition – crafting unique experiences at compelling prices. Rotman-Utp Publishing, Toronto

Ntv (2021) Wahrheit oder Bluff? Diese 3 Tricks verschweigt Ihr Stromanbieter, 14 März 2021 https://wwwn-tvde/ratgeber/Diese-3-Tricks-verschweigt-Ihr-Stromanbieter-article22418175html. Accessed 25 Mar 2021

Pan X, Luo X (2006) Service capabilities in value appropriation: a conceptualization and investigation of internet retailers, Working Paper, Indiana University, Bloomington

Reinartz WJ, Krafft M (2001) Überprüfung des Zusammenhangs von Kundenbindungsdauer und Kundenertragswert. ZfB – Z Betriebswirt 71(11):1263–1281

Rust RT, Lemon KN, Zeithaml VA (2004) Return on marketing: using customer equity to focus marketing strategy. J Mark 68(1):109–127

Schnäbele P (1997) Mass customized marketing: effiziente Individualisierung von Vermarktungsobjekten und -prozessen. Schnäbele, Deutscher Universitäts-Verlag, Wiesbaden

Slotegraaf RJ, Moorman C, Inman J (2003) The role of firm resources in returns to market deployment. J Mark Res 40(3):295–309

Stauss B (1994) Total quality management und marketing. Marketing – ZFP 16(3):149–159

Stöhr A, Budzinski O, Jasper J (2020) Die Neue E. ON auf dem deutschen Strommarkt Wettbewerbliche Auswirkungen der innogy-Übernahme. List Forum für Wirtschafts- und Finanzpolitik 45(3):295–317

Venkatesan R, Kumar V, Bohling T (2007) Optimal CRM using Bayesian decision theory: an application for customer selection. J Mark Res 44(4):579–594

Krämer A (2024) New Mobility–vom 9-Euro-Ticket zur Verkehrswende? Springer Fachmedien, Wiesbaden

Part IV

Customer Value-Centered Management: Management and Controlling of the Interfaces Between Benefit, Price and Costs

10.1 Introduction: The Relationship Between Price and Benefit

"Long ago, Ben Graham taught me that 'Price is what you pay; value is what you get'. Whether we're talking about socks or stocks, I like buying quality merchandise when it is marked down."—Warren Buffet

With his statement, Warren Buffet expresses that there is a difference between the perceived quality and value of a product or service and the price that the consumer pays for it. Obviously, the star investor prefers situations in which the value clearly exceeds the product price.

He is not alone in this. Chapter 4 described the concept of customer benefit. A high customer benefit, for example due to an outstanding product, high brand loyalty or the perception of a lack of alternatives, translates into a high willingness to pay. This makes one direction of impact clear, namely from benefit to price (Fig. 10.1). However, there is also an effect in the opposite direction if the price influences the customer benefit. On the one hand, this can occur through the level of the price, if buyers equate a higher price with better quality (price-quality correlation). On the other hand, it is possible to use the instruments of behavioral pricing and rely on price-tactical and price-optical effects. These elements were discussed in Chap. 5. The subject of further considerations will be the question of how customer benefits can be monetized and to what extent this makes sense.

If a company succeeds in satisfying customers with regard to their expectations through products or services, this results in a satisfaction of needs, i.e., customer benefit is created (Morar 2013). In the case of perceived value, customers compare the subjectively assessed benefit ("What value do I receive?") and the sacrifice ("How high are my expenses in order to receive this value?"), while customer satisfaction arises when the expected price is lower than the value actually delivered. The two concepts can therefore be seen as different but complementary (Korda and

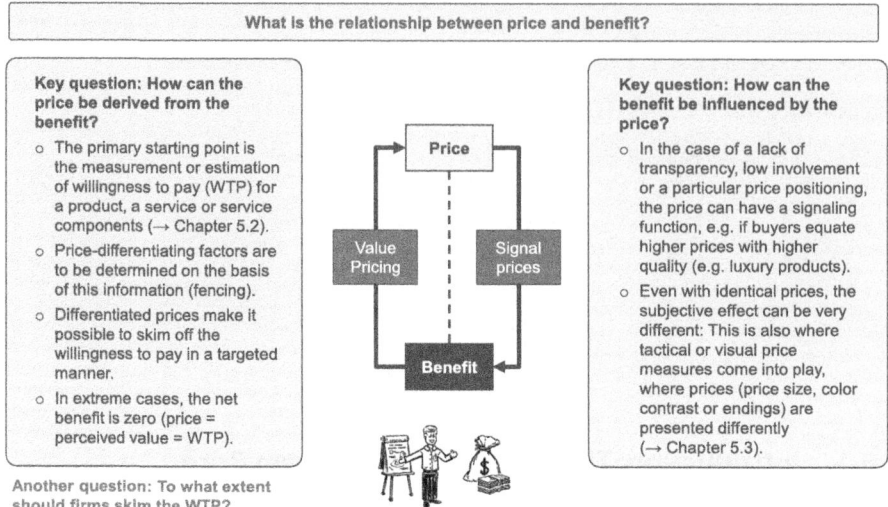

Fig. 10.1 The relationship between price and benefit

Snoj 2010). From this perspective, it quickly becomes clear how essential price is in this context.

A high perceived value results when the customer realizes a positive net benefit (value > price). This can also be translated as a good price-performance ratio. Such a perception then generally also leads to customer satisfaction. If the price is increased by the supplier with an identical perception of quality, the net benefit for the customer decreases (equivalent to the consumer surplus), but the producer surplus increases. The price increase can—but does not have to—lead to reduced customer satisfaction (e.g., not if the price increase is well justified from the customer's perspective).

According to Anselmsson et al. (2014), the possibility of achieving a price premium arises from the following aspects:

- Brand awareness
- Perceived quality benefits (products, services, processes, etc.)
- Social self-image of the company (CSR)
- Origin
- Social image
- Uniqueness.

Market situations with volatile commodity prices, growing competitive pressure, and changing customer expectations require a precise analysis of the potential in the pricing of products and services (see Mack et al. 2015). While the classic cost-based approach to pricing (cost-plus approach)—as well as competition-oriented pricing—has advantages when little market information is available, these approaches are less suitable for meeting real customer benefits in the market (Krämer and Schmutz 2020). Against this backdrop, customer benefit-oriented pricing, known as value-based pricing, has been recommended for many years. The cornerstones of costs, competition, and customer (3-C pricing: costs, competition, customer) are usually only presented alongside each other and in isolation when it comes to the question of "optimal pricing." In this context, value-based pricing is often emphasized as a superior approach in which pricing is derived from the customer's willingness to pay.

In fact—especially in times of dynamically changing framework conditions—there are a number of interactions and dependencies that prohibit an isolated view and demand an integrated approach.

Academics who have dedicated themselves to price research repeatedly complain about a gap between an approach to professional price determination and the practice of price management. Bergers and Fassnacht (2017, p. 51) cite the "inappropriate use" of cost-plus pricing in this context. This gives the impression that there is a clearly superior method of pricing that has not yet been recognized as such by practitioners. So far, little light has been shed on why the practice of value-based pricing has not or could not establish itself (Schmutz and Reinecke 2020).

Other authors point to the problems of purely competition-oriented pricing (Fisher et al. 2017; Kossmann 2008). While academia and consulting companies predominantly propagate the use of cost- or competition-oriented pricing as suboptimal and instead offer value-based pricing as a solution (Hinterhuber 2008; Liozu et al. 2015; Töytäri et al. 2015), practice seems to "follow suit" only with a delay and reluctance. Value-based pricing focuses primarily on the customer's willingness to pay, with some obvious advantages: Firstly, it is generally agreed that price is the marketing tool with the greatest (immediate) leverage (Iyer et al. 2015; Roll and Krampitz 2017). Secondly, it is argued that the price sensitivity of customers is often lower than is estimated by suppliers (Hinterhuber 2004). Following this argument—and subsuming the superiority of value-based over cost- or competition-based pricing (Hinterhuber 2008)—there is indeed a "theory-practice gap" (Liozu et al. 2015; Bergers and Fassnacht 2017; Simon and Fassnacht 2016). In the justification of this gap, it is obviously assumed that in an optimal state, every company implements the value-based pricing approach.

However, in the sometimes overly positive presentation of the possibilities of value-based pricing, some questions are severely neglected, e.g., "How is value defined as the basis for price determination?" On the one hand, the focus is on the value that is generated for the potential buyer, and on the other hand on the value that arises for the company from the completed transaction. On the one hand, this divergence offers several starting points for determining value and, on the other hand, shows that there is no strategy-related classification of pricing methods (Krämer and Schmutz 2020).

In practice, pricing models have become established over the last 10 years that are almost impossible to reconcile with traditional pricing based on consumers' willingness to pay. This applies to freemium and subscription models (Dropbox, SurveyMonkey, Amazon Prime) through to for-free offers in the B2C sector

(WhatsApp, Facebook, etc., see Krämer and Kalka 2017). A recent study came to the conclusion that the willingness to pay for the use of Facebook is USD 48 per month (Brynjolfsson et al. 2019). In this case, the added value generated is not skimmed off in terms of price. This can hardly be reconciled with classic value-based pricing. If users have an average willingness to pay of USD 48 per month, Facebook could also offer its service as a subscription at a price of USD 9.99 or USD 19.99 per month without losing large customer segments. Facebook has decided not to do this because the company is aiming for a maximum traffic on the platform, which in turn forms the basis for advertising revenue as the central source of income within the business model.

The same applies to the WhatsApp messenger service. After WhatsApp was initially offered free of charge, the company introduced a subscription price model in 2013 (not for IOS devices). However, in 2016 the messenger service became free again. This cannot be explained by the fact that the willingness to pay for the service is close to zero. On the contrary: the authors' own studies, which examined the perceived value and willingness to pay for WhatsApp in Germany, also confirm significant willingness to pay on average, but here, too, willingness to pay is very fragmented. Some frequent users see a high personal value in the app because it is the central communication medium, while others use the app more sporadically or see other free alternatives to the messenger service. In fact, there are also classic starting points for price differentiation, but these are deliberately avoided. Here, too, the key figure of user volume is given extremely high weighting as a central parameter for the value of the platform.

The deliberate avoidance of skimming off willingness to pay is to a large extent also the basis for the freemium price model, in which users do not have to make a monetary sacrifice for a basic service.

While these pricing models leave willingness to pay out of scope, changing framework conditions are also creating opportunities for providers to estimate willingness to pay in real time and determine it in a dynamically personalized way, so that the consumer surplus approaches zero, such as in the travel industry (Krämer et al. 2017; Krämer 2018). This is realistic because the opportunities for customer-specific data collection have improved due to the interplay of increased internet use, stronger internet sales activities, and the spread of data exchange.

10.2 Benefits and Customer Value as Cornerstones for Pricing

10.2.1 Starting Points for Determining the Price—Or: Why Cost and Competition-Oriented Pricing Are Suboptimal

The basic thinking models for price setting can be derived from the orientation of the business models (Ohmae 1983), whereby the primary orientation can be the company's own expenses, or cost focus, the orientation towards competitors, or competitive focus and the understanding of the needs and value of potential buyers, or customer focus (Fig. 10.2). The continuation of this logic results in correspond-ing derivations for price determination. If there is a clear understanding of the com-pany's own cost structure and a cost calculation for each product, then cost-plus pricing can also be useful. Cost-plus pricing is often cited as a prominent example (Nagle and Müller 2017; Hinterhuber 2008).

The cost-plus pricing model gives the impression of financial security. However, in many industries, it is not possible to calculate the unit costs of a product precisely before determining the price, as unit costs depend on sales figures (Nagle and Müller 2017). Despite the weaknesses (Fig. 10.2), empirical studies confirm the widespread use of cost-based pricing in practice (Shim and Sudit 1995; Liozu et al. 2015). Iyer et al. (2015) go particularly far in their interpretation when they place a correspond-ing approach in the context of irrational decisions.

While the approach of cost-plus is sometimes devaluated, the academic discus-sion often overlooks the fact that situations can arise in business practice in which a cost-plus approach supports the pricing decision in a meaningful way, e.g., in the spare parts business (large number of products, little customer and competitor infor-mation) or in professional services (e.g., legal advice, consulting), where alternative fee forms have been discussed for decades, but billing according to daily or hourly rates (analogous to cost-plus pricing) continues to be the standard (Hanna and Dodge 2017). A more dynamic view of the pricing process reveals another advan-tage of cost orientation: the justification of price adjustments. One example is the fruit juice producer Beckers Bester (Koeppel 2020), which had to implement a price increase after a disastrous harvest year (2017) and whose management turned directly to the end customer with an explanation of the cost increase and the neces-sary price increase in retail (and the promise to withdraw the price increase as soon as possible).

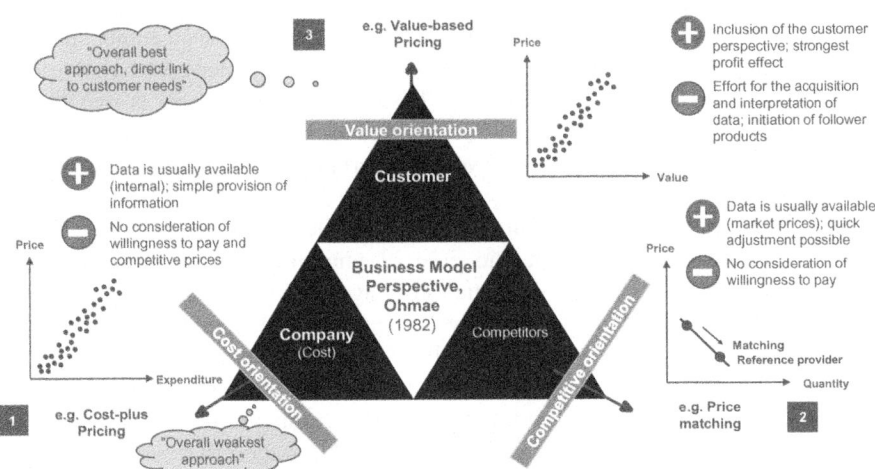

Fig. 10.2 From the business strategy to the pricing model

Competition-based pricing performs little better than cost-based pricing in scientific assessments (Simon and Fassnacht 2016). A particularly prominent example of this is "price matching," in which a company orients itself directly to the pricing of one or more of its most important competitors (Fig. 10.2). An inappropriately strong price reduction is often described as a consequence of strongly focussing on competitors, which suggests a cognitive bias or an anchor effect (Totzek and Alavi 2010).

While both cost-based and competition-based pricing methods are based on the most readily available information (own costs, market prices), value-based pricing is based on the value generated at the interface with the customer. The basis here is an understanding of which customer values which product and service features and to what extent (Hinterhuber 2004). This requires knowledge of consumer needs, which are used as the basis for benefit-based customer segmentation (see Trevenen 2012). The changed technological, social, and economic conditions today even make it possible to completely (dynamically) individualize pricing (Krämer and Kalka 2017; Krämer 2018).

10.2.2 Value-Based Pricing: Clear Reasons for Use, But Also Limitations

In the literature, value-based pricing is strongly combined with the concept of willingness to pay. Examples are "we define value as the customer's maximum willingness to pay" (Liozu et al. 2012) or "it uses data on the perceived customer value of the product as the main factor for determining the final selling price" (cf. Hinterhuber and Liozu 2012, p. 71). The strong focus on WTP indirectly leads to an "underweighting" of the view of costs. In extreme cases, the "marginal costs = zero assumption" in the case of high fixed costs results in a singular focus on maximum sales price points. It is easy to overlook the fact that cost analyses can provide a clear framework for pricing, e.g., by providing short- and long-term price floors. The situation is even more different in the B2B sector, where the customer structure is very heterogeneous. Here, Shin et al. (2012) propose customer-cost-based pricing to eliminate unprofitable customers. The basic consideration here is that, firstly, costs are very widely spread across customers and, secondly, it is not possible to achieve a sufficient level of cost recovery for certain customers, even with higher unit revenues.

The "marginal costs = zero assumption" can also lead to wrong decisions from a strategic perspective. In the specific case of emerging price competition, this assumption feeds the idea that in a situation of aggressive competition, sharp price reductions are possible and strategically justifiable (for example, with the aim of securing one's own market share). After all, fixed costs are not relevant to decision-making in the case of short-term price adjustments. In the worst-case scenario, this approach can lead to companies going from a price competition to an outright price war (Wilger and Krämer 2020). Guilding et al. (2005) suggest this correlation when they state:

"In a highly competitive market, accurate cost information would appear to be a particularly important resource for marketing and sales personnel concerned with how low they can price a product and still cover variable costs (if a short-term 'variable costing' philosophy is adopted) or fixed and variable costs (if a long-term 'full-costing' philosophy is adopted)."

From a concrete company perspective, the classification "cost-based pricing = weak approach" vs. "value-based pricing = best approach" (Hinterhuber 2004) is therefore not sufficient. Rather, special features such as the number of products to be priced, speed of price changes, perceived similarity of products, homogeneity of competition, or transparency in the market should be considered (Fig. 10.3). For example, there are good conditions for value-based pricing in the case of Apple where there are few products and a clear USP. This is different in the case of discounters in the food retail sector (e.g., Lidl) or in the spare parts business with an almost unmanageable number of product categories. The high proportion of direct costs in the retail sector means that the industry places a relatively high value on cost mark-ups (Guilding et al. 2005).

The number of products for which a price has to be determined is often even higher in the spare parts business than in food retailing. Here, the volume in terms of special machinery or aircraft can comprise several hundred thousand products (Wickboldt and Kliewer 2018). To name just one order of magnitude: The largest commercial aircraft, the Airbus A380, consists of around 2.5 million individual parts. There is little product similarity in the different kinds of spare parts with regard to a comparison with each other, as well as a comparison with competitor products.

Apple is a striking example of a company with a limited number of products and low product similarity in that the iPhone accounts for a significant share of the technology group's total revenue. This concentration on one product family justifies a

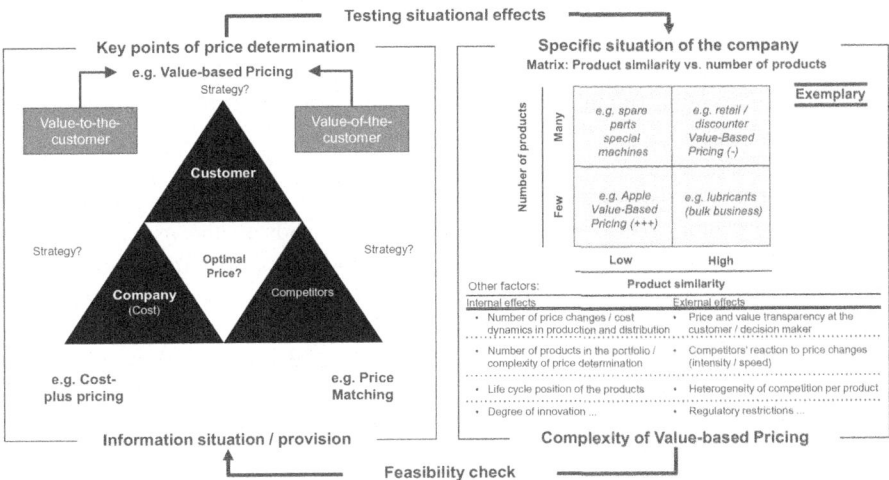

Fig. 10.3 Pricing methods and the company-specific view

considerable investment in determining willingness to pay. The optimal pricing of a latest generation iPhone is neither trivial nor extremely complex. De Giovanni and Zaccour (2019), for example, show that the launch price of the iPhone 4 to 7 models remained identical in the UK. The well-known marketing "skimming strategy" has long since established itself: A very high price is charged at market launch, then the sales figures are checked to see which part of the potential demand is covered. A decision is then made as to when the price should be successively lowered. This familiar approach also reflects a way of fencing segments with different willingness to pay and skimming off willingness to pay.

In addition, there are a number of internal factors (e.g., the number of price changes, the dynamics of cost development, etc.) or external effects (competitors' reaction to price changes, heterogeneity of the competition, etc.) that must be considered when setting price levels. Particularly in the case of genuine innovations, where there is no existing price comparison point, pricing based on perceived or anticipated added value is more likely to be successful. The specific situation for pricing is determined by the supplier's orientation and strategic requirements (e.g., short-term improvement of the profit situation), while at the same time influencing the concrete feasibility of value-based pricing.

Hinterhuber (2008) lists the barriers to the use of value-based pricing and mentions problems such as in:

- Determining value (companies are not able to correctly assess the value they offer their customers).
- Communicating value (companies are not able to properly communicate the value they offer their customers).
- Market segmentation (companies are not able to segment and differentiate customers according to their needs and price sensitivity).
- The management of the sales force (individual members of the team do not handle pricing the same way and thus give customers the impression of inconsistency or arbitrariness).
- The support of the management, if it for example stresses the importance of its value-based pricing and at the same time issues aggressive volume targets to the sales department.

These barriers to use relate to points that essentially come into play within the organization. Caution is advised if this discussion leads to the assessment that value-based pricing is feasible in any case, and that its successful implementation is only a question of willingness. For some suppliers—as has been shown—there are very convincing arguments for value-based pricing, especially in the case of superior performance. For example, Hilti, a company specializing in fastening technology, states "We are proud to be more expensive than our competitors" (cf. Belz and Bieger 2006, p. 302). The examples can be extended at will (e.g., by suppliers such as Festool in the power tools sector or Miele in the household appliances sector). However, this should not obscure the fact that value-based pricing cannot be successfully implemented in every company and in every situation.

10.2.3 Different Perspectives on Value Orientation

As mentioned at the beginning, an in-depth discussion of value orientation requires a closer look at the now overused term "customer value." Derived terms such as "potential value," "actual value," and "perceived value," as discussed by Nagle and Müller (2017), reflect the diverse ways in which the concept is applied. In their empirical analysis, Liozu et al. (2012) arrive at a diffuse and contradictory understanding of value-based pricing, even within individual companies, and point to at least twelve different definitions in the academic literature.

It is recommended to differentiate at the meta-level whether customer value is defined as the value that the customer perceives (value-to-the-customer) or as the value that the customer represents for the company (value-of-the-customer). Belz and Bieger (2006, p. 20) already describe this dual perspective when they point out that "customer value" can be understood as an umbrella term for the value "from" and "for" customers. Both perspectives are fundamentally different (one from the perspective of the end customer/consumer, the other from the perspective of the company/seller). Combining both dimensions results in a matrix (value-to-value segmentation) that can be used to support decision-making (see Bongaerts and Krämer 2014; Burgartz and Krämer 2015a). The specific steps are described in Chap. 9.

Examples of a recalibration of value perspectives (increase in producer surplus at the expense of consumer surplus) include the price increase at Netflix in the USA (+12–14%) in 2020 or Amazon Prime in Germany in 2017 (+41%). This is particularly evident in the transition from free services to paid services.

This was briefly the case with WhatsApp. BlaBlaCar, the market leader for carpooling, added charges to its service in 2016 (see Krämer and Kalka 2017, p. 90). The mere mixing of these two fundamentally different interpretations of the word "value," first value in terms of value-to-the-customer and second value in terms of value-of-the-customer, leads to misunderstandings and ambiguities in value-based pricing. Furthermore, the method is weak when it comes to clearly defining the price range that cost-based and competition-based pricing can deliver. The lack of such a price corridor is particularly precarious in B2B business. Here, the final price is decided in negotiations between sales and the individual customer. A price negotiation under value-based pricing, with the associated value-based sales arguments, always opens up a discussion about value and thus degradation. In the worst case, the pricing method can even damage the product and the brand in its practical implementation.

10.2.4 No Value-Based Pricing Without the Competitive and Cost Perspective

The three basic directions in price determination described at the beginning are usually presented monolithically in pure form, whereby the impression is reinforced that the decision in favor of "one direction" also means turning away from the others. This section aims to refute precisely this conclusion. To prove this, the conceptual interdependencies of the individual basic directions are considered simultaneously in the next step to specify the framework for an integrated pricing process. As an illustration, a simple market situation is described below (based on Dolan and Gourville 2009), which consists of two suppliers (hereinafter referred to as "Supplier 1" and the competitor "Supplier 2," Fig. 10.3). In a rational decision, the customer buys the product from supplier 1, as the net benefit from perceived value minus the price is greater than that of the competition (Fig. 10.4, case A, delta 1 > delta 2). While the cost situation is irrelevant for the consumer, the situation is different from the supplier's perspective: the difference between the price achieved and the variable costs (= contribution margin) ultimately represents the incentive for the supplier to sell the product.

In a modified scenario (Fig. 10.4, case B), all parameters for Provider 1 remain unchanged. Changes initially affect the cost situation of the competitor company (Provider 2), then subsequently its pricing strategy: cost savings are passed on to consumers through reduced prices. As a result, the consumer decision situation changes in favor of Provider 2 (delta 2 > delta 1).

This means that the outcome of an isolated cost-based strategy is nevertheless influenced by the competition due to external circumstances (external decisions). This is because even without a change in pricing strategy, purchasing decisions tend to favor the competitor. For example, the Irish low-cost airline Ryanair announced an open price war upon its market entry in Germany (2016) and justified this with a superior cost structure, particularly compared to its main competitor Lufthansa (Krämer et al. 2016).

This mechanism means that the dimensions of costs and competition are so closely interlinked that it appears difficult or even impossible to consider them separately in implementation.

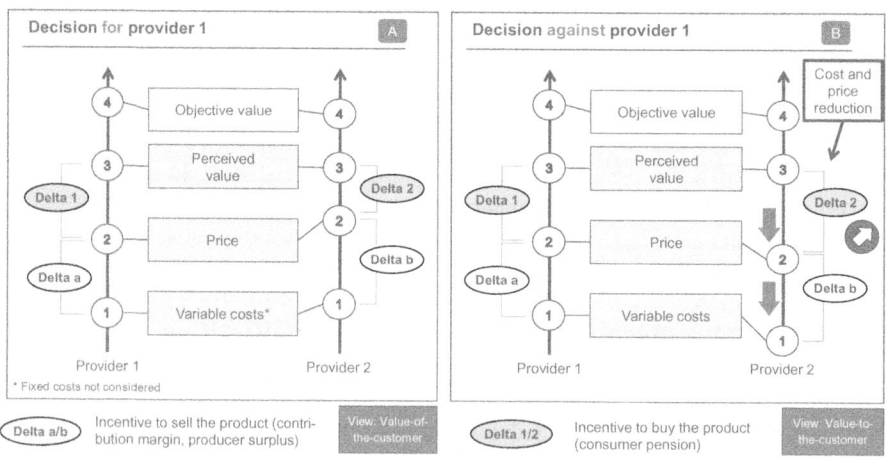

Fig. 10.4 The consumer decision taking perceived value into account

Specific framework conditions such as complete information, market transparency and stable preferences (see Lowe et al. 2013 for a critical review) apply for a solid justification of a consumer decision on the net customer benefit (rational decision). This reveals a direct influence of the dimensions of competition and costs on value-based pricing (regardless of the underlying definition of value). Both ideas of customer value are necessarily dependent on the competitive situation and pricing. And this in turn on internal and external costs as the example above clearly describes. In this interlinked chain, value-based pricing inevitably joins the somewhat more conventional and practical pricing methods as an important determinant of pricing but is not necessarily able to outperform the other methods in terms of effectiveness and implementation.

In summary, it can be stated that the suggested imbalance in the performance of the individual pricing methods leads to a separation of pricing method and context. Likewise, the three approaches should not be seen as silos standing next to each other, but rather as common pillars of a price (or a pricing strategy). To stay with this image: they support the individual pricing decisions and each influence the stability and therefore the success of the entire pricing construct.

10.2.5   Challenges and Recommendations for Practice

The interdependencies identified give rise to challenges for practical management, the key points of which can be described as follows:

1. Moving away from a monolithic discussion of the "3-Cs" for pricing.

   The cost-plus approach can provide initial relevant indications for a final price and the lower price limit. This facilitates orientation in the rest of the pricing process and in sales discussions. It should therefore not initially be seen as inferior to the other approaches, but at least on an equal footing with its strengths and weaknesses. The superiority of value-based pricing usually results from the deficits of the other two approaches. Pure value-based pricing may be possible if competition and cost structure are thin or even non-existent as a basis for information. Normally, the three pillars can only provide a superior approach in combination—so costs, competition, and customer are not so much isolated cornerstones, but rather interesting and value-adding in their interdependencies.

2. Pricing as a management competence.

   When it comes to information management, provision, and price implementation, automated solutions can relieve the burden on those responsible in the company. However, the core decisions remain with management—even with a relatively transparent and well-founded information structure; see Apple's sales problems with the iPhone in China at the end of 2018. The primary starting point must be the question of which "customer value" strategy is pursued by the company (Belz and Bieger 2006) and how the aspects of "value for the customer" or "value of the customer" are weighted. Approaches such as relationship pricing or customer value pricing (see Krämer and Kalka 2017, p. 88), which focus on the longer-term customer relationship, are therefore very interesting.

3. "Price satisficing rather than price optimizing".

Similar to the behavior of consumers (and managers), which can only be described in theory as completely rational and reason-driven, individuals instead try to make the best possible decisions under conditions of limited information ("bounded rationality"). If price determination is based on the consumer's perceived value and willingness to pay, these are variable parameters (Töytäri et al. 2015; Lowe et al. 2013). The willingness to pay becomes a variable parameter that can be easily influenced in some cases (Chap. 5). Particularly in industries with rapid changes in price and competitive position, the pressure to make a decision often outweighs the benefits of a 100% secure solution (Roll and Krampitz 2017). Gigerenzer and Goldstein (1996) formulate the target system as "satisficing rather than optimizing" for a framework with limited information and uncertainty, which can be transferred to price management. In principle, this means that in certain decision-making situations, an approximately good (80%) solution should be considered sufficient and no approximation to a better solution makes sense if a) this is not an option in terms of time or b) this can only be achieved with disproportionately high effort.

As many authors have already noted, value-based pricing has only gained limited acceptance in practical application. This is partly attributed to the attachment to proven pricing methods (inertia effect), elsewhere classified as cognitive bias and highlighted as irrational management behavior (see above). As a result of this tenor, value-based pricing has made a name for itself in academic circles as a superior pricing method, but one that has been almost unassailably placed on a pedestal and which is difficult to apply in practice. In other words, the implementation of value-based pricing seems unrealistic in many situations due to a lack of appropriate data and processes as well as a lack of customer acceptance. However, whether value based pricing is used or not, it should not be forgotten that an economic principle also applies here, i.e., the revenue must exceed costs. Whether this is the case depends on the specifics of the company and industry.

The thesis of the theory-practice gap implies, firstly, a one-sided superiority of value-based pricing as a pricing method and, secondly, a need to catch up in practice with regard to the greater inclusion of the customer perspective. In the classification attempted here and the presentation of the dependencies, however, the term "value" loses its "sharpness," so the description as a myth (blurred, glorified, etc.) is apt. The VUCA-related influence of changing market conditions on price management in companies, which calls for new pricing methods, integrated and dynamic approaches, and fast decision support in practice, requires additional attention by academia.

10.3 Changing Development Trends in Price Management

As has been shown, the ability to price products and services according to their value to the customer is closely linked to the provision of data and process support in pricing. These aspects are described in more detail below.

10.3.1 Customer Data as a Breeding Ground for Value-Based Pricing: Changing Data Management

If pricing decisions are to be made on the basis of the customer's perceived value of products or services, sufficient customer knowledge is required above all. The continuous provision of customer data is better than ad-hoc customer surveys, on the basis of which prices are later optimized. Ideally, this should be automated and available in real time. While the term "big data" is often understood to mean gaining knowledge from previously unevaluable unstructured data or different data sources (Chap. 3), it is also possible to obtain a better and deeper view of customers by linking different data sources in a customer-centric view of an individual person (end customer B2C) or an individual company (customer B2B). This has long been the case in the field of eCommerce, where market leader Amazon, for example, not only has a complete history of transactions for each customer via a customer account, but also preferences (e.g., based on search behavior) and ultimately also information on price sensitivity, even depending on the current environment or location.

New data sources are not always necessary to obtain relevant information as a basis for price management decisions. In many cases, in addition to sales and CRM data in general, data from customer experience management in particular is becoming increasingly important (see Fig. 10.5). Against this backdrop, it is also understandable why SAP, a leading global provider of business software solutions, agreed to pay a purchase price of USD 8 billion for a company focused on market research such as Qualtrics at the end of 2018. Qualtrics was founded in 2002 and initially focused on supporting schools and universities in conducting online studies. Extremely strong revenue growth occurred when the company focused primarily on the corporate segment (Lazarow 2020). In March 2017, CEO Smith launched a new product, the Qualtrics XM Platform™, the world's first experience management (XM) platform that enables companies to receive continuous live feedback to prioritize needs and optimize customer, product, employee, and brand experiences. Smith explained "This platform is a game changer. Traditionally all of this information has been siloed. For the first time organizations can look at their customer, employee, product and brand data together in one place and understand how they all influence each other. It allows the [client] company to build incredible products that people will love, delight the customers at every single touch point, build a phenomenal employee culture, and build an iconic brand." Nothing less than the end of information silos was announced. Well-known companies such as Allianz, JetBlue and Michelin began to operate their business with the XM platform.

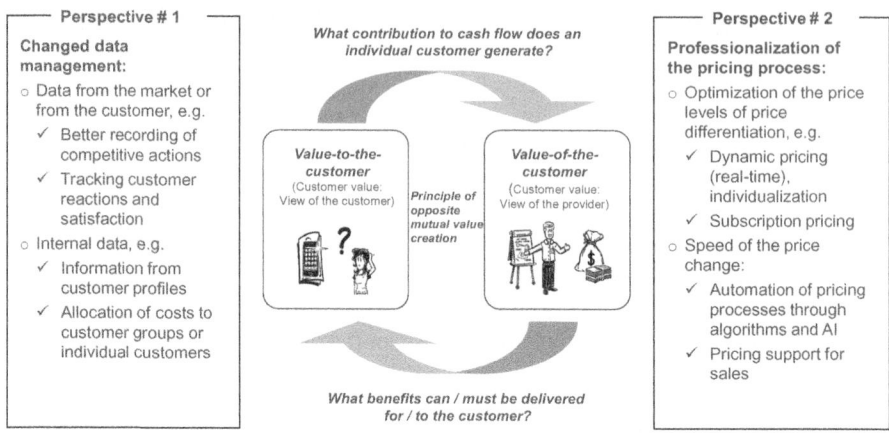

Fig. 10.5 Two strands change the view of price management (Krämer and Burgartz 2020)

There are three key figures to consider in this company acquisition. Firstly, the valuation of the company, which was founded in 2002, was only USD 2 billion just three years previously. Secondly, Qualtrics' turnover amounted to less than USD 400 million in 2018. Thirdly, based on the customer base, the purchase price is just under USD 900,000 per customer. Viewed in isolation, the key figures indicate a highly speculative nature; from the perspective of an overarching business strategy, however, the acquisition appears well-founded: "Together, SAP and Qualtrics will define a new standard, similar to how markets have changed through personalized operating systems, mobile devices and social networks," commented the then SAP CEO McDermott. In January 2021, SAP floated its subsidiary Qualtrics on the stock exchange. According to its CFO, SAP is estimated to have generated around USD 2.4 billion (€2 billion) in revenue from the sale of the shares. However, the true value lies in the 423 million Qualtrics shares that majority owner SAP continues to hold. This share package was worth USD 21.7 billion shortly after the IPO (as of Feb. 2021).

Better information regarding customer requirements favors the use of the value-based pricing method. It is based on an open, direct exchange with the customer or individual customer segments and is based, for example, on the pricing of additional benefits or the perceived value for a customer or customer segment compared to the price of the next best alternative of the customer.

The primary starting point is value-to-the-customer, i.e., the benefit of the offer as perceived by the customer.

10.3.2 Improved Decision-Making Processes: Professionalization of Pricing Processes

Changing market conditions mean that companies are accelerating their pricing processes on the one hand and increasingly differentiating themselves on the other. The faster offers and prices change in the market, the faster companies must be able to react to avoid losing market share or margins. In order to achieve this in an increasingly complex world, companies are trying to support decisions (decision support systems) or completely automate pricing mechanisms (see Mack et al. 2015; Krämer and Kalka 2017).

The background to increasing price differentiation is the ability to better match customers' willingness to pay with several price points than is the case with a standard price. In the final stage, this will lead to individualized pricing. In the B2B sector, this is possible if differentiated discounts, delivery conditions, and bonuses result in different effective prices depending on the customer. This is not only the case in the manufacturing industry, but also in the service sector. For example, studies on fee determination for consultants show that project costs are often differentiated according to the customer's industry, the size of the customer, the scope of the order, etc. (Deelmann and Krämer 2020).

A further step can be to make price differentiation dynamic: Dynamic pricing is currently being discussed and piloted as an option for differentiated pricing in many B2C markets and in retail. This extends as far as food retail (Merkle and Krämer 2021). This is linked to the hope of being able to react flexibly to changes in the market including new suppliers, changed prices, etc. but also in one's own cost structure such as warehousing and/or expiry dates. However, the focus on internal cornerstones is not enough. The decision-making process must also take external factors into account, such as customer perception, competitor reactions and the partners' view of the value creation stages (Krämer and Merkle 2021; see also Chap. 1).

Subscription pricing takes a completely different approach. Here, the customer pays on an ongoing basis, for example monthly, and receives a defined scope of delivery. This can be fixed as seen with newspapers or freely definable by the customer as seen in streaming subscriptions. The subscription is based on the price simplification lever and emphasizes the focus on building a long-term business relationship. Finally, subscription pricing essentially dispenses with customer-specific price segmentation; effectively, price differentiation is usually very limited and relates to target groups, such as the Amazon Prime offer for students, or at service levels as seen with Netflix (service streaming with advertisement, standard and premium service).

The value-of-the-customer arises from the time perspective: customers see the subscription as part of their lives and as satisfaction of basic needs, do not think about the meaningfulness of the subscription on an ongoing basis and in fact remain loyal to the provider, who in turn generates a continuous cash flow through the customer relationship.

10.4   A Changed Understanding of Value-Based Pricing

10.4.1 The Ambivalent Value Perspective

A closer look at customer value-oriented pricing reveals a certain ambivalence: after all, it encompasses two different aspects, namely customer value as "value-to-the-customer" in terms of what benefits the company generates for the individual customer and customer value as "value-of-the-customer" in terms of what benefits the company generates from the customer relationship. These are two sides of the same coin, as shown in Fig. 10.6 (Burgartz and Krämer 2014, 2015b). As a result, companies must decide which perspective they give more weight to, a more short-term price optimization via the individual transaction or a more medium-term focus on the contribution margin of the entire customer relationship. Against this background, the current developments in price management are also easy to classify. A greater flexibilization of prices is being discussed that goes beyond the familiar examples of mobility service providers such as air, rail, rental cars, hotels, and petrol stations. The so-called dynamic pricing in which the price can fluctuate significantly over short periods of time is also increasingly being used at concerts and sporting events. Tests for use in supermarkets are also underway. In the final stage of development, the flexibilization of prices will possibly amount to dynamic personalized pricing, as is already technically feasible in eCommerce today. At the time of a specific inquiry, the customer is assigned a price that matches the person's willingness to pay as closely as possible. Relevant information for this can be where the customer is located, their search behavior or transaction history, or which operating system they are using (Fig. 10.6).

However, skimming off the willingness to pay also has an impact on the customer relationship. For example, customers react negatively when they experience

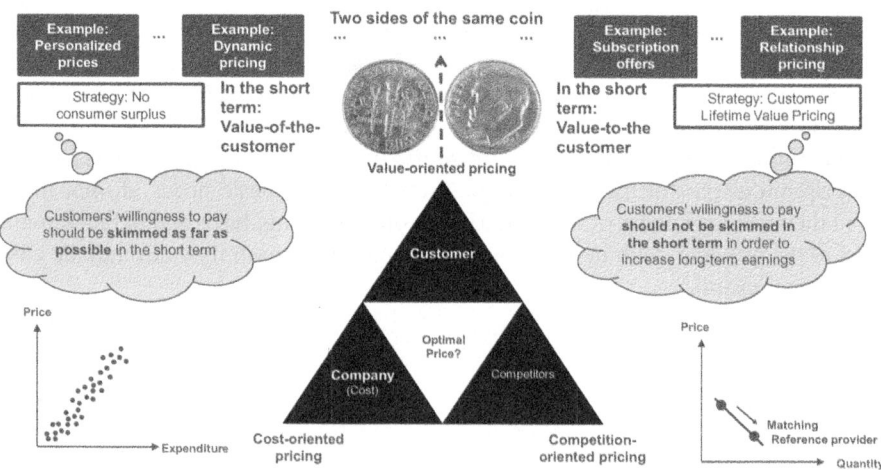

Fig. 10.6 Different objectives of value-based pricing (Krämer and Burgartz 2020)

a flexibilization of prices, especially in the case of sharp price jumps "upwards." From a consumer perspective, the evaluation of individualized prices in real time is even more negative.

If the second side of the coin is weighted more heavily (short-term focus on value for the customer, renunciation of complete monetization of customer benefits), companies arrive at different pricing models. At the same time as the trend towards price dynamization, a new era of subscription management and relationship pricing has been identified (Krämer 2020).

The increasing use of subscription offers reflects an ongoing change in the way companies view the customer relationship (subscription offers are only one facet of this): Participatory pricing mechanisms such as "pay-what-you-want" will be discussed further in Chap. 5. The focus shifts away from the individual transaction, in which an attempt is made to meet the customer's willingness to pay as precisely as possible (this generally requires a minimum degree of price differentiation). Instead, it focuses on the customer relationship as a whole and the value generated over the duration of the customer relationship.

Non-linear subscription price models are particularly effective in convincing customers to focus a large part of their consumption on just one provider. Customers are rewarded for their commitment to a company. Even if the customer's willingness to pay is known, this should not be completely skimmed off. Rather, the strategy is to build trust and customer loyalty through value positioning, with corresponding positive effects on market share and medium-term cash flow. This requires a different, i.e., detailed and dynamic view of the customer relationship that goes far beyond a short-term view of sales (Krämer and Burgartz 2019). The retail company real, for example, introduced a discount program called "realPro" to the market at the end of 2019 that is reminiscent of the well-known BahnCard or Amazon Prime models. Customers were given the opportunity to save 20% on food (or 10% on alcoholic beverages) for an annual contribution of €69. For customers, participation in realPro pays off after an annual spend of €345 or four to five large purchases (Fuchs 2019). Given the average gross margin in the German retail sector of 33%, this approach entails a considerable entrepreneurial risk, but also the opportunity to increase market share in the highly competitive food retail sector.

A customer who has previously spent €1000 on groceries (€200 at real, €800 at other retailers) can reduce their expenditure as a realPro subscriber to €869 (€69 fee + €800 purchase value) and thus effectively shop 13% cheaper at real. With a gross margin of 33%, real earns €66 in the first case and €199 in the second case (€130 margin and €69 card fee). However, this represents the maximum effect with a complete shift in demand in favor of real. In the case of previous expenditure of €1000 per year at real (€330 gross margin), real loses approximately €130 (€200 discount for the customer minus €69 card fee) if the customer's purchase quantities remain constant. Consequently, two facets are decisive: firstly, the participants' previous average expenditure and secondly, the impact of program participation on expenditure at real. However, the retail company is not in a position to evaluate the medium-term effects of the discount card. Following the takeover of real by the Russian investor SCP, the realPro program ended (Schrader 2020).

As this rough calculation shows, regardless of the pricing instruments used, better customer knowledge is increasingly important.

If it is possible to estimate the spending structure of customers, their purchasing volumes, buying rhythms, and reactions, risks from innovative pricing models cannot be eliminated for suppliers, but they can be significantly reduced. This makes CRM an integral part of price management.

10.4.2 Short-Term Focus on Value-to-the-Customer: The Trend Towards Subscription Offers

Subscription offers are nothing new. They have been established instruments for decades, for example in the area of mobility (e.g., season tickets in transport associations or Deutsche Bahn's BahnCard) or in the media sector with newspaper and magazine subscriptions. However, the subscription says nothing about the price model: this can be a fixed price offer, for example. Or individual prices are defined for each product or service. Two-tier tariffs, which consist of a basic price (e.g., basic fee) and a discounted price per transaction, are also frequently found (Fig. 10.7).

This is the case, for example, with the BahnCard or Amazon Prime (if you consider the annual fee as a one-off payment and the free delivery as a price reduction for the individual order). After subscription marketing was considered antiquated for some time, it has experienced a new upswing in the last 10 years, particularly due to increasing digitalization. Even with regard to automobiles, so beloved by Germans, subscription is now available. For example, cluno.de offers car use on a subscription basis at a monthly package price excluding refueling (see Fig. 10.7). The major car manufacturers have adopted similar pricing models after also

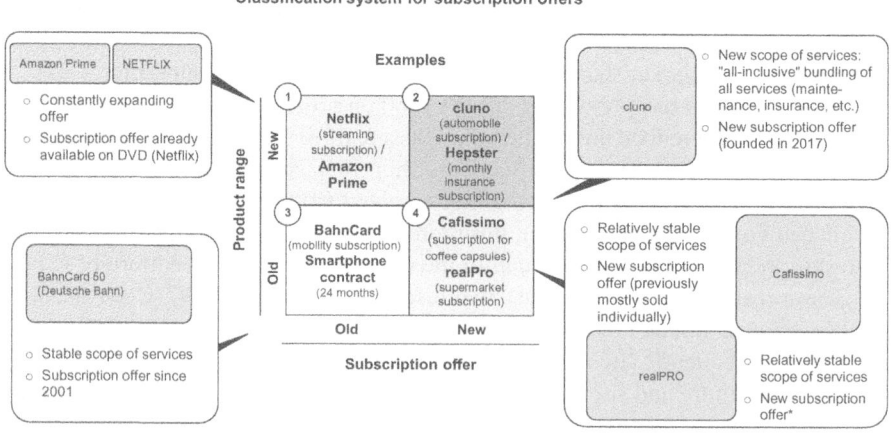

* For an annual fee of 69 euros, members receive a permanent 20 percent discount on food, drinks, drugstore products and pet food; terminated in 2020.

Fig. 10.7 Systematization of subscription offers (Krämer and Burgartz 2020)

identifying a significant market. For example, VW Board Member for Sales Klaus Zellmer stated at the beginning of Sep. 2021 (ntv 2021):

> "We estimate that around 20 percent of our revenue could come from subscriptions and other short-term mobility offers by 2030."

Subscriptions are now also offered for bicycles. The strong surge in demand for bicycles triggered by the coronavirus crisis, in which Weimer notes there was a 40–50% increase in 2020 compared to the previous year was one driver. Providers such as Swapfiets and Dance offer the use of bicycles on a subscription basis. Dance offers its customers their own e-bike for €79 per month. They promise to take care of it within 24 hours in the event of damage (Weimer 2021).

By contrast, Amazon's Prime subscription is based on a two-tier tariff consisting of an annual fee (€69) and discounts for individual transactions (free and faster delivery in online shops, some free music and video consumption, etc.). Netflix offers its service in different service levels as a flat-rate subscription. In July 2019, the Pricing Lab study (Hercher and Krämer 2020) analyzed the use of subscriptions in different product areas at the individual level.

Among those surveyed, almost 80% of German consumers use a subscription in at least one product area (on average 2.7 areas with a subscription across all respondents). The most frequently mentioned subscriptions relate to landline connections (telephone), the Internet, and mobile phone contracts. However, there is also a clear age dependency: in the under-30 age group, subscriptions for video and music streaming, for sport and for public transport are more common than average. While companies such as Spotify or Netflix are often discussed in public, consumers consider the subscriptions they use for telephony and the internet to be particularly important personally.

10.4.3 Dollar Shave Club Case Study: Subscription-Based Business Model with a Focus on Customer Proximity

The connection between the subscription pricing model, customer relationship, and company value becomes particularly clear when start-ups that offer subscriptions in order to address an existing customer need differently than the established providers in the market are examined. Dollar Shave Club was founded in 2011 and changed the marketing of razors in the USA within a very short space of time by going against the strategy of the major providers in the market, above all Gillette. Dollar Shave Club offers the razor as a monthly subscription (three different performance levels). While the company's awareness initially remained low in the start-up phase, this changed after a viral video in 2012 reached a broad mass of potential users and Dollar Shave Club became a company known practically overnight. Within the following four years, the start-up's market share rose to circa 8%. The company's success was partly due to how Dollar Shave Club cleverly differentiated itself from

Gillette with a new marketing concept and thus managed to gain and expand direct access to the end customer (see Esty and Fisher 2019).

According to Randall et al. (2016), the subscription offer was ultimately able to meet two fundamental needs that remained unfulfilled by Gillette's decades-old business model. Firstly, the convenience factor: for consumers who are pressed for time, a service such as automatic delivery is valuable because consumers no longer have to drive to a store or remember to buy a product they need all the time. Secondly, the decision support factor: potential buyers can be overwhelmed by the choice between a multitude of product alternatives. The choice of three different products, differentiated by price and performance, as with Dollar Shave Club, often seems sufficient for many consumers. Due to the special customer interaction, Halligan (2020) describes the company not as a tech-, but as an experience-disruptor. A third factor is the desire of the consumer for a fair price. This was also associated with a high degree of emotionality. Gillette's high margins were determined both by its dominant market position (70% market share)—also a prerequisite for strong pricing power—and by the sale of lock-in product systems (razor and blade, see Granig et al. 2015, p. 24). In particular, the subsequent purchase of blades at an incomprehensibly high price led to customer anger. Even though Gillette's management was convinced that its customers regarded the brand as an indispensable part of their consumption, the de facto market leader was vulnerable (Ingrassia 2020). The dominant market position and the high level of customer satisfaction measured in market research masked Gillette's vulnerability: the lack of customer physical and mental proximity not only led to an incorrect assessment of customer needs, including increasing performance requirements, but also to a lack of agility regarding response time to market changes. The introduction of a new high-performance product, the focus on comparative advertising, and the attempt to copy ("Gillette Shave Club") were moderately successful, but ultimately risky.

A key advantage of Dollar Shave Club's subscription offer is direct (and permanent) access to end customers and interaction with them. At the same time, the cost risk is limited. The flow of information from the customer to the provider formed the basis for active customer relationship management. In just a few years, the company was able to gather significantly more information about end customers than the market-dominating company Gillette, which had hardly any access to end customers due to its multi-level distribution. The market leader's market share fell to less than 60% in just a few years. Five years after it was founded, Dollar Shave Club was sold to Gillette's competitor Unilever. The purchase price of USD 1 billion was five times the annual turnover (USD 180–200 million). The buyer felt that this multiple was justified, with the issue of customer proximity and data playing a particularly important role; the number of subscribers had risen to 3.2 million by 2016. The direct customer business model gives Unilever "unique insights into consumer data," according to Kees Kruythoff, President of Unilever North America (see Terlep 2016). As the example of Dollar Shave Club shows, changing market conditions including digitalization and different customer preferences open the door to innovative business models and disruption. However, adjustments are also possible within existing business models, as the following example of the OTC pharmaceutical market demonstrates.

Even before the digital revolution, which has made it possible for new companies such as Dollar Shave Club (1) to change entire industries, (2) have a disruptive effect, and (3) generate a high company value in a short space of time, relatively small companies were able to operate extremely successfully because they focused on their strengths and clear customer benefits.

Hidden champions, unknown (global) market leaders, play a major role in the economic success of an economy, especially in Germany. The term "hidden champions" was first used in the 1990s by Simon (1996) and describes a particularly successful subgroup of medium-sized companies. Hidden champions are defined by three criteria: Market leadership, turnover and brand recognition. Accordingly, a company is considered a hidden champion if it (1) is one of the top three companies on the global market or the number one on a continent, (2) generates a turnover of less than five billion euros, and (3) has a low level of public awareness. MEDICE Arzneimittel Pütter from Iserlohn, which was founded in 1949, is also listed in a study by the state of North Rhine-Westphalia on the hidden champions in the state (FZM 2021). The company describes itself as follows: "The MEDICE Health Family develops and distributes innovative and diverse healthcare solutions. From the onset to acute symptoms, suitable prevention or treatment concepts are created for every stage of the disease, in which pharmaceutical, digital and nutritional expertise are intertwined and interwoven (MEDICE 2024)." The success of the hidden champions is also due to the fact that they know exactly what value they deliver to their customers and are able to translate superior performance into a price premium.

10.5 Interview with Fabian Beger, Global Head Strategic Development OTC at MEDICE Arzneimittel

Question: What changes have the coronavirus crisis and other crises brought?

Fabian Beger: If you look at the pharmaceutical market, we have noticed a clear shift towards digital sales channels, especially during the lockdown. In the pharmaceutical market, we are primarily talking about specialized.

Mail-order pharmacies, which have a significantly higher sales volume and logistical scalability, have a completely different calculation than a stationary pharmacy, which means that mail-order pharmacies can generally offer the end consumer significantly lower prices. This effect described above has been reflected, for example, in the rising share prices of "Shop Apotheke" and "DocMorris"—especially in the first months of the coronavirus pandemic. In the long term the digital channel will certainly benefit from this strong digital shift, as many new customers have been acquired. This means that—due to the price transparency prevailing in the mail order business more and more low-cost preparations (generics) are preferred today than were years ago. The "Made in Germany" seal of approval and the quality of the medicines are also not as important for mail-order pharmacies as they are for bricks-and-mortar pharmacies. Medium-sized companies in particular are committed to public pharmacies because we are seeing a significant drop in prices, especially in the mail-order business, and at the same time it is important to maintain and further develop the quality of advice for patients on site.

This development began long before the outbreak of the coronavirus crisis: The share of sales generated by mail-order pharmacies in the overall market has increased from 16% to 20% in the last five years. During the coronavirus lockdown, the share even reached 25% at times. It is expected that the share of sales will stabilize at around 23%. As a result, the trend is strengthening, but not at the speed we have seen in other sectors. This is also due to the fact that we do not yet have a giant like Amazon, as the pharmaceutical market is much more regulated, for example due to the need for a pharmacy license. What we are seeing, however, is that many mail-order pharmacies are selling via Amazon and are therefore becoming dependent on it to a certain extent. Nevertheless, it can be said that Amazon is only as strong as one of the largest mail-order pharmacies. What surprised us was that the average customer of a mail-order pharmacy is in their early 50 s, which means that these are not so much digitally savvy patients, but rather customers who buy medicines regularly, for example because they are undergoing long-term therapy or buying bulk packs for their medicine cabinet.

Question: What kind of benefit argumentation is there? Who are the target groups?

Fabian Beger: As an OTC, or over the counter manufacturer, we differentiate between three target groups:

Patients, pharmacists and doctors. The decisive factor here is the impact the respective target group has on the sale of a product. There are certain indications where patients themselves make the purchase decision based on good experiences with a medicine or brand awareness. This direct approach can take place digitally or in analog form through traditional media, but also within a presence at the POS in the pharmacy. For many OTC-relevant symptoms, however, the pharmacy is the first port of call. We all know it: if I spontaneously have a sore throat, I go to the pharmacy and ask for the best product and my purchase decision depends on the advice of the PTA (pharmaceutical technical assistants). Therefore, the benefit argument in the pharmacy is highly relevant, since both the benefit for the patient and the pharmacy must emerge. PThis can be of an economic nature, such as an increased unit benefit, but also qualitative, such as training for the team.

There has been a change in strategy with regard to pharmacy support, which will be reinforced in the coming years. Previously, the market was very much characterized by "sell-in," with stockpiling campaigns, for example during the cold season, in an attempt to build up as much stock pressure as possible. Now, "sell-out" is the new currency, as "sell-in" logically follows "sell-out." Pharmacies' expectations of manufacturers have developed accordingly, with pharmacies always demanding a strategic partnership with qualified sales advice. As a result, the requirements profile of a sales representative is currently changing significantly.

However, pharmacies are not the only point of contact for certain symptoms; the majority of patients go directly to the doctor, depending on the severity. The doctor, in turn, has a completely different view and expectation of benefits than a pharmacy, which also requires a differentiated approach. Doctors do not earn directly from

OTC sales, but charge for their services. It is therefore of primary importance for the doctor that patients feel well looked after and that the treatment is effective. At the same time, the doctor is of course dependent on patients ultimately remaining with the practice or recommending it to others. The doctor is therefore more concerned with the quality of treatment than with "sales," which is why a different type of sales force is needed here than in the pharmacy. Scientific studies, for example, are also very helpful in arguing the benefits, as the scientific level is significantly higher and certain patient images play a major role. The following insight is important: in the extended "buying center" described above, a healthcare professional can have more leverage than convincing 20–30 end customers. We have to take this into account in our marketing activities.

Question: How do you create differentiation values?

Fabian Beger: Against the background of the changed market development and the expanded target group definition, we see a new differentiation advantage in the fact that we ensure a balanced target group approach and support—always in the "patient—pharmacist—doctor" triangle. The differentiation value lies in the fact that we support the benefit argumentation with regard to all three customer groups simultaneously and thus ensure a consistent presence in the market. On the one hand, this requires a redistribution of marketing budgets, and on the other hand, new skills become important. A conversation with a doctor must take place "at eye level," as in today's predatory markets, it is above all the content-related arguments that need to be convincing. We will therefore be introducing a new organization in customer care in the future, which provides for even closer cooperation between the traditional pharmacy sales force and the pharmaceutical sales representatives at the doctor's by defining common goals and creating synergies from both target groups.

Question: What significance does price have in the benefits argument?

Fabian Beger: Although the growing importance of mail-order pharmacies as described above is increasing price transparency, we tend to have a low level of price awareness, particularly in the OTC market. This is due to the fact that patients generally only buy certain preparations, such as cold remedies, twice a year on average, meaning that price awareness and comparability are significantly lower than with traditional FMCG products.

Just as in other sectors, brands with a high level of brand awareness have a significantly greater price margin, as users are reluctant to switch products if they have had a good experience with the product and have therefore built up a certain level of brand loyalty. In this context, it should also be noted that customers with a low level of information and limited involvement may also see the higher price as an indicator of higher quality.

At the same time, the higher price means a higher margin for the pharmacist. This view has been gaining ground in recent years, particularly among pharmacists, because pharmacies are being managed more commercially overall.

The interlocutor:

Fabian Beger (M.Sc.)

Head of Germany Primary & Consumer Care at MEDICE Arzneimittel.

Email: F.Beger@medice.de.

10.6 Outlook: Customer Data as the Basis for Price Management

As shown, both strategies can be categorized under the term value-based pricing, namely on the one hand the strategy of extracting as much consumer surplus as possible, and on the other hand the strategy of foregoing precisely this in favor of building a long-term customer relationship. Ultimately, however, this makes the description of value-based pricing extremely elastic or amorphous.

Value-based pricing strategies are not necessarily aimed at fully monetizing customer benefits in the short term (this is usually associated with the term). Rather, one objective can be to forego the exploitation of willingness to pay and instead increase the value of the company via the lever of customer loyalty and recommendation. This also explains why there has been a boom in subscription management in recent years. There are interesting developments in this area. The example of Dollar Shave Club illustrates how subscriptions can be used to undermine established business models (such as Gillette's). Digital subscriptions in the publishing industry have led to an increase in the industry's profitability (Chap. 7). The Prime subscription is a key revenue driver for eCommerce giant Amazon (Chap. 14). Freemium models (e.g., Spotify for music streaming, SurveyMonkey for online market research or simple-show video maker, Chap. 4) are very popular (subscribers are gained from a pool of customers with free use), as key services are available at no charge (Chap. 14).

Despite all the differences, what the subscription models have in common is that the chain of success starts with the facet of customer proximity and leads to an increase in customer value, namely the value for the customer and the value for the company.

References

Anselmsson J, Bondesson NV, Johansson U (2014) Brand image and customers' willingness to pay a price premium for food brands. J Prod Bran Manag 23(2):90–102

Belz C, Bieger T (2006) Customer-Value: Kundenvorteile schaffen Unternehmensvorteile. MI Wirtschaftsbuch, Thexis, St. Gallen

Bergers D, Fassnacht M (2017) Debiasing strategies in the price management process. Mark Rev St Gallen 34(6):50–58

Bongaerts R, Krämer A (2014) Value-to-Value-Segmentierung im Vertrieb. Mark Rev St Gallen 32(4):12–20

Brynjolfsson E, Collis A, Eggers F (2019) Using massive online choice experiments to measure changes in well-being. Proc Natl Acad Sci 116(15):7250–7255

Burgartz T, Krämer A (2014) Customer relationship controlling – IT-gestütztes customer value management. Controlling 26(4–5):264–271

Burgartz T, Krämer A (2015a) Customer value controlling – combining different value perspectives. Bus and Manag Stud 1(2):11–19

Burgartz T, Krämer A (2015b) Measures to understand and control customer relationship and loyalty. In: Mack et al (eds) Managing in a VUCA World. Springer, New York, pp 99–114

De Giovanni P, Zaccour G (2019) Optimal quality improvements and pricing strategies with active and passive product returns. Omega 88:248–262

Deelmann T, Krämer A (2020) Consulting: Ein Lehr-Lern- und Lesebuch zur Unternehmensberatung. Erich Schmidt Verlag, Berlin

Dolan RJ, Gourville JT (2009) Principles of pricing. Harvard Business School, Boston

Esty B, Fisher D (2019) Gillette, cutting prices to regain share. HBS Case 2019(720–378)

Fisher M, Gallino S, Li J (2017) Competition-based dynamic pricing in online retailing: a methodology validated with field experiments. Manag Sci 64(6):2496–2514

Forschungszentrum Mittelstand (FZM) der Universität Trier (2021) Hidden Champions in Nordrhein-Westfalen, Studie im Auftrag des Ministeriums für Wirtschaft, Innovation, Digitalisierung und Energie des Landes Nordrhein-Westfalen. Trier

Fuchs G (2019) Supermarkt Real startet digitales Vorteilsprogramm mit 20 Prozent Rabatt, t3n vom 15.11.2019. https://t3n.de/news/supermarkt-real-vorteilsprogramm-realpro-1222002/

Gigerenzer G, Goldstein DG (1996) Reasoning the fast and frugal way: models of bounded rationality. Psychol Rev 103:650–669

Granig P, Hartlieb E, Lingenhel D (2015) Geschäftsmodellinnovationen: Vom Trend zum Geschäftsmodell

Guilding C, Drury C, Tayles M (2005) An empirical investigation of the importance of cost-plus pricing. Manag Audit J 20(2):125–137

Halligan B (2020) The experience disruptors, sloan management review, vom 27.2.2020. https://sloanreview.mit.edu/article/the-experience-disrupters/

Hanna N, Dodge HR (2017) Pricing: policies and procedures. Macmillan International Higher Education, MACMILLAN, London

Hercher J, Krämer A (2020) "Eine Welt voller Abonnements", Pricing Lab 2020: Rogator/exeo untersuchen Präferenzen der deutschen Verbraucher für Abo-Angebote. Bonn, Jan. 2020

Hinterhuber A (2004) Towards value-based pricing – an integrative framework for decision making. Ind Mark Manage 33(8):765–778

Hinterhuber A (2008) Customer value-based pricing strategies: why companies resist. J Bus Strateg 29(4):41–50

Hinterhuber A, Liozu S (2012) Is it time to rethink your pricing strategy? MIT Sloan Manag Rev 53(4):69–73

Ingrassia L (2020) Billion dollar brand club: how dollar shave club, Warby Parker, and other disruptors are remaking what we buy. Henry Holt and Company, New York

Iyer GR, Xiao SH, Sharma A, Nicholson M (2015) Behavioral issues in price setting in businessto-business marketing: a framework for analysis. Ind Mark Manage 47:6–16

Koeppel S (2020) Fallstudie: Preiskommunikation bei beckers bester. In: Kalka R, Krämer A (eds) Preiskommunikation. Springer Gabler, Wiesbaden, pp 339–350

Korda AP, Snoj B (2010) Development, validity and reliability of perceived service quality in retail banking and its relationship with perceived value and customer satisfaction. Manag Glob Transit 8(2):187–205

Kossmann J (2008) Die Implementierung der Preispolitik in Business-to-Business-Unternehmen. GIM-Verlag, Nürnberg

Krämer A (2018) Customer Centricity und deren Monetarisierung am Beispiel Amazon Prime. Mark Rev St Gallen 35(4):13–20

Krämer A (2020) Preisvereinfachung versus Preisdifferenzierung. In: Kalka R, Krämer A (eds) Preiskommunikation – Strategische Herausforderungen und innovative Anwendungsfelder. Springer Gabler, Wiesbaden, pp 73–88

Krämer A, Burgartz T (2019) Kundenwert und Kundenprofitabilität: Nicht zu komplex und nicht zu einfach. Sales Excellence 2(7/8):40–43

Krämer A, Burgartz T (2020) Kundenwertorientiertes Pricing – Die beiden unterschiedlichen Facetten des Kundenwerts. Controlling 32(Spezialausgabe):58–63

Krämer A, Kalka R (2017) How digital disruption changes pricing strategies and price models. In: Khare A, Schatz R, Stewart B (eds) Phantom ex machina: digital disruption's role in business model transformation. Springer, Wiesbaden, pp 87–103

Krämer A, Merkle W (2021) Dynamisch oder nicht!? Welche Chancen und Risiken bietet der Einsatz von Dynamic Pricing im stationären Handel? Mark Theory 83(11):78–81

Krämer A, Schmutz I (2020) Mythos Value-Based Pricing: Der Versuch einer (wertfreien) Einordnung. Mark Rev St Gallen 37(2):44–53

Krämer A, Jung M, Burgartz T (2016) A small step from price competition to price war: understanding causes, effects and possible countermeasures. Int Bus Res 9(3):1–13

Krämer A, Friesen M, Shelton T (2017) Are airline passengers ready for individualized pricing? A study of German consumers. J Reve Pric Manag 16(6):1–6

Lazarow A (2020) Beyond silicon valley. Harvard Business Review. http://knowen-production. s3.amazonaws.com/uploads/attachment/file/4910/When%2BStartups%2BSucceed%2Bin%2 BUnlikely%2BPlaces.pdf. Accessed 11 Apr 2021

Liozu S, Hinterhuber A, Boland R, Perelli S (2012) The conceptualization of value-based pricing in industrial firms. J Rev Pric Manag 11(1):12–34

Liozu S, Boland D, Hinterhuber A, Perelli S (2015) Mindful pricing: transforming organizations through value based pricing. In: Robinson L (ed) Marketing dynamism & sustainability: things change, things stay the same…. Springer, Cham, pp 412–421

Lowe B, Lowe J, Lynch D (2013) Behavioral aspects of pricing. In: Hinterhuber A, Liozu S (eds) Innovation in pricing. Routledge, Abingdon, pp 357–375

Mack O, Khare A, Krämer A, Burgartz T (2015) Managing in a VUCA World. Springer, New York

MEDICE (2024) Unternehmen. https://medice.com/de-de/Unternehmen. Accessed 18 Nov 2024

Merkle W, Krämer A (2021) Händler brauchen für Dynamic Pricing eine Gesamtstrategie. Lebensmittelzeitung 12(3):46

Morar DD (2013) An overview of the consumer value literature perceived value. International conference, marketing from information to decision. 6: Aufl., Babeş-Bolyai University, Cluj-Napoca, pp 169–186

Nagle TT, Müller G (2017) The strategy and tactics of pricing: a guide to growing more profitably. Routledge, New York

NTV (2021) "Zwischen Leasing und Sharing" VW bietet jetzt E-Autos im Abo an, NTV vom 1.9.2021, https://www.n-tv.de/wirtschaft/VW-bietet-jetzt-E-Autos-im-Abo-an-article22777994.html. Accessed 3 Sept 2021

Ohmae K (1983) The mind of the strategist. Penguin, Harmondsworth

Randall C, Lewis A, Davis A (2016) How subscriptions are creating winners and losers in retail. Harv Bus Rev 18(5):1–6

Roll O, Krampitz S (2017) Pricing 4.0: Neue Wege jenseits des Value Pricing. Mark Rev St Gallen 34(6):60–66

Schmutz IK, Reinecke S (2020) Gibt's nicht, geht nicht! Eine Konzeptionalisierung von Informationsdefiziten im Preisprozess. Mark Rev St Gallen 37(6):64–73

Schrader P (2020) Real Pro endet 2021, aber Walmart+ und Tesco Clubcard Plus setzen den Trend: Werden Supermärkte zu Mitglieds-Clubs? Supermarktblog vom 29.9.2020. https://www. supermarktblog.com/2020/09/29/real-pro-endet-2021-aber-walmart-und-tesco-clubcard-plus-setzenden-trend-werden-supermaerkte-zu-mitglieds-clubs/. Accessed 13 Apr 2021

Shim E, Sudit EF (1995) How manufacturers price products. Strateg Finance 76(8):37

Shin J, Sudhir K, Yoon DH (2012) When to "fire" customers: customer cost-based pricing. Manag Sci 58(5):932–947

Simon H (1996) You don't have to be German to be a "hidden champion". Bus Strateg Rev 7(2):1–13

Simon H, Fassnacht M (2016) Preismanagement, 4. Aufl. Gabler, Wiesbaden

Terlep S (2016) Unilever kauft für 1 Milliarde Dollar Startup Dollar Shave Club. https://www.finanznachrichten.de/nachrichten-2016-07/38025040-unilever-kauft-fuer-1-milliarde-dollarstartup-dollar-shave-club-015.htm. Accessed 5 Mar 2020

Totzek D, Alavi S (2010) Professionalisierung des Preismanagements auf Business-to-Business-Märkten: Die Rolle der Marktorientierung und der Unternehmenskultur. Schmalenbachs Zeitschrift für betriebswirtschaftliche Forschung 62(5):533–562

Töytäri P, Rajala R, Alejandro TB (2015) Organizational and institutional barriers to value-based pricing in industrial relationships. Ind Mark Manage 47:53–64

Trevenen L (2012) Why segmentation matters. In: Hinterhuber A, Liozu S (eds) Innovation in pricing. Routledge, Abingdon, pp 151–163

Weimer M (2021) E-Bike-Startup der Soundcloud-Erfinder startet: Hat dieses Rad das Zeug zum Hit? Gründerszene vom 31.8.2021, https://www.businessinsider.de/gruenderszene/automotivemobility/e-bike-startup-der-soundcloud-erfinder-startet-hat-dieses-rad-das-zeug-zum-hit/. Accessed 3 Sept 2021

Wickboldt C, Kliewer N (2018) Value based pricing meets data science: a concept for automated spare part valuation. Multikonferenz Wirtschaftsinformatik 2018:269–279

Wilger G, Krämer A (2020) Signaling gegenüber Wettbewerbern – Erkennen und Verhindern von Preiswettbewerb und "Preiskrieg". In: Kalka R, Krämer A (eds) Preiskommunikation – Strategische Herausforderungen und innovative Anwendungsfelder. Springer Gabler, Wiesbaden, pp 129–149

Price-Cost Perspective: Impact Patterns of Top-Down and Bottom-Up Approaches

11

11.1 Excessive Focus on Price at the Expense of Costs?

"The thought makes him pale when he asks: What does it cost?"—Wilhelm Busch.

While from the perspective of the typical price-sensitive buyer the price paid represents a strong sacrificial component ("the thought makes him pale"), decision-makers in the company sometimes try to completely disregard the cost perspective, e.g., in order to reduce the complexity of decision-making or because it is not possible to allocate the entire costs to the individual product according to their cause. The following considerations are dedicated to the possibly daring hypothesis that the cost perspective is neglected in value management because many decision-makers perceive price as the primary and most effective starting point for generating sustainable profits. To this end, some typical arguments for the dominance of the price factor are first examined in more detail. These are illustrated in Fig. 11.1. They relate to the narratives that (1) price is the decisive independent determinant of profit, (2) price must be considered the strongest profit lever, and (3) price is the only lever in marketing that has a direct effect (resulting in a time advantage, among other things). The respective perspectives are explained in the following chapters.

11.1.1 Price as the Independent Variable

According to Simon and Fassnacht (2016), the price-sales and cost functions determine how the price influences profit via the various intermediate stages. Accordingly, there are exactly three paths in this system along which this influence acts:

Price → Turnover → Profit
Price →Sales volume → Turnover → Profit
Price →Sales volume → Costs → Profit

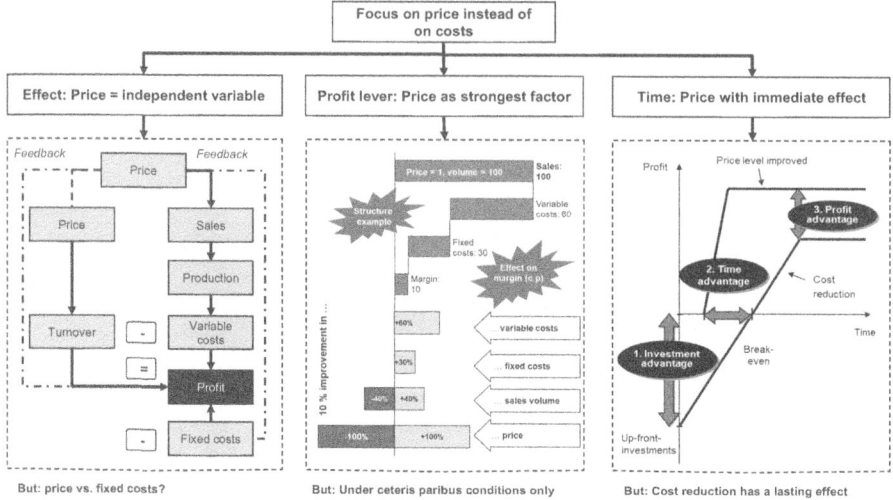

Fig. 11.1 Focus on the price perspective at the expense of the cost perspective

Costs are often divided into variable and fixed costs. The variable costs are co-determined by the interdependency: price → sales volume → production. If the production volume changes, there is a proportional change in the variable costs. The fixed costs are included in the following equation as an invariable variable:

Profit = turnover (price × sales volume) – variable costs – fixed costs

This consideration alone results in a compelling focus on price. Simon and Fassnacht (2016) explain that "the interrelationships and the resulting chains of effects prove to be much more complex" and point out that the price effects are "not only multidimensional, but also interdependent and sometimes contradictory." However, they do not address the following directions of impact:

- Fixed costs → Price → Turnover → Profit or
- Price → Sales planning → Fixed costs.

Looking at these chains of effects would inevitably result in greater attention being paid to the issue of costs (in Fig. 11.1, left section). For example, when discussing the emergence of price competition and the transition to price wars, overcapacity often plays a role as a trigger (Wilger and Krämer 2005a, 2025; Heil and Helsen 2001). Due to the high burden of fixed costs, price managers feel compelled to react to price reductions, which they interpret as an attack and threat to their existence by the competition, with price cuts. This example alone illustrates how strongly costs can influence pricing (Wilger and Krämer 2005b). It is also easily conceivable that excessive price expectations on the part of management can lead to incorrect sales planning, leading in turn to a high fixed cost burden.

Against this background, it seems sensible to take a more holistic and dynamic view of the dependencies between price and costs than is usually the case.

11.1.2 Price as the Biggest Profit Driver

A popular approach to illustrate the dominant effect of price as a driver of profit is to simulate changes of, for example, 10% (improvement) in a direct comparison and under otherwise comparable conditions for the factors price, quantity, variable, and fixed costs (Baker et al. 2010). In the example (Fig. 11.1, middle section), there is a turnover of 100 (100 units at a price of 1), the variable costs are 60 units, and the fixed costs are 30 units. The operating margin is 10 units. The 10% change in price leads to the strongest profit effects compared to the change in the other variables considered. This consideration also leads directly to the price factor and gives the impression that price is necessarily—regardless of the specific business context— by far the strongest profit lever.

This thought experiment can be found repeatedly in various publications, including in the modification in which the largest US or European companies are used as examples instead of an abstract corporate example. Such examples are effective influencers of opinion, especially when consultants "sell" pricing projects. They not only draw attention to the price, but also lead to corresponding expectations with regard to strong profit effects. However, the prerequisite assumption that all other things are and remain equal contains an inadmissible, gross simplification that excludes any interdependence and thus ignores the fact that as a rule, a price change leads to an effect on sales volume.

11.1.3 Price and the Time Advantage

Preconceptions regarding the relevance of the price lever and its superiority compared to other approaches to increasing profits can also be illustrated by analyzing the effect of a price change compared to a cost-cutting measure (Fig. 11.1, right-hand side).

Simon and Fassnacht (2016) reveal a blind spot while explaining this effect:

> "The investment advantage means that, unlike with cost reduction or marketing invest-ments, less capital flows out in advance with price optimization. The time advantage means that the positive profit effects of the price occur more quickly. And the profit advantage expresses the fact that the profit increase achievable through price measures is particu-larly high."

It is important to put this into perspective. It is undeniable that a direct comparison of a price measure, e.g., with a renovation project, results in considerable differ-ences in terms of the effect over time. Prices can often—but not always—be changed relatively quickly. However, a rapid change in prices with an immediate improve-ment in the profit situation is only realistic if the price-sales effect, i.e., the price elasticity of demand, is correctly assessed. Therefore, the opportunity of the time advantage is always associated with a risk, namely that of having misjudged the reaction of demand to a price change, but then the damage has been done and may be irreversible.

Furthermore, it is doubtful that pricing projects necessarily lead to a stronger effect on earnings than cost-cutting measures. The opposite argument can also be made that cost effects have a more lasting and therefore more sustainable effect than price adjustments. Overall, the evidence justifying pricing primacy is relatively weak.

11.2   The Interplay Between Price and Costs

Costs alone are an incomplete benchmark for optimized pricing. The added value or the customer benefit achieved is often not adequately reflected by cost-oriented pricing and the value of the products and services is not considered from the customer's perspective. This means that the customer's willingness to pay cannot be optimally exploited. Even if the discussion on more precise pricing is very much characterized by the inclusion of customer benefit in the sense of a fair benefit assessment of a product-service bundle from the customer's perspective (Wolf 2019; Bruhn 2019), the consideration of the cost structure when setting prices should not be neglected. This is because an additional service often means not only an additional benefit for the customer, but typically also additional costs for the provider.

Ideally pricing simulates the cost structure without being significantly determined by it. In addition, the market price and the customer's benefit expectations are often unknown, e.g., in the case of individual services or innovations. It can therefore be difficult or practically impossible to precisely determine a customer's willingness to pay. In this case, cost-based pricing serves as an approximate solution, also for determining the lower price limit. According to Rese and Wulfhorst (2015), five influencing factors can be identified that drive a price floor:

- Amount of input costs
- Distribution of overheads
- Assumptions behind the planned costs
- Organizational influences on the level of costs and
- Effect of incentive systems on the credibility of cost approaches.

Cost-oriented pricing can still be observed in most companies. The only question here is, based on which costs? For many companies, the total cost block is largely determined by fixed costs, at least in the short to medium term. In many cases, only the marginal costs are used for a price decision. The very strong focus on marginal costs is also reinforced by the intensification of the perceived intensity of competition. This highlights the danger of a price war. A customer-related cost view presupposes that the costs of all customer processes (order processing, customer care, etc.) are known and can be allocated accordingly (see Fig. 11.2).

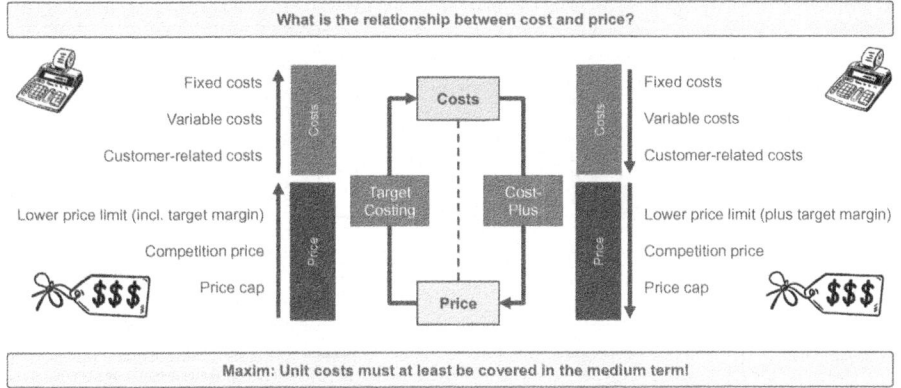

Fig. 11.2 The direction of impact of cost-plus and target costing

Against the background of conventional pricing for a product or service (cost-plus), the calculation is carried out bottom-up by adding the so-called service production costs and taking a target margin into account.

In contrast, target costing or target cost management uses a top-down approach: Based on the possible market price, the target costs to be achieved are determined after deducting the target margin. If the standard costs (internal company cost calculation) of operational service provision are higher than the target costs, there is a need for action in cost management (Klenger 2000; Schawel and Billing 2018).

11.3   From Costs to Price: Cost-Plus or the Bottom-Up Approach with a Clear Goal

Cost-plus pricing (mark-up pricing) describes the simplest and still most common pricing method (see Fig. 11.3). As a rule, a fixed profit mark-up is calculated on all allocable unit costs incurred to determine the offer price in order to ensure the targeted profitability (Dholakia 2018). Various approaches to cost-plus pricing have also been the subject of academic discussion for some time (Barusman et al. 2020; Guilding et al. 2005). The decisive factor for an exact calculation is a detailed recording of the costs and an allocation to individual customers (segments). To this end, it is necessary to define attributable, customer-related costs with acceptable effort depending on the industry and the organization of the company. This can be illustrated through the following examples.

- Packaging and shipping costs
- Service and customer support costs
- Commission payments and discounts
- Order-related costs
- Costs due to individual customer behavior (complaints, advice, type of communication).

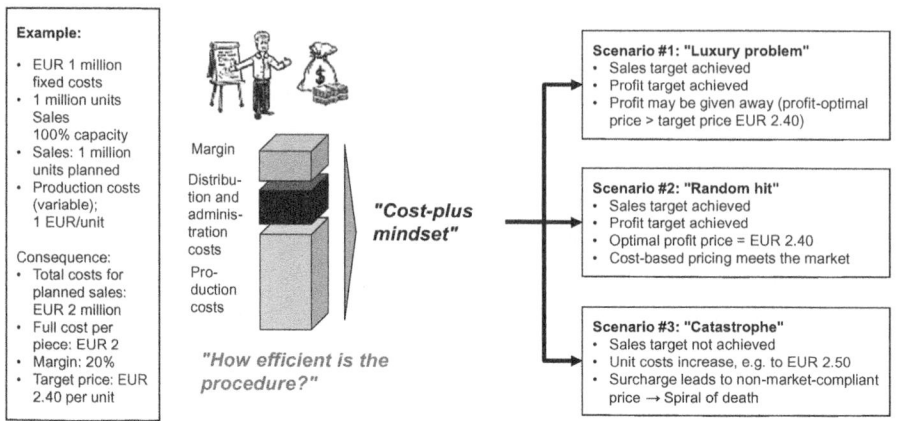

Fig. 11.3 The basic logic of cost-plus pricing and the effects (scenarios)

The limits of direct allocation via the direct costs and overheads clusters lie in the respective cost type and, above all, in the corresponding effort required to record costs. For example, marketing costs, such as advertising, trade fairs, etc., cannot usually be allocated to individual customers.

When used prudently, the strategic and tactical advantages of cost-plus pricing are strong differentiation, greater customer confidence, reduced risk of price wars, and stable, predictable profits for the company. No other pricing method is easier to communicate or justify. What is often overlooked in academic discussions is that in practice, situations can arise where a cost-plus approach is a sufficient methodology and supports the pricing decision.

For example, in the spare parts business (large number of products, little customer and competitor information) or in professional services (e.g., legal advice, consulting). In the case of pricing in consulting, the gap between theory ("cost-based pricing = inefficient") and practice (pricing based on daily rates, derived from costs) is particularly wide. In the area of professional services, alternative fee forms have been discussed for decades, but billing according to daily or hourly rates (analogous to cost-plus pricing) continues to be the standard (Hanna and Dodge 2017; Deelmann and Krämer 2020).

The price increase must be communicated to customers in a comprehensible manner. A reasonable explanation for a price increase is the argument of increased costs. Accordingly, a dynamic view of the pricing process reveals a not insignificant communication advantage (Krämer and Kalka 2025): The justification of price adjustments. One example is the fruit juice producer Beckers Bester, which had to implement a price increase after a disastrous harvest year (2017) and whose management addressed the end customer directly with an explanation of the cost increase and the necessary price increase in retail (and the promise to withdraw the price increase as soon as possible; Koeppel 2025). This example is remarkable in view of the multi-level distribution and pricing expertise of retailers. This approach is also common practice in areas with a direct customer focus, e.g., public transport or energy suppliers (Krämer and Schmutz 2020).

The clothing retailer Everlane goes one step further by illustrating its value proposition of "radical transparency" through cost mark-ups (Bohn 2017). For each item of clothing sold, Everlane provides a detailed breakdown of the costs of materials, labor, duties, and transportation, as well as a mark-up. In this way, customers are shown how Everlane attaches importance to paying production workers fair wages and then encouraging customers to buy products to increase the value of the company (Dholakia 2018).

The transparent cost surcharge, which is comprehensible to the customer, offers companies the opportunity to avoid misunderstanding on the part of the customer. For example, consumers perceived the price increases at Uber (extreme market situations), the dynamic pricing of Coca-Cola vending machines depending on the outside temperature or the variable tariffs of electricity suppliers as pure "rip-offs" in the sense of value-oriented pricing by companies. Cost-plus providers are less exposed to this risk and signal fair prices (Dholakia 2018). For companies with a cost advantage or an interest in using price transparency as a differentiator, the cost-plus is a powerful strategic tool. Cost-based pricing is an effective tactic for providers who want to communicate fair prices and gain the trust of their customers.

The disadvantage, however, is that the price may be below the customer's willingness to pay and thus give away valuable margins or be above the calculated limit and prevent any sales prospects. These relationships are illustrated in Fig. 11.3. In the example calculation, the unit costs are €2.00, based on a concrete assumption regarding total sales (in this case full capacity utilization). The target price is calculated by adding a margin to the unit costs. Cost-plus pricing can lead to different scenarios. Three key points are listed as examples.

In the "luxury problem" scenario, the target figures are achieved exactly. The problem is that full capacity utilization might also have been achieved if the selling price had been higher. In the target calculation, the margin is €0.4 million (€0.4 per unit * one million units sold). The margin effect is easy to grasp if the optimum price is 3 and the total margin would then be €one million (€1.0 per unit * one million units sold), i.e., 150% higher. A scenario in which the target price determined via cost-plus pricing actually corresponds to the profit-optimal price of €2.40 is described as a random hit. If the mark-up calculation leads to a price that is not in line with the market, this can lead to catastrophic consequences for a firm.

Another disadvantage of the cost-plus method is the often system-based and therefore unreflected link between price and costs. If a company succeeds in reducing costs, this harbors the risk of an unintentional price reduction.

One of the most well-known users of the cost-plus method is the U.S. Department of Defense (DoD). Its usage has drawn considerable ire from tax payers and activists alike. In her book *The Shock Doctrine*, Naomi Klein relates that:

"as far as Halliburton was concerned, keeping the customer satisfied was good business – it guaranteed more contracts, and because profits were calculated as a percentage of costs, the higher the costs, the higher the profits. "Don't worry, it's cost-plus," was a saying made famous in Baghdad's Green Zone, but the deluxe war spending was pioneered during the Clinton era" (Klein 2007, p. 292).

Cost-plus pricing can encourage innovation in military technologies by removing the fear of cost overruns and distributing risk between the supplier and the DoD.

However, the lure of excess profits has not gone unnoticed by Klein and others, and the opportunity it provides for dominance via first mover advantage may be thwarted by the temptation cost-plus creates in military suppliers to slow production time (Thompson 2024). The story of the thousand-dollar hammer has legendary status amid critics of cost-plus pricing within the military-industrial complex. As multiple conflicts continue to develop through the second half of this decade, it remains to be seen whether it will be the pricing method of choice for governments in the years to come.

11.4   From Price to Cost: Target Costing or Top-Down Approach with a View to the Market

11.4.1 Theoretical Framework

The current business environment is characterized by high competition. In order to be successful, companies must adapt quickly and flexibly to the prevailing VUCA conditions, in particular to increased customer requirements.

Gradually, costs are viewed from a strategic perspective and cost planning is carried out in the pre-production phase, as this phase has the greatest influence on the future success of a product. The different perceptions of costs and the associated behavior also require the development and use of suitable tools for strategic management, such as target costing. Vedder (2008) states that the origin of such a costing technique dates back to the 1970s, when private sector income in Japan experienced a rapid increase and people began to satisfy more needs.

Target costing is a systematic profit planning process and, in contrast to the inward-looking traditional cost methods (cost-plus method), is based on market and customer expectations. As a management technique, target costing supports pricing decisions based on certain factors such as competition, customer-related costs, and comparable products (Brünger and Faupel 2010; Ansan et al. 2006; Alinezhad Sarokolaee et al. 2012). These factors leave management little room for maneuver in controlling the sales price and the only way to increase the profit margin with a quasi-predetermined market price is through cost control over the entire product life cycle (research, development, production, and marketing; see Nicolini et al. 2000; Pennanen et al. 2011; Perry and Barnes 2000). Target costing is therefore the calculation of costs by deducting a profit margin desired by the company from the market price of a product and, against this background, defines the costs required to manufacture a product with a marketable quality and to guarantee or achieve a certain profit margin (Horvath et al. 2020; Weber and Schäffer 2020).

Target costing is an interdisciplinary topic of business administration, accounting, management, and supply chain. Despite its academic and practical implications, target costing has not been sufficiently researched, especially in terms of methodology. For example, studies have attempted to use a combination of quantitative and qualitative research methods to support the introduction of target costing (Potkány and Škultétyová 2019; Zanella and Oyelere 2020). Sakurai 1989 describes target costing as a cost management tool that can reduce the total cost of a product over its entire life cycle with the help of the production, engineering, R&D, marketing, and accounting departments. Other representatives focus on the interaction of different tools and propose an integrated framework for strategic cost management based on target costing, in combination with activity-based costing and product life cycle costing (Hematfar et al. 2013; Alwisy et al. 2018; Ferreira and Oliveira 2020).

Monden and Lee (1993) state that target costing is defined as an organization-wide profit management activity during the new product development phase that includes the following:

1. Planning products with customer-friendly quality.
2. Determination of the target costs (including the target investment costs) for the new product to achieve the target profit required in the medium to long term under the current market conditions.
3. Developing ways in which the product design can achieve the target cost while meeting customer needs for quality and fast delivery.

One of the most important strategies for gaining a competitive advantage is certainly the differentiation of products and services. Target costing is very useful here and aims to integrate market- and customer-oriented cost management. Novák and Popesko (2014), Potkány et al. (2012) and Dejnega (2010) also share this insight into the greater importance of cost management, cost behavior analyses, and corresponding cost projection on adequate cost systems.

Krstevski and Mancheski (2018) state that most definitions of target costing include a process based on a competitive market environment, market prices, cost and investment decisions, cost planning, management and cross-functional team involvement, up to and including management accounting. Ahn et al. (2018) identify nine different research directions that include advancements to the traditional target costing methodology, including consideration of information uncertainty, dynamic target costs, consideration of indirect costs, and accuracy of analysis.

Kocakülâh and Austill (2006) state in their study that the target costing concept arose from the need of manufacturers to improve product cost management and product development. The traditional cost management, accumulation, and distribution methods, which have been used for decades and still predominate in the manufacturing and service sectors, have not always led to the desired insights as tools for product development, planning and strategic cost management. This is mainly because they focus on product costs and not on customer expectations and the product design itself. It is precisely in this area that the great potential of target costing is seen.

In their study on target costing, Potkány and Škultétyová (2019) focused on the price level accepted by the consumer. This study showed that, assuming an existing target price, target costing using value analysis principles played a decisive role.

The basic idea of target costing was to determine the upper limit of acceptable costs that must not be exceeded during production. This limit is not determined according to the basic technical and economic standards of consumption, but on the contrary as the surplus of the target price after deducting the target profit.

The application of the target costing methodology can be substantiated by a target cost index (TCI) (Horváth 1993). This index describes the fulfillment or non-fulfillment of the quality of a product with simultaneous acceptance or non-acceptance of the price by the customer. The ideal state is achieved when the planned cost level for the product components corresponds to the value with which this component contributes to the fulfillment of customer preferences. However, this state is almost impossible to achieve. Therefore, according to Coenenberg et al. (2016), the tolerance cost zone can also be defined in this context, which leaves a certain amount of leeway in the balancing act of mirroring the relative importance of the product components from the customer's perspective with the intended costs for these components from the company's perspective (Ehrlenspiel et al. 2007).

The application of target costing has generated a wide range of experience in different industries and illustrates its adaptability to very different framework conditions. For example, Schildmacher (2021) examines target costing for the automotive industry, Aladwan et al. (2018) in the hotel management sector, Lima et al. (2016) in the agricultural sector, and Macuda and Orlinski (2017) in healthcare facilities. However, perhaps the most famous example of target costing occurred in the 1980s with the rise of Swatch. Traditional manufacturers were faced with a disruptor from Japan, technology that suddenly rendered Swiss watches much more expensive than the competition. As the "quartz crisis" flooded the market with cheap, reliable timepieces, the Swatch Group responded to this existential threat by re-engineering their product starting from a desired price point (Anwar 2012; The Brand Hopper 2023). They dropped the number of parts by half, welded pieces in and introduced plastic bands, creating a new type of watch that had the cache of being authentically Swiss at a price point unheard of until then among its peers.

11.4.2 Case Study: Target Costing at Dacia

The Dacia brand is a particularly striking example of target costing in car manufacturing. Here, too, the crucial question is "What should a product cost?" Dacia has been a great success for Renault since the car manufacturer bought the Romanian brand from the communist era in 1999. Dacia's secret is to offer no-frills cars that do without unnecessary technology. Under Renault's management, Dacia's sales figures have risen almost every year, giving it a market share of 3% in Europe. Dacia models are also sold worldwide as Renault models under the carmaker's Global Access Program for low-cost vehicles. Dacia calls its development process "Design to Cost." A cost target is set for a particular part and designers, engineers, and suppliers work together to meet this price. The target costing approach gave Renault the opportunity to use a Less Expensive Alternative (LEA) to address market segments that were not previously the manufacturer's primary target group or that, from a

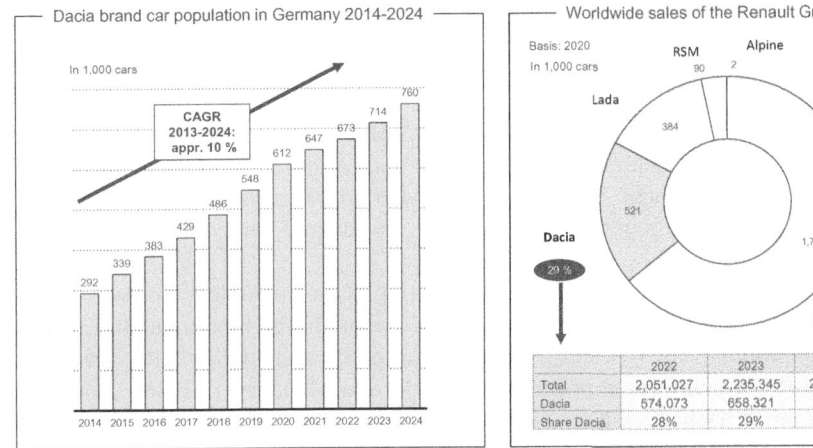

Fig. 11.4   Key sales figures for the Dacia car brand (stock and sales in units of vehicles)

previous perspective, entailed high cannibalization risks. The provider is pursuing a clear "Penetration Strategy." The low entry-level price is the starting point. For 2019, a study on end customer prices for cars concluded that Dacia models cost 56% less than the average market price. As Fig. 11.4 shows, the Dacia brand is growing steadily in the highly competitive German car market. While the number of cars sold in 2014 was 292,000, this figure increased to 760,000 by 2024.

Converted, this means an annual growth rate of approximately 6% (CAGR 2013–2021). Within Renault's global vehicle sales, Dacia achieved a share of 29% in 2020.

Seidenschwarz and Böhme (2010) explain:

"The vision in 2004 was: €5000 entry-level price. The central anchor point of the price strategy was a simple and clear price positioning based on the maxim: noticeably the cheapest car in the target segment. This maxim was always aimed at customers who do not just look at the price, but consciously weigh up price and value proposition."

Against this background, the following success factors are decisive:

- Simple model range (six models, few equipment variants, eight engines).
- Simple sales organization (the sales talk should last a maximum of 30 minutes, 5% dealer margin, no discounts, offer at approx. a quarter of Renault dealers).
- Simple development and production (use of the existing Renault platform, use of Renault components).
- Simple marketing with clear messages.

Dacia's turnover is estimated at around €1,778 million in 2021. According to the forecast, a market volume of €2640 million will be reached in 2025; this corresponds to expected annual sales growth of 10.4% (CAGR 2021–2025). The volume-weighted average price per unit was €8,700 in 2021.

The Dacia pricing strategy has remained relatively unchanged over time. It aims to keep the price level of Dacia models as low as possible and to accept the lowest possible margin in order to maintain its position in the market (Funaru and Funaru 2011).

Gopalakrishnan et al. (2004) and Sharaf-Addin et al. (2018) come to further conclusions in other sectors, highlighting the current need for new approaches to strategic cost management. Target costing is also proposed as an effective tool for service companies, although companies here are always guided by the cost-plus approach.

Overall, it can be assumed that target costing is an instrument that can reveal potential reserves of the company and offer solutions for the functional differentiation of the product. The risk lies in precise market research and in determining the relative costs of certain components. Krstevski and Mancheski (2018) show that target costing in itself is not a revolution in the planning process. However, the focus on the customer's willingness to pay in combination with demand-oriented allocation enables significant progress in competitiveness.

11.5   Outlook: Understanding the Interdependencies Between Costs and Pricing

A more intensive examination of the price-cost axis has shown that it makes perfect sense to question the seemingly dominant role of price and at least demand equalization of costs. Both cost-based pricing and target price-oriented cost analysis have a right to exist. Market-oriented corporate management must therefore continue to look for new approaches in the future in order to meet the new customer expectations of transparent prices on the one hand and to enable a more efficient planning process in the sense of a more inward-looking cost transparency with the possibility of short-term control and influence on the other.

As the description of the cost-plus pricing and target pricing approaches has shown, there are different ways of establishing a direct relationship between costs and prices. Both instruments have strengths and weaknesses. For this reason alone, it is advisable to combine as many different approaches as possible. Figure 11.5 attempts to illustrate this. In principle, a cost-plus calculation can be converted into target costing (the opposite direction is also sensible and possible). While the cost-plus approach follows the "bottom-up" logic, the target costing approach starts with the target turnover or profit. Retrograde calculations are then made, resulting in the "permitted costs" as the target figure. In conclusion, despite all the euphoria surrounding value-based pricing (based on the customer's perceived value) or participative pricing (the customer is actively involved in pricing and, in extreme cases, decides on the price), i.e., approaches which focus on the customer, taking costs into account as well remains essential.

The costs must always be considered when placing the customer at the center of consideration. The company can only achieve long-term success if the long-term unit costs are covered. Even—or especially—in times of new VUCA framework conditions, this maxim remains valid.

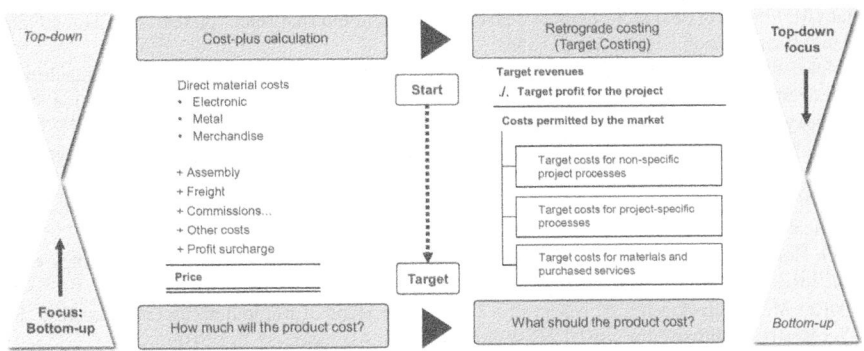

Fig. 11.5 The conversion of the cost-plus pricing approach into target costing

References

Ahn H, Clermont M, Schwetschke S (2018) Research on target costing: past, present and future. Manag Rev Quart 68(3):321–354

Aladwan M, Alsinglawi O, Alhawatmeh O (2018) The applicability of target costing in Jordanian hotels industry. Acad Acc Finan Stu J 22(3):1–13

Alinezhad Sarokolaee M, Taghizadeh V, Ebrati M (2012) The relationship between target costing and value-based pricing and presenting an aggregate model based on customers' expectations. Proc Soc Behav Sci 41:74–83

Alwisy A, Bouferguene A, Al-Hussein M (2018) Framework for target cost modelling in construction projects. Int J Constr Manag 20(3):1–16

Ansan S, Bell U, Okano H (2006) Target costing: uncharted research territory. Handb Manag Acc Res 2:507–530

Anwar ST (2012) Selling Time: Swatch Group and the Global Watch Industry. https://onlinelibrary.wiley.com/doi/full/10.1002/tie.21497

Baker WL, Marn MV, Zawada CC (2010) The price advantage, 2. Aufl. John Wiley, Hoboken

Barusman A, Yuliana MT, Mirfazli E (2020) Analysis of implementation cost plus pricing method in the decision on the determination of product sales prices. Intern J Adv Sci Techn 29(06):1832–1838

Bohn A (2017) Voll transparent. Voll transparent (fluter.de)

Bruhn M (2019) Qualitätsmanagement für Dienstleistungen. Handbuch für ein erfolgreiches Qualitätsmanagement. Grundlagen – Konzepte – Methoden. Springer, Heidelberg

Brünger C, Faupel C (2010) Target Costing: Pragmatische Ansätze für eine erfolgreiche Anwendung. ZfCM Control Manag 54(3):170–174

Coenenberg A, Fisher T, Günther T (2016) Kostenrechnung und Kostenanalyse. Schäffer-Poeschel, Stuttgart

Deelmann T, Krämer A (2020) Consulting: Ein Lehr-, Lern- und Lesebuch zur Unternehmensberatung. Erich Schmidt Verlag, Berlin

Dejnega O (2010) Methods activity based costing and time-driven activity based costing and their using in practice by measuring costs of processes. EMI Econ Manag Inno 2(1):11–19

Dholakia U (2018) When cost-plus pricing is a good idea. In: Harvard Business Review Digital Article, July 12. https://hbr.org/2018/07/when-cost-plus-pricing-is-a-good-idea

Ehrlenspiel K, Kiewert A, Lindemann U (2007) Cost-efficient design. Springer, Berlin

Ferreira MM, Oliveira SRM (2020) Integrated framework for strategic cost management based on target costing, ABC and product life cycle in PDP: empirical experience. Global J Bus Econ Manag Current Issue 10(1):31–43

Funaru M, Funaru G (2011) Strategies of Dacia Renault on International Markets. Bull Transilvania Univ Brasov Econ Sci Ser 4(1):31–36

Gopalakrishnan B, Kokatnur A, Gupta DP (2004) Application of target costing in machining. Proceedings SPIE 5605, Intelligent Systems in Design and Manufacturing V., (Philadelphia, Pennsylvania, United States) 11:238–250

Guilding C, Drury C, Tayles M (2005) An empirical investigation of the importance of cost-plus pricing February. Manag Aud J 20(2)

Hanna N, Dodge HR (2017) Pricing: policies and procedures. Macmillan International Higher Education

Heil O, Helsen K (2001) Toward an understanding of price wars: their nature and how they erupt. Int J Res Mark 18(1–2):83–98

Hematfar M, Sanati-Arasteh A, Nooryan S (2013) The steps of implementing target costing. Soc Sci Res Netw https://doi.org/10.2139/ssrn.1455184. Accessed 15 Jan 2019

Horváth P (1993) Target costing: state-of-the-art-report. Consortium of Advanced Manufacturing-International, Texas

Horváth P, Gleich R, Seiter M (2020) Controlling, 14. Aufl, München

Klein N (2007) The shock doctrine: the rise of disaster capitalism. Penguin

Klenger F (2000) Operatives controlling, 5. Aufl. München

Kocakülâh MC, Austill D (2006) Product development and cost management using target costing: a discussion and case analysis. J Bus Econ Res 4(2):61–72

Koeppel S (2025) Fallstudie: Preiskommunikation bei beckers bester. In: Preiskommunikation. Springer Gabler, Wiesbaden, pp 359–370

Krämer A, Kalka R (2025) Maßnahmen und Argumente in der Preisveränderungskommunikation gegenüber Endkunden. In: Preiskommunikation. Springer Gabler, Wiesbaden, pp 165–188

Krämer A, Schmutz I (2020) Mythos Value Based Pricing-der Versuch einer (wertfreien) Einordnung. Mark Rev St Gallen 2:44–53

Krstevski D, Mancheski G (2018) The utilization of target costing in the telecom industry. Int J Bus Manag 2(3):21–26

Lima AC, Silveira J, Silva S, Ching H (2016) Target costing: exploring the concept and its relation to competitiveness in agribusiness. Custos e Agronegocio 12(3):11–25

Macuda M, Orlinski R (2017) Target costing – a remedy for hospitals' ills? Przedsiebiorczosc I Zarzadzanie 18(1):113–123

Monden Y, Lee J (1993) How a Japanese auto maker reduces costs. Manag Acc 75(2):22–26

Nicolini D, Tomkins C, Holti R, Oldman A, Smalley M (2000) Can target costing and whole life costing be applied in the construction industry? Br J Manag 11(4):303–325

Novák P, Popesko B (2014) Cost variability and cost behaviour in manufacturing enterprises. Econ Soc 7(4):89–103

Pennanen A, Ballard G, Haahtela Y (2011) Target costing and designing to targets in construction. J Financ Manag Prop Constr 16(1):52–63

Perry JG, Barnes M (2000) Target cost contracts: an analysis of the interplay between fee, target, share and price. Eng Constr Archit Manag 7(2):202–209

Potkány M, Škultétyová M (2019) Research into customer preferences of potential buyers of simple wood-based houses for the purpose of using the target costing. Open Eng 9(1):390–396

Potkány M, Hajduková A, Teplická K (2012) Target costing calculation in the woodworking industry to support demand at the time of global recessvion. Drewno 55(187):89–104

Rese M, Wulfhorst V (2015) Preise und Kosten – Preisbeurteilung im Industriegüterbereich. In: Backhaus K, Voeth M (eds) Handbuch business-to-business-marketing. Springer Gabler, Wiesbaden, pp 517–535

Sakurai M (1989) Target costing and how to use it. J Cos Manag Manuf Indus 1989:39–50

Schawel C, Billing F (2018) Zielkostenmanagement/Target Costing, Kennzahlen und Konzepte der Unternehmensführung. Top 100 Management Tools, S 377–379

Schildmacher R (2021) Weiterentwicklung des Target Costing unter besonderer Berücksichtigung der Automobilindustrie. Springer, Wiesbaden

Seidenschwarz W, Böhme H (2010) Target costing im Low-Price-Segment am Beispiel Dacia. Controlling 2:120–126

Sharaf-Addin HH, Omar N, Sulaiman S (2018) Relationship between organizational capabilities. Implementation decision on target costing and organisational performance: an empirical study of Malaysian automotive industry. Pertanika J Soc Scie Humanit 26(2):615–641

Simon H, Fassnacht M (2016) Preismanagement: Strategie – Analyse – Entscheidung – Umsetzung. Springer Gabler, Wiesbaden

The Brand Hopper (2023) Exploring swatch marketing strategies & marketing mix. https://thebrandhopper.com/2023/08/27/exploring-the-swatch-groups-marketing-strategies-mix-4ps/. Accessed 11 June 2025

Thompson M (2024) Wary or weary of fixed price contracts. https://www.jedonline.com/2024/03/04/wary-or-weary-of-fixed-price-contracts/ Journal of Electromagnetic Dominance

Vedder H (2008) The target costing approach. Berlin

Weber J, Schäffer U (2020) Einführung in das Controlling, 16. Aufl. Stuttgart

Wilger G, Krämer A (2005a) Richtiges Verhalten im Preiskrieg. Planung Anal 5:34–38

Wilger G, Krämer A (2005b) Zwischen Preiskrieg und Paradigmenwechsel – Ansätze für ein strategisches Pricing in der Verlagsbranche. Res Res 2:56–57

Wilger G, Krämer A (2025) Signaling gegenüber Wettbewerbern–Erkennen und Verhindern von Preiswettbewerb und "Preiskrieg". In: Preiskommunikation. Springer Gabler, Wiesbaden, pp 141–163

Wolf S (2019) Analyse der Determinanten modularer Dienstleistungs- und Organisationsarchitekturen. Springer, Wiesbaden

Zanella F, Oyelere P (2020) Competitive environment and corporate constructs of price and costs in the UAE. Corpor Owner Control 17(4):129–141

Cost-Benefit Perspective: Navigating the Conflict Between Transparent and Target Pricing

12

12.1   The Interplay Between Costs and Benefits

"Today, company bosses have to say that our employees are our most important asset. What a load of nonsense. Employees are our biggest cost block and many are so lazy that we constantly have to kick their asses. Every boss actually thinks that, but nobody wants to admit it."—Michael O'Leary

With this statement, the head of Ryanair is expressing the opinion that employees are a pure cost factor for the management of the low-cost airline and not an investment in good service or customer experience. The inventor of the low-cost business model, the US airline Southwest, takes a completely different view. Here, employee satisfaction is seen as a prerequisite for high customer satisfaction.

While the correlations between benefit and price or cost and price are deeply rooted in the minds of marketing decision makers, the focus is less on the interactions between benefit and cost. This is reflected in value-based pricing, where the price is determined by customer benefit and willingness to pay, and cost-based pricing, in which the price is determined on the basis of unit costs. Here, too, there are two directions of impact. On the one hand, it is necessary to ask how costs influence customer benefits and, on the other, what effects changes in benefits have on the level or structure of costs. The latter starts at the point which product managers ask themselves whether an existing or newly designed product meets existing customer expectations. If additional product or service features are integrated, this leads to changes in the perceived value for the customer, but in most cases also to increased costs. It is important to find the right balance here. Target pricing is a suitable methodological approach to this conundrum (Fig. 12.1).

The first direction of impact (costs → benefits) concerns an aspect often ignored in microeconomics but covered by behavioral pricing. This line of research focuses, among other things, on explaining consumer decisions in situations with limited price information that cannot be explained using traditional theories. The core idea

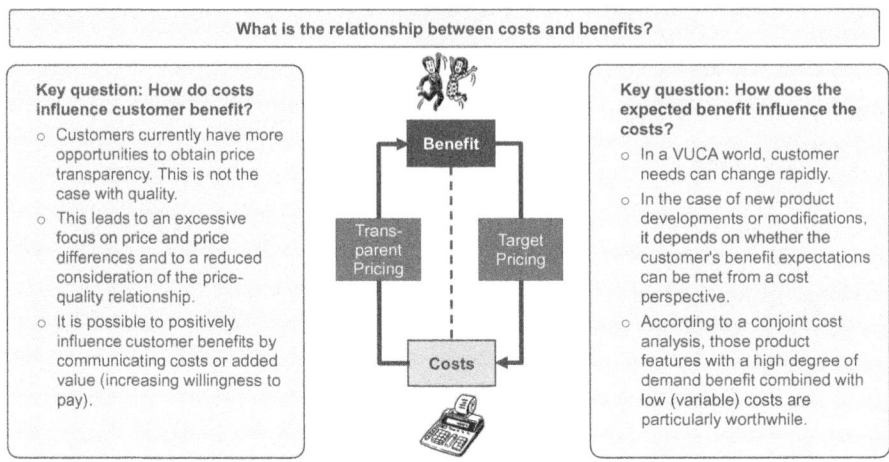

Fig. 12.1   Relationship between costs and benefits

of transparent pricing is to disclose pricing to customers by openly presenting costs along the supply chain in price communication (Somervuori 2014). The primary target group is potential buyers, including those whose willingness to pay was previously not high enough to buy a product. Both methods, transparent pricing and target pricing, are discussed in more detail below.

12.2   From Costs to Benefits: Transparent Pricing or "Pay What It Costs Plus"

12.2.1 When Does It Make Sense for Providers to "Lay Their Cards on the Table"?

To clarify the basic logic of transparent pricing, it is useful to refer to information economics, which divides products into search, experience and trust goods. Due to the changed technological framework conditions, it is now much easier for potential buyers to obtain transparency regarding the price of products. In addition to general search engines, special comparison and price portals can provide support. This change alone means that price is becoming more prominent in the mindset of consumers as other factors are added and reinforce price sensitivity. At the same time, consumers are finding it more difficult to assess differences in quality. As a result, price is sometimes used as a substitute indicator for assessing product quality. While the level of the price is known and transparent, suppliers have so far had no incentive to describe and explain how the price is calculated. The common assumption is that the customer does not need to know this and that the competition should not know this. Therefore, in the past, the interfaces between costs and price and between price and benefit were considered. In such a model, costs play no role for the individual consumer.

The transparent pricing approach challenges this maxim. In this alternative strategy, the price is determined deliberately disclosed in part, in terms of communication of costs or margin, or in full, with disclosure about both (Mohan et al. 2020; Fu at al. 2025). This distinguishes transparent pricing from related marketing practices such as social marketing, cause-related marketing and pay-what-you-want. Carter and Curry (2010) use controlled experiments in various product categories with different samples to prove that transparent prices systematically change consumers' utility functions and choice behavior. The results support explanations from both neoclassical and behavioral economic theory (inequity aversion, procedural justice and altruism). While classical theory assumes that price transparency has little impact on consumer behavior, behavioral economists argue that consumers relax their "self-interest" in the face of transparent prices, which leads to counterintuitive preferences. By disclosing its entire cost and margin calculation, the company aims to build trust. This only proves effective if consumers are interested in transparency — a point that studies show has grown in importance over recent years.

The coronavirus pandemic has reinforced the trends towards greater sustainability, regional production and the desire for fewer mass-produced products and more quality products such as meat and other foods (Qi 2021; Busch et al. 2021). Production processes are becoming increasingly relevant (Štefko and Steffek 2018). This is where a radically transparent pricing policy comes in. Wine and textiles are typical product categories for which consumers have little objective information on quality. Karpik (2011) describes this as follows: "In France ... tens of thousands of wine varieties are produced, which differ in their individuality and special characteristics. So there is general uncertainty about quality." This description can easily be transferred to other countries and product categories.

Avins (2017) reports on the Californian wine producer Mark Tarlov, whose marketing concept is aimed at the end customer, the wine drinker. He discloses the entire value chain. The sum of the individual costs results in US$15.10 per bottle. A margin of US$12.35 is added to this figure, so that the customer is presented with a final price of US$27.45. The reasoning behind this complete transparency is very simple:

"Understanding why wine costs what it costs gives you a sense of what is valuable."

Further examples are shown in Fig. 12.2. The company Everlane is frequently mentioned (Brown 2013; Detweiler 2025) and has a kind of pioneer status. However, some providers do not offer complete transparency, as in the example shown for wine.

EVELO, a provider of electric bicycles, addresses the criticism on its own website that e-bikes are very expensive and uses the Aurora model to explain how the sales price of US$2524 (EVELO 2021) was calculated. After the production costs of US$1066.67 (two decimal places!) are noted, 14 further cost items are explained until finally a profit per unit of US$255.65, 10.1% of the sales price, is shown.

The customer's interpretation of the information on costs and margin and ultimately the sales price aims to support the potential buyer's feeling of price fairness.

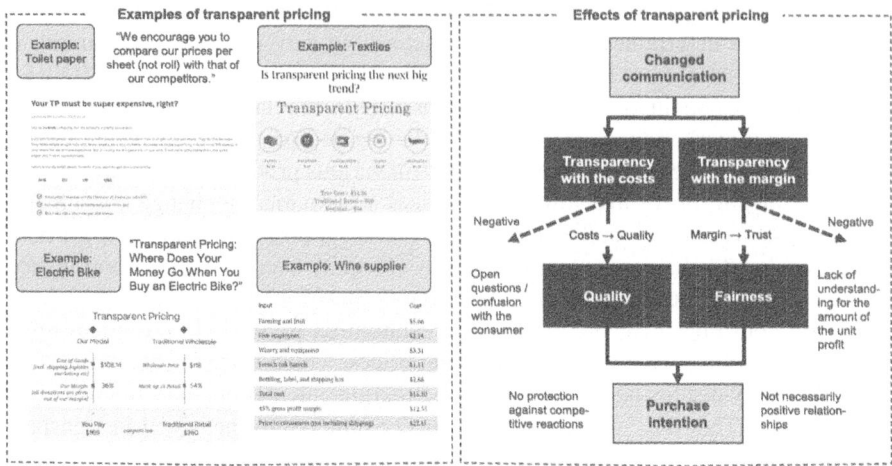

Fig. 12.2 Transparent pricing: examples and the path from communication to purchase intention

In their study, Ferguson and Ellen (2013) focused on the perception of price fairness and transparent pricing when the sales price is increased and prove that the price fairness effects on the consumer are more positive in the case of voluntary disclosure of costs by suppliers than when this information is provided to the customer by third parties. This should ultimately increase price acceptance, willingness to pay and the intention to buy.

The study by Jung et al. (2020) also confirms how the disclosure of costs and margin as components of the sales price influences the customer's perception of price fairness. However, it was pointed out that the information provided by transparent pricing is not rated positively by all customers. If consumers rate the information provided as less useful, this can have a negative impact. In their study, Kim et al. (2020) found a correlation between price fairness and purchase intention. According to this, purchase intention decreases if the price is perceived as unfair in the context of transparent pricing. In contrast, purchase intention increases if the price is perceived as fair.

At this point, it seems worthwhile to subdivide the concept of price fairness into sub- areas and individual facets. Diller (2008), for example, sees the following elements:

- Price consistency: Consistency means that the interaction procedures between the partners always follow the same "rule conformities," i.e., that they all act according to the same price formulas, for example.
- Price reliability: This can concern compliance with the prices set at the time of signing the contract (B2B), but also price information that the consumer regards as binding (B2C).

- Price honesty: This is closely related to the trust factor: "The customer expects accurate, easily comprehensible, unadulterated and complete information concerning prices, conditions and services."

Figure 12.2 illustrates those interdependencies. In a positive scenario, disclosing costs can enhance perceived quality (i.e., 'what is expensive must be of high quality'), while revealing profit margins can improve price perception and foster a sense of paying a fair price. These positive effects are not inevitable. It is possible that potential buyers will be annoyed by the size of the margin because the reason for it remains unclear or, from their point of view, unjustified.

12.2.2 How Does Price Transparency Influence Consumers' Willingness to Pay?

Behavioral science offers a variety of explanations as to why transparent pricing can be effective. Aspects such as trust and fairness play a role here, as does the process of information processing.

The effect of transparent pricing can be explained if the following theories are taken into account (for further details see Kalka et al. 2023):

- **Equity theory:** This deals with the perceived fairness in exchange relationships between transaction partners, such as customer and seller (Homburg and Koschate 2005). The focus here is on the relationship between input and output. Input is therefore defined as the expenses incurred in the form of costs, time, or personal commitment on the part of one transaction partner. The output represents the consideration of the other transaction partner. The input is weighed against the output in the so-called input/output ratio to arrive at the result of "equity" or "inequity." If the ratio between the transaction partners matches, the transaction is considered fair, also known as an equity transaction. "Equity" is defined as the ratio. If this ratio does not apply, the transaction is assessed as less fair or unfair, also known as "inequity."
- **Anchoring-and-adjustment concept:** If customers are unsure about the price, they look for points of reference, also known as anchors. These serve as a comparison to be able to evaluate a price. In the development of the anchoring and adjustment concept, the assumption that people would choose a starting point, e.g. an extreme value, in the absence of internal information plays a central role (Northcraft and Neale 1987; Furnham and Boo 2011). The expected price is adjusted either upwards or downwards along this extreme value. The adjustment is completed when a plausible value has been found by the individual. An anchor price is therefore used to find a suitable and acceptable price that is above or below the anchor price. The anchor price can be a price experience from past purchases, expectations of a price or be made up of accessible information. It is therefore not surprising that studies show that the estimated prices for cars from luxury manufacturers, such as Audi or Mercedes, are consistently higher than those for popular cars, i.e., manufacturers that tend to serve the mass market. The

difference is due to the fact that people associate car manufacturers with certain characteristics in their memory. This is the basis for semi- conscious anchoring. In the examples mentioned above, such as fashion products or wine, the brand factor—in contrast to established brands—does not play a dominant role, as these are relatively new business models with a low level of awareness. However, an anchoring can take place if, for example, consumers have learned from observation that T-shirts are available at prices of €5 each and are associated with correspondingly low costs. If the costs of €20 per T-shirt are disclosed to the consumer, this can lead to an adaptation of the cost perception.

• **Dual-entitlement principle:** This construct also picks up on the aspect of reference or anchor prices (Kahneman et al. 1986), at the center of which is a reference transaction. In this respect, there are two different demands, namely from the perspective of the buyer (customer) and from the perspective of the supplier with regard to a reference profit. Test subjects showed an acceptance for an increase in sales prices in retail if no sufficient profits would otherwise be realized (dual entitlement). It is important to note that in the event of a simultaneous threat to the claims of both parties, the supplier's profit claim takes precedence over the customer's (price) claim. As a consequence, a customer can judge a price increase or a high price to be fair even though his own claim has been violated.

12.3   From Benefits to Costs: Target Pricing or "Conjoint + COST"

12.3.1 When and How Do Existing Products and Services Need to Be Adapted?

When answering the question of whether, based on an existing product, a product extension with additional features is more suitable or whether a reduction of the individual product features is more appropriate or sensible, there are different decision paths (Fig. 12.3). In each case, the decision lies in the area of conflict as to whether a higher benefit will be achieved after a product has been adapted in comparison to the additional costs incurred or whether the future benefit will dominate the costs if the product is upgraded with additional, benefit-creating features. If the benefits outweigh the costs, an extension is justified; however, if the investments required by innovations or higher-quality product features exceed the expected benefits, extension should be avoided from a profitability standpoint.

A reduction in product features can also make sense and create a greater benefit than the costs express. If a decision is made in favor of a reduction, the cost reduction should be significantly higher than the loss of benefit perceived by the customer. The example of Dacia (Chap. 11) has illustrated how the benefits and costs of services were weighed against each other in a low-cost approach. Low-cost carriers have successfully implemented similar approaches air travel industry. The providers achieve a low target price by radically changing their business model. Other

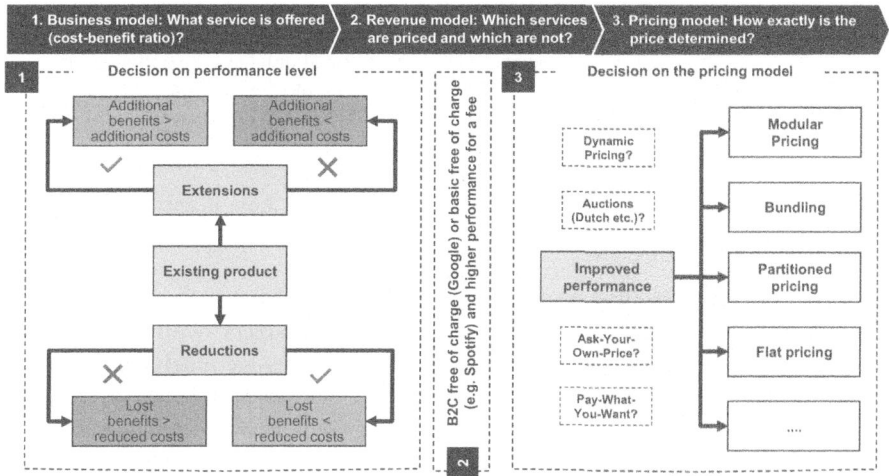

Fig. 12.3 Decisions on service level and pricing model

examples can be found in the areas of rail travel and rental cars (SNCF's "Ouigo" brand, Firefly's low-cost offer for rental cars, to name but a few), as well as in banking and insurance. The examples extend to professional services such as market research (Krämer 2018) and consulting (Deelmann and Krämer 2020), driven primarily by the network economy. If, on the other hand, a rather negligible cost saving leads to a noticeable loss of benefit from the customer's perspective, reducing the features is not an option, at least for this existing product. In the opposite direction, there are examples in many markets where customers pay a high price premium for extended services. This is the case with Apple, for example, when devices such as the iPhone offer extended storage options at a relatively high surcharge.

12.3.2 Different Ways of Translating the Changed "Perceived Value" in Customer Value (Value-of-the-Customer)

12.3.2.1 From the Change in Perceived Value to the Pricing Model

The identification of promising service changes is only a partial objective. In the case of an important service enhancement from the customer's point of view, a decision must be made as to how and whether this service benefit should be monetized. This leads to the question of which services should be priced and only then to the question of suitable pricing models (Fig. 12.3 right). The company must decide in what form it can succeed in exploiting the different willingness to pay for different levels of service. However, the terms business, revenue, and pricing model are sometimes confused (Frohmann 2018; Skiera et al. 2005; Krämer and Kalka 2025).

The following sequence should be strictly adhered to when proceeding:

1. Business model → 2. Revenue model → 3. Price model.

Skiera et al. (2005) explain:

"Once the revenue source has been determined, a decision must then be made as to which revenue partner should be priced. Intermediaries in particular, such as providers of auction platforms (e.g. eBay) or used car exchanges (e.g. Autoscout24.de), have the option of pricing both the buyer and the seller. Only after the source of revenue ("what is priced") and the revenue partner ("who is priced") have been determined can the pricing model itself be discussed."

Different approaches are available, with examples of key points being highlighted below.

12.3.2.2 Modular Pricing or the Offer of Price Modules

A very simple and catchy way of tapping into potential buyers' willingness to pay and at the same time giving customers the feeling that they are receiving a product that meets their needs is to offer modular price components (Krämer 2025). The application is particularly easy to explain using the example of equipping a new car: Here, the willingness to pay for additional services (optional extras) varies considerably. The customer is offered a choice of a variety of equipment features, with different levels of performance available at different prices. Using an online configurator, people who are in the process of selecting and deciding whether to buy a new car are able to put together a car according to their own wishes and price preferences. The prerequisite for the effective use of this pricing model is, firstly, knowledge of the willingness to pay and, secondly, acceptance by buyers of a correspondingly differentiated pricing structure, which can also be tedious for the customer. Modular pricing is widely used in many other sectors, such as insurance, mechanical engineering, and real estate.

12.3.2.3 Price Bundling

Bundling is a combined offer of two or more services at a total price (cf. Simon and Fassnacht 2016, p. 272). This pricing model is popular, for example, with software packages that contain several application programs, with cable network operators and telephone providers such as Telekom or Vodafone (combination of telephony, text messages and internet use) and with providers of internet or mobile phone contracts that have access to streaming services (Krämer 2025). Overall, the price of the bundle generally undermines the added prices of the individual products. This effect is amplified if the discount of the bundle is explicitly communicated compared to the sum of the individual prices of the partial services. If different bundle offers are offered side by side, also as a contrast to the purchase of individual products, price differentiation (with self-selection by the customer) takes place.

Price bundling is not so much about exactly skimming off the willingness to pay for each service, but rather defining the package of services in such a way that the added willingness to pay is met. Bundling is always a good idea when the willingness to pay for individual services is very heterogeneous. For example, the ten-theater package contains performances with a very high degree of attractiveness (the buyer of the package would also book these individually), but also events with medium or low attractiveness (the user of the bundle would not book these individually). The consumer therefore buys more services with the bundle than in the scenario without bundling (Fuerderer et al. 2013; Koderisch et al. 2007). Consumers and providers can benefit, the consumer through more consumption at a lower price, the provider through higher sales and possibly higher profits.

12.3.2.4 Price Partitioning

Price partitioning is to be understood as a "counter-strategy to the bundling of products." While price bundling is about offering services with different average willingness to pay as a combined offer, price partitioning reverses this process, i.e., services that were previously bundled together are offered separately. Price partitioning is intended to influence the consumer's price perception in connection with a transaction. As Bertini and Wathieu (2008) argue, an online or catalog retailer has the option of selling DVDs, for example, for US$23.45 including shipping and handling or for US$16.95 plus US$6.50 for shipping. Despite these offers being objectively identical in terms of the final price, customers' perception processes can differ. This is also confirmed by the results of an experimental study by Krämer (2017) on the selection decision regarding product purchases online vs. stationary with different handling of shipping costs, shown additively or included. Overall, there are relatively strong effects on demand, depending on whether shipping costs are included in the online offer or not. There is little evidence to support the theory that additional costs are only disproportionately taken into account in price perception (Morwitz et al. 1998).

The practice of price splitting has become established in some industries, while it is less relevant in others. Instead of charging a simple, all-inclusive price, companies offer additional fees and surcharges for various service components of an offer. The end result is a lower price for the basic product, but this cannot be realized as further expenses are required to use the product such as for delivery or services,

Positive effects on consumption arise when the partitioning of prices leads to a feeling of a low price (Morwitz et al. 1998) or when customers see an undifferentiated and unfair advantage in the bundling of services. One explanation for a positive assessment of partitioned prices is that consumers initially focus on the base price and consider it attractive. They have the choice to buy additional services or not.

12.3.2.5 Flat Pricing

On closer inspection, different trends within price management must be taken into account, each of which favors a differentiated conception of price models. In some cases, these are contradictory, for example when it is discussed how customers' willingness to pay can be better exploited through price differentiation, while in the opposite school of thought the strategy of price simplification is pursued (Krämer 2025), for example through a subscription. In the case of subscriptions, different price models can be differentiated. These include flat-price offers (such as Netflix or Spotify) or two-tier systems (BahnCard, Amazon Prime). While many academics and practitioners assumed that subscription price models had long since passed their zenith, subscription models are experiencing a boom due to the strong digitalization or parallel to it (Rudolph et al. 2017). They can be found in many business models today. In clear contrast to modular pricing, a flat price offer is not aimed at exploiting willingness to pay in the short term. However, this does not mean that there is no focus on the "value of the customer" aspect; the aim is rather to increase value over the customer life cycle.

12.3.2.6 Deciding on the "Right" Pricing Model

The pricing models shown have only been presented in their pure form. In reality, mixed forms are often found. It may come as a surprise that the results on the advantageousness of complete prices or disaggregated prices are not unambiguous (Bambauer and Gierl 2008). The same applies to differentiated prices and flat-price offers. Obviously, this depends on the individual strategy of the company. For example, different providers in the same sector can offer different pricing models and strategies (Krämer and Kalka 2016; Krämer 2015). The airline industry is an example where low-cost providers offer an à la carte price (Nason 2009). Ryanair, the leading provider in this segment in Europe, separates the prices for the flight, for additional baggage, for meals or seat reservations, etc., while in the USA Southwest, as the "inventor" of the low-cost concept, offers a simple complete price ("transfarency") and thus attempts to positively differentiate itself from the industry standards.

Dominant companies in their sector rely on a flat-pricing offer that does not allow for strong price differentiation. This is the case with the streaming service Netflix, for example, although it is obvious that the willingness to pay for the service offered is likely to vary extremely (it is low for occasional users and higher for customers who stream several hours of series a day; this is only partially covered by the different service levels).

By mixing different pricing models, the question of the "right" pricing model often does not even arise, but rather the question of the right interplay, i.e., the pricing system. Providers such as Amazon, for example, use pricing models such as dynamic pricing and subscription systems (Amazon Prime) side by side (Krämer and Kalka 2016). Mobility service providers such as Deutsche Bahn offer services integrated into the ticket price (City Ticket), but also services that are modular, i.e., priced separately, such as seat reservations.

12.4   Processes and Tools: From Product Change to Economic Success

Deriving the costs to fulfill customer benefits is a major challenge of strategic product management. In the search for the perfect product to meet all customer expectations, the company's own costs often stand in the way. It is becoming increasingly challenging for companies to profitably "extract" the maximum benefit from a product while adhering to specified (internal and external) cost levels. Target pricing determines the price, which reflects the product and performance requirements of the market. In contrast to the cost- based approach, a target price is assumed that reflects the average willingness of customers to pay. A target profit is determined on the basis of the target price (Li 2023). The difference between the target price and the target profit represents the target costs (allowable costs). The target costs are compared with the planned standard costs incurred (drifting costs). If the standard costs are higher than the target costs, cost reduction measures must be derived (Horváth and Möller 2003). In particular, the aspect of willingness to pay is crucial. Due to the close integration of target pricing with target costing (Fig. 12.4 left) and a rather one-sided location in controlling, it seems to make sense to include information from market research and combine it synergistically. When it comes to uncovering willingness to pay, conjoint analysis can be used in conjunction with a cost analysis of each individual product feature. The determination of the customer benefits of each component of the product is compared with the respective cost share. Ideally, each individual customer benefit should correspond to its cost share. If there is an unbalanced relationship between customer benefit and cost share, the cost reduction measures are to be applied for each component. If the customer benefit predominates, a functional improvement should only be sought if the customer considers it to be worthy of improvement. Otherwise, cost advantages should be exploited.

In this way, cost specifications can be considered as early as the product development stage and customer preferences can be addressed in a targeted manner. Furthermore, a continuous improvement process is initiated and disproportionalities in the cost structure are uncovered. However, the concept is only applicable to radical innovations to a limited extent due to the non-existent market price. In general, target pricing supports pricing or price optimization, but should be supplemented by other instruments (such as value pricing).

To identify a profit-maximizing model variant, Bauer et al. (1995) propose a method (conjoint + COST) that requires the partial utility values of all characteristic values, the total utility values of the competing products and additionally the variable costs as data input from the conjoint measurement. The realistic simulation of a purchase decision using a conjoint analysis determines not only the customer

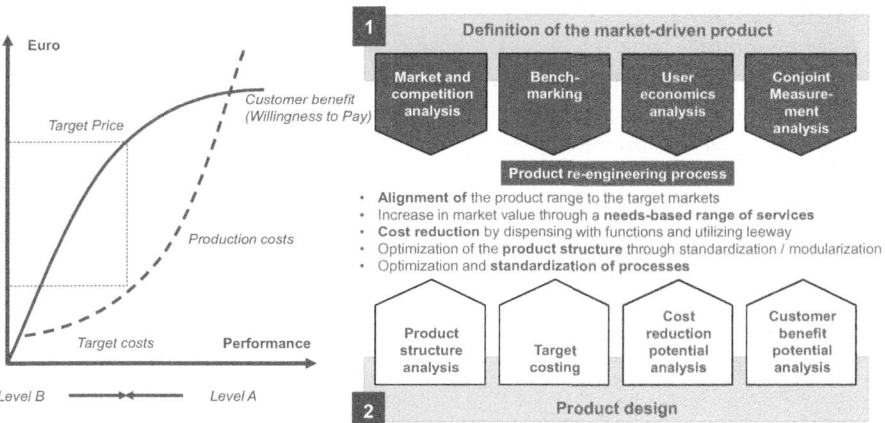

Fig. 12.4 Analysis path for generating target prices and target costs

preference for product characteristics such as design or quality, but also the assessment of the willingness to pay, in that a characteristic value in a product or service bundle to be evaluated represents the price. This means that potential customers also decide on their own willingness to pay for each bundle (Schmaus 2013).

The possibilities of measuring and determining customer needs were discussed in Chap. 4. The project of a successful new product development or extension raises the question of providing as much information as possible to achieve an optimal balance between added or reduced benefits at added or reduced costs—with the aim of seeing existing products as the starting point for a customer value-centric approach through improved performance. Innovations, trends, market developments, and user behavior must be equally assessed from the perspective of a market-driven product. The recommendation to bundle all relevant information means that a market and competition analysis, benchmarking and knowledge of consumer, and usage habits must be balanced with an analysis of the product and cost structure as well as customer benefit potential (Fig. 12.4).

The findings from the following areas of analysis are particularly noteworthy:

- **Market and competitor analyses** create an understanding of market development and market dynamics in all relevant customer and target markets (Scheed and Scherer 2018). The masses of data available through digitalization and connectivity offer new sources and opportunities for data collection and evaluation for market and competition analysis. Suitable big data applications and systems can be used to provide additional information about the market and competition (Seidler-de Alwis 2018).
- **Benchmarking** is a particularly valuable procedure for the alignment of cost acceptance on the market and provides information about the currently dominant expectations of the customer (benefit expectations) as well as the degree of fulfillment by competitors (see Chap. 14). With the help of key figures, the comparison between your own company and the best-practice company can be assessed with regard to customer-centric processes via the drivers costs and benefits (Meier 2001).
- **User economics** analyses provide transparency for a needs-based range of services from the user's perspective. A cost-benefit analysis by the customer provides information on potential cost reductions that can be achieved while maintaining at least the same level of benefits.
- **Conjoint measurement** analyses focus on the individually preferred customer benefit and uncover potentials that trigger a superior benefit fulfillment for the customer in the market despite higher costs (see Sect. 4.2.4). This is a crucial source of information for target pricing, especially in the early phase of product and customer relationship development. Detailed knowledge of benefit preferences enables target pricing by skimming off the willingness to pay (Gustaffson et al. 2007).

12.5 Interview Prof. Dr. Regine Kalka

When considering the dependencies between costs and benefits, pricing is usually seen as an attempt to offer an economically optimized service by comparing the benefits from the perspective of potential customers and the respective costs. What aspects need to be taken into account?

Regine Kalka: In pricing, which looks at the relationship between costs and benefits for customers, there are various aspects that need to be considered to offer an economically optimized service. As a rule, the customer's perception of the benefit takes center stage. The aim is to understand what individual value customers attach to the product or service. This individual perceived value can be made up of functional, emotional and/or social benefit aspects. The benefit level from the customer's perspective is then compared with a specific performance level, considering the costs of the service. This involves cost structures and cost control, i.e. precise knowledge of the cost structures of the product or service. The fixed and variable costs should be analyzed to determine the minimum price.

By combining these aspects, a price can be developed that not only covers the costs, but also optimally reflects the perceived benefits and utilizes the customer's willingness to pay. Even if this is usually assumed: Better performance does not necessarily mean higher costs. Companies can raise the level of service without necessarily increasing costs. Firstly, this is possible if efficiency increases are realized, for example through more efficient processes, automation or the use of innovative technologies. Secondly, it is possible to utilize economies of scale, for example when larger production volumes reduce unit costs. Target pricing is a pricing strategy in which the company sets the price of a product based on the customer's willingness to pay and market requirements. The starting point is therefore the benefit dimension. The production and development costs are then organized in such a way that they correspond to this target price and the desired profit margin.

How is it possible to influence customer benefit on the basis of information on production costs?

Regine Kalka: Information on production costs can have a positive influence on perceived customer benefits if it is used in a targeted and transparent manner. If companies disclose how the price of a product is made up (e.g., material costs, production, transport), this can increase customer trust (trust dimension): Customers often feel more comfortable when they know that a product is fairly priced, and they feel that it is not overpriced. This can increase the benefit from the customer's perspective, especially in the case of high-quality or ethically produced products:

1. Information about production costs can be used to emphasize the quality and durability of the product. For example, higher material or production costs can emphasize the importance placed on high-quality raw materials or elaborate manufacturing processes, which increases the perceived value and thus the benefit of the product (quality communication dimension).

2. Customers are increasingly paying attention to fair and sustainable manufacturing conditions. If companies disclose production costs and show that part of the price goes towards fair wages, environmentally friendly materials, or sustainable processes, this increases the attractiveness for customers for whom such aspects are important. Transparency regarding sustainability can increase the intangible benefits of the product for customers, as they also support their own values with their purchase (sustainability dimension). In addition, the communication of production costs can be embedded in a "story," e.g., how and where the product was made and by whom, i.e. by which employee. This creates an emotional connection that increases customer benefit.
3. In some markets or for certain products, a higher price can be justified by the production costs. If customers understand that a product costs more due to high quality materials, local craftsmanship or specialized production processes, this can increase the perceived value and encourage purchase. Companies can thus show that the higher price is not arbitrary, but based on real costs, which makes customers more aware of the value of the product (price communication dimension).

What examples of transparent pricing do you have in mind?

Regine Kalka: A frequently cited example is Everlane (fashion industry), which has developed Radical Transparency. It discloses in detail how the prices of its products are made up, including material, labor and transport costs as well as the profit margin. Everlane also explains why certain products are more expensive and how fair labor conditions are affect costs. This transparency has helped Everlane build trust with price-conscious and ethical customers. Another example is Patagonia (outdoor clothing): Here, it is clearly communicated that part of the price is higher due to sustainability standards, which helps customers understand the value of the brand and the ideal added value. This openness has helped Patagonia to reach a loyal and environmentally conscious customer group. Outdoor furniture manufacturer Bloom also tries to justify its prices to customers. Bloom communicates that its purely handmade production only on demand, direct sales, deliberate avoidance of warehousing, transparency of working conditions, and support for social projects mean that its products are offered with sustainable quality at a fair price. This gives the customer the feeling that they are buying something handmade and of high quality and doing something good at the same time. This increases their personally perceived added value. Going one step further, Allbirds is an example of the shoe manufacturing sector: Allbirds discloses the costs incurred for materials, production, and transport and how these costs affect the final price. It also explains how the use of sustainable resources such as merino wool or sugar cane influences production costs.

The next example from the food industry shows that transparent pricing does not necessarily have to be successful. Transparent pricing can also fail in some cases, especially if it is not implemented carefully or does not fit the target group and market positioning. Whole Foods has tried to explain the higher price of organic and fair-trade products through transparent pricing. While some customers appreciated this transparency, many still felt the prices were too expensive. The attempt to justify premium prices through transparency led to the company being perceived by customers as a "Whole Paycheck" (an expensive place), giving it the image of an overpriced luxury supermarket. Blue Apron, a meal kit delivery service, tried to show transparency by disclosing the cost of ingredients and packaging. However, many customers felt the prices were too high as they could find the same or similar food cheaper in supermarkets. The transparency unexpectedly revealed how high Blue Apron's profit margins were, which led to customers perceiving the price as excessive. This ultimately led to a decline in customer loyalty.

Transparent pricing can increase customers' willingness to pay by building trust, increasing the perceived value of the product and providing a sense of fairness. There are several ways in which transparent pricing can be used specifically to increase customers' willingness to pay. If it is possible to build trust through openness by transparently explaining how the price is made up, trust is created as customers have the feeling that nothing is being kept from them. The perceived value from the customer's point of view increases if, for example, the breakdown of costs (e.g., material, labor costs, shipping) makes it easier for customers to understand why a product has a certain price or if transparency about profit margins improves the customer's perception of fairness. The perceived value from the customer's perspective increases if, for example, the breakdown of costs (e.g., material, labor costs, shipping) makes it easier for customers to understand why a product has a certain price or if transparency about profit margins improves the customer's perception of fairness, but there are also risks, as the two examples have shown, which can arise if the disclosure of costs leads customers to view prices as too overpriced or the company's profit margins as too high. It is therefore essential to correctly assess price fairness from the customer's perspective.

Prof. Dr. Regine Kalka has been Professor of Marketing and Communication at Düsseldorf University of Applied Sciences since 2003 and a member of the University Council since 2018. She was previously a Vice President at a trade fair company and a senior consultant at an international management consultancy. Her research focuses on pricing, trade fair management, and brand management. She is also the author of numerous publications in these areas and a freelance consultant.

12.6 Outlook

The changed framework conditions—intensified once again by multiple macroeconomic factors—are having an impact on price management. One strand of impact is the discussion of innovative pricing models ("pay-what-you-want," "name your own price," etc.), another is the stronger focus on behavioral aspects of price management and another is the transfer of familiar pricing models to new sectors (e.g., dynamic pricing, subscription systems) and their further development (Krämer and Kalka 2025).

The inclusion and consideration of the reciprocal effects between benefits and costs are an interface that has not yet been sufficiently recognized in the context of customer value-centered management. A more in-depth analysis reveals a previously underestimated importance of the two parameters alongside price. It becomes clear that instruments such as transparent pricing (costs → benefits) and target pricing (benefits → costs) can provide companies with valuable information and opportunities for action for a more differentiated market approach. Both approaches include the aspect of customer centricity, albeit with different modes of action. Transparent pricing is based on the principles of behavioral pricing, while target pricing is compatible with neoclassical theory.

When used correctly, the supposedly opposing drivers of customer value prove to be a viable aid in assessing and weighing up internal and market-related circumstances. Product managers are thus able to better categorize an existing or newly designed product that meets existing customer expectations along a business, revenue, and pricing model.In particular, the final decision support for the right price model or for the exact price determination means added value. The cost-benefit assessment of each business relationship over the customer life cycle is also necessary in terms of "value of the customer" in terms of generation of a genuine contribution to the company's results by the customer.

References

Avins J (2017) This startup is taking the mystery out of wine pricing – and making the good stuff cheaper. QUARTZ v. 15.1.2017, https://qz.com/884169/the-good-stuff-for-less-meet-alit-the-everlane-of-wine. Accessed 30 Apr 2025

Bambauer S, Gierl H (2008) Should marketers use price partitioning or total prices? In: Lee AY, Duluth DS (Hrsg) Adv Consum Res 35:262–268

Bauer HH, Herrmann A, Mengen A (1995) Conioint + COST: Nicht Marktanteile, sondern Gewinne maximieren! Controlling 6(4):339-345

Bertini M, Wathieu L (2008) Research note – attention arousal through price partitioning. Mark Sci 27(2):236–246

Brown R (2013) Everlane's take on supply and demand. Wwd, 30.12.2023,http://wwd.com/accessories-news/handbags/everlanes-take-on-supply-and-demand-7326470/. Accessed 29 Apr 2025

Busch G, Bayer E, Iweala S, Mehlhose C, Risius A, Rubach C, Spiller A (2021) Einkaufs- und Ernährungsverhalten sowie Resilienz des Ernährungssystems aus Sicht der Bevölkerung: Eine Studie während der Corona-Pandemie im November 2020. Ergebnisse der dritten Befragungswelle (No. 2102). Diskussionsbeitrag

Carter RE, Curry DJ (2010) Transparent pricing: theory, tests, and implications for marketing practice. J Acad Mark Sci 38(6):759–774

Deelmann T, Krämer A (2020) Consulting: Ein Lehr-, Lern- und Lesebuch zur Unternehmensberatung. Erich Schmidt Verlag, Berlin

Detweiler L (2025) How e-commerce brands and retailers are building trust with transparent pricing. Omnia Retail, February10, 2025, https://www.omniaretail.com/blog/how-e-commerce-brands-and-retailers-are-building-trust-with-transparentpricing. Accessed 29 Apr 2025

Diller H (2008) Price fairness. J Prod & Bran Manag 17(5):353–355

EVELO (2021) Transparent pricing: where does your money go when you buy an electric bike? https://evelo.com/blogs/learn/transparent-pricing-where-does-your-money-go-when-you-buyan-electric-bike. Accessed 4 Oct 2021

Ferguson JL, Ellen PS (2013) Transparency in pricing and its effect on perceived price fairness. J Prod Bran Manag 22(5/6):404–412

Frohmann F (2018) Digitales Pricing. Springer-Gabler, Wiesbaden

Fu W, Shang, G, Tong X (2025) Budget Disclosure in Crowdfunding: Information Asymmetry and Cost Transparency.Manufacturing & Service Operations Management 27(2):659–678

Fuerderer R, Herrmann A, Wuebker G (2013) Optimal bundling: marketing strategies for improving economic performance. Springer Science & Business Media

Furnham A, Boo HC (2011) A literature review of the anchoring effect. J Socio-Econ 40(1):35–42

Gustaffson A, Herrmann A, Huber F (2007) Conjoint measurement methods and applications, 4. Aufl, Springer. Berlin, Heidelberg, New York

Homburg C, Koschate N (2005) Behavioral Pricing Forschung im Überblick. Z Betriebswirt 75(5):501–524

Horváth P, Möller K (2003) Target pricing und profit planning. Handbuch Preispolitik:455–480

Jung S, Cho HJ, Jin BE (2020) Does effective cost transparency increase price fairness? An analysis of apparel brand strategies. J Brand Manag 27(5):495–507

Kahneman D, Knetsch JL, Thaler R (1986) Fairness as a constraint on profit seeking: entitlements in the market. Am Econ Rev 76:728–741

Kalka R, Krämer A, Ziehe N (2023) Der Irrweg der ewigen Neukundengewinnung–Hunting oder Farming als Ziele imMarketing. In Stammkundenbindung versus Neukundengewinnung: Marketing und Vertrieb im Spannungsfeld von Huntingund Farming, Springer Fachmedien, Wiesbaden, pp. 29–48

Karpik L (2011) Mehr Wert: Die Ökonomie des Einzigartigen, vol 74. campus

Kim NL, Kim G, Rothenberg L (2020) Is honesty the best policy? Examining the role of price and production transparency in fashion marketing. Sustain For 12(17):6800

Koderisch M, Wuebker G, Baumgarten J, Baillie J (2007) Bundling in banking – a powerful strategy to increase profits. J Finan Ser Mark 11(3):268–276

Krämer A (2015) Pricing in a VUCA world – how to optimize prices, if the economic, social and legal framework changes rapidly. In: Mack O, Khare A, Krämer A, Burgartz T (eds) Managing in a VUCA world. Springer, New York, pp 115–128

Krämer A (2017) Multi-channel pricing: channel-specific marketing from the perspective of consumers and companies. Mark Rev St Gallen 34(5):78–86

Krämer A (2018) Price Wars: how to turn it to your advantage, International Pricing Forum 2018, Paris, June 18th, 2018

Krämer A (2025) Preisvereinfachung versus Preisdifferenzierung. In Preiskommunikation: Strategische Herausforderungen und innovative Anwendungsfelder (pp. 81-99). Wiesbaden: Springer Fachmedien Wiesbaden

Krämer A, Kalka R (2016) How digital disruption changes pricing strategies and price models. In: Khare A, Schatz R, Stewart B (eds) Phantom ex machina: digital disruption's role in business model transformation. Springer, Berlin, pp 87–103

Krämer A, Kalka R (2025) Neue Perspektiven für die Preiskommunikation in einer digitalen Welt. In Preiskommunikation: Strategische Herausforderungen und innovative Anwendungsfelder (pp. 479-500), Springer Fachmedien, Wiesbaden

Li W (2023) Pricing Strategies in a Dynamic Market. In Strategic Management Accounting in a Network Economy (pp. 183–209). Singapore: Springer Nature Singapore

Meier R (2001) Customer care excellence – with benchmarking to success. Customer care management. Gabler Publishing House, pp 13–38

Mohan B, Buell RW, John LK (2020) Lifting the veil: The benefits of cost transparency. Marketing Science 39(6):1105–1121

Morwitz VG, Greenleaf EA, Johnson EJ (1998) Divide and prosper: consumers' reactions to partitioned prices. J Mark Res 35:453–463

Nason SD (2009) The future of a la carte pricing in the airline industry. J Revenue Pricing Manag 8(5):467–468

Northcraft GB, Neale MA (1987) Experts, amateurs, and real estate: an anchoring-and-adjustment perspective on property pricing decisions. Organ Behav Hum Decis Process 39(1):84–97

Qi X (2021) Green food consumption: studies on consumers' purchase intentions and the intention-behavior gap in the Chinese context (Doctoral dissertation)

Rudolph T, Bischof SF, Böttger TM, Weiler N (2017) Disruption at the door: a taxonomy on subscription models in retailing. Market Rev St Gallen 34(5):18–25

Scheed B, Scherer P (2018) MARKT – Strategische Markt- und Wettbewerbsanalyse und strategische Marktplanung, Strategic Sales Management. Springer Gabler, Wiesbaden, pp 17–57

Schmaus P (2013) Conjoint analyses in target costing. Controlling 25(12):686–689

Seidler-de Alwis R (2018) Market and competitive analysis in times of big data and digitalization. In: Schade F, Georgy U (eds) Practical handbook of information marketing: Convergent strategies, methods and concepts. De Gruyter Saur, Berlin, Boston, pp 59–70

Simon H, Fassnacht M (2016) Preismanagement: Strategie – Analyse – Entscheidung – Umsetzung. Springer Gabler, Wiesbaden

Skiera B, Spann M, Walz U (2005) Revenue sources and pricing models for the business-to-consumer sector on the Internet. Inf Syst 47(4):285–293

Somervuori O (2014) Profiling behavioral pricing research in marketing. J Prod Bran Manag 23(6):462–474

Štefko R, Steffek V (2018) Key issues in slow fashion: current challenges and future perspectives. Sustainability 10(7):2270 (Online)

Part V

Outlook: Customer Value-Centered Management in a VUCA World

The Path to a Customer Value-Centered Company

13

13.1 Value-Centricity and Customer-Centricity: A Contradiction?

"You can't manage what you don't measure."—Peter Drucker

In the sense of a control loop, it is important to define and continuously measure the key success drivers to give management the opportunity to make decisions based on them. This correlation described by Peter Drucker underlines the dependency of performance indicators on the one hand and the quality of management decisions on the other. Profitability and liquidity figures in particular were not sufficiently taken into account or even neglected in many companies. The corona crisis has made companies around the world aware of how important it is to generate profitability from the customer relationship and to build up reserves in order to be prepared for "bad times."

A return on sales of 7.5% was still estimated for the German SME sector in 2019, but this level fell sharply with the outbreak of the coronavirus crisis (KfW 2020). Most economies experienced both a supply and a demand shock (Bofinger et al. 2020). The reasoning is very simple: the individual customer relationship is the central nucleus for generating profits. If companies succeed in managing their customer portfolio in a profit-oriented manner, especially in a crisis, it is also likely that sustainable profits can be generated (Lies 2021). As a result, companies should focus on the value of the customer relationship.

At the same time, the coronavirus pandemic has given a second perspective a new boost, namely the focus on the customer experience. In their book *Outside-In*, published in 2012, Manning and Bodine drew a picture of a pyramid comprising three levels. The customer experience should be needs-based, simple, and pleasant. Each time customers come into contact or interact with a product, service, person, or automated system, they rate how well the contact or interaction helped them achieve their goals, how much effort they had to put into the contact/interaction, and

A. Krämer et al., *Customer Value-centered Management*, Future of Business and Finance, https://doi.org/10.1007/978-3-031-90497-4_13

how much they enjoyed the interaction (Manning and Bodine 2012). The authors proclaimed an "age of the customer—a time when focus on the customer matters more than any other strategic imperative." In a crisis, companies have understood how important the principle of a perfect customer experience is, in many cases abruptly (just think of the many retail companies that were only able to generate sales online due to the closure of brick-and-mortar stores during the lockdown). This perspective focuses the company's full attention on the customer's perspective, with the aim of understanding customer needs as deeply as possible and then generating value for the individual customer ("if we convince the customer, we are successful").

In academia—as in business practice—the two perspectives are usually viewed in isolation. However, it adds value to combine the two strands, i.e., the view of customer value, as value-of-the-customer on the one hand and value-to-the-customer on the other (Chap. 9). This is made possible by value-to-value segmentation (see Fig. 13.1). Here, customers are assigned to a manageable number of clusters (e.g., 2*2, 3*3), firstly according to primary needs ("Which benefit factor primarily determines the purchase?") and secondly according to the contribution margin or customer lifetime value (CLV). At this point, it should be pointed out once again that there are a variety of ways to segment customers—this could be done according to socio-demographic aspects, purchasing patterns or customer value, for example (Malthouse 2016). As Verhoef and Langerak (2002) describe and illustrate with examples, a singular overly simplified customer value segmentation runs the risk of creating the wrong customer value.

Decisions regarding the prioritization of customers can be based on erroneous assumptions if the full span of customer needs (value from the customer's perspective) is not taken into account. However, the proposed value-to-value segmentation ensures that both value dimensions are explicitly considered.

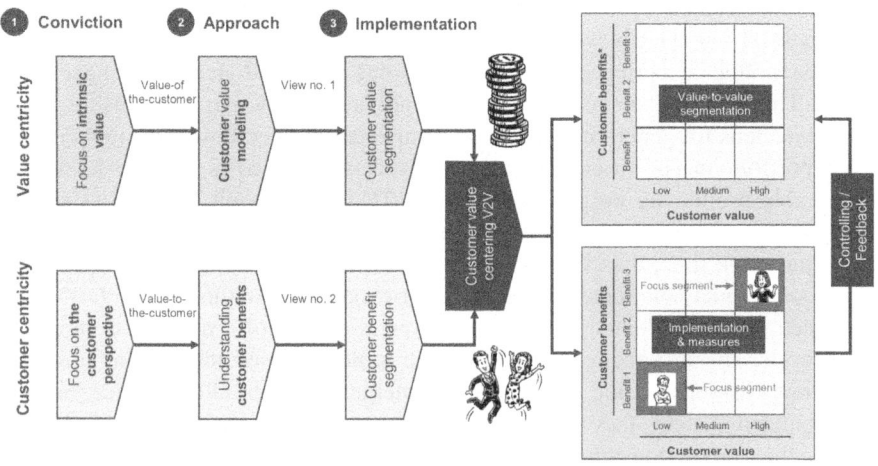

* Primary needs; e.g. price/brand-oriented buyers, etc.

Fig. 13.1 The concept of customer value-centered management

Once segmentation has taken place, the customer value segments can be used to support operational marketing. This concerns the aspects of automation and personalization as well as the optimization of customer contact points.

Measuring the two value dimensions is not trivial, but it is feasible. It should also be borne in mind that the classification of customers can change over time. In some cases, abrupt changes can occur. For example, Krämer et al. (2021) found that customer coverage within the local transport industry changed significantly with the outbreak of the coronavirus crisis and the subsequent lockdowns. On the one hand, previous season ticket holders parted with their season tickets (sharp drop in revenue and contribution margin), while on the other hand, regular customers remained loyal to the transport companies, although in practice, with limited mobility, e.g., due to working from home, the break-even point (usage at which it is worth owning a season ticket) was not reached. In this case, constant revenue results in an increased customer contribution margin. It is also clear that the corona-related surge in online sales had a positive impact on the customer value of, for example, Amazon Prime customers.

As a result, a snapshot is initially required when considering CLV. Exactly how the calculation is carried out depends on the company-specific situation. However, it is important that an estimate, an attempt at quantification, is made at all. If the customer relationship is assessed as economically problematic, it is necessary to check whether a negative CLV or a CLV that is low in relation to other customers can be improved. In extreme cases—where no possibilities can be identified to change the customer relationship into a sufficiently profitable situation—the company may also decide to terminate a customer relationship.

13.2 Personalization and Automation in Marketing and Sales

13.2.1 Personalization and Automation in Product Design, Sales, and Communication

Over the last decade, changes in the structuring and aggregation of data have been observed in the development of data management. A distinction must be made between different layers, which can be defined in terms of business content or data technology (Burgartz and Krämer 2016).

In terms of changes in the process steps of customer data management, the degree of automation is increasing across the process steps. Initially, data input was based on manual recording, data analysis was largely manual and decisions were made on an individual basis. Today, complete automation is feasible, but it has its limits in terms of content (Krämer and Tachilzik 2016). As soon as technology loses its "bottleneck status," a new bottleneck arises: with the realization that the technical maximum is not the same as the (economic) optimum in terms of content, the technical expertise of marketing and sales becomes (once again) more important.

The automation of data management will be particularly interesting if it is possible to develop data networking into a learning system (see Chap. 3), but here, too, the specialist input of marketing and sales staff will be required for the foreseeable future. By segmenting customers, enriching the data in CRM and defining business rules, the conditions can be created to standardize marketing processes and thus make them more automatable. This is demonstrated below using activities within the framework of a current understanding of marketing:

- Use of relevant data to improve the customer experience: Information and offers for customers are increasingly being made available in real time and individually. As soon as transaction data is linked to a customer account or at least contact data, numerous possibilities can offer added value for the customer, for example by (1) sending information about the status of the delivery or the possibility of changing the predicted time or day of delivery (e.g., online retail), (2) providing information about flight delays or gate changes at airports or offers, (3) options for upselling (e.g., booking a comfortable seat on the plane or train or changing booking class after the ticket booking has been completed) or (4) simulating the booking process on the train or a change of booking class after the ticket booking has been completed) or (4) simulation of a vehicle purchase using an online configurator. The list can be extended at will.
- Customer feedback as a learning system: While it was previously the case that customer satisfaction was measured in detail as a core element of relationship management (at the individual level, not the individual transaction as the key element), the trend in satisfaction measurement in recent years has been towards a transactional orientation (Markey et al. 2009) and a shortening and focus on core parameters such as overall satisfaction and the intention to recommend. The success of the Net Promoter Score (NPS) can also be explained against this background (Reichheld 2003). The main advantage of the tool lies in its simplicity (Bendle and Bagga 2016), as users only answer one simple question (How likely is it that you would recommend X to a friend or colleague?). The increasing utilization of corporate fan pages on Facebook serves the strategic objective of fostering customer advocacy, typically measured through the top two positive response categories to indicate promoter status (1) level: "Like," (2) level: "Share." Even after online purchases, customers are increasingly being automatically asked to recommend the product on Facebook ("Share this purchase with your friends") if a Facebook cookie or account is recognized on the end device (Tachilzik 2013). The spread of the internet, a stronger customer focus in marketing areas (creation of CRM databases with corresponding contact information such as email etc.), and the accessibility of inexpensive market research software have significantly improved the cost-efficient measurement of customer satisfaction. The US company Surveymonkey is a particularly good example of a disruptive business model that enables companies and private individuals to conduct online studies themselves. As part of DIY market research, companies are able to obtain feedback from customers quickly and cost-effectively in order to be able to react promptly (Krämer 2018b).
- Product innovation and change through digitalization: While the publishing industry has long struggled to create a link between the "old offline world" and

the digital world, a number of intermediaries have attempted to better meet information and media consumption needs through individually created news. These are not publishers, but providers of editorial content tailored to the reader profile. Flipboard is the market leader in this small but rapidly developing market for social magazines (Macmanus 2011). The publisher C.H. Beck offers a large proportion of legal literature online as a subscription. Constantly updated legislation sets strict rules for the traditional book business. However, the production cycles for standard textbooks have the disadvantage that some of the law is already out of date when the edition is published. As part of the subscription, customers receive direct access to the updated online version of the standard works, so the reader always has an "up-to-date product."

- Differentiated customer management to increase customer retention: In many cases, customer lifetime value is essentially driven by the duration of the business relationship with the customer. The longer this relationship lasts, the higher the cumulative revenue from the customer relationship. For example, Gupta et al. (2004) have shown that it is worth far more to increase the customer retention rate by 1% than to increase the new customer rate by the same percentage. Customer churn is predictable to a certain extent. If it is possible to determine the probability of customer churn and at the same time the value of an individual customer, business rules can be used to automatically initiate customer-specific measures. At the same time, forecasting options can be improved by increasing both the quality and quantity of data. This enables companies to better identify the drivers of customer behavior. In addition, automated routines are required for a larger customer base to enable decision-making support in individual cases and in real time.

Figure 13.2 shows the dependencies between targeted segment-oriented marketing and big data as well as a central customer account. Ideally, information is provided from the big data that can be assigned to the individual customers, e.g., input on the central dimensions such as customer needs and customer contribution margin (Bongaerts and Krämer 2014). On this basis, targeted marketing measures, such as in the areas of customer feedback, customer management or direct marketing campaigns, etc. can then be initiated.

13.2.2 Personalization and Automation in Pricing

The topic of "dynamic pricing" is currently the subject of much controversy (Puscher 2016). As Paul Krugman (2000) has already described, dynamic pricing is a new version of the "age-old" practice of price discrimination. What is new is that dynamic pricing is also made possible from a profit-cost perspective in mass markets. A common form of dynamic pricing is to change prices over time. Prices are increased on days or time windows when purchasing power is expected to be higher and reduced accordingly during periods of low demand. These are typical patterns for airlines, rail travel, hotels, and rental cars. These companies rely on highly automated yield management systems (Cross et al. 2011) to simultaneously improve

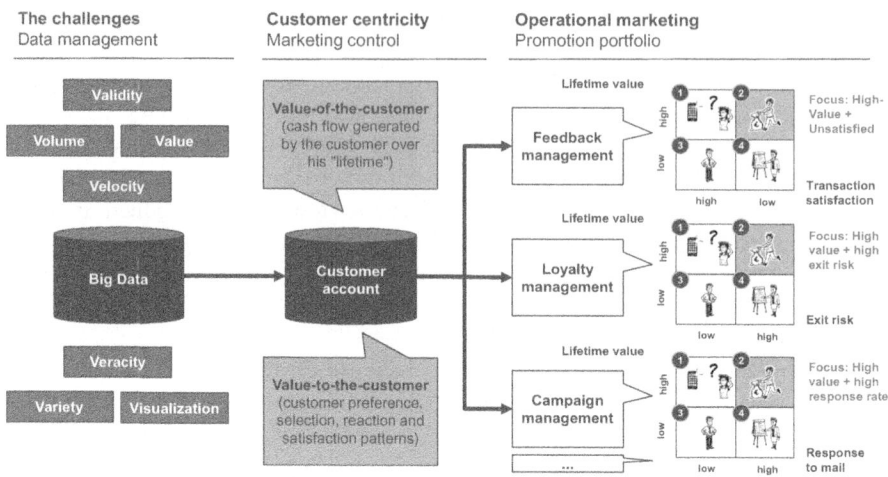

Fig. 13.2 Customer value-centered management in operational implementation (Krämer et al. 2016d)

capacity utilization and overall revenue. To this end, the availability of different price levels or fare quotas is changed. More recently, the use of dynamic pricing has also been discussed in stationary retail. The automation of pricing processes fundamentally entails the risk of price wars if price reductions by one provider lead to corresponding price reductions by competitors in the short term, thereby triggering an "unwanted dynamic" (Krämer et al. 2016a).

In principle, it is also possible to calculate individual prices using customer information (purchases already made, browsers used, place of residence, etc.) to skim off as much of the consumer's maximum willingness to pay as possible. However, this is viewed comparatively critically (particularly in relation to the internet giants Google, Facebook, and Amazon, see Bernasek and Mongan 2015; Krämer and Burgartz 2016). As a representative survey shows, 44% of German Amazon customers, for example, are of the opinion that Amazon cannot afford to offer its customers different prices according to their profile. More than 50% of Amazon customers are even of the opinion that they would no longer shop with the online retailer (Krämer and Kalka 2017) if they engage in this practice. Nevertheless, Amazon is one of the pioneers of dynamic pricing.

Flexible pricing promises high business management potential, which suggests that a corresponding IT project should be set up. Nevertheless it is essential to include the customer perspective, as a price can vary not only over time, but also depending on the customer. The introduction of dynamic pricing is associated with further refinements, such as (dynamic) personalized pricing (Krämer et al. 2018; Priester et al. 2020). Personalized pricing is when a customer is shown an individual price based on personal data that is not offered to other customers. With personalized dynamic pricing (PDP), the price is changed for each person and purchase situation.

This step in which a customer receives exactly the price they are willing to pay depending on their specific personality profile, previous search and purchasing behavior and their general willingness to pay (Adams 2017; Adolphs 2020), theoretically promises even more sales effects than dynamic pricing, but is all the more problematic for the customer relationship (Reinartz et al. 2017; Krämer et al. 2016b). This also makes it clear that the concept of dynamic pricing requires clear classification and differentiation. Figure 13.3 offers a suggestion for this. It is important to note, for example, that a PDP is not the same as a personalized discount coupon. The coupon is not dynamic. The customer decides whether the coupon is redeemed or not, and the redemption of the coupon necessarily leads to a price reduction.

Empirical studies on the practical significance of a PDP come to different conclusions, possibly also because it is very difficult to prove methodologically. For example, ibi research and trinnovative (2020) conclude that "personalized pricing does not exist on the market and is not actively used by providers," while Krämer (2018a) demonstrates this selectively using the example of Amazon.

Certain much-discussed aspects of pricing, such as personalization and automation, are both an opportunity and a risk. They are by no means a one-way street, and there are considerable differences, at least in the comparison of pricing and other marketing elements. On the one hand, an automated and personalized approach to the customer through a product tailored to their needs can increase customer loyalty and at the same time reduce the costs of customer care; on the other hand, the transfer of these principles to pricing involves considerable risks. These are particularly high if personalized, dynamic pricing is used from the company's perspective. In the worst case scenario, customers find that they are offered different prices for an identical product depending on their personal circumstances. However, the reasons for this are not clear to the customer. In addition to legal aspects, which are not

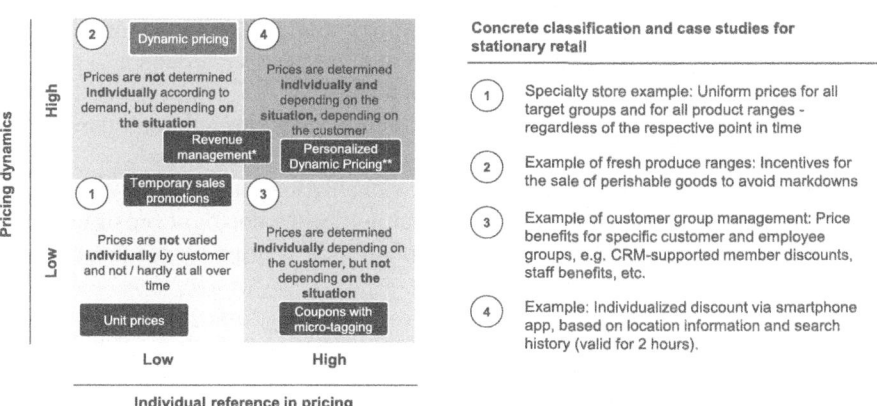

* Dynamic pricing is sometimes equated with revenue management (RM); however, RM involves simultaneous price and volume control, i.e. it includes not only price differentiation but also a change in supply quotas (Krämer, Friesen & Shelton, 2018).
** Customers receive an individual price offer at the time of inquiry, e.g. based on profile data (see Priester et al. 2020).

Fig. 13.3 Dynamics and individual reference in pricing

discussed in detail here (GDPR), the risks with regard to a loss of trust should not be underestimated (Krämer and Mauer 2023). The question also arises as to how customer loyalty can actually be maintained if customers have the feeling that their willingness to pay is being completely siphoned off (in this case, the consumer surplus = 0).

13.3   Customer Service Processes: Data-Driven and Thought Through to the End

13.3.1 Service Problems in Times of Digitalization?

One would think that most companies today would have understood the link between service quality and sales, whether through bitter experience or good business sense. As a rule, satisfied customers spend more and are more loyal. CEOs of companies large and small are recognizing the importance of providing better customer service to create and then exploit potential for strategic competitive advantage. Some now emphasize customer service more than product quality and price. This makes it even more surprising when problems caused by poor customer service become more frequent. Estimates based on customer surveys on the termination of customer relationships indicate that in 2018, poor customer service cost companies in the USA more than USD 75 billion per year (Hyken 2018). Just as worrying is the realization that this figure has risen significantly compared to previous measurements. Around 67% of customers have become "serial switchers," i.e., customers who are willing to switch brands due to a poor customer experience.

Reasons for this may be if:

- Customers do not feel (sufficiently) valued, e.g., because they see themselves as loyal regular customers who deserve a certain treatment.
- Customers are not able to talk to a person who can give them the answers they are looking for, i.e., they have the feeling of being "passed around as a problem case until the problem has hopefully solved itself."
- Customers experience rude and unhelpful employees, even though they would describe themselves as polite and friendly.
- Customers are kept "on hold" for an unreasonably long time, which can include waiting for the service to be provided (waiting for the doctor or repair person at home), waiting for urgently needed information or waiting for feedback, e.g., a complaint.

A study by Ovum (2016) points to a discrepancy between customer behavior and contact center support. For example, due to changes in technology, customers readily use digital channels to search for information, but are often unable to resolve issues through these channels. Contact centers should be able to better understand digital behavior and provide integrated support offerings that meet the needs of the connected, mobile customer. However, the reality is often suboptimal. For example,

62% of customers believe it takes five or more different interactions for their issues to be resolved, while more than half of contact center managers believe customers typically receive answers within one to two touchpoints (and the customer issue is resolved). More than 80% of consumers confirm that they have terminated a customer relationship at least once due to poor service. These problems have been recognized to some extent, with the realization that it is imperative to measure and control the quality of customer contacts.

The analysis of the customer journey and the associated customer touchpoint management have become particularly important for brand management during digitalization and technological progress, as the diversity and heterogeneity of customer touchpoints have increased significantly. On the one hand, it is important to differentiate between contact sources that customers are generally passively exposed to (push touchpoints) and those that customers actively select (pull touchpoints). On the other hand, a distinction must be made as to whether the contact is with the manufacturer or the retailer. This second aspect is particularly relevant, for example, for brand producers in multi-level distribution—such as in food retailing—where important pull touchpoints essentially occur before or during the purchase of food in the store. If consumers have an increasing need for knowledge when buying food and are more enlightened and critical, the pull contact points play a key role in optimizing the customer journey. If the customer experience is positively perceived, this impacts the brand's image. The pull contact points with the manufacturer form the interface between the customer experience and the customer journey.

13.3.2   A Case Study: Telephone Hotlines

Service telephone hotlines play a special role in the context of active pull contact points. In times of digitalization, telephone hotlines may be seen as an "old-fashioned" form of communication, but they make it easier for customers to contact the manufacturer directly if they have urgent questions or problems. According to studies on the importance of different contact channels in customer service (Sommerhäuser 2018), it is important for consumers to communicate with a service employee in person, especially for complex issues. Other studies (Ovum 2016) found that 72% of respondents first search for information online or look for a solution to a problem before picking up the phone. At the same time, around two thirds of consumers also state that their problem was solved the first time they contacted them personally on the phone. This means that the hotline performs better than live chat (21% problem resolution), the website/ FAQ (13% problem resolution) and email contact (10% problem resolution). Customer-initiated, non-promotional dialog therefore has the potential to have a particularly positive influence on customer satisfaction and thus strengthen customer loyalty.

Against this backdrop, an empirical study (a collaboration between Düsseldorf University of Applied Sciences, exeo Strategic Consulting AG and Rogator AG) examined the pull contact points for food as well as the accessibility and service quality of food manufacturers' telephone hotlines (Kalka and Krämer 2018). The approach was multi-stage. In the first stage, the pull contact points were identified as part of a representative survey of German consumers aged 18 and over (online, $n = 520$, March 2017). In the second stage, a random field survey was conducted in stationary retail stores to determine the existence of telephone hotlines on food product packaging. In the third stage, the customer experience was examined as part of mystery calls by investigating the accessibility and service quality (quality of answers and problem-solving skills) of food manufacturers' telephone hotlines. A final fourth step comprised qualitative interviews with relevant marketing decision-makers in the company. As part of the empirical study (stage 1), the interviewees were asked to indicate which contact sources they had already used for questions about food and which they considered to be the most important contact points. First of all, store employees and product information in bricks-and-mortar stores are the most important points of contact for questions about food (58% of responses and 35% of respondents mention these). This correlation is even more pronounced among older consumers. Roughly one third of consumers engage in direct contact with the brand manufacturer. Of these, four-fifths of contact points do not involve direct interaction (email, product information on the home page), while one-fifth involve direct interaction with the manufacturer (use of telephone hotline and live chat on the website). The results of the customer survey are shown in Fig. 13.4 (left-hand side).

Although the direct customer-initiated contact points with food manufacturers play a less significant role in terms of quantity compared to the other contact points (8% of consumers state that they have already used a manufacturer's telephone hot-line; 12% have contacted the manufacturer by email), they can still have a decisive influence during the customer journey and for customer experience management, especially when customers are highly involved or have urgent questions from the consumer's point of view. If customers expect an immediate response from the man-ufacturer, email and product information on the website are less likely to be used as

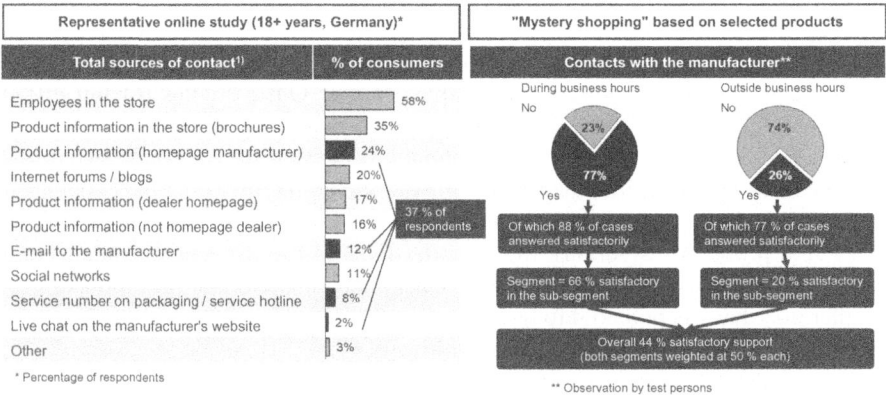

Fig. 13.4 Research results on the quality of customer hotlines in the food retail sector

sources of contact; instead, a service number or live chat on the website should be used. Another important point: in direct contact with the end customer, branded goods manufacturers can manage the customer process better and in a more targeted manner than is the case with direct contact in grocery stores.

As part of a field study, the project team randomly examined 1153 food packaging samples of manufacturer brand products from 9 different product categories. Between 49 and 141 different individual products were recorded in each category. A service number or telephone hotline was identifiable on 28% of the product packaging, while 72% of the products did not display a telephone service on the packaging. Only 1% of manufacturers with a telephone hotline indicated business hours or availability. Overall, it can therefore be stated that service hotlines in times of digitalization are obviously not a necessary touchpoint from the company's point of view and, if they are used, they are not controlled via contact times.

Mystery calls were carried out (step 3) to test the accessibility and service quality of the telephone hotlines of food manufacturers identified in the survey on a random basis. Test callers used a predefined scenario and a standardized guideline to check the behavior of the telephone hotline staff and the telephone call process and evaluated them based on objective criteria. After eliminating telephone numbers that were recorded more than once due to products from the same manufacturer, a total of 104 telephone hotlines w e r e analyzed, which were contacted both during business hours from Monday to Friday between 9 a.m. and 6 p.m. and outside these business hours, including weekends (Fig. 13.4, right-hand side). In addition to the aspect of accessibility, the problem-solving competence was also examined.

Overall, only 44% of telephone calls were answered satisfactorily (average of 68% during business hours and 20% outside of business hours). It is striking that 23% of telephone numbers were unavailable during business hours and 74% outside of business hours, although only 1% of products with a telephone number were available.

The telephone hotline was not indicated as having specific business hours and therefore contact seekers would generally have to assume 24/7 availability. "Unavailable" specifically means that the call was not answered, or the number was not taken. In the case of availability, questions could be answered satisfactorily in 88% of cases within business hours and in 77% of cases outside of business hours. The result shows that a solution to the problem could only be found in 20% of contacts made outside business hours. In the event of an urgent customer inquiry, this results in a considerable "frustration potential" for consumers "seeking help," combined with a corresponding risk for the lifetime value of a disappointed customer.

At first glance, telephone hotlines for food products appear to be of little importance from the customer and manufacturer's perspective. However, a closer look at the pull touchpoints initiated by the customer reveals a certain relevance. In a qualitative telephone survey of manufacturers who offer telephone hotlines, it was uniformly confirmed that telephone hotlines are generally considered less important than other touchpoints. However, it was emphasized that older customers still prefer to make contact by telephone. In addition, most of the qualitative interviews with marketing representatives pointed out that personal and individual advice is better at generating customer trust and that complaints can be handled most quickly via phone calls, as all the necessary information can be requested immediately, as in the case of iglo (Kalka and Krämer 2018):

> "It is important to us that our customers can reach iglo quickly and easily, whether by phone, email, post or social media, without having to search for a contact option for a long time. The quickest way to do this is via our free consumer service hotline." Ute Sievert, Consumer Service & Quality Management, Iglo GmbH.

It can also be assumed that the level of involvement, the need for information, and the urgency to clarify questions directly with the manufacturer are comparatively high for food. Most manufacturers pay too little attention to this customer touch-point and experience medium. Against the backdrop of more cost-effective and meaningful digital customer touchpoints, such as live chat, which can be better integrated as part of marketing automation, this is understandable to a certain extent. However, this is not necessarily understandable from a customer experience management perspective. Companies that (still) attach importance to the telephone hotline and offer the consumer a corresponding contact option can be expected to deal with customer concerns satisfactorily, i.e., the company must be available via the hotline and the contact person on the company side must have some ability to solve the customer's problem. If you're going to do it, do it right!

13.3.3 Deficits in Customer Service: Not an Isolated Case

The question that arises in this context is whether the deficits in customer service are firstly planned (i.e., accepted) or secondly whether the companies have overlooked certain customer needs and expectations of service quality. In the first explanatory approach, it should be noted that it is a legitimate decision for companies to unilaterally terminate selected customer relationships or reduce the service offering to increase the company's profitability (Mittal et al. 2008; Shin et al. 2012; Zeithaml, et al. 2001). Divestment (or demarketing) is a serious relationship intervention that is not based on mutual consent, but solely on the provider's assessment of the relationship. However, initial findings from research and numerous examples from practice are worrying, proving that rejected customers or customers with bad experiences in contact with the provider "fight back" emotionally and effectively (Lepthien et al. 2017).

The second explanatory approach raises the question of why companies have not understood important customer expectations or have not taken sufficient measures to ensure adequate service quality in the face of existing customer understanding. This could also be related to the fact that decision-makers in the company underestimate the extent of poor service perception. The consequences can be that there are severe complaints from customers or that particularly blatant cases appear on social networks and then lead to public discussions.

The example of Deutsche Bahn illustrates how an increase in the number of complaints has led to the digitalization of a long overdue customer process. Never have so many people in Germany contacted the arbitration board for public transport as in the coronavirus year 2020. The reasons for this were problems with flight and rail travel cancellations, especially with refunds. The customers' lack of understanding mainly concerned the lack of transparency in the processes and the waiting times. A particular annoyance for many rail customers was the reporting of delays, which were handled in a lengthy bureaucratic process. Rail customers who were either on delayed trains or who missed connections due to delays and were therefore already sufficiently affected had to fill in a so-called passenger rights form and either send it to Deutsche Bahn (German Rail, DB) by post or hand it in at a travel center at the station together with their ticket. For this passenger rights form to be processed properly, a great deal of detailed information was required, for example the train numbers of the affected trains. In May 2021, DB declared (NN 2021) that the company would fulfill a promise and "rail customers will be able to submit their compensation digitally with just a few clicks from 1 June" and that it would be "quick, easy, and transparent." To apply for compensation, the affected long-distance or regional train journey must be selected on the user interface of the website or mobile app, and the process should take no longer than five minutes. In this context, many travelers wondered why the state-owned company held on to outdated, complicated, and environmentally harmful processes for so long—after all, digital refund applications have been offered by other European train companies for years (Hüfner 2021). The train journey itself cannot be digitized, but all processes that are necessary from the customer's point of view before, during and after the journey can (Krämer and Bongaerts 2017).

Even more depressing are situation reports from online banking customers who find themselves in an existentially threatening situation, e.g., because they realize that they have been robbed and then try to understand the problem and find a solution. For example, the Business Insider portal (Schlenk 2018) reports on an N26 (fully digital bank) customer who discovered €80,000 was stolen and who then contacted the bank's customer service. Here are excerpts from the conversation:

"...
Customer: What is my account balance (…). Customer: Previously it was around €80,000 (…).
N26: Axel, I urgently need to clarify a few things directly with my colleagues. Can you stay in the chat?
Customer: Yes.
N26: There's not even more than €30 left in your account at the moment, sorry. Customer: Excuse me?
N26: 12,26 €. (…).
N26: Contact the police immediately. We will do our best to support you in resolving this case.
Customer: I can't believe it.
N26: Please be patient.
Customer: I would like a telephone number where I can speak to someone personally. N26: Unfortunately, we no longer offer a telephone service, sorry."

13.3.4 Value-to-Value Perspective: Finding the Right Balance

The increased discussion on the implementation of digitalization and automation in marketing and sales will only add value if it succeeds in meeting customer needs and thereby improving the customer relationship. As different as the examples presented (telephone hotlines, complaint management at Deutsche Bahn or customer service at N26) may be, what they all have in common is that customers—especially those with increased involvement (e.g., enquiries to the manufacturer about the safety of food, the possibility of compensation in the event of a complaint, etc.) have clear requirements for what they consider to be a (basic) hygiene service that a service provider must fulfill because customers take this for granted. No matter how much a company is interested in the digitalization of marketing and sales, if it is not able to offer a quick and pragmatic solution to a problem in this situation, there is a risk of an immediate and lasting loss of trust and image. Even from a perspective that focuses on the value of the customer and refers to the cost perspective, such an approach can only be explained to a limited extent, namely if it is assumed that a customer relationship will continue despite poor performance. However, this cannot be assumed under the changed VUCA, social media, and customer demand inflation framework conditions.

As can be seen, efficient marketing and sales measures require both facets of customer value to be taken into account. Measures must have a value for the customer (or also: a sacrifice of service accepted by the company must not lead to a deterioration in the customer relationship) and they must (considering all direct and indirect effects) result in an increase in the cumulative customer coverage contribution, at least in the medium term. The win-win relationship within the two customer value perspectives is not automatic. However, many examples can be found where there is an imbalance in corporate practice. A focus primarily on value to the customer or alternatively only on value of the customer does not create a sufficient basis for sustainable customer relationship management.

13.4 Big Data in Marketing and Sales: No Blind Trust in Algorithms and Artificial Intelligence

Finding the right balance between the two perspectives of customer value is a key achievement of corporate management and control. In this context, further consequences arise, e.g., how the buzzword big data is to be classified and how it is to be used in the sense of customer value-centered management.

There are two basic approaches to using big data to support decision-making (Fig. 13.5), which Krämer and Tachilzik (2016) compare. In the "technology-oriented" approach, as much data as possible is brought together in the hope of identifying previously unrecognized correlations. In contrast, the "business model-oriented" approach reverses the process steps (top-down): First, relevant measures to improve the company's results are identified. In the next step, the relevant sensitive parameters for profitability are determined. The decisive point is

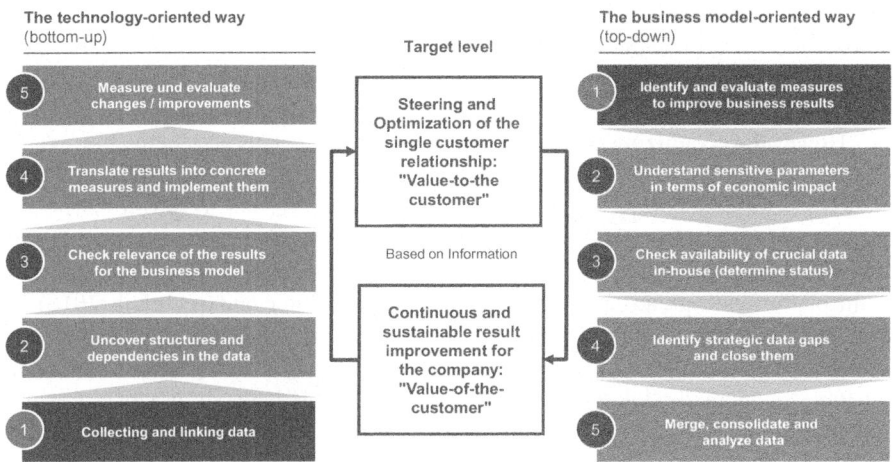

Fig. 13.5 Technology-oriented vs. business model-oriented approach

therefore not so much the amount of data and analytics, but the business understanding of those involved. Finally, the available data is reviewed (Krämer and Tachilzik 2016; Krämer et al. 2016c).The customer relationship level is the nucleus: This is where central data for decision support is collected.

While the special features of big data are usually seen in connection with a technology-oriented approach (the hope is to identify correlations from the interplay of different data that were previously not perceived in this way or lacked convincing quantification), the advantages of a business model-oriented approach should not be underestimated. In the technology-oriented approach, the process begins with the collection and provision of data. Building on this, dependencies in the data are examined, i.e., correlations. The next steps involve examining how the findings can be used to positively change a business case. It is often assumed that all that is needed is a sufficient amount of data and analysis capacity (see the interview in Sect. 3.3.1). Mayer-Schönberger and Cukier (2013) begin their book with the example of data scientist Oren Etzioni, who in 2003 discovered that he had paid significantly more for a flight ticket than his fellow traveller, then used big data to calculate a prediction model based on this to determine when the cheapest ticket prices could be realized, founded a company with this idea (Farecast), which was later acquired by Microsoft (2008, for USD 110 million, later integrated into the Bing search engine). This anecdote also suggests the myth of "a lot helps a lot" or "big data can easily change the world."

However, there are doubts as to whether the search for correlations is sufficient, as Harford (2014) points out when he first describes how Google managed to make better and faster predictions about the spread of influenza at a later stage.

As the outbreak began, it failed completely with its own forecasts: "Google's engineers weren't trying to figure out what caused what. They were merely finding statistical patterns in the data. They cared about correlation rather than causation.

This is common in big data analysis. Figuring out what causes what is hard (impossible, some say). Figuring out what is correlated with what is much cheaper and easier." He concludes, "Big data do not solve the problem that has obsessed statisticians and scientists for centuries: the problem of insight, of inferring what is going on." However, recognizing correlations in data is a start. This step helps, for example, to formulate hypotheses and then test a cause-and-effect relationship.

Against this backdrop, it is advisable to use big data, but to devote sufficient energy to understanding causalities (see Sect. 3). In this context, the discussed business model-oriented approach, which reverses the sequence of steps in the process chain of the widespread narrative, is interesting (Krämer and Tachilzik 2016). It starts by considering which parameters are particularly sensitive for the business model. It then attempts to test its own hypotheses using existing or new data and existing or new methodologies (big data can be valuable here). In practice, it is not uncommon to come across data gaps. These can be partially closed by interlinking data. In some cases, it can be useful to carry out targeted studies to clarify certain unexplained dependencies and causalities. These can be A/B tests, but, e.g., also experimental online studies.

In contrast to a free, agile, and unstructured process (technology-oriented approach), the business model-oriented approach offers the opportunity to consider the two customer value perspectives (value-to-the-customer and value-of-the-customer) from start to finish.

The rise of the platform can be regarded as one key characteristic of the "digital revolution." Platforms generate benefits in different ways. One key value provided is that they help to match supply and demand with low search cost and at the same time act as an intermediary between the buyer and the seller (Xue et al. 2020[1]). Overall, digital platforms facilitate the flow of information and the execution of transactions. As Özdilek (2024)[2] describes, there has been an increasing focus on the practical applications of platforms within real estate during the last two decade, particularly in relation to PropTech (Property Technology). Platforms such as Realtor.com, Zillow.com, Airbnb.com, and Booking.com have begun determining the way properties are advertised, rented, and shared and are disruptive for traditional business models of real estate, rooted in physical attributes—including land, buildings, and infrastructure. Here, processes such as informatization, servicization, automatization, e-spatialization, dematerialization, and humanization generate value and ensure a personalized customer experience. In the USA, for example Zillow entered the market in the early 2000s and continuously covered every step of the real estate process. Today, there are three segments—Home Sales, Internet Media and Technology (IMT), and its very popular Zestimate, its ongoing/live database of home prices. Hoffman et al. (2024)[3] explain, "the brand, Zillow, is now synonymous with real estate."

Developments similar to those in the USA have also taken place in Europe. In 1998, ImmoScout24 (ImmobilienScout24 until mid-2020) was founded as the first nationwide online marketplace for real estate under the name EIB—Elektronische Immobilienbörse (EIB). The portal was initially aimed at business customers, and as of 2000 private individuals were also able to advertise on the platform.

Scout24 operates ImmoScout24, a digital advertising platform for the real estate market. According to its own information, ImmobilienScout24 is the leading platform for digital real estate advertisements in Germany. In addition to searches and offers, it also offers guides, tips, and analysis tools for tenants and landlords. The sale of AutoScout24, FinanceScout24 and Finanzcheck to Hellman & Friedman was completed in spring 2020. In 2023, Scout24 generated revenue of EUR 509 million. Earnings after taxes amounted to EUR 179 million. This translates into a return on sales of 35%. In November 2024, the market capitalization reached a value of more than EUR 6 billion. In comparison, the US online marketplace Zillow achieved sales of USD 1.945 billion in 2023, compared to earnings after taxes of USD -158 million (market capitalization in November 2024 approximately USD 16 billion).

The example of Scout24 shows how the aspects of "value-of-the-customer" and "value-to-the-customer" are connected. The successful increase in company value is related to the fact that the platform succeeds in implementing customer centricity based on various data sources in such a way that, for example, the individual participants experience a high degree of personalization. This perceived value then leads to increased company value via a suitable revenue model.

13.5 Interview Tobias Hartmann, Scout24

In a nutshell, what makes Scout24 SE and its Immoscout24 platform so special?

Tobias Hartmann: Scout24 is one of the leading digital companies operating digital real estate platforms in Germany and Austria. With our brand ImmoScout24, we offer an interconnected platform and services for residential and commercial real estate. We connect homeowners, real estate agents, tenants, and buyers, thus bringing together all participants engaging in property transactions, and we have been doing so for over 26 years, but we are more than a platform: We operate a unique three-sided marketplace, where we bring our three core customer groups—namely professionals, homeowners and seekers—together.

Our product portfolio and our value chain cover the entire real estate transaction: products for selling, buying, financing, letting, renting, assessing and managing real estate. We make it easier for people looking for a new home, we support homeowners to find suitable buyers or tenants and manage their properties, and we support agents in marketing properties efficiently or in acquiring new mandates. We have emerged from the classifieds industry, and we are now offering a unique product portfolio for professional customers, private consumers and a real focus on homeowners. Most of our B2C and B2B customers have a subscription product with Scout24 (Fig. 13.6).

What role does customer centricity play for Scout24? What needs do your customers have?

Tobias Hartmann: Customer centricity is crucial for our success. It revolves around deeply understanding and addressing the needs of our three core customer groups: professionals, seekers, and homeowners depending on the market situation.

Scout24's three-sided marketplace:
**Connecting professionals, seekers
and homeowners and creating an
even more efficient matchmaking**

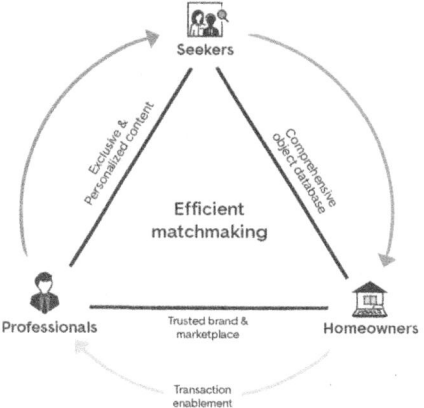

Scout24 is one of the leading digital companies in
Germany. With the digital marketplace ImmoScout24,
for residential and commercial real estate, we
successfully bring together homeowners, real estate
agents, tenants, and buyers – and we have been doing
so for 25 years. With more than 19 million users per
month on the website or in the app, ImmoScout24 is
the market leader for digital real estate listing and
search. To digitise the process of real estate
transactions, ImmoScout24 is continually developing
new products and building up a networked, data-rich
ecosystem for renting, buying, and commercial real
estate in Germany and Austria.

Fig. 13.6   Business Model Scout24

Let me briefly introduce the needs of our three customers—which can change
depending on the market situation—alongside our three-sided marketplace.

Professional customers, mainly agents, generate business by marketing and
eventually selling or renting out objects, acquire new mandates, build a brand and
efficiently steer their business. We address those needs by offering agent member-
ships that include efficient tools for agents to create visibility and market their
objects. We also provide them with high quality buyer or seller leads, valuations and
training. Seekers, mainly private consumers, are looking to rent or buy their dream
home. They are looking for a seamless search experience, maximum market transparency, a smooth buy or rent process and more convenience during their decision
making. We cater those needs with our object supply and a personalized search
experience. We support them in their search with our TenantPlus and BuyerPlus
subscription products. The last side of our three-sided marketplace are homeowners.
Depending on their situation homeowners want to get more information about their
property, sell their property for the highest price or find the right tenant. For that
Scout24 has established a dedicated homeowner hub. Homeowners can register
their object and then choose what they want to do: rent, sale, finance, manage or just
receive market insights. We provide them with the latest market data on demand,
possible price developments and, if needed, agents to support them.

With our three-sided marketplace we cover all market participants. With our
focus on interconnectivity, we can facilitate our customers' needs, as it essentially

means connecting our three core customer groups with each other to create an even more efficient matchmaking. For example: If a homeowner registers their object on our PropertyHub and chooses to rent it, we can then match seekers based on their search profile with the listed object of the homeowner. This creates value for both parties: the homeowner is supported with his property, and we receive more insights on object data and the intent of the homeowner.

To conclude, customer centricity at Scout24 means creating value for all customer groups by providing tailored support, leveraging data and technology, and fostering long-term relationships. This approach ensures that professionals, seekers, and homeowners can navigate the complex real estate market more effectively. Our entire ecosystem and our strategy with a focus on interconnectivity are built around our three customer groups.

Is customer centricity possible without big data and AI? How do you get insights into their needs?

Tobias Hartmann: When it comes to AI and Big Data, both are essential to facilitate customer centricity. There are two levels how we use AI and Big Data at Scout24 in the process of collecting, storing, and analyzing. The first step is to identify the customer needs. At Scout24 we have three buckets of data. (1) Exclusive data coming from the supply side and the top of the funnel (seeker) side, which enables us to generate firsthand insights and intent. (2) Data with historical insights from operating the platform. (3) Third party licensed data which we use to enrich our own data assets and AI models. With the help of AI, we can analyze and combine this data, and with AI based research we are able to generate a deep understanding on how our customers function, what they do, what they need and what their intent is.

After identifying the customers' needs, the second level is delivering value to our customers with new product features based on AI. We look at our existing products and, based on the insights we retrieved from step one, add AI features to our products that cater to the needs of our customers. For example, we use AI to provide a better lead qualification to agents, we implemented an AI search on our website for seekers and we also offer an ESG data prediction model. One concrete example for our seekers: If a seeker is looking to rent an apartment, they can save their personal search profile with ImmoScout24. We then use our data pool in combination with machine learning to make personalized suggestions for homes or apartments to users based on their search history and profile. They get tailored suggestions, and we increase their chances of finding their dream home.

To sum it up, by using AI and adding AI capabilities to our platform, the outcomes for our customers and stakeholders are: more personalized content and a truly personalized user experience and product features as well as improved matchmaking through interconnected products. Additionally, we provide market insights, data analytics and create market transparency in an increasingly complex market.

Can you be more specific, how you create customer value and why it is important to focus on your customers?

Tobias Hartmann: By providing our customer groups alongside the object life cycle with most relevant data and products, we create a deep engagement and a better and faster matchmaking. To simplify: we turn experience and engagement into value and subscription products. This is quite unique within the industry.

Let me give you one concrete example: Our goal remains unchanged to be the preferred partner for our professional customers by helping them to drive their business. To do so, we offer great value: With our platform we can not only provide the biggest reach, but as well the highest quality of buyers. We offer them tools to stand out and reach maximum visibility for buyers, and we offer our CRM systems and standardized tools and processes to act more efficiently in a more complex environment. Additionally, we can support our professional customers not only with data for valuations, but as well with training and toolsets to be capable of consulting buyers and sellers as well as tenants and landlords in the best possible way. For this we created a membership model which is specifically tailored to those needs.

For seekers, we focus on innovating the search experience, making it easier to find properties that match their needs. With our TenantPlus and BuyerPlus subscriptions, we offer additional features and support during the search phase. With LivingPlus we will extend the value proposition of our Plus products beyond the search process and move into a continuous relationship with the seeker. Due to the shortage of supply, finding a rental apartment is a massive hustle in Germany. Over time we have continuously enhanced pricing and the paywall logic which is a significant trigger to purchase our Plus products as certain listings are only visible to TenantPlus subscribers. To give an example: A homeowner decides to sell or rent out his property via the PropertyHub. The seeker found this new home with BuyerPlus or TenantPlus subscription and will then maintain a relationship with Scout24 with LivingPlus to enjoy further benefits as a tenant after moving into the new apartment.

For the homeowner, we see them as the key decision maker for what happens to a property. They decide, if and when they want to sell or rent out their property and therefore decide, when an object comes on the market. The customer value here is great, as we need the homeowner to further cater to the need for new objects for our professional customers and seekers. Our goal is helping homeowners to manage their assets digitally as best as possible through our PropertyHub—by providing market insights, personalized content, support, and advice for decision-making around their real estate. The PropertyHub is therefore a key element for our customer lifecycle management.

To sum this up: by focusing on our customers, understanding their needs and offering them value-add products to accomplish their goals, we can drive loyalty and develop a true customer relationship. This eventually leads to a growing customer base and increasing customer engagement.

Interview partner:

Tobias Hartmann has been Chief Executive Officer (CEO) of Scout24 SE since November 2018. He has more than two decades of international management experience in launching, developing, and growing consumer product and platform solutions businesses. He has worked for both privately held and publicly listed companies in Europe and the USA. Hartmann previously worked among others for eBay Inc., Hellofresh SE, Loyalty Partner, and Roland Berger Strategy Consultants.

13.6 Customer Value-Centered Management: A Holistic Approach

A company's customer-centric focus is not a product of chance. Even if the facets of personalization and automation in customer management, consistency in customer contact and an understanding of the "right" use of big data discussed in this chapter have been given particular attention, it should be emphasized that a change from product to customer orientation is primarily a matter for company management. It is therefore also clear that customer value centricity must be manifested in correspondingly clearly defined goals. These should include both "sides of the same coin," i.e., the value from the customer's perspective (customer satisfaction score, churn rate, customer effort score, recommendation rate) and the value from the company's perspective (change in customer contribution margins, cost development per customer, proportion of customers with a negative contribution margin, etc.).

The demand for customer value centricity forces a change in corporate culture. This includes values such as trust, listening, a sense of responsibility, cooperation, respect, and openness (feedback) among all employees. Leaders have a strong role model function here. For example, when Jeff Bezos characterized his company Amazon as the most customer-centric company, it was clear to him that this had to be lived by him and his management team. Various guidelines were set for this. The question is how to communicate internally and externally how extremely customer-centric a company is and how this can be linked to the management team. The requirement that one chair remains unoccupied at Amazon management meetings and is reserved for "the customer" is almost legendary (Kreuter 2015). This is intended to remind those present of key issues:

- "How does the topic under discussion present itself from the customer's perspective?"
- "What would the customers say—have we put ourselves sufficiently in the customer's shoes and involved them enough?"
- "Have we asked customers about this or what feedback have they given?"

Jeff Bezos' communication with employees when there were customer problems was no less mythologized (Bort 2018). If an employee receives a message from the boss that contains nothing but a question mark, it is a matter of the utmost urgency—usually in connection with a direct customer complaint. For Bezos, his email address jeff@amazon.com is a way to stay in touch with customers. At the same time, a myth was born. The head of the internet giant could be reached by any of his customers, or at least that is the narrative.

References

Adams T (2017) Surge Pricing comes to the supermarket. Abruf am 4. Juni 2017. https://www.theguardian.com/technology/2017/jun/04/surge-pricing-comes-to-the-supermarket-dynamicpersonal-data

Adolphs K (2020) Erfolgreiches individuelles Pricing – Kunden verstehen und die richtige Strategie entwickeln. https://www.marktforschung.de/dossiers/themendossiers/pricing-undpreisforschung/dossier/erfolgreiches-individuelles-pricing-kunden-verstehen-und-die-richtigestrategie-entwickeln/. Accessed 10 Nov 2020

Bendle N, Bagga C (2016) The metrics that marketers muddle. MIT Sloan Manag Rev 57:73–82

Bernasek A, Mongan D (2015) All you can pay: how companies use our data empty our wallets. Bold Type Books, New York

Bofinger P, Dullien S, Felbermayr G, Fuest C, Hüther M, Südekum J, di Mauro BW (2020) Wirtschaftliche Implikationen der Corona-Krise und wirtschaftspolitische Maßnahmen. Wirtschaftsdienst 100(4):259–265

Bongaerts R, Krämer A (2014) Value-to-Value-Segmentierung im Vertrieb. Mark Rev St Gallen 32(4):12–20

Bort J (2018) Jeff Bezos erklärt, warum er E-Mails mit nur einem Zeichen verschickt, das Managern das Fürchten lehrt. Bus Insid 30(4):2018. https://www.businessinsider.de/karriere/arbeitsleben/bezos-erklaert-gefuerchtete-e-mails-mit-nur-einem-zeichen-2018-4/

Burgartz T, Krämer A (2016) Measures to understand and control customer relationship and loyalty. In: Mack et al (eds) Managing in a VUCA World. Springer, New York, pp 99–114

Cross RG, Higbie JA, Cross ZN (2011) Milestones in the application of analytical pricing and revenue management. J Reve Pric Manag 10(1):8–18

Gupta S, Lehmann D, Stuart J (2004) Valuing customers. J Mark Res 41(1):7–18

Harford T (2014) Big data: a big mistake? Significance 11(5):14–19

Hoffman DL, Gilliard DJ, Baalbaki-Yassine S (2024) Zillow Group, Inc.: Changing the Way Americans Buy Homes. J Mark Devel Competit 18(3):1–12

Hüfner D (2021) Bahn erstattet Tickets jetzt online: Droht Verspätungs-Startups das Ende? Gruenderszene.de v. 01 Jun 2021. https://www.businessinsider.de/gruenderszene/automotive-mobility/deutsche-bahn-online-erstattung-startups/. Accessed 2 June 2021

Hyken S (2018) Businesses lose $75 billion due To poor customer service. Forbes, v. 17.5.2018. https://www.forbes.com/sites/shephyken/2018/05/17/businesses-lose-75-billion-due-to-poorcustomer-service/?sh=896be3616f92. Accessed 28 May 2021

ibi research/trinnovative (2020) Schlussbericht – Empirie zu personalisierten Preisen im E-Commerce. Regensburg

Kalka R, Krämer A (2018) Kein Anschluss unter dieser Nummer? MARKENARTIKEL 79(1–2):53–55

KfW (2020) KfW-Mittelstandspanel 2020: Unternehmen erwarten durch Corona-Krise historisch schlechte Geschäftsentwicklung. https://www.kfw.de/KfW-Konzern/Newsroom/Aktuelles/Pressemitteilungen-Details_613056.html. Accessed 31 Aug 2021

Krämer A (2018a) Dynamic personalized pricing – The next generation of pricing?! Vortrag bei der GOR-Arbeitsgruppe Pricing und Revenue Management am 19. Jan. 2018 (in Hannover)

Krämer A (2018b) Price Wars: how to turn it to your advantage, International Pricing Forum 2018, Paris, June 18th

Krämer A, Bongaerts R (2017) Wie Digitalisierung die Wettbewerbsposition der Bahn verändert. Internationales Verkehrswesen 69(2):26–30

Krämer A, Burgartz T (2016) Controlling von innovativen Preismodellen Controlling 28(6):329–337

Krämer A, Kalka R (2017) How digital disruption changes pricing strategies and price model. In: Khare A, Schatz R, Stewart B (eds) Phantom ex machina: digital disruption's role in business model transformation. Springer, Wiesbaden

Krämer A, Tachilzik T (2016) Die Zukunft von Big Data im Vertrieb. Sales Management Review 25(2):64–71

Krämer A, Mauer R (2023) Datenschutz für Entscheider in Marketing und Vertrieb. Springer Books, Wiesbaden

Krämer A, Jung M, Burgartz T (2016a) A small step from price competition to price war: understanding causes. Effects and possible countermeasures. Int Bus Res 9(3):1–13

Krämer A, Kalka R, Ziehe N (2016b) Personalisiertes und dynamisches Pricing aus Einzelhandels- und Verbrauchersicht. Mark Rev St Gallen 33(6):28–37

Krämer A, Tachilzik T, Bongaerts R (2016c) Automatisierung im Kundenbeziehungsmanagement: Chance oder Risiko für Unternehmen? Mark Rev St Gallen 33(4):10–17

Krämer A, Tachilzik T, Bongaerts R (2016d) Technology and disruption: how the new customer relationship influences the corporate strategy. In: Khare A, Schatz R, Stewart B (eds) Phantom ex machina: digital disruption's role in business model transformation. Springer, Cham, pp 53–70

Krämer A, Friesen M, Shelton T (2018) Are airline passengers ready for personalized dynamic pricing? A study of German consumers. J Rev Pric Manag 17(2):115–120

Krämer A, Bongaerts R, Reinhold T (2021) Kundenwert – die zwei Seiten einer Medaille: Valueto-Value-Segmentierung für die traffiQ Frankfurt. IVW 73(3):80–83

Kreuter D (2015) Jeff Bezos und der leere Stuhl oder warum Ihr Kunde kaufen sollte. Cash. Online v. 23.07.2015. https://www.cash-online.de/berater/2015/jeff-bezos/264033. Accessed 11 June 2025

Krugman P (2000) What Price Fairness? N.Y. TIMES, Oct. 4, 2000, A35

Lepthien A, Papies D, Clement M, Melnyk V (2017) The ugly side of customer management – consumer reactions to firm-initiated contract terminations. Int J Res Mark 34(4):829–850

Lies J (2021) Krisenmarketing: Gezielt handeln in der Corona-Krise und bei anderen unerwarteten Ereignissen. Schäffer-Poeschel, Stuttgart

Macmanus R (2011) Social magazines: What's their business model? http://readwrite.com/2011/01/18/social_magazines_business_model. Accessed 12 Apr 2020

Malthouse EC (2016) Customer relationship management strategy: more important now than ever before. The new advertising: branding, content, and consumer relationships in the data-driven social media Era. Praeger, Westport, Connecticut, pp 111–134

Manning H, Bodine K (2012) Outside in: the power of putting customers at the center of your business. Houghton Mifflin Harcourt, Boston

Markey R, Reichheld F, Dullweber A (2009) Closing the customer feedback loop. Harv Bus Rev 87(12):43–47

Mayer-Schönberger V, Cukier K (2013) Big data: a revolution that will transform how we live, work, and think. Houghton Mifflin Harcourt, Boston

Mittal V, Sarkees M, Murshed F (2008) The right way to manage unprofitable customers. Harv Bus Rev 86(4):94–103

NN (2021) Entschädigung per Online-Formular. Tagesschau Online v. 24.5.2021. https://www.tagesschau.de/wirtschaft/verbraucher/bahn-entschaedigung-online-antrag-101.html. Accessed 28 May 2021

Ovum (2016) Get it right: deliver the omni-channel support customers want. https://az766929.vo.msecnd.net/document-library/boldchat/pdf/en/boldchat-whitepaper-ovum-logmein.pdf. Accessed 28 May 2021

Özdilek Ü (2024) From bricks to bytes: transforming real estate into the core platform of the digital ecosystem. Platforms 2(4):165–179

Priester A, Robbert T, Roth S (2020) A special price just for you: effects of personalized dynamic pricing on consumer fairness perceptions. J Reve Prici Manag 19:99–112

Puscher F (2016) Was falsches Pricing kostet. Absatzwirtschaft 59(4):32–36

Reichheld F (2003) The one number you need to grow. Harv Bus Rev 12:2–10

Reinartz W, Haucap J, Wiegand N, Hunold M (2017) Preisdifferenzierung und -dispersion im Handel. Ausgewählte Schriften der IFH-Förderer

Schlenk T (2018) Einem N26-Kunden werden 80.000 Euro gestohlen — und die Bank ist überfordert. https://www.businessinsider.de/wirtschaft/einem-n26-kunden-werden-80000-eurogestohlen-und-die-bank-ist-ueberfordert-2019-3/. Accessed 6 June 2021

Shin J, Sudhir K, Yoon DH (2012) When to "fire" customers: customer cost-based pricing. Manag Sci 58(5):932–947

Sommerhäuser L (2018) Kundenservice: Echte Gespräche gewünscht. IT-Zoom 27.06.2018. https://www.it-zoom.de/it-mittelstand/e/kundenservice-echte-gespraeche-gewuenscht-20050/. Accessed 11 June 2025

Tachilzik T (2013) Social CRM im Unternehmensbetrieb, Vortrag Konferenz DMEXCO, Köln, 18. September 2013

Verhoef PC, Langerak F (2002) Eleven misconceptions about customer relationship management. Bus Strateg Rev 13(4):70–76

Xue C, Tian W, Zhao X (2020) The literature review of platform economy. Sci Program 2020(1):8877128

Zeithaml VA, Rust RT, Lemon KN (2001) The customer pyramid: creating and serving profitable customers. Calif Manag Rev 43(4):118–142

Learning from the Most Successful Companies: What Works and What Doesn't

14

14.1 Introduction: The Value of Benchmarking

"You can't just impose a best practice. It has to be adapted to your own company's style."—Arun Maua

If a company pursues the goal of (further) developing itself noticeably and quickly in the direction of "customer value centricity," the question arises as to which companies are following "best practices."

And which have implemented processes that seem transferable to one's own company? This question leads to the instrument of benchmarking, i.e., the identification of the highest standards of excellence for products, services, or processes and the subsequent implementation of the necessary improvements to achieve these standards. Pragmatically, the question can be asked "Why reinvent the wheel?" The benchmarking method is not so much a competitive analysis or a numbers game, nor is it to be equated with spying or copying. This is what the preceding quote from Maua means with "It has to be adapted…." Rather, it refers to a process that is intended to prepare the ground for creative breakthroughs (Pryor 1989). In the list of the most important tools in management examined and evaluated by the management consultancy Bain & Company, benchmarking regularly achieves top rankings (Rigby and Bilodeau 2018). When used correctly, benchmarking can lead to rapid suggestions for improvement.

However, some limitations must be taken into account:

- Benchmarking only provides limited information about what customers actually want. If the product or service is outdated, even the best production processes will not be able to make it competitive. In Porter's sense, "copying is not a strategy": if benchmarking is seen as simply copying "best-in-class" services, this may lead to a "Dead end," e.g., because the requirements of your own customers and the specific positioning of your own company are not given sufficient consideration.

- The involvement of employees in the process is urgently required. Benchmarking should firstly be seen as a continuous process, which secondly takes place with the involvement of employees. Only the involvement of employees can ensure that a willingness for change and support for change management can be achieved.
- A prerequisite for success is sufficient openness and willingness to change. If some companies reject benchmarking because it is assumed that their weaknesses would be exposed, the methodology is misplaced here.

In addition, a distinction must be made as to what the benchmarking specifically refers to. According to Bhutta and Huq (1999), a distinction must be made:

- Performance benchmarking, where the focus is on performance parameters ("How well does our company perform in terms of …?").
- Process benchmarking, in which methods and processes are examined (e.g., "What steps does the comparison company see in complaint management and how can the complaint handling processes of its own company be improved on this basis?").
- Strategic benchmarking, in which special attention is paid to the strategic orientation of comparable companies and the positioning of one's own company in relation to them.
- Internal benchmarking, in which a comparison is made between different departments or areas of the company.
- Competitive benchmarking, which refers to the analysis of the strongest competition: Once the best-in-class provider has been identified (Töpfer and Mann 2013), the next step is to understand what this company does better than the others.
- Functional benchmarking, in which functions and processes are only considered in the company's own industry, as opposed to.
- Generic benchmarking, where this restriction does not apply (completely foreign industries are also included).

This list can also be extended to include the aspects of value benchmarking or customer relationship benchmarking in the context of these explanations. The focus here could be on facets such as strong customer loyalty, intensive recommendation, or customer understanding. Finally, Zhang et al. (2016) argue that customers are the most important intangible assets of a company. It is therefore necessary for companies to have the ability to anticipate customer value. In this context, the researchers examine the relationship between customer value anticipation, product innovation, and value generation from the customer's perspective. Apple is highlighted as a particularly striking example. The conclusion is that:

> "This study also provides guidelines for practitioners in terms of how to increase customer lifetime value. First, the results show that firms should not only be better than their competitors at innovating and creating new products, but also be good at anticipating customers' value. Customer value anticipation capabilities can be an important resource for firms to enhance their competitive advantages."

Apple is regarded as a company that is able to anticipate customer benefits to a particularly high degree and is considered to have the ability to monetize these customer benefits. The example of Apple will therefore be examined in more detail as a benchmark for the topic of "value capturing." In addition to Fresenius and Hewlett Packard, Habel et al. (2020) also name Amazon as a company that is particularly customer-oriented. Due to its own claim to be the most customer-centric company in the world (Simons 2014), Amazon seems predestined as a benchmark for the topic of "value delivering." Almquist et al. (2016) also name Apple and Amazon as top representatives that deliver customer benefits in a variety of individual facets. In their empirical study, they identify around 30 different customer benefits (divided into 4 areas: Social Impact, Life-Changing, Emotional and Functional). Amazon achieves high ratings in eight functional benefit dimensions.

14.2   Amazon as a Benchmark for Value Delivery

Amazon is a prime example of a business strategy that is both based on and benefits from the internet. It conducts its business with its partners directly and exclusively via the Internet (for the sake of simplicity, the activities of recent years in offline retailing are excluded here). As Mahadevan (2000) pointed out, Amazon's business model requires "a comprehensive adaptation of the information system and business processes to meet customer requirements (and service experiences) online."

Amazon offers a wide range of services, which are only briefly listed here because they are also direct sources of revenue (the percentages relate to the contribution of the service to the company's total revenue in the 2019/2020 financial year):

- Own sales: Amazon generated revenue of around USD 163 billion (approx. 51%) via online stores in the 2019/2020 financial year. In addition to the sale of physical products, Amazon established a new market for e-books by introducing Kindle to the market. Amazon has launched its own product range with phones, tablets, TVs and mobile OS.
- Amazon marketplace: revenue from commissions and other fees from sellers. Online stores accounted for revenues of around USD 63 billion (approx. 20%) in 2019/2020.
- Amazon Music and Videos: The business model includes sales and a streaming service for music and videos (including star websites such as IMDB and twitch.tv).
- Amazon Gaming: The Amazon Digital Game Store sells games from third-party providers and is active in the market with its subsidiary Amazon Game Studios.

- Amazon Web Services: The company is one of the world's leading IT infrastructure providers and generated revenues of around USD 40 billion (approx. 12%) in 2019/20. Amazon Mechanical Turk is part of this division.
- Amazon Prime: The company offers a premium membership for all its services through Amazon Prime.
- Amazon patents: Amazon holds more than 1000 patents, many of which are licensed from other companies.
- Amazon Fresh: This is Amazon's entry into the grocery market. These are also delivered. Amazon has owned the Whole Food Market chain in the USA since 2017 and is opening its own grocery stores without cash registers. In 2019/20, stationary stores accounted for revenues of around USD 17 billion (approx. 5%).
- Amazon Merch: Amazon is expanding into the print on demand (POD) market for T-shirts.
- Advertising revenue: In recent years, Amazon has also increasingly generated revenue from advertising on the platform. The Other segment, which includes advertising revenue and credit cards, for example, generated revenue of around USD 17 billion in 2019/2020 (approx. 5%). In the first quarter of 2021, revenue was roughly 50% higher than in QI 2020, with profit tripling. The share determined by advertising is becoming increasingly large and is already likely to exceed the profit share of the cloud business (Herrmann 2021).

This brief overview alone makes it clear that Amazon is much more than just a large online retailer. Its activities serve to create and further develop an ecosystem with the customer (or customer account) at its center. Transactions are processed via a central account, so that the company has a wealth of information at its disposal. As a platform provider that offers the placement of personalized advertising, Amazon will be a strong and potent competitor to both Google and Facebook in the foreseeable future (Krämer 2018). Customer data plays an important role in this.

14.2.1 Special Understanding for the Customer: Customer First

A fundamental feature that is deeply rooted in Amazon's business model is the idea that the customer always comes first. Jeff Bezos established this principle as a basic philosophy very early on. Further special features of the design of the Amazon shopping portal can be explained based on this idea. To this end, Klaus (2013) proposed a model that relates to psychological factors, functionalities and engagement. All processes are designed to give the customer confidence that they have made a good decision when purchasing on the platform. The confidence of being offered a good price is only one element; lean processes and clarity are others. To make the decision easier for the buyer, Amazon pioneered big data-based product recommendations at an early stage in its development. Anshari et al. (2019) explain "Some of the examples for customers' profiling of services; Amazon.com developed a system of product recommendation based on their analysis on customers' previous purchases data." While many internet users now perceive product recommendations as standard, Amazon is considered to have established this service (it is referred to as "item-based collaborative filtering"). This has been offered since 1998 and enables a personalized presentation of offers (Smith and Linden 2017).

Based on the argumentation of Venkatesan (2017), the model can be expanded to include the engagement factor (see Fig. 14.1). The development of Amazon Dash, the Amazon Associates affiliate program (participants are given the opportunity to advertise products and earn up to 10% in referral fees) and the crowdsourcing marketplace called Amazon Mechanical Turk (aim: to improve customer feedback and also learn from customers' knowledge about products, introduced in 2005) are cited as starting points for generating customer engagement.

14.2.2 Special Understanding of Competition: Marketplace and Coopetition

Today's eCommerce giant started out as an online bookseller and has evolved over the years into a consumer shopping portal by diversifying its product range. The next important step for Amazon was to expand its business model with the introduction of Amazon Marketplace in November 2000, a marketplace for third-party sellers. The roll-out took place in stages, initially on Amazon.com's international websites, then in the UK and Germany in 2002 and in France, Canada and Japan in 2003. This change in the business model is significant in that it reflects the contribution of coopetition, i.e., collaboration with competitors, to increasing value creation and as a driver of growth (Ritala et al. 2014). Amazon thus also demonstrates a particular ability to radically question and further develop its own business models in the platform economy.

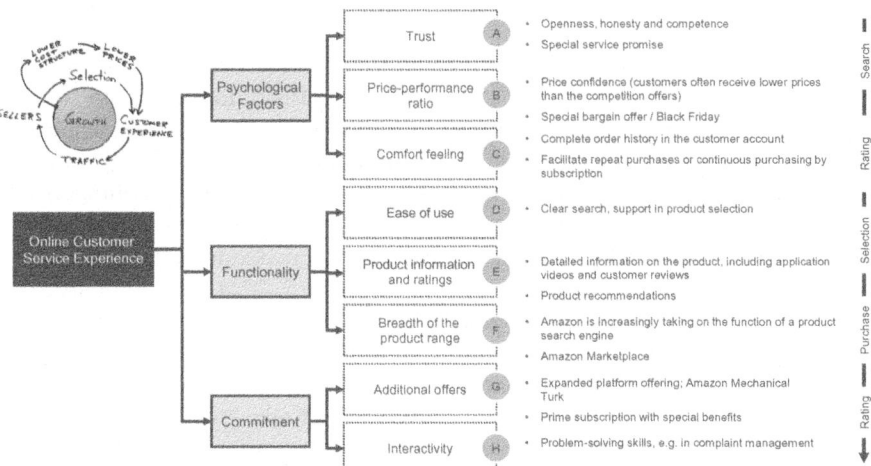

Fig. 14.1 Amazon: Conceptual model for the Online Customer Service Experience (OCSE)

Amazon Marketplace was the first implementation of Amazon's coopetition-based business model (others were to follow later, as illustrated by the creation of Amazon Web Services). Basically, it allows sellers to use the e-commerce services and tools to present their products alongside Amazon on the same product detail page on the website, pursuing what Jeff Bezos called a "single-store strategy." There is a clear customer benefit associated with this, and that is to provide the potential buyer with a single point of contact and options ranging from buying a new product from Amazon, to buying a used product from Amazon, to buying a new or used product from another seller via the Amazon marketplace (i.e., a competitor of Amazon). This represented a major shift in the business model because it triggered a transformation from a retailer to a true marketplace (Chua 2011). According to the saying "It's good to have choices," Amazon offers added value to the customer and accepts that the customer buys a competitor's product instead of directly from Amazon.

14.2.3 Special Understanding of Customer Loyalty: Amazon Prime

As Ashley et al. (2016) explain, some service and retail companies have switched from free to fee-based loyalty programs in order to cover program costs. Amazon Prime is a particularly prominent example of this. In its "home country," the USA, the number of members has grown from ten million (2012) to 90 million (2018). Prime experienced another growth spurt during the coronavirus pandemic. When publishing the last Letter to the Shareholders in his role as CEO (Apr. 2020), Jeff Bezos put the number of Prime customers worldwide at around 200 million (Palmer 2021).

Amazon Prime is a fee-based loyalty program that offers free or reduced shipping costs for selected items and special offers for members (free premium shipping, reduced fees for express shipping, €5 per item). Other benefits include very different facets, such as free use of the Kindle lending library for e-books, unlimited storage space for digital photos (in Amazon Cloud Drive), free access to Amazon Prime Instant Video and premium access to Amazon BuyVIP (customers and their family members receive access to special offers nine hours before the start of the sale). Since 2019, the Prime subscription has also included a free credit card. The annual subscription to Amazon Prime in Germany was offered at a price of €69 in 2022. From September 15, 2022, the price was increased to €89.90, which corresponds to an increase of around 30%. On February 5, 2024, Amazon introduced advertising in Prime Video. To continue streaming content ad-free, users can book an additional option for €2.99 per month. For customers, this means either a significant deterioration in perceived performance (advertisingwhen streaming) or a price increase of $12 \times €2.99 = €35.88$ (+30%; Krämer and Kalka 2025).

Not all services have the same relevance from the customer's perspective. As Fig. 14.2 shows, Prime members are mainly familiar with the core features of the

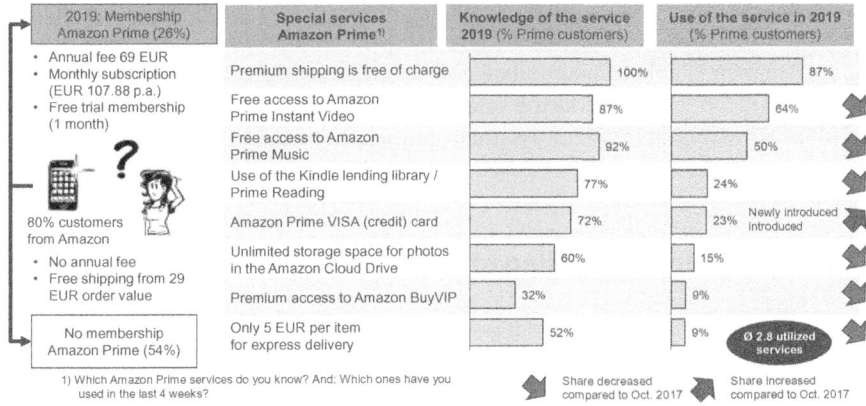

Fig. 14.2 Knowledge and use of Amazon Prime services by members (July 2019)

service bundle. Free premium shipping and video and music streaming are particularly relevant from a customer perspective (> 50% usage rate in the last 4 weeks).

In order to understand Amazon's rapid growth, the impact of Amazon Prime must be examined in more detail. The paid subscription acts as a driver for sales per customer. Jeff Bezos explains (McAlone 2016) "… they buy more on Amazon than non-Prime members, and one of the reasons they do that is once they pay their annual fee, they're looking around to see, 'How can I get more value out of the program?' And so they look across more categories—they store more."

Overall, the Prime service results in the classic ideal-typical effects of customer loyalty (Krämer 2018). The most important are:

- Shift in consumer decisions in favor of the platform.
- Recommendation effects.
- Increase in the number of transactions.
- Reduction in price sensitivity.

It remains questionable whether sustained high growth and high customer satisfaction and intention to recommend are possible. The OpinionTRAIN study (Krämer and Hercher 2021) comes to the conclusion that Amazon has achieved very high values in Germany in the past in terms of intention to recommend, reaching a Net Promoter Score of +24 and (see Chaps. 1 and 13). However, when looking at the NPS time series, a strongly negative trend for Amazon becomes apparent, both for customers with and without a Prime subscription. A deterioration was observed compared to previous ratings. While the customer segment Prime subscription still reached a level of just under +80 in 2017, the NPS was only +43 in 2021. However, it is not clear whether the values measured are more determined by the coronavirus crisis or rather reflect the consolidation of a negative NPS trend for Amazon. What is clear, however, is that it is becoming increasingly difficult for the internet giant to inspire existing customers. Over time, Amazon started to put more weight on the value-of-the-customer perspective. As Walke et al. (2025) point out: "Through a combination of targeted advertising, dynamic pricing algorithms, and data-driven insights, Amazon is able to manipulate consumer perceptions to its advantage. The perception of deep discounts during sales events is carefully curated, with the company often adjusting prices in ways that optimise both the perceived value to the customer and Amazon's profit margins.

14.2.4   Special Understanding of Pricing: Dynamic Pricing

Phan and Vogel (2010) already address the interactions between price differentiation and CRM and come to the conclusion that differentiated pricing can have a negative impact on the customer relationship and cite a frequently cited example: Based on cookies collected from customers' computers, Amazon offered particularly lower prices to new customers in 2000. When regular customers found out that they were paying more for the same items, an emotionally charged public discussion developed, which ended in an apology from the company and the payment of refunds. The damage to Amazon's image was not insignificant. Although this test of personalized or at least segment-based pricing failed, dynamic pricing is very important in the Amazon business model. Its successful use in eCommerce means that the implementation of dynamic pricing is currently also being discussed in bricks-and-mortar retail (Merkle and Krämer 2021).

This point reveals a clear risk for the customer relationship (Krämer and Kalka 2016). When asked about the approach of flexible pricing (this has long been common practice at Amazon), Amazon Prime customers are predominantly critical of dynamic pricing (Krämer and Hercher 2021): 39% do not find its use for household appliances, for example, to be useful. Across 20 different product categories, acceptance among Prime customers is relatively critical, similar to the overall value. This is remarkable in that Amazon is considered a pioneer of dynamic pricing. Product prices can change several times a day on the platform. This reveals a clear contradiction: on the one hand, the Prime subscriber customer segment is a key lever for further growth. On the other hand, there is a great risk of annoying these customers if regular customers are increasingly aware of price changes (around two thirds of Prime customers do this) and consider flexible pricing to be unfair.

The possibilities offered by Amazon already go beyond dynamic pricing. The next stage of development is described as Personalized Dynamic Pricing (Krämer 2025). As the example from the year 2000 mentioned above illustrates, Amazon has many years of experience in this area. Based on the collected customer information, Amazon is not only able to improve the customer experience, e.g., by presenting product reviews or displaying products that other customers have also purchased. In addition, the best possible conditions are created for 1:1 marketing, characterized by individualized products, services, communicative approach, and ultimately also by the price, which is adjusted in real time to changing market conditions. The interaction of AI and marketing automation enables Amazon not only to become "part of the household" using Alexa, but also to adapt offers to the needs of individual customers without delay. This also applies to the estimation of individual willing-ness to pay and its use for pricing. If an Amazon customer takes out a Prime sub-scription, these opportunities improve because the intensity of platform use increases (Krämer 2018).

14.2.5 Outlook: Adjustment of the Business Model

The description of the special features of the Amazon business model alone could fill entire books. Despite its size, Amazon has always seen itself as an agile com-pany that is prepared to invest heavily in innovation and take considerable risks. The low margins of the business have made the company extremely sensitive to costs, even more so than in traditional brick-and-mortar retail. In most cases, investments have not resulted in a direct leap in sales, but only over time. All the more reason to emphasize the effect of a long-term strategy. Dennis and Nonnenmann (2014) state "One of the key factors to Amazon's success is the implementation of their long-term strategy. The strategy includes low margins, high customer satisfaction, low prices, rapid shipment, and low profitability". It is worth noting that Amazon was not taken seriously by the financial world and investors for a long time. In particular, the company's low profitability was frequently criticized: "Amazon is a fantastic company with a lot of potential in the future, but one thing they could improve is their overall profitability by marginally increasing their prices." Just a few years later, the picture has changed. Amazon has enjoyed a long phase of rising profits since 2015.

The previous descriptions of Amazon, for example, refer to the interface between Amazon and the end customer (B2C). At the same time, Amazon also focuses on the lucrative segment of corporate customers. With Amazon Business, customers have access to more than 250 million products. Driven by the goal of constantly expand-ing its business areas and maintaining its massive growth, e-procurement must be a relevant business area for Amazon. The activities in this area in recent years are therefore only logical. Similar to the private customer business, this means that Amazon is moving to the interface between customers and suppliers and wants to own the B2B customer relationship in the future.

As in the private customer business, the aim here is to stand out positively from the competition. At the same time, it is becoming more difficult to identify real benchmarks, i.e., companies that master certain processes better than one's own company does. The following example from Skymetrix can only be compared with the online retailer Amazon to a limited extent. While Amazon defines the relevant market ever more broadly, Skymetrix occupies a relatively narrow market (airline procurement processes), but with no regional limits. This combination is possible given that many airlines have similar needs in terms of operational processes, which do not differ greatly in North America from Australia.

14.3   Interview Michael Scheidler, Skymetrix

Please describe the company Skymetrix: What makes Skymetrix so special as a company?

Michael Scheidler: Skymetrix is on a mission to transform fuel and cost management for airlines so they can maximize success. Success could mean increasing profitability, improving efficiency, staying competitive, or growing sustainably. We use our cloud-based, next-generation platform to do this, combined with our expertise in fuel and cost management best practice. Our company was formed in 2021 following the merger of two leaders in the aviation fuel and cost management space — Airpas and FuelPlus. Together, we have over 140 customers, 40+ years of experience in the field, and well-established strategic partnerships with industry bodies like IATA. Every year, we manage over 30% of commercial aviation fuel and more than $76bn of direct flight charges for airlines. Our headquarters and development center are in Europe, but we operate worldwide, with customers in the Middle East, Africa, the Americas, Asia, and Europe.

The special feature of our company is its uniqueness. We offer individual product categories that are unique in the market and often not interchangeable. This makes us special, as does our long-term customer relationship. We have some customers that we have been looking after for a very long time, and they appreciate our reliability. The decision for this type of software is not made every year. These are decisions that are made for the medium term.

To what extent is Skymetrix similar to or different from the competition in terms of market orientation, for example product portfolio and pricing? And who are your most important competitors?

Michael Scheidler: Our market orientation is based primarily on the needs of our customers. The customers in the airline industry seem similar, but on closer inspection they are not. We therefore have to meet the fragmented demands of the market. To achieve this, we do not focus on the competition, but on feedback from customer relationships. The better we understand the needs of the airlines, the better we are protected from the competition. The specific competitive situation is just as fragmented. Theoretically, customers always have the option of creating a cost management tool themselves; in many cases, there are also very specialized providers that cover part of Skymetrix's range of services, but hardly any providers with the same portfolio.

As we see ourselves as the market leader, we understand that it makes little sense to orient ourselves towards competitors. On the contrary: our focus is on setting industry standards.

What role does customer value play in Skymetrix's business model?

Michael Scheidler: Customer value has a dual meaning for our business. The first is the value we offer our customers. Purchasing processes in our business are designed for the medium term. It is not about a decision that is repeated every year. This is why price plays a role as a decision-making factor, but often more in the dimension of cost of total ownership, i.e., a consideration over a longer period of time. The price dimension is therefore a facet of the overall package that the customer purchases. The fact that our team has many years of expertise in the airline market often plays a role here.

The second meaning of customer value is the value that the customer has for Skymetrix over a longer relationship period. We work hard to ensure that we manage each individual customer relationship in such a way as to ensure high customer satisfaction and a high intention to recommend: we continuously measure the Net Promoter Score and see it as an important KPI, but each individual customer relationship should also be profitable. To this end, we look at customer profitability indicators and develop approaches to change them for the better.

This chapter deals with the question of what can be learned from the most successful companies in terms of both what to do and what not to do. Apple and Amazon were discussed in some depth. What can Skymetrix learn from these and similar organizations?

Michael Scheidler: It can always be useful to take a closer look at external benchmarks and consider which best practices can be applied to your own company. Apple is very good at monetizing the value it provides to customers. This is possible when the market includes a sufficiently large group of customers who are very design-oriented and willing to pay a high price. This can be a cornerstone of pricing. However, too little attention is often paid to costs in pricing because value-based pricing suggests that production costs are not really important. In fact, we can learn something from Amazon, or retail companies in general, in this regard. Companies that have had to work with low margins for a long time and still have to do so successfully with a strong awareness of costs. Transferring this cost perspective to a software area characterized by high fixed costs is challenging but makes sense.

Interview partner:

Dr. Michael Scheidler started his career at Lufthansa and has held senior roles at Roland Berger, Deutsche Bahn Thomas Cook, Rivus Fleet Solutions and EO Charging—one of Europe's fastest growing companies. He also has expertise in transformational change and data-driven analytics. Michael has been the CEO of Skymetrix since May 2022.

14.4 Apple as a Benchmark for Value Capturing

Apple's best-known products include the Macintosh computer, the iPod, the iPhone, and iTunes, an application for the company's content and applications. Apple succeeds in creating systemic value for customers through the interplay of different instances. Apple focuses on the "connectedness" factor through design and user-friendliness. At the same time, the closed Apple system (in the sense of being bound) offers efficient protection against competitors because it is so difficult to create similar or better offers. The downside is that this limits the accessible market. Mikkonen et al. (2009) see iTunes (App Store) as a content engine that enables Apple to create value. For example, when a customer buys a song from the iTunes Store and saves it to their computer's hard disk, they have several options for listening to it. The ease of use and familiar usability from device to device reinforces the customer's positive user experience.

In a nutshell, Apple's business model is designed to integrate consumers into its ecosystem and then keep them there. It is a mixture of a connected and tethered strategy. It gives Apple control over the entire value chain and thus the unique ability to maintain a low-cost sourcing strategy while maintaining high price points in the market and retaining consumers through high switching costs (Montgomerie and Roscoe 2013). This results in an unusual situation: Apple not only generates a high contribution margin per device sold in absolute terms, but also covers a large part of the value added of individual industries in relative terms. In 2010, it was estimated that Apple claimed 58% of the value of an iPhone for itself (Kraemer et al. 2011). According to Orr (2023) in 2022, Apple's operating profit share of the worldwide smartphone market reached a high of 85%.

14.4.1 Concentration on Lucrative Market Segments

Apple's positioning can be clearly outlined. The company only focuses on one market segment, that of high-end customers, in contrast to its competitor Samsung, which positions itself across a broad market coverage (Tien et al. 2019). In 2007, Steve Jobs announced the market launch of the iPhone:

> "One percent market share equals ten million units. This is a giant market. If you [sell] just 1% market share, you are going to sell ten million phones—this is exactly what we are going to try and do in 2008, our first full year in the market—grab 1% market share and go from there... We think we are going to have the best product in the world, and we are going to go for it, see if we can get 1% market share—ten million units in 2008."

At the market launch (June 30, 2007), the iPhone was offered in two versions, a 4 GB version at US$499 and an 8 GB version at US$599. The queues that became famous in subsequent years could already be observed in 2007. It is said that 270,000 devices were sold within the first 30 hours. In September 2007, however, the price of the iPhone was reduced by US$200 to US$399 which led to negative assessments in the financial markets, but also among Apple customers. In marketing science, this is seen as an example of a skimming price strategy. Following heavy criticism, Steve Job felt compelled to offer existing buyers a discount of US$100 (Chulkov and Nizovtsev 2014). This example illustrates the difficulty of finding the right price for a product that customers first have to get to know due to its novelty in order to recognize its value. Apple saw the price reduction as a necessary step to reach a sufficiently large customer base. As a rule, such difficulties no longer arose with subsequent product generations. On the contrary: the positioning of new product types via a very high price, which is then successively reduced over time, became the industry standard.

Apple may not dominate the market, but it is extremely profitable: with a market share of around 15%, the company generates around 80% of global profits from

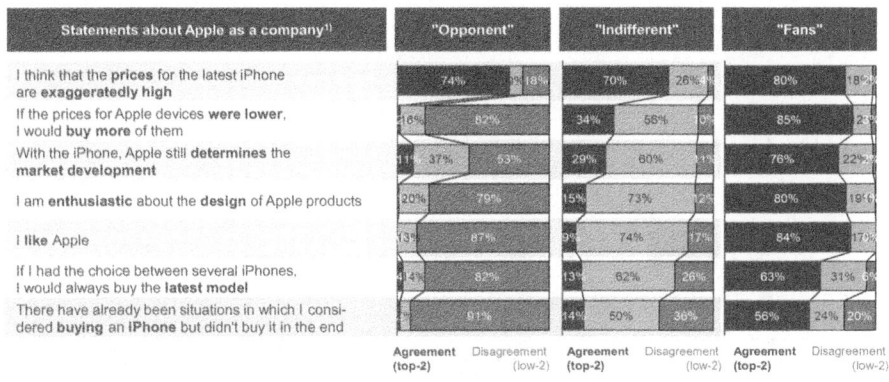

Fig. 14.3   Results of a cluster analysis of consumers based on statements about Apple (2017)

smartphones. At the same time, the iPhone is the most important profit driver for the Group. According to the results of the Pricing Lab 2017 study (Krämer and Hercher 2018), Apple devices are used in a quarter of German households. The proportion of Apple customers in the <30 age group is significantly higher at 47%, but lower among senior citizens. When it comes to statements about Apple as a company, criticism of the pricing ("excessively high prices") stands out. Around 70% of respondents agree with the statement "I think the prices for the latest iPhone are too high" (8% disagree). Based on a cluster analysis, three segments can be identified. Around 29% of respondents can be assigned to the segment of "Apple fans." Although they are critical of the pricing, they are enthusiastic about the design of the products and like Apple (see Fig. 14.3).

14.4.2   Skimming Off the Willingness to Pay

Irrespective of the consumer segment ("opponents," "indifferents," or "fans" of Apple), excessively high prices for the latest iPhone are criticized. This reflects the fact that Apple's primary objective is to exploit the resulting customer benefits and the associated willingness to pay above-average prices to stay in the Apple ecosystem. As part of the skimming strategy, customers who see a high value in owning an iPhone of the latest generation pay a very high price. However, customers who value owning an iPhone, but not necessarily the latest generation, are also willing to pay a price premium.

In order to analyze this further, an analysis of the willingness to pay of potential smartphone buyers was carried out based on a survey from 2017. The iPhone 6 s (32 GB) was deliberately chosen rather than a current product to measure consumers' willingness to pay. This model was presented to the public back in Sep. 2015 (launch price US$649 in the USA for the 16 GB device). It was sold in Germany at

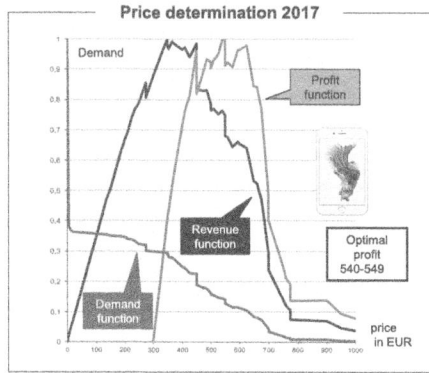
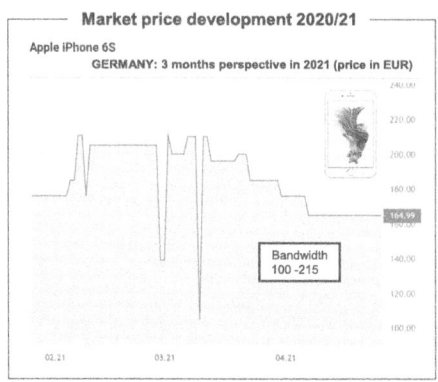

Fig. 14.4 iPhone 6s: Price optimization in 2017 and price level in 2020/21 (Germany)

the time of the study (i.e., around 2 years later) at electronics retailers and directly from Apple at a price of €519 (Oct. 2017). The willingness to pay was measured in the online survey based on the PSM (Price Sensitivity Measurement) Plus approach developed by exeo (see Sect. 14.5). This showed that more than 60% of the test subjects are not prepared to buy an iPhone 6 s (see Fig. 14.4, left-hand side). Around 15% are willing to pay € 519 or more (i.e., at or above the actual price). The willingness to pay varies greatly between the market segments. While "Apple opponents" are willing to pay an average of €48, the "Apple fans" segment reaches a value of just under €300. This makes it clear that the relevant sales market for the iPhone is clearly limited. The maximum profitable price of the iPhone 6 s is around €525 to €540, which is on a par with the current market price. With this pricing, Apple skims off the market's willingness to pay relatively well (Krämer 2017).

As can be seen (Fig. 14.4, right-hand side), the market price for the iPhone 6 s in Apr. 2021 is only around €160. Apple itself no longer offers the device for sale. In Apr. 2021, the range of sales prices at Apple starts at 579 (iPhone X) and extends to the iPhone 12 Pro from €1149. Apple found out that the issue of price can also be overstretched when it launched the iPhone X in 2017, when exceeding the €1000 price mark was the subject of particularly fierce negative discussion on social media (Frohmann 2018, p. 157). Nevertheless, the impression is growing that even in the case of obvious overpricing, the damage to Apple remains limited. In the "worst case scenario," this leads to a downward price adjustment, whereby the high price anchor ("originally more than €1000 expensive") remains in the minds of consumers.

14.5 Profitability as the Basis for Company Valuation

14.5.1 Amazon: Cash Flow as the Basis for Innovation and Innovation as the Basis for Growth

When publishing the last Letter to the Shareholders in his role as CEO, Jeff Bezos emphasized the importance of Prime customers for the further growth of the Group

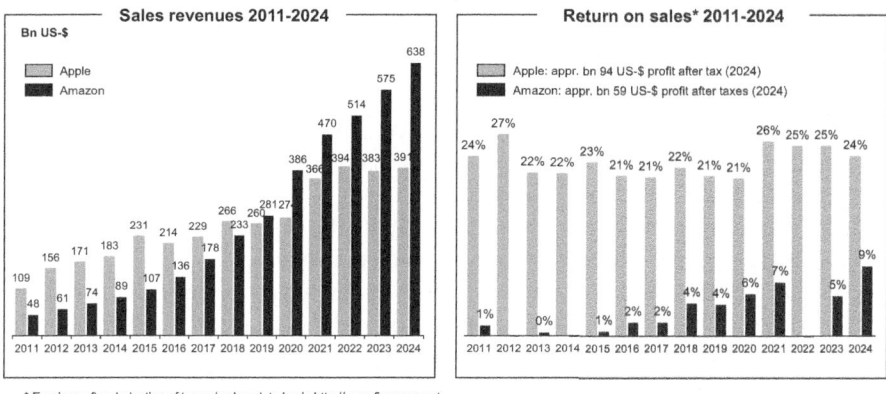

* Earnings after deduction of taxes / sales; data basis http://www.finanzen.net.

Fig. 14.5 Revenues and return on sales: Apple vs. Amazon (2011–2020)

(Palmer 2021), based on the high benefits for customers. According to Amazon's estimates, the time saved on trips to brick-and-mortar retailers alone is worth a total of USD 126 billion to customers (200 million customers, 75 hours saved per year, valued at USD 10 per hour).

The development of the share price reflects the hope of rising profits: while the price was around € 130 per share in April 2011, Amazon shares reached around € 2800 (US$3300) 10 years later. This represents a market capitalization of around € 1.4 trillion. Shareholders participate in the company's success through an extremely high share price, not through a profit distribution (there is no distribution). Amazon always finances its growth from existing cash flow. In the years 2011–2020, Amazon only achieved a return on sales of >2% in 3 separate years (Fig. 14.5). The comparatively high figures in 2018–2020 of 4–5% return on sales gave the eCommerce giant's share price another particularly strong boost. This is convincing for financial analysts because Amazon shows no signs of falling behind in terms of sales growth. Despite its size, Amazon continues to grow at high rates. Growth in 2020 was particularly strong due to coronavirus. Compared to 2019 (USD 281 billion), the company generated sales of USD 386 billion (+37%) in 2020. In 2024 sales revenues reached USD 638 billion.

14.5.2 Apple: Cash Flow as a Risk Buffer for "Bad Times"

Apple's particular appreciation of extensive cash reserves is best understood by looking at the state of the company at the time of Steve Jobs' return to Apple in 1997. Apple's position back then was diametrically opposed to what the company stands for today. The company was characterized by a significant amount of bureaucracy, extremely broad-based, with an almost unmanageable number of product variants and a low level of innovation (Lashinsky 2012). The company was close to illiquidity.

The following key points document Apple's transformation from a crisis company to the most valuable company in the world:

- 1998: Apple restructures its product range, the Apple Newton is discontinued and the iMac is introduced instead. There were to be only a few models: A home computer and a mobile device, one for normal users and one for professionals (today MacBook, MacBookPro, iMac, Mac Pro).
- 2001: Apple opens its first retail store. With the Apple Store, the company addresses consumers directly—the first iPod is introduced.
- 2003: The iTunes Store for music and movie downloads became the first commercially successful download portal and played a decisive role in shaping this market. Today, the iTunes Store and the App Store, which opened in 2008, are two of the world's largest distribution channels for digital goods.
- 2007: Apple launches the iPhone and Apple TV.
- 2008: Apple introduces the MacBook Air, the lightest and thinnest Mac notebook Apple has ever produced.
- 2010: Presentation of the iPad.

Even after the death of company founder Steve Jobs (2011), Apple continued to deliver top economic performance. CEO Tim Cook also benefited from this personally: his income in 2017, for example, amounted to US$100 million (comprising a basic salary of USD three million, a bonus of USD nine million and share options of US$88 million). The Group led by Cook was the first company to exceed the trillion mark on the stock market. While the share price was still close to USD 13 in 2013, it exceeded the USD 170 mark in Feb. 2022. Apple is one of the few companies to achieve a sustainable return on sales of more than 20% (revenue of USD 274 billion was offset by an after-tax profit of USD 57 billion in 2020) and is characterized by cash reserves of more than USD 220 billion (the highest level of USD 285 billion was achieved in QI 2018). In the Interbrand agency ranking, Apple occupied the top spot in 2020 with a brand value of USD 323 billion (Interbrand 2021). One year later (2021), the brand value was forecast to be USD 408 billion. In 2024, Apple reached a historic milestone: According to the Kantar BrandZ Most Valuable Global Brands Report, Apple became the first company in the world whose brand value exceeded the threshold of 1 trillion US dollars.

Apple rejected the criticism voiced by shareholders and financial analysts that Apple was not using its cash reserves in a targeted manner (Wilhelm 2014). In fact, Apple was also reluctant to pay dividends to shareholders. In the years 2014–2020, the dividend per share was 45–80 US cents. The fear of illiquidity is deeply rooted in Apple's DNA.

14.6 Apple and Amazon: Successful with Different Customer Value Weighting

With Amazon Prime, the online retailer is succeeding in occupying an increasingly strong position not only in the area of purchasing decisions, but also in household media consumption (Amazon Prime Video was the second most used video streaming service in Germany in 2021, behind Netflix). The Prime program not only serves Amazon to increase customer equity in the B2C segment, but also indirectly to develop Amazon into the central consumption platform. The more time consumers spend here, the more qualified data they provide (indirectly, unconsciously), the more interesting Amazon becomes as a partner for the advertising industry and thus a competitor to Facebook and Google. The driver for Amazon's business success is not only the transaction (purchase) and the associated income, such as commission, but also the time in which the platform is used by customers or information seekers. Here too, Prime customers and non-customers differ significantly from one another.

Against this backdrop, it is relevant how consumers rate Amazon and Google in a direct comparison: Google has noticeable disadvantages compared to Amazon in terms of consumer preferences (Krämer 2018). In the "Pricing Lab" study in 2017, 53% of respondents in Germany stated that they first look at Amazon when they intend to buy products (Prime customers: 63%, agreement top 2 values). Only about one-fifth (21%) of consumers favor Google in a direct comparison. Galloway (2017) reports similar results for the USA. Even among consumers who use Google intensively as a search engine, there is a preference for Amazon when searching for products. With its Prime service, Amazon also has a very effective tool for increasing customer loyalty to the provider. In this case, customer loyalty not only means a better position in the consumer's mindset, combined with shifts in sales in favor of the online retailer, but also more and better customer information—especially on actual purchasing behavior. This also increases the leverage in the use of artificial intelligence.

While Amazon primarily focused on sales growth for years and only later switched to exploiting pricing potential in retail, Apple is remaining true to its strategy of offering a closed ecosystem with a limited number of products. The iPhone plays an important role in this because sales and profits increasingly focus on this product.

As Apple does not rely on exorbitant customer growth, high margins per device are still possible. However, without new areas for growth, there are clear limits to leaps in market capitalization.

Both companies are value-oriented, and are among the world's most valuable companies, but they prioritize the value facets of value-to-the-customer and value-of-the-customer very differently and are ultimately successful despite these differences. This demonstrates how amorphous terms such as value management or value-based pricing are (Krämer and Schmutz 2020). Amazon's growth strategy is based on "value delivery." The customer sees the Amazon platform as a central purchasing option that promises not only low prices, but also simple processes and good service. The Prime subscription serves to strengthen customer loyalty and increase purchase volume. Apple, on the other hand, focuses on a relatively small customer segment that promises high margins. The emphasis here is on the aspect of "value capture," i.e., skimming off as much of the willingness to pay as possible.

It is important to note from the comparative analysis of Amazon and Apple's business models that, firstly, a benchmark can only ever provide limited information and the findings cannot be used as a predictor for the future. The successes of both companies must always be seen in their historical context. Caution is advised with approaches or concepts such as Blue Ocean Strategy, which often refer to the afore-mentioned examples of Apple and Amazon (Alam and Islam 2017), but only once they have proven to be recognizably successful. The causal chain, "Apple is successful because the company is customer-oriented and innovative, ... if our company is customer-oriented and innovative, we will be successful!" is certainly a clear misunderstanding. Statements such as "make the competition irrelevant" can also be described as crude or even naïve for a market strategy. Secondly, the two companies each offer a bundle of best practices. The list of benchmarks can be extended to include any number of other companies, with Apple and Amazon demonstrating particularly well the range of ways in which customer value-centered management can be understood.

Despite all that benchmarking can achieve, it remains the primary task and responsibility of management to scrutinize potential for improvement in customer processes or interfaces and mechanisms of action in their own business model in order to build sustainable differentiation from the competition and a bond with the most loyal and best customers. Gaining an overview of best practices is always illuminating. However, the real ambition must be to become the benchmark for other companies.

References

Alam S, Islam MT (2017) Impact of blue ocean strategy on organizational performance: a literature review toward implementation logic. IOSR J Bus Manag 19(1):1–19

Almquist E, Senior J, Bloch N (2016) The elements of value. Harv Bus Rev 94(9):47–53

Anshari M, Almunawar MN, Lim SA, Al-Mudimigh A (2019) Customer relationship management and big data enabled: personalization & customization of services. Appl Comp Inform 15(2):94–101

Ashley C, Gillespie EA, Noble SM (2016) The effect of loyalty program fees on program perceptions and engagement. J Bus Res 69(2):964–973

Bhutta KS, Huq F (1999) Benchmarking–best practices: an integrated approach. Benchma An Int J 6(3):254–268

Chua AY (2011) How Web 2.0 supports customer relationship management in Amazon. Int J Elect Cust Relat Manag 5(3–4):288–304

Chulkov D, Nizovtsev D (2014) Economics of apple iphone: price discrimination or pricing error? J Int Acad Cas Stud 20(1):49–54

Dennis B, Nonnenmann S (2014) Amazon: is profitability a possibility? Exp Jo Bus Manag 2(1):9–13

Frohmann F (2018) Digitales pricing. Springer Gabler, Wiesbaden

Galloway S (2017) The four: the hidden DNA of Amazon, Apple, Facebook and Google. Random House, London

Habel J, Kassemeier R, Alavi S, Haaf P, Schmitz C, Wieseke J (2020) When do customers perceive customer centricity? The role of a firm's and salespeople's customer orientation. J Perso Sell Sal Manag 40(1):25–42

Herrmann C (2021) Werbung schlägt Shop und Cloud – Amazons dritter Gigant erwacht. N-tv.de https://wwwn-tvde/wirtschaft/Amazons-dritter-Gigant-erwacht-article22547346html. Accessed 12 May 2021

Interbrand (2021) Best global brands. https://wwwinterbrandcom/best-global-brands/. Accessed 26 Apr 2021

Klaus P (2013) The case of Amazon.com: towards a conceptual framework of online customer service experience (OCSE) using the emerging consensus technique (ECT). J Serv Mark 27(6):443–457

Kraemer KL, Linden G, Dedrick J (2011) Capturing value in global networks: Apple's iPad and iPhone. Research supported by grants from the Alfred P. Sloan Foundation and the US National Science Foundation (CISE/IIS)

Krämer A (2017) Van Westendorp Reloaded: Wie sich auf Basis des PSM-Ansatzes (doch) gute Preisentscheidungen treffen lassen. Vortrag auf der Research & Results Messe, am 25(10):2017. in München

Krämer A (2018) Customer Centricity und deren Monetarisierung am Beispiel Amazon Prime. Mark Rev St Gallen 35(4):13–20

Krämer A (2025) Dynamische und individuelle Preise aus Unternehmens- und Verbrauchersicht. In: Kalka R, Krämer A (eds) Preiskommunikation – Strategische Herausforderungen und innovative Anwendungsfelder. Springer Gabler, Wiesbaden, pp 101–120

Krämer A, Hercher J (2018) Apple: Spitzenleistung nicht nur bei Produkt und Kundenbeziehung, sondern auch beim Pricing Studie "Pricing Lab" untersucht das Pricing von Apple, Bonn. https://doi.org/10.13140/RG.2.2.20203.64801. Accessed 18 Jan 2018

Krämer A, Hercher J (2021) "Amazon: Das Prime-Abo als Motor für die Amazon-Wachstumsgeschichte", Rogator/exeo untersuchen die Kundenbeziehung zu Amazon und den Einfluss auf das Einkaufsverhalten („OpinionTRAIN"), 30. März 2021. https://www.pressebox.de/presse-mitteilung/rogator-ag/Das-Prime-Abo-als-Motor-fuer-die-Amazon-Wachstumsgeschichte/boxid/1051980?utm_source=Belegmail&utm_medium=Email&utm_campaign=Aktiv. Accessed 24 Apr 2021

Krämer A, Kalka R (2016) How digital disruption changes pricing strategies and price models. In: Khare A, Schatz R, Stewart B (eds) Phantom ex machina: digital disruption's role in business model transformation. Springer, Cham, pp 87–103

Krämer A, Schmutz I (2020) Mythos value-based pricing: Der Versuch einer (wertfreien) Einordnung. Mark Rev St Gallen 37(2):44–53

Krämer A, Kalka R (2025) Maßnahmen und Argumente in der Preisveränderungskommunikation gegenüber Endkunden. In:Preiskommunikation: Strategische Herausforderungen und innovative Anwendungsfelder (pp. 165-188), Springer Fachmedien,Wiesbaden

Lashinsky A (2012) Inside Apple: How America's most admired—and secretive—company really works. Hachette, UK

Mahadevan B (2000) Business models for internet-based e-commerce: an anatomy. Calif Manag Rev 42(4):55–69

McAlone N. (2016) Amazon CEO Jeff Bezos said something about Prime Video that should scare Netflix. https://wwwbusinessinsiderde/amazon-ceo-jeff-bezos-said-something-about-primevideo-that-should-scare-netflix-2016-6?r=US&IR=T. Accessed 23 Apr 2021

Merkle W, Krämer A (2021) Händler brauchen für Dynamic Pricing eine Gesamtstrategie. Lebensmittelzeitung 12(3):46

Mikkonen K, Seppänen M, Pynnönen M (2009) Building theory for systemic customer value: case apple. In: The Proceedings of the 4th European Conference on Entrepreneurship and Innovation (ECEI) (S 683–690)

Montgomerie J, Roscoe S (2013) Owning the consumer – getting to the core of the Apple business model. Account Forum 37(4):290–299

Orr A (2023) Apple collects nearly all of the profit in the worldwide smartphone market. appleinsider, Feb 03, 2023,https://appleinsider.com/articles/23/02/03/apple-collects-nearly-all-of-the-profit-in-the-worldwide-smartphone-market?utm_source=chatgpt.com. Accessed 12 May 2025

Palmer A (2021) Jeff Bezos says Amazon needs to do a better job for employees in his final shareholder letter as CEO. https://wwwcnbccom/2021/04/15/jeff-bezos-releases-final-letter-toamazon-shareholdershtml. Accessed 23 Apr 2021

Phan DD, Vogel DR (2010) A model of customer relationship management and business intelligence systems for catalogue and online retailers. Inform Manag 47(2):69–77

Pryor LS (1989) Benchmarking: a self-improvement strategy. J Bus Strateg 10(6):28–32

Rigby D, Bilodeau B (2018) Management tools & trends. https://wwwbaincom/insights/management-tools-and-trends-2017/. Accessed 21 Apr 2021

Ritala P, Golnam A, Wegmann A (2014) Coopetition-based business models: the case of Amazon.com. Indus Mark Manag 43(2):236–249

Simons R (2014) Choosing the right customer. Harv Bus Rev 92(3):48–55

Smith B, Linden G (2017) Two decades of recommender systems at Amazon.com. IEEE Internet Comput 21(3):12–18

Tien NH, Long NT, Chi DTP (2019) Price policy in international marketing. Comparative analysis between Samsung and Apple. Int J Res Mark Manag Sal 1(2):144–147

Töpfer A, Mann A (2013) Benchmarking: Lernen von den Besten. In: Töpfer A (ed) Benchmarking – Der Weg zu Best Practice. Springer, Wiesbaden

Venkatesan R (2017) Executing on a customer engagement strategy. J Acad Mark Sci 45:289–293

Wilhelm A (2014) Apple CEO Tim Cook says iPhone expansion plans include 50 more carriers this quarter | TechCrunch. [online] TechCrunch http://techcrunchcom/2014/02/07/apple-ceotim-cook-says-iphone-expansion-plans-include-50-more-carriers-this-quarter/. Accessed 26 Apr 2021

Walke M, Tomar NS, Ghanwat G, Kapse M, Sharma V (2025) Price Dynamics Unveiled: A Comparative Study on Pre-Sale, On-Sale, and Post-Sale Day Prices on Amazon. Australasian Accounting, Business and Finance Journal 19(1):137–152

Zhang H, Liang X, Wang S (2016) Customer value anticipation, product innovativeness, and customer lifetime value: The moderating role of advertising strategy. J Bus Res 69(9):3725–3730

The Challenge: Managing Increasingly Uncertain Environmental Conditions

15

15.1 VUCA Environmental Conditions and the Need for Customer Value-Centered Management

"It is not enough to know, one must also apply it; it is not enough to want, one must also do it."—Johann Wolfgang von Goethe

The aim of these concluding observations is to ensure, in the spirit of agile management, that customer value-centric management is introduced in the basic elements, even if the operationalization of the customer value dimensions is not yet 100% secure. In this respect, the aspect "…you also have to do it" is deliberately placed first in this chapter. In theory, the use of Customer Lifetime Value is catchy, convincing, and compelling (Anderl et al. n.d.). It is true that it is complex to forecast the future total profit from a customer. However, from a long-term perspective, this perspective is the key parameter for making investment decisions. Thus, at first glance, irrational marketing and acquisition costs as well as subsidized and unprofitable loss-leader offers can be justified, provided that proof of an increase in medium or long-term customer value can be provided.

At the same time, science has identified a key performance indicator to support and legitimize management decisions in the direction of active value management, but also to create overall transparency in decision-making. The monetary customer lifetime value (CLV) as a representation of the value contributions over the entire life cycle of a customer (Reichheld and Sasser 1990) is a—if not the—recognized control parameter for a wide range of corporate issues (Heidemann et al. 2009).

At the same time, however, it has been observed in practice that the CLV approach is not given the importance it is given in science. It is confirmed that many companies "stop at" a relatively simple sales-based ABC customer analysis or implement other very simplified customer value concepts. This reveals a major entrepreneurial challenge. The goal cannot be to dispense with a serious consideration of customer value. However, companies often feel overwhelmed by the complexity of advanced

A. Krämer et al., *Customer Value-centered Management*, Future of Business and Finance, https://doi.org/10.1007/978-3-031-90497-4_15

mathematical CLV models (Verhoef and Langerak 2002) or do not feel able to provide sufficient resources. In this respect, it is not surprising that studies such as that by Mengen and Wanker (2015) for the energy industry come to the conclusion that comprehensive customer value management is "still in its infancy." To be fair, it must be acknowledged that elaborate CLV models — especially those incorporating parameters such as retention rates or recommendation effects — can easily push analysts to their limits.

The question then arises as to whether reliable data is even available to properly model the corresponding impact mechanisms. This can sometimes lead to despair. The finer the customer value model is to be differentiated, the more obvious it becomes how many different variables need to be considered. In this case, the following saying attributed to Aristotle proves to be true:

"The more I know, the more I know that I don't know."—Aristotle

The trick in this context is to find the right balance between cost and return. It is important that the CLV does not become a fictitious control variable that is detached from the company's practice, but rather that it is sufficiently accepted by the employees. Projects that provide for the implementation of customer value accounting always include a strong change management component. The facet of empowerment also plays a role here.

At this point at the latest, it becomes clear that the provision of customer-specific data represents a central challenge for the implementation of customer value-centered management, yet the objection of Reimer and Becker (2011) should be taken seriously: "However, many companies still struggle to concretely identify the customer data which can be used as control measures in different phases of a customer relationship (e.g., by measuring the effectiveness for implementing actions and optimizing campaigns), or is relevant for the analysis of customer behavior (e.g., by means of determining customer profitability, Customer Lifetime Values (CLV) and Customer Equity)."

In this context, the superiority of a top-down approach to data analysis is clearly evident, a process that first defines the relevant parameters and then attempts to provide the required information in a targeted manner. As an alternative to calculating customer value, there is also discussion of using substitute indicators for CLV, such as the degree of customer satisfaction or the length of the customer relationship. Unfortunately, recent empirical research shows that a positive correlation cannot necessarily be assumed. Groening et al. (2019) state "The idea that high levels of customer satisfaction and high levels of loyalty always lead to high profitability has many exceptions." This is not intended to diminish the strategic importance of the customer satisfaction indicator, but rather to dispel the misconception that an increase in customer satisfaction is synonymous with increased customer equity. The same applies to the Net Promoter Score indicator, which plays an important role in practice and is sometimes considered to correlate positively with customer equity, while the scientific community remains rather critical (Artz 2017). In the meantime, enthusiasm for the supposed "key performance indicator star" NPS is also crumbling in business practice. In a highly regarded article in Forbes magazine, Shevlin (2019) calls for "It's Time To Retire The Net Promoter Score" and justifies this with "It measures intention, not behavior." Criticism has also become louder from a scientific perspective in recent years (Cazzaro and Chiodini 2023).

Regardless of which specific implementation a company chooses: It is important that the logic of customer value measurement is implemented and that this is viewed as a continuous process. This statement is fundamentally valid, but is becoming even more important due to the increasingly VUCA environment. In dynamic markets with stronger structural breaks, the customer relationship becomes the central instance (see Fig. 15.1).

It would be premature to deduce from the much-discussed VUCA framework conditions that they render both the necessity and the power of a customer value approach obsolete. After all, volatility in markets is noticeably increasing, uncertainty in corporate decision-making is heightened, seemingly obvious correlations are turning out to be complex and attempts to master the growing "mountain of data" and different sources of information give the impression of contradiction and ambiguity. On closer inspection, however, the changed—and more difficult—environmental conditions do not lead to an invalidation of customer value as an entrepreneurial target.

In contrast to the NPS as an entrepreneurial target figure, decision-makers in companies need to take a closer look at customer value (including the success chain from customer proximity to value enhancement for customers and companies). Simplistic indicators, such as the NPS, are increasingly out of place, suggesting simple and obvious correlations that may not exist (Chap. 1). This is particularly the case if it is not possible to consistently remedy shortcomings in the company based on the NPS (in this case, more complex surveys are required that allow cause-and-effect relationships to be assigned).

Ultimately, very few companies can directly influence or even create framework conditions or trends. As a rule, these must be accepted as given. In crisis situations,

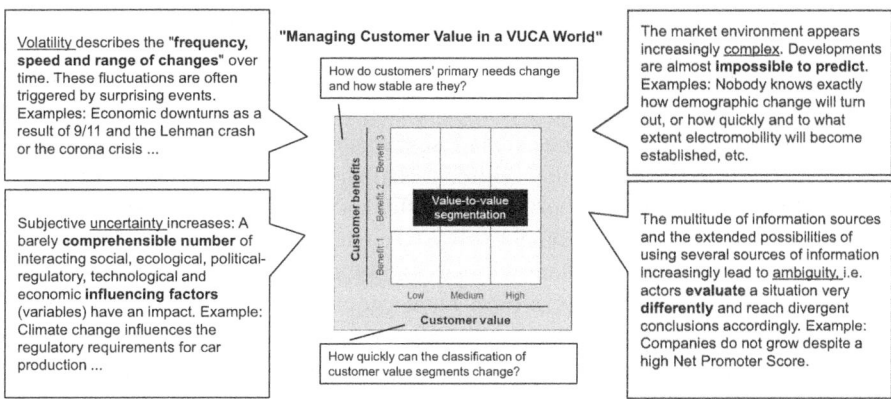

Fig. 15.1 Customer value-centered management and VUCA framework conditions

it becomes clear how the needs structure of people (customers or company leaders) can be greatly altered. The perception that the world is "coming apart at the seams"—as was the case with the outbreak of the coronavirus pandemic—offers different reaction patterns. Resignation is just one of them ("we can no longer rely on anything"), while another relies on resilience ("we have made it this far and will continue to do so"). In the study by exeo and Rogator (Krämer and Hercher 2020) shortly after the outbreak of the COVID-19 crisis (Apr./May 2020), the participants (four European countries) were asked the question: "Please think about the phase when the coronavirus restrictions are lifted: How long do you think it will take for the economy to return to the level it was at before the corona crisis?" A good third of respondents said a period of up to one year. However, the longer the pandemic lasts, the greater the realization that far-reaching, lasting changes can be expected in various areas of society and thus also the economy (in a repeat survey in Aug./Sep 2021, this proportion was at the same level).

Companies that have proven to be particularly adaptable in the crisis situation are those that have derived concrete actions from their proximity to customers and their understanding of changing customer needs by offering new products or services or establishing new sales channels and communication channels. However, this also highlights the strategic importance of customer value-centered management. This should be anchored as a central function in corporate management.

15.2   Aligning the Business Model "Customer Value-Centered"

With increasing digitalization and big data, the role of CRM in organizations is changing. The new way of managing the customer relationship shows a development from the classic goal of "collecting customer data" and adding customers to defined product campaigns to a customer-centric CRM approach. Customers only want to be contacted by companies when it is relevant and only via their preferred communication channel. Personal interaction is no longer a must. Messenger apps, social media forums, automated chats, and self-service portals complement the traditional channels (telephone, post and email) in CRM. In an ideal world, required information is directly available in the self-service portal and only relevant product offers build a customer-centric approach. Offering the right product at the right time can now be achieved through the extensive use of smartphone and messenger apps. One-stop shopping with one click will be a challenge for all companies across all sectors. Real-time analysis of the "next best offer" is no longer limited to stores with less customized products. Customers will ask for customized offers in a high-value and complex product environment without going through a time-consuming selection process. Vacation bookings or even a new car can be offered and purchased on a "final customized" basis. The cultural shift towards companies knowing or even actively managing the customer journey will be reflected in the fact that only relevant product offers or even direct product deliveries will be requested. Companies with a high match of relevant offers will dominate in this world.

Simple and convenient CRM processes will replace complicated and non-transparent processes in sales. Companies that can analyze customer data automatically can focus their valuable personal CRM processes on the right customers to generate added value. This new CRM has a strong self-service focus that enables the validation of data by the customer themselves, offers automated, relevant customer activities (next best action) and generates a company-wide data source for customer data.

Ultimately, the changed strategic role of CRM means that the business model must be aligned accordingly. Based on the business model canvas proposed by Osterwalder et al. (2010), the decisive adjustments are visually highlighted (see Fig. 15.2). The central element of the business model is the focus on the customer. The consistently modified core elements are (1) customer data management, (2) the generation of perceptible customer benefits, and (3) value extraction, i.e., the conversion of customer benefits into cash flow for the company. All parts of the traditional business model are therefore affected (Krämer et al. 2016b):

1. Customer data management:

Understanding the way in which customers assess and evaluate a service or product is crucial to achieving a competitive advantage. This is where customer data management comes into play. Ultimately, it forms the basis for recognizing value potential from proximity to the customer. The basis for this is in turn data that is ideally linked directly to the customer account. Collis (2019) refers to this aspect of the business model as the "value potential." Disruptive technologies are both an opportunity and a challenge for corporate strategy. The ability to extract valid information from big data and convert it into smart data will become a competitive factor: on the one hand, customers can be offered customized products and services (this is also possible in terms of price if customers are presented with individual prices in a dynamic process), and on the other hand, customer value management

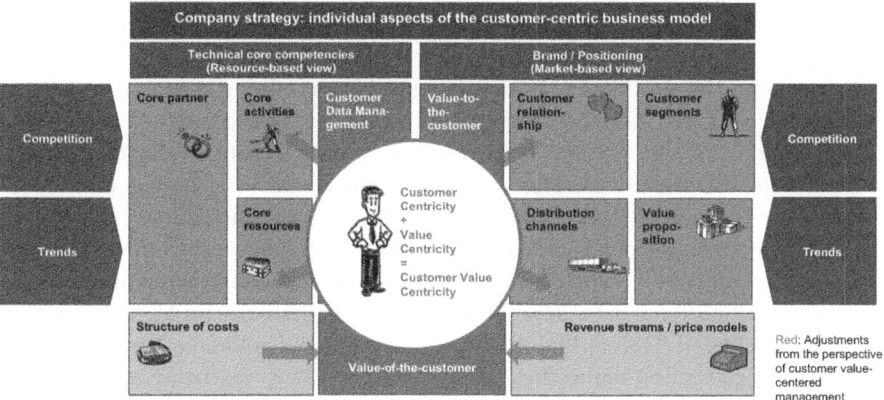

Fig. 15.2 Customer value-centered business model

can be monitored and controlled in real time. The answer to this challenge will not be to collect as much different customer data as possible, but to focus on strategically relevant information and also to address the question of whether companies should (or must) offer their customers compensation for providing data. In the end, this will result in a win-win situation. Only if consumers see a tangible benefit will there be a lasting willingness to consent to individual data storage.

2. Generating customer benefits for customers/users:

   Recognizing and creating value for the customer, i.e., customer benefit, is considered an essential prerequisite for the long-term survival and success of a company (Porter 1996; Graf and Maas 2008). Understanding how customers evaluate and rate a service or product is crucial to achieving a competitive advantage. Apart from a few who view consumer decisions as consistently irrational, the central explanatory pattern for consumer decisions consists of potential buyers who expect an increase in value (in the sense of a net benefit, i.e., perceived value minus the price paid) and who select precisely the offer that offers the highest expected increase in value among all the offers compared (Kotler and Bliemel 2001; Krämer and Schmutz 2020).

3. Value extraction, i.e., the conversion of customer benefit into cash flow for the company:

   As has been shown so far, the questions of how customer value can be generated and how companies can then monetize customer value are usually two separate strands of research. Cleland and Bruno (1997) assume a relationship between customer value and shareholder value, but postulate that the only permanently successful strategy is to focus on both. A company must "ensure that its customer value strategies deliver rigorous revenues to … create wealth for shareholders." However, this harmony is not mandatory. After all, numerous examples can be used to show that high customer value does not go hand in hand with a sufficient profit situation for the provider (Krämer and Kalka 2016). To name just a few:

- WhatsApp: The messenger service quickly became the leading application in this area (Sect. 10.1). Since the app became free for all end users (B2C) following its acquisition by Facebook, the question of what a profitable business model could look like has arisen. This example is representative of providers that rely on strong user growth with the "for free" revenue model (Krämer and Wilger 2025). However, the changed legal situation regarding data protection (GDPR in Europe) significantly limits the opportunities to generate revenue through the provision of personal data. In September 2021, the Irish data protection authority imposed a fine of €225 million because WhatsApp did not make it transparent to Irish data protection authorities which customer data was being used and for what purpose. In 2023, WhatsApp generated estimated revenues of around USD 1.3 billion, mainly through its business services such as the WhatsApp Business

API and click-to-WhatsApp ads. Despite this revenue, WhatsApp's direct contribution to Meta's total revenue remains small.

- Flixbus: The company achieves a very competitive market. After the market liberalization in Germany (2013), the company became the market leader within a short period of time and put a lot of pressure on its competitor DB Fernverkehr. However, the low price level and the special business model with bus companies as cooperation partners result in low margins. The offer of low-cost trips leads to a high perceived value for users—often travelers under the age of 30 who have a limited budget for travel. The problem for the realized, effective market price level is less the competitive prices of the railroads than the aggressive marketing strategies of intramodal competitors. The competition for market share in this new market for long-distance bus travel led to a price war in Germany in 2015, which was largely driven by the provider Megabus with anchor prices of EUR 1 per trip (Krämer et al. 2016a; Wilger and Krämer 2015). Following the withdrawal of Megabus and the market entry of BlaBlaBus, the French provider adopted this strategy and in winter 2019/spring 2020 offered promotional prices of € 0.99 per trip on a larger scale (Krämer et al. 2019).This destructive price war was abruptly interrupted by the outbreak of the coronavirus pandemic. In 2023, Flix SE achieved an EBITDA margin of 5.2% on sales of around EUR 2 billion and thus profitable growth.
- Spotify: The company has developed into the leading music streaming platform with high popularity ratings among users. Although the freemium revenue model generates direct revenue for at least some users (via the subscription model), revenue is generated through advertising for non-subscribers. The key issue is that the marginal costs for usage are not zero or close to zero, as is the case with many other platform providers. Costs (especially license fees for the music industry) also increase with usage, resulting in a negative operating result for years (approx. USD-662 million after-tax result in 2020). Spotify recorded annual losses between 2020 and 2023. In 2023, the loss amounted to around 532 million EUR, despite sales of around 13.25 billion EUR. However, in 2024, the operating result amounted to 1.37 billion EUR (change in subscription price and cost reductions).

It is important to find the right balance in the weighting of the facets of value generation (creation of customer benefits) and monetization of customer benefits. In the short term, this can certainly be one-sided, e.g., if the targeted skimming of willingness to pay is dispensed with from the company's perspective in order to achieve growth and customer targets. However, it can also be the provider's primary objective to skim off the willingness to pay as completely as possible. Apple is a good example of this. In both cases, the management of customer data is a basic prerequisite. The concepts of customer centricity on the one hand and value centricity on the other can therefore be used to derive the demand for customer value centricity—customer value-centered management. The argumentation in both the "value-to-the-customer" and "value-of-the- customer" strands should be data-driven.

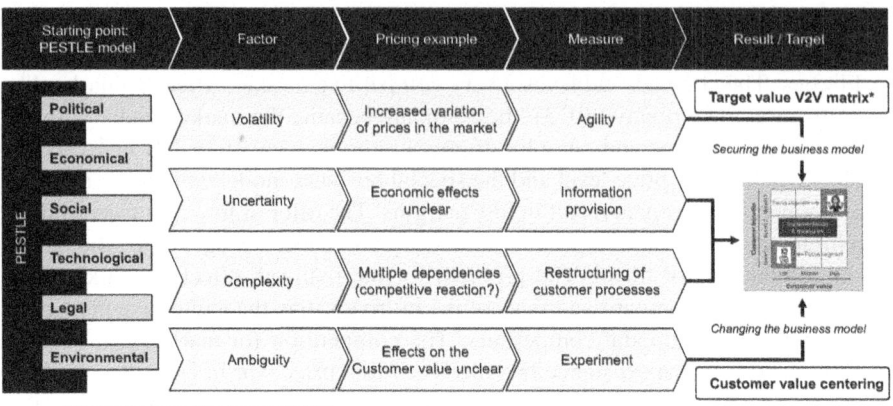

* Value-to-value segmentation shown as an example.

Fig. 15.3 Customer value-centered management as a process—example of price management

15.3   Customer Value-Centered Management: Creating Conditions and New Priorities

The VUCA framework conditions, which have already been discussed more intensively in the last decade, but whose relevance must be reclassified due to the coronavirus pandemic, do not emerge of their own accord. The PESTLE model can be used, for example, to identify the initial points (see Fig. 15.3). These can be political, economic, social, technological, legal, or environmental triggers, or a combination of these (Fernando 2019). In the perception of corporate decision-makers, this results in the four VUCA dimensions. Bennett and Lemoine (2014) take up the problem areas and derive a standard of action for each aspect as a kind of countermeasure. They set (1) agility as the response to volatility; (2) the provision of information as the response to uncertainty; (3) the provision of process restructuring as the response to complexity; and (4) the prioritizing experimentation as a response to ambiguity.

Unfortunately, there is a tendency to view the strands of measures, e.g., agility, as a general solution pattern (i.e., rather one-sided, undifferentiated) ("only agile companies can survive"). Rather than a monolithic emphasis on individual approaches, the right mix is essential for the survival of customer value-centered corporate management.

This insight is not new, but it is still valid and should therefore have a sufficient place in the discussion. Snowden and Boone (2007) already attempted to use the Cynefin framework to help managers determine the prevailing operational context so that they can make appropriate decisions. Each area requires different actions. Simple and complicated contexts assume an ordered universe in which cause-and-effect relationships are perceptible and correct answers can be determined based on the facts. Complex and chaotic contexts are disordered—there is no immediately recognizable relationship between cause and effect—and the way forward is determined based on emergent patterns.

15.3.1 Agility as a Response to the VUCA Phenomenon of "Volatility"

The concept of agility is now firmly established in modern management literature and increasingly also in management. The fascination with agility is also related to the fact that companies and managers expect competitive advantages and ultimately an economic impact from it. Studies that show that organizations with very agile capabilities not only generate more revenue, but also generate higher profits than companies that have been classified as non-agile (Wang et al. 2014), are therefore well received.

In 1982, agility was mentioned for the first time in a corporate context, namely as "the capacity to react quickly to rapidly changing circumstances" (cf. Brown and Agnew 1982, S. 29). Organizational agility expresses the entirety of a company's ability to thrive and succeed in an unpredictable and rapidly changing environment. It is therefore understandable that the terms agility and resilience are often mentioned in the same breath. Fernando (2019) sees the ability to respond quickly as the core definition. This ability depends on three criteria: Responsiveness, adaptability, and control. Today, the demand for agility appears in very different contexts, from politics ("our political leadership must become more agile") to the recommendation of "agile pricing" in price management (Maessen and Haller 2020). This points to a trend toward an inflationary use of the term with consistently positive connotations.

The expectations associated with an agile organization are also positive: "… to detect opportunities and threats, assemble the needed assets and capabilities to launch an appropriate response, judge the benefits and risks of initiating an action, and execute actions with competitive speed and success" (Lee et al. 2015). Success comes when outdated, outmoded processes or hierarchical levels are rethought. However, it is also legitimate to ask where the limits of agility lie. Above all, it should be noted that agility must always be considered in connection with strategic management and works in this context (Walter 2020).

15.3.2 Providing Information in Response to the VUCA Phenomenon of "Uncertainty"

If there are uncertainties regarding decisions, the provision of data appears to be an option for eliminating or at least reducing these uncertainties. This aspect does not only concern the aspect of big data but goes beyond this. Managers would like to see the provision of relevant KPIs in real time. In some cases, the priority seems to be fast availability above all. However, the main challenge is then to provide sufficient quality assurance.

In addition to the speed of information provision, the networking of different data sources plays a major role. The interplay of big data and traditional marketing analytics can be advantageous here. According to Saidali et al. (2019), the following effects should be aimed for:

- Faster and better decision support.
- Improvement of (customer) processes.
- Better understanding of (changing) customer needs.
- Uncovering risks.

The desire of company decision-makers for quickly available KPIs that are able to describe the situation of their own business sufficiently well is understandable. After all, managers are under time and performance pressure. Such real-time tools are therefore the focus of attention today. Technological changes make real-time data delivery seem possible by increasing the performance of existing internal reporting tools, making computer capacity available at lower cost or, for example, using automated routines to provide immediate results (e.g., measuring the satisfaction of purchasing processes directly after the purchase has been completed online).

However, not all processes can be mapped fully automatically, at least not with the aim of providing information that can be used directly for decision-making.

For more in-depth analyses, e.g., uncovering new cause-and-effect relationships, semi-manual processes will be required. Here, not only data analysis skills but also business understanding play an important role.

15.3.3 Restructuring Customer Processes in Response to the VUCA Phenomenon of "Complexity"

The term complexity refers to the interconnectivity and interdependence of multiple dimensions in a system. The different layers intermingle and make it impossible to get an overview of how things are connected. Decision-making is consequently very convoluted and consists of a web of reaction and counter-reaction (Sinha and Sinha 2020). Ultimately, choosing the right alternative becomes almost impossible. This applies in particular to customer relationship management and the risk that the company's employees will assess aspects such as customer needs and satisfaction levels differently to the customers themselves. One measure that can be taken is to review and, if necessary, change customer processes. The focus should be on two aspects and issues in particular: (1) the customer experience and (2) customer engagement:

- Are the customer processes designed in such a way that they are simple, transparent and ultimately satisfactory from the customer's point of view, but also sufficiently recognize cost reduction potential or opportunities to increase sales per customer?
- Are customers sufficiently involved in existing activities? Does customer engagement lead to clearly positive economic effects for the company?

In today's networked world, knowledge of customer behavior is essential. The more unpredictable environmental conditions become, and the more unstable customer relationships develop, the more proximity to customers becomes a strategic competitive advantage for providers. Many companies launch special initiatives to promote customer engagement. The aim is to motivate customers to provide feedback or to interact with the company. One of several effects is so-called value co-creation (companies and customers work together to improve products or services). However, the effects are not clearly positive. For example, the customer feedback requested can have negative effects, such as on the brand image (Hollebeek et al. 2021). The study by Beckers et al. (2018) examines the value-related consequences of company-initiated customer engagement measures from the shareholders' perspective and comes to the conclusion that corresponding initiatives by companies to retain customers reduce their market capitalization on average.

The reason given for this is that shareholders consider the risk of failure of these initiatives to be particularly high.

15.3.4 Testing as a Response to the VUCA Phenomenon "Ambiguity"

In a complex context, according to Snowden and Boone (2007), the right answers cannot be found at all; rather, revealing patterns emerge when management conducts experiments that can also fail. This is the realm of the "unknown unknowns" in which much of today's business world operates. In this context, managers must first probe, then perceive and then react. In the field of e-commerce, among others, this reasoning has led to a veritable euphoria regarding A–B testing. As Bhat et al. (2020) explain, A–B testing is playing an increasingly important role in e-commerce today, and tests have become indispensable as a basis for decision-making. The area of application ranges from the optimization of content and graphics for online advertising to the design of optimal layouts and product ranges for websites. However, the use of large amounts of data does not guarantee accurate conclusions on cause-effect relationships, especially if the dependent variable is not only dependent on the experimental factor (independent variable), but also on a large number of other variables. Against this background, there is also the risk of a one-sided focus on A/B tests as the ultimate maxim for the validation of decisions.

Testing and trial and error not only describe highly scientific experiments, but also the "trial and error" approach. Clemens Bauer, Head of Marketing at Rewe, answers the question "How do you decide which message to place in which channel?" with "At the moment, nobody can really tell you. The only thing that helps is to try and test" (Campillo-Lundbeck 2021).

Despite all the advantages of testing effects under real-life conditions, there are also opportunities to examine mechanisms of action in marketing before a live test takes place. For example, different forms of price presentation can be examined as part of experimental online studies (Krämer 2025). During an online interview, experimental groups (e.g., with 150–300 test subjects) are formed in real time, each of which receives (slightly) modified presentations of prices (e.g., changed price ending, reference anchor, color, etc.). These test groups are formed randomly and are therefore structurally identical. This creates the prerequisites for experimental test arrangements.

The same applies to the implementation of concept tests, in which verbally or graphically substantiated product ideas are subjected to an evaluation well in advance of the market launch..

Market research studies can therefore play an important role in helping to make the right selection decisions as part of filter processes (start with a large number of concepts, end with a vote for the best-rated variant) before product launch.

15.3.5 The Need for an Overarching Approach

The rules of corporate management or common approaches in marketing and sales that have worked well in the past cannot simply be extrapolated to the present. The "directive" style of managers who expect their orders to be followed and implemented without contradiction cannot work in a VUCA world. Instead, a management style is required that consciously gives employees freedom. Organizational changes are therefore essential. At the interface to the customer, all relevant processes must be scrutinized to determine whether they are designed to meet needs. Regardless of the expansion of freedom and increased flexibility, strategic targets should be achieved. To check this, a manageable set of KPIs based on a functioning and efficient data management system is required. These cornerstones of the customer-centric company apply equally to the customer-value-centric company (Chap. 8).

On closer inspection, the correlations described above reveal strong similarities to the much-discussed design thinking process. Gordon et al. (2019) distinguish between five phases based on the Stanford D-School Model:

- Empathy: In this step, the preferences of the users are observed and their needs are determined ("needs assessment").
- Define: This phase expands awareness of people's needs and preferences. The aim is to get to know the core problems of customers/users as well as possible.
- Ideate: Here, the design thinker or team develops ideas for solutions to customer problems in a process that evaluates both the quantity and quality of options.
- Prototype: This involves narrowing down the ideation results towards a rough, early solution to the problem. Here it is accepted that the status quo does not represent a finished, completely conclusive solution. Rather, it is to be understood as a sketch, a model or an early working solution.
- Test: Finally, an iterative process is used to try out what works and what doesn't in order to determine the necessary modification of the basic prototype. This takes as long as it takes to find a product design that meets the target.

Principles that have already been discussed become recognizable in this approach: The aspects of leadership (assigning a group of employees the skills to independently develop a solution to a customer problem that leads to better economic results), agility (claiming to "enter the race" even with an 80% solution—the main thing is that the customer problem is solved quickly), and customer centricity (perspective of looking at existing processes backwards from the customer).

In a VUCA world, there are a multitude of challenges that companies face. To successfully meet them, organizations must be able to adapt and learn. They must also be able to respond quickly to changes and minimize risks. The use of AI can help with this. Potential applications of AI in the VUCA world across all industries include the automation of business processes, prediction of outcomes, decision support, improved customer relations, and personalized offers for customers.

15.4 Interview with Luke van Skyhawk, Hypatos

Could you briefly describe the positioning of Hypatos, what special characteristics do you particularly emphasize here?

Luke van Skyhawk: Hypatos is a technology spin-off that was founded in Potsdam. The purpose is to focus on large customers, enterprise customers, with a product that can be integrated into the processes and also into the system landscape of enterprise customers. The product is a deep-tech product that we are positioning on the market as an embedded generative AI solution.

Embedded generative AI means that the larger customers already have a certain system landscape for the purchase-to-pay and order-to-cash processes, as well as in the HR area. However, these solutions generally do not achieve the automation rates that are possible with the new technology, with generative AI.

In terms of corporate communication, we are trying to automate document-heavy processes. Communication between companies is basically very difficult to standardize. There are many different options for standardization, such as e-invoicing formats or electronic data formats, but standardizing these formats is a major challenge. And this is precisely where we intervene, so to speak, in the area that is highly transactional, which is difficult to achieve through standardization using electronic formats, and this is simply the case in communication between companies.

Automating document-based processes means, firstly, extracting the information from the documents (e.g., a PDF, an e-mail, an electronic file). The second is to do something with this information, i.e., to really understand the context. The third step is to improve the quality of the customer's data and use the documents to make comparisons with the systems. The documents represent the most up-to-date information because they are generated by the customer. As soon as information differs from the master data, this is an indication of an anomaly or a potential fraud check.

At Hypatos, I am responsible for the organization that is more in contact with the customers, the revenue organization. Under the revenue organization are the Customer Success departments, service teams with the clear goal of increasing customer value, as well as from the customer's perspective. We have professional services teams because the product offered requires specialized skills to carry out this implementation. As a rule, these are larger implementation projects. Pre-Sales is the organization that specializes in identifying the pain points of potential customers.

A fraud check could also be a change of master data. In the case of a move, the account data has not yet been stored, but a new credit card has been used for payment. Is this then the current data?

Luke van Skyhawk: This does not always have to be fraud. As a rule, it is simply an unmaintained or older master data record or simply a change. The autonomous thing here is that the AI can basically identify this and can then communicate with the supplier. This goes in the direction of a chatbot, where an attempt is made to solve precisely this problem without the involvement of employees on the customer side. By using AI, a certain consistency is achieved in the actions carried out and a relatively good ability to react.

A guest with a customer account makes a purchase with different transaction data because a credit card is replaced by a stored EC account during the payment process. Does the AI recognize this new situation?

Luke van Skyhawk: Of course, what we often see in a business-to-business context is one-off master data and the exchange of information about documents. A change to the data is only reflected in the document. In the business-to-customer area, you often find direct feedback. A purchase-to-pay process always goes via the purchase requisitions, then via the order, the delivery bill and the delivery note invoice. An attempt is made to post the invoice in the accounts-payable area. Certain accounting information is then already available in the order.

The alternative to using an AI would be manual input. In what order of magnitude can the savings effect be expected?

Luke van Skyhawk: The problem with incoming invoice processing is the enormous number of invoices that are recorded, coded, and matched. Here we try to identify step by step for each process step where a high level of automation could be achieved. This means that we mainly identify the value for the customer via the automation rates, which are then reflected in cost factors, but also in quality factors. Thanks to the consistency provided by AI, automation results in fewer errors. For employees, this means less data processing volume. The AI also makes suggestions for other processes.

In other words, an inventory is carried out with the customer and the AI starts where the quality level of the processes needs to be optimized?

Luke van Skyhawk: This is then mainly quantified by the number of employees or hours invested in a certain process step, or by the error rates or penalties. Penalties are incurred if account assignments are created incorrectly and additional payments are generated during the VAT audit, and these are, so to speak, the value measurement points that we use, the metrics, and we win the customer by identifying these metrics and presenting these individual use cases in an integrated way in a pilot and either achieving these success metrics or not. Our pricing is value-based pricing. This means that our pricing is already based on a basic list price. But after we have identified this value through workshops, an individual price is set based on the value that the customer can generate from the solution, and it is also an individual price for the customer. We agree prices with customers and depending on the automation rates, the price evolves. The higher the automation, the higher the license fees for the customer.

In addition to quality and costs, how big is the time effect? In other words, how much faster can a process be completed with AI? Is that the actual added value in the end or is it really more about costs?

Luke van Skyhawk: Here we are in the area of payment terms that cannot be met in the old process because the processing of receipts and documents, in the case of invoices but also in the order-to-cash area, cannot be carried out so quickly. Throughput times of 8 to 30 days in manual invoice processing mean that the cost of a document is usually 5 to 12 euros. With AI, however, the company only needs 2–3 minutes, and even if the documents have to be checked again, this checking time is of course much shorter. In other words, what we are now seeing as a result with our customers is that 75, 80, even up to 85, 90 percent of invoices are processed completely automatically on the incoming side.

So you work in an area where there is already a certain degree of automation?

Luke van Skyhawk: It is a highly transactional area that is already achieving some success with current solutions via ERP systems, other workflow automation solutions and RPA bots. These technologies are not capable of mapping this next step of contextual understanding. The topics of data governance and data security also play an important role.

Certain "hallucinations" of generative AI, i.e., information that never happened or information that is not true, are a major problem in a business context. The solution is to restrict the solution space of the AI. As soon as you ask a large AI model, a basic model such as a GPT, a question, the AI tries to access the entire treasure trove of data. In our case, however, the solution space of the AI is restricted in such a way that the AI is not tempted to give any answers that do not make sense.

With regard to dynamic pricing, do you see a problem with the use of AI when we think about the data protection aspect in Germany, or Europe, with the General Data Protection Regulation?

Luke van Skyhawk: In the EU in particular, data may not be used for purposes other than the primary purpose, and if it is used for another purpose, consent must first be obtained. The question is to what extent it is possible to generalize, anonymize, and pseudonymize in order to be able to say that we need to adapt to this type of customer group as follows.

Are there any other customer value components that your product generates?

Luke van Skyhawk: It is potentially feasible to use AI for various use cases. Basically, we have full flexibility for different use cases, and these use cases can also take place between an insurance company and policyholders. In other words, the policyholder would be the customer of an insurance company with a claim, who wants to report the claim and expects a quick response to simplify the claims reporting process. Here we work with a chatbot, a simple WhatsApp message or an email, for example.

Interview partner:
Luke van Skyhawk.
Chief Revenue Officer, Hypatos.

15.5   Customer Value-Centered Management: Rethinking Corporate Management

In a world with VUCA conditions, it is no longer enough to focus on market share and relative costs. Collis (2019) compares the established giants of yesterday—at the turn of the millennium, the largest US companies in terms of market capitalization were GE, Microsoft, Exxon, Citibank and Walmart—with the "upstarts" that have, in part, displaced them: in 2019, Microsoft, Amazon, Alphabet, Apple, and Facebook (Meta) topped the rankings. The disruptions they have catalyzed are rooted in their new approaches, using different technologies or satisfying customer needs in a completely different way. Focusing solely on the value capturing dimension is risky because customer needs are not sufficiently taken into account. A business model that is strongly focused on customer needs carries the risk of not being able to realize sufficient profits to ensure the company's continued existence. To visualize the problem, it is enough to look at prominent disruptors such as Uber or its competitor DiDi (ride service) as well as WhatsApp and its competitor Discord (messenger service, chat). WhatsApp itself generates little direct revenue (more important for the meta ecosystem; Kraus et al. 2022). Discord generates revenue through Nitro subscriptions, but according to several sources, is not yet profitable. Uber reported its first annual operating profit in 2023 after many years of high losses. Didi was profitable for a while, but had to undergo significant restructuring following regulatory pressure in China (data protection, etc.). They generate a high level of customer benefit, but are in most cases not profitable. In the case of WhatsApp, for example, this is determined by the "for free" pricing model for end users. These business models are radical; they offer a low-cost satisfaction of consumer needs. The monetization of value is downstream, but must occur at some point, as for example WhatsApp, which offers special services to business customers for a fee. Customer value-centered management helps to find the right balance, a win for the customer and a win for the company. Only a holistic approach ensures that a company can be managed in a customer value-centered way, combining two value perspectives: Firstly, the value that the company generates for the customer ("perceived value") and secondly, the value that the company derives from the customer relationship in terms of monetary and non-monetary effects.

References

Anderl E, März A, Schumann JH, Wangenheim FV, Ackermann S (n.d.) Kann man mit kostenfreien Dienstleistungen Geld verdienen? CLIC – Center for Leading Innovation & Cooperation, Leipzig

Artz M (2017) NPS – the one measure you really need to grow? Control Manag Rev 61(1):32–38

Beckers SF, Van Doorn J, Verhoef PC (2018) Good, better, engaged? The effect of company initiated customer engagement behavior on shareholder value. J Acad Mark Sci 46(3):366–383

Bennett N, Lemoine GJ (2014) What a difference a word makes: understanding threats to performance in a VUCA world. Bus Horiz 57(3):311–317

Bhat N, Farias VF, Moallemi CC, Sinha D (2020) Near-optimal AB testing. Manag Sci 66(10):4477–4495

Brown JL, Agnew NM (1982) Corporate agility. Bus Horizons 25(2):29–33

Campillo-Lundbeck S (2021) Wie Clemens Bauer das Marketing fit für die digitale Ära machen will und und welche Rolle Test&Learn Ansätze dabei spielen; planung&analyse v. 05. Juli 2021. https://www.horizont.net/planung-analyse/nachrichten/rewe-wie-clemensbauer-das-marketing-fit-fuer-die-digitale-aera-machen-will-und-und-welche-rolletestlearn-ansaetze-dabei-spielen-191522?utm_source=%2Fmeta%2Fnewsflash%2Fpua&utm_medium=newsletter&utm_campaign=nl44912&utm_term=a51ab59de814cb28cb3324a0d3e23d18. Accessed 5 July 2021

Cleland AS, Bruno AV (1997) Building customer and shareholder value. Strat Leadersh 25(3):22–28

Collis DJ (2019) Why has strategy become irrelevant? Understanding the complete strategy landscape. Understanding the complete strategy landscape (September 11, 2019). Harvard Business School Strategy Unit Working Paper (20–027)

Cazzaro M, Chiodini, PM (2023) Statistical validation of critical aspects of the Net Promoter Score, The TQM Journal 35(9):191-209

Fernando R (2019) Agile strategy: how to create a strategy ready for anything. Pearson

Gordon A, Rohrbeck R, Schwarz JO (2019) Escaping the "faster horses" trap: bridging strategic foresight and design-based innovation. Technol Innov Manag Rev 9(8):30–42

Graf A, Maas P (2008) Customer value from a customer perspective: a comprehensive review. Journal für Betriebswirtschaft 58(1):1–20

Groening C, Krafft M, Mittal V, Pallas F (2019) Strategic customer management: collect a mixture of customers

Heidemann J, Kamprath N, Görz Q (2009) Customer lifetime value – Entwicklungspfade. Einsatzpotenziale und Herausforderungen Journal für Betriebswirtschaft 59(4):183–199

Hollebeek LD, Sharma TG, Pandey R, Sanyal P, Clark MK (2021) Fifteen years of customer engagement research: a bibliometric and network analysis. J Prod & Bran Manag, Accepted Paper, University of Reading

Kotler P, Bliemel FW (2001) Marketing-management: Analysen, Planung und Verwirklichung. 10. Aufl, Schäffer-Poeschel, Stuttgart

Krämer A (2025) Preiskommunikation in Zeiten des „Behavioral Pricing ". In: Preiskommunikation: Strategische Herausforderungen und innovative Anwendungsfelder (pp. 29–53), Springer Fachmedien, Wiesbaden

Krämer A, Hercher J (2020) „Trotz unterschiedlicher Maßnahmen: Breite Unterstützung für die europäischen Regierungen in der Corona-Krise", OpinionTRAIN: Rogator/exeo untersuchen veränderte Einstellungen und Werte in Deutschland. Österreich, der Schweiz und in Schweden, Bonn 20. Mai 2020

Krämer A, Kalka R (2016) How digital disruption changes pricing strategies and price model. In: Khare A, Schatz R, Stewart B (eds) Phantom ex machina: digital disruption's role in business model transformation. Springer, Cham

Krämer A, Schmutz I (2020) Mythos value-based pricing: Der Versuch einer (wertfreien) Einordnung. Mark Rev St Gallen 37(2):44–53

Krämer A, Wilger G (2025) Kommunikation bei der Änderung von Preissystemen. In: Preiskommunikation: Strategische Herausforderungen und innovative Anwendungsfelder (pp. 189–210), Springer Fachmedien, Wiesbaden

Krämer A, Jung M, Burgartz T (2016a) A small step from price competition to price war – understanding causes, effects and possible countermeasures. Int Bus Res 9(3):1–13

Krämer A, Tachilzik T, Bongaerts R (2016b) Technology and disruption: how the new customer relationship influences the corporate strategy. In: Khare A, Schatz R, Stewart B (eds) Phantom ex machina: Digital disruption's role in business MODEL transformation. Springer, Wiesbaden, pp 53–70

Krämer A, Bongaerts R, Wilger G (2019) Wettbewerb um die führende Mobilitätsplattform für Fernreisen. Internationales Verkehrswesen 71(4):20–24

Kraus S, Kanbach DK, Krysta PM, Steinhoff MM, Tomini N (2022) Facebook and the creation of the metaverse: radical business model innovationor incremental transformation?. International Journal of Entrepreneurial Behavior & Research 28(9): 52-77

Lee OKD, Sambamurthy V, Lim KH, Wei KK (2015) How does it ambidexterity impact organizational agility? Inform Syst Res 26(2):398–417

Maessen A, Haller T (2020) Agile Pricing: In: 4 Schritten zur effektiven Preisgestaltung in volatilen Zeiten, marktforschung.de v. 1.12.2020. https://www.marktforschung.de/dossiers/themendossiers/pricing-und-preisforschung/dossier/agile-pricing-in-4-schritten-zur effektivenpreisgestaltung-in-volatilen-zeiten/. Accessed 4 July 2021

Mengen A, Wanker M (2015) Status quo des Kundenwertmanagements in der Energiewirtschaft. Arbeitspapier

Osterwalder A, Pigneur Y, Wegberg J (2010) Business model generation. Wiley, Hoboken

Porter ME (1996) What is strategy? Harv Bus Rev 44:61–78

Reichheld FF, Sasser WEJ (1990) Zero defections: quality comes to services. Harv Bus Rev 68(5):105–111

Reimer K, Becker JU (2011) Revisiting the use of customer information for CRM, Arbeitspapiere des Lehrstuhls für Innovation. Neue Medien und Marketing, Econstor

Saidali J, Rahich H, Tabaa Y, Medouri A (2019) The combination between big data and marketing strategies to gain valuable business insights for better production success. Procedia Manufacturing 32:1017–1023

Shevlin R (2019) It's time to retire the net promoter score (And here's what to replace it with). Forbes online v. https://www.forbes.com/sites/ronshevlin/2019/05/21/its-time-to-retire-the-netpromoter-score/?sh=8e77a4d6bbb9. Accessed 21 May 2021

Sinha D, Sinha S (2020) Managing in a VUCA world: possibilities and pitfalls. J Technol Manag Grow Econ 11(1):17–21

Snowden DJ, Boone ME (2007) A leader's framework for decision making. Harv Bus Rev 85(11):68–76

Verhoef PC, Langerak F (2002) Eleven misconceptions about customer relationship management. Bus Strateg Rev 13(4):70–76

Walter AT (2020) Organizational agility: ill-defined and somewhat confusing? A systematic literature review and conceptualization. Manag Rev Quarter 71:343–391

Wang Z, Pan SL, Ouyang TH, Chou TC (2014) Achieving IT-enabled enterprise agility in China: an IT organizational identity perspective. IEEE Trans Eng Manag 61(1):182–195

Wilger G, Krämer A (2015) Fernbusse bringen Bewegung in den Mobilitätsmarkt. Studie MobilitätsTRENDS (exeo Strategic Consulting AG/Rogator AG). planung&analyse 5:55